The Horse Conformation Handbook

The Horse Conformation Handbook

Heather Smith Thomas

With illustrations by Jo Anna Rissanen

Storey Publishing

*The mission of Storey Publishing is to serve our customers by publishing practical information
that encourages personal independence in harmony with the environment.*

Edited by Deborah Burns and Marie Salter
Art direction and design by Vicky Vaughn
Cover photograph/frontispiece: Thoroughbred racing legend and 1973 Triple Crown winner, Secretariat.
  His conformation was exceptional and is considered near perfect by many. It gave him a long, easy
  stride and the power and endurance to be a winner. © 1974 by Tony Leonard, recipient of the Inter-
  national Photographic Council's Lifetime Achievement Award in 2004, after more than 40 years as
  an equine photographer.
Interior photographs: Courtesy of the author, opposite; © Sharon Fibelkorn 340, 364, 365; Elaine Nash
  357, 358; © Bob Langrish xii, 26, 48, 66, 80, 104, 140, 170, 192, 204, 220, 232, 252, 268, 308, 360-363;
  © Tony Leonard 7, 191, 351
Illustrations by Jo Anna Rissanen
Text production by Liseann Karandisecky, Jennifer Jepson Smith, and Jessica Armstrong
Indexed by Susan Olason/Indexes & Knowledge Maps

The information in this book is true and complete to the best of our knowledge. All recommendations
are made without guarantee on the part of the author or Storey Publishing. The author and publisher
disclaim any liability in connection with the use of this information. For additional information, please
contact Storey Publishing, 210 MASS MoCA Way, North Adams, MA 01247.

Storey books are available for special premium and promotional uses and for customized editions.
For further information, please call (800) 793-9396.

Printed in the United States by Von Hoffmann
10 9 8 7 6 5 4 3 2 1

Library of Congress Cataloging-in-Publication Data

Thomas, Heather Smith, 1944–
    The horse conformation handbook / Heather Smith Thomas.
        p. cm.
    Includes index.
    ISBN-13: 978-1-58017-558-6; ISBN-10: 1-58017-558-9 (pbk. : alk. paper)
    ISBN-13: 978-1-58017-559-3; ISBN-10: 1-58017-559-7 (hardcover : alk. paper)
    1. Horses—Conformation. 2. Horses—Anatomy. I. Title.

SF279.T49 2005
63.1'0891—dc22
                                                              2004025045

To Nellace and Nokhomis ("Nikki"), the two best horses I've been privileged to ride during my lifetime working cattle in the mountains of eastern central Idaho. Mother and daughter, these two equine athletes inspired and awed me with their ability to outrun, outmaneuver, and outthink the most devious cow, no matter how steep, rocky, or slippery the terrain.

They spoiled me, because they elevated my expectations. They started me on a lifelong study of conformation and taught me the most about this fascinating subject.

Nellace and Nikki, 1962

Nikki and Nikkolis, 1973

CONTENTS

PREFACE

What makes a good horse? Often, it's a combination of factors: genetics (conformation and attitude, which encompasses that elusive quality we call "heart"), good care, and training.

Nellace was a Thoroughbred, born in 1953 on a ranch near ours. She was raised by an old man who shared our cattle range. He had bred good Thoroughbred ranch horses for decades; the Quarter Horse did not yet exist as a breed during most of his breeding program. My dad bought Nellace as a yearling. She was sired by Cheyenne Chief, a Thoroughbred Remount stallion whose forte was versatility. Another neighbor, the rancher who stood him at stud, won races every year at the county fair; right after the races, he would use him as a pick-up horse in the rodeo arena, helping cowboys safely off the bucking horses if they made their rides. This tough job can be done only by an agile, well-trained horse with a cool head.

Cheyenne Chief's sire was Pillory, a racehorse who nearly won the Triple Crown in 1922. He won the Preakness and Belmont Stakes but didn't enter the Kentucky Derby. His offspring combined speed with agility. Cheyenne Chief sired many good ranch horses that made their livings chasing cows.

Nellace was our family's best cow horse. She gave birth to Nikki in 1962, the year I graduated from high school and started college. Nikki's sire was El Khamis, a well-built little Arabian stallion whose owner, my 4-H leader Jerry Ravndal, used him for cattle work, roping and holding calves at branding time, packing deer out of the hills in hunting season, and teaching 4-H kids the finer points of dressage. Nikki took after her sire in size — she was only 14.3 hands high — but she combined the best of both parents in her well-balanced conformation and catty agility.

Nikki was my horse, raised as a 4-H project and ranch horse. She later went with me when my husband and I started our own cattle ranch. I'd be hard put to guess how many thousands of miles I rode her — checking, moving, and sorting cattle on the range; bringing home the occasional cow to doctor or sell; sorting out the "heavy" cows at calving time and bringing them in from the often muddy or frozen field, with treacherous footing, to the maternity pen. She would be exuberant and in high spirits if she hadn't been ridden for a while, but she settled down to perfect seriousness when we went after a cow; I was always confident that the two of us would get the job done efficiently and safely. I used her for cattle work until she was 26 years old, when she had to be put down due to complications from an allergic reaction, then continued on with her son Nikkolis (three-fourths Arabian) who was nearly as good at chasing cows as she was.

Nellace and Nikki had the type of conformation that makes for durability and versatility. They were able to run fast, jump logs and rocks, stop and turn swiftly, gallop downhill full speed after a cow (with perfect balance and control without being rough or stumbling), hit a bog or a slick spot at full speed and collect and keep going without falling. They had natural talent, enhanced with good training. Their surefootedness and balance (their "agility ability"), stemmed from good conformation: ideal leg and body angles that enabled them to move with grace, precision, speed, and stamina — through a long life of hard work in steep country. This type of work takes a harsh toll on most horses' joints, eventually creating arthritis, stiffness, and impaired ability, yet those two mares stayed sound.

Very few horses possess the conformation needed for this kind of dependability in a strenuous athletic career. Some horses can do a great job of cow cutting on good footing in a level arena but don't have the agility or stamina for this type of work all day long in steep terrain. I came to realize that Nellace and Nikki embodied near-perfect "ideal" conformation that is so difficult to find in modern horses.

●　　●　　●

The horseman's goal is to breed or select individuals that come as close to ideal conformation as possible. This book is meant to serve as a guide to help you find your own Nellace or Nikki — the best horse for your specific needs in any equine sport or career, but focusing mainly on riding horses. The first part focuses on anatomy and general conformation principles; the second part walks you through important steps in evaluating a horse. This collective knowledge will help you see beyond a horse's beauty to recognize the hallmarks of good conformation, soundness, and athletic potential — invaluable tools no matter what type of decision you need to make. Whether judging or selecting a horse, buying a new horse, making breeding decisions, or determining your horse's suitability for a certain sport or activity, this book will help you. You'll also learn more about horses and how they function, which will help you become a better horseman.

ACKNOWLEDGMENTS

Much of the information in this book is drawn from more than 45 years of working with and writing about horses. I've talked with and interviewed many knowledgeable people on various topics pertaining to conformation, soundness, and lameness over the years. I thank them all, and for the purposes of this book I especially wish to thank:

- Mike Barter, equine dentist, Ardmore, Oklahoma
- Elizabeth Graves, horsewoman, horse show judge, and educator, who gives clinics on better ways to select and ride gaited horses of all breeds, Spring Grove, Minnesota
- C. Wayne McIlwraith, BVSc, PhD, DSc, FRCVS, Dipl. ACVS, Director of Equine Orthopedic Research Center, Colorado State University, Fort Collins, Colorado
- Tia Nelson, DVM, veterinarian/farrier specializing in restoring lame horses to soundness, Helena, Montana
- Robert Schneider, DVM, MS, Professor of Orthopedic Surgery, Washington State University, whose private practice specializes in lameness problems, Pullman, Washington
- Heidi Smith, DVM, retired veterinarian and breeder of Arabian endurance horses, Tendoy, Idaho
- Lee Ziegler, breeder and judge of gaited horses of all breeds, Black Forest, Colorado

Preliminaries

A WELL-BUILT RIDING HORSE can run faster, farther, and more nimbly than any other animal with a rider on its back. This athletic prowess springs from the form and function of the equine body. A horse with good conformation is more comfortable to ride and easier to train than a horse with poor conformation, because he can handle himself better and move in any direction with ease and flexibility.

We often ask horses to perform tasks that are more demanding than anything they would do naturally. We ask them to travel at high speeds while carrying a rider,

A horse with good conformation is athletic, moves with fluidity and grace, and is easier to ride and train than a horse with poor conformation. Learning how to recognize desirable qualities will help you select the best horse for your needs.

often for distances far greater than they would run in the wild to elude a predator. We may ask a horse to jump higher over obstacles than he would ever jump in nature, or to spin and dodge after a cow or a polo ball. Our expectations often put a horse's body under much greater stress and strain than a free-roaming wild horse would ever encounter.

To reduce the risks of physical injury, the horses we ride must have excellent conformation and fluid, efficient action — attributes that help, rather than hinder, job performance. Learning how to recognize these qualities will help you choose the best horse for the job.

Why Conformation Is Important

When selecting or evaluating a horse, there are many factors to consider: breed, breed type (how the horse embodies the characteristics of his breed or type), pedigree, color, disposition, and personality. Most important is conformation, particularly if a horse is a candidate for an athletic career, long years of sound service, or breeding. Avoid the disappointment and heartbreak of a career-ending injury or arthritic disability by selecting a horse with conformation as close to the ideal as possible; make sure the various aspects of his build are well suited to the activity.

Some of the "rules" of good conformation are based on physics and geometry — structural strength, leverage forces, and proper angles, for instance — and these help us understand why, when performing similar tasks, some horses stay sound and others do not. They also help explain why some aspects of conformation favor the jumper, draft horse, racehorse, or other equine specialist.

A horse with good conformation has no obvious faults that detract from his general makeup. In addition, he usually has grace and "presence," that indefinable something that catches the eye and gives the impression that he is a good one. It is this presence and a pleasing overall appearance, coupled with fluidity and grace, that help convince a horseman that he has found a winner.

Athletic ability can be a somewhat elusive quality; you can't always tell by looking at a horse whether he will be an outstanding performer. Some good-looking horses don't move as well as expected, and some not-so-good-looking ones move very well and excel in athletic careers. Each horse is an individual and has a variety of strengths and weaknesses.

The adage that winners of races come in all shapes also applies to jumpers, pleasure horses, stock horses, and dressage horses, but generally this is the exception, not the rule. Most of the best equine athletes possess certain qualities of good conformation that enable them to perform with greater agility, precision, speed, and stamina than horses with poor conformation.

Evaluating potential for future soundness is always a gamble, and good conformation may not always guarantee good performance. A horse also must have the heart and strength of will to do his best. Conformation greatly influences a horse's "way of going" and ability to move correctly, making it the principal factor that determines whether he will be a good athlete or a poor one.

Generally, the horse with good conformation and proper body and leg angles experiences less wear and tear on joints and other structures. He is more apt to stay sound during a long life of athletic service than a horse with serious flaws.

Some Definitions

Blemish: A visible lump, thickening, or scar. A blemish is not considered an unsoundness unless it interferes with a moving part, the ability of the horse to work, or has the potential to cause lameness with hard work. A blemish is *not* a fault of the horse's conformation. A blemish might be a scar, a healed splint due to a kick on the outside of the cannon bone, or wind puffs at the fetlock joint due to strain on the joint capsules from overwork.

Conformation: How a horse's body is put together; specifically, his body shape, the configuration of the parts of the body, the relationship between those structures, and how they function. Conformation determines how a horse moves and how well or poorly his body can withstand the effects of that movement, specifically stress and concussion.

Fault: An undesirable aspect of conformation, such as sickle hocks, splayed feet or pigeon toes, a too-short neck, or some other flaw. In some instances, a fault may lead to an unsoundness if the horse is worked hard.

Sound horse: A healthy horse with no injuries or impairments.

Unsound horse: A horse with a physical injury or abnormality that interferes with his usefulness.

Unsoundness: Anything that makes a horse lame or unsafe to ride, impairs the stamina needed for an ordinary day's work, or otherwise makes him unable to perform normally.

Unsoundness

Poor conformation predisposes horses for certain unsoundnesses, and poor conformation can be inherited. If the sire or dam has crooked legs, for example, the foal may have crooked legs. Navicular syndrome (chronic pain involving the navicular bone and its surrounding structures) used to be considered an inherited problem, but what is actually inherited is the foot and leg structure that makes a horse more prone to navicular trauma. Some types of conformation can make a horse more likely to develop ringbone, splints, curb, or some other type of injury and breakdown or impairment.

Injuries from accidents are responsible for some types of unsoundness: a dislocated stifle caused by a kick, blindness due to a blow to the eye, or sidebone caused by a wire cut, for example. Other types of unsoundness, such as a bowed tendon, bucked shins, and certain types of splints, can result from excessive strain and overwork. Many problems caused by strain and trauma tend to occur more readily and be more severe in a horse with poor conformation than in one with good conformation. The feet and legs of a horse with good conformation suffer less strain from the outset, because the force is distributed equally along the well-formed structure, rather than there being too much pull or concussion on any one part of the leg.

SEVERITY

An unsoundness can be mild or severe, depending in part on the horse's function. An unsoundness, such as a bowed tendon or bone spavin, can hinder a horse used for racing, endurance competition, chasing wild cattle all day in steep mountains, jumping, or some other strenuous activity, but it may not hinder a horse used for quiet pleasure riding or as a child's first mount. Even horses selected for pleasure riding or for a child may harbor some types of unsoundness that can become worse with use. A horse with poor conformation or an old injury due to poor conformation may not be lame today, but that does not guarantee that he will not be lame tomorrow.

A prospective child's horse must be safe to ride at faster gaits in case the youngster decides to try some speed, but a horse used for this type of riding will not undergo as much stress as he would in a career of endurance competition or eventing. A horse that has foundered (but is correctively shod to travel comfortably) or has an old injury that flares up only when he is used hard may still be able to perform adequately as a pleasure horse for a rider who does not make long or strenuous rides.

The Veterinarian's Role

If you are unsure about a horse's conformation, particularly regarding suitability for a certain purpose or sport, or are wondering whether a horse will hold up and stay sound, have an equine veterinarian evaluate the horse. A pre-purchase soundness examination is always wise when selecting a horse for an athletic career. Choose a veterinarian who specializes in equine health and lameness and have her examine the horse and give you an informed opinion about the horse's future usefulness. In a pre-purchase exam, the veterinarian checks for lameness, respiratory impairment, and any other unsoundness.

PART I

Anatomy and Principles of Conformation

To understand basic horse conformation, it helps to become familiar with the underlying structures of the body, the skeletal bones; this will be our focus in chapters 2 through 9.

Conformation depends primarily on bone structure and only marginally on musculature and fat cover. Even though all horses have the same basic skeletal structure, bone lengths and their relationships with one another vary from horse to horse, resulting in different body proportions. Small differences can sometimes have a significant impact on how well a horse can perform a certain task. Fundamental differences exist among breeds and among individuals within a particular breed.

Understanding horse conformation begins with basic lessons about the equine skeleton, a movable framework constructed of bones and connected by joints, which are held together by ligaments. When muscles contract, pulling on tendons attached to the bones, the bones move.

Basic Anatomy

HORSES ARE ATHLETES. As prey animals in their natural habitat, their survival depended on quickness and speed, the ability to leap into action and spin away from a pouncing predator. The horse's flexible, agile neck allows him to swiftly swing his head to either side or raise it to look over his back and behind himself. Horses also had to be able to outrun predators. Any horse that couldn't bolt away from the wolves or big cats that stalked the grazing herd soon became dinner.

After domesticating horses, humans took advantage of their athletic ability and selectively bred them for various purposes. As a result, certain types of horses are

To understand how a horse moves and to determine the likelihood of future soundness and success in a certain career, you need a basic understanding of equine anatomy, especially the skeletal and muscle systems. Conformation affects a horse's athletic ability.

swifter than their wild counterparts; others are superior in their ability to jump, dodge after a cow, or pull heavy wagons. These athletic accomplishments are possible because of the way the horse's body is formed. When breeding or selecting horses for specific purposes, we must have a good eye for the aspects of conformation that promote soundness and enable a horse to excel in what we want him to do.

Form Follows Function

When evaluating a horse, it's important to consider his conformation and how it affects his health, soundness, and ability to perform his job. To understand how the horse moves and to evaluate his chances for athletic success in a certain task or sport, we must have a basic understanding of equine anatomy, especially the horse's skeletal and muscle systems.

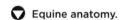 Equine anatomy.

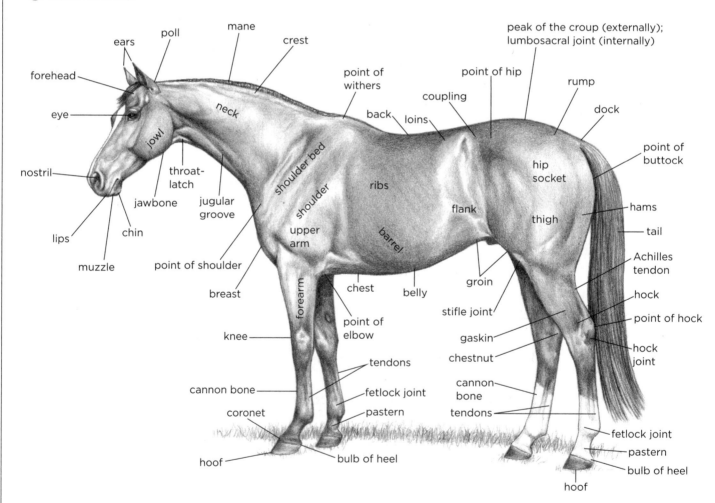

You can more easily visualize how the horse's skeletal system works when you realize that nearly every part of the horse's body, except the tail, corresponds to a similar part of the human body.

Comparative Anatomy: Horses vs. Humans

The horse's ancestors had multiple toes (comparable to our toes and fingers), but the modern horse retained only the widened and elongated middle toe. Humans have one anatomical feature that the horse and other four-legged animals do not have — the clavicle, or collarbone — but in most other aspects our anatomies are similar.

FRONT LEGS

The bones of the equine front leg are similar to those of the human arm, arranged in the same order: shoulder blade, humerus (upper arm), elbow, and radius and ulna in the forearm. There are a few minor differences. The two arm bones (radius and ulna) are fused together in the horse and the ulna is smaller, but the upper end remains as the point of the elbow. In humans, these two arm bones are separate but parallel in the forearm. This allows the human forearm to rotate at the elbow, whereas the horse's forearm cannot rotate. Thus, in the horse's front leg, the knee, which is equivalent to the human wrist, must move forward in a straight line. This is critical to the action and stability of the horse's leg in supporting and propelling his body.

Another difference is that the human arm is free moving and independent from the shoulder joint down, whereas the horse's humerus, equivalent to the arm bone, is attached to the chest wall by skin and muscles. It has a fair range of movement, although it is encased in the body of the horse. The range of motion of the horse's upper arm is limited, as a human's would be if someone were to tie a rope around the chest and upper arms, leaving the arms free only from the elbows down.

HIND LEGS

In a horse's hind leg, the femur (the upper leg bone, or thighbone) is also bound to the body by muscle and skin. This gives the visual impression that the horse's hind leg begins at the stifle, just as you might think a horse's front leg begins at the elbow, but it actually starts where the pelvis joins the spine. The bones and joints of the equine hind leg are similar to the bones and joints of the human leg. The horse's stifle has the same structure as the human knee, with the patella, or kneecap, being the same.

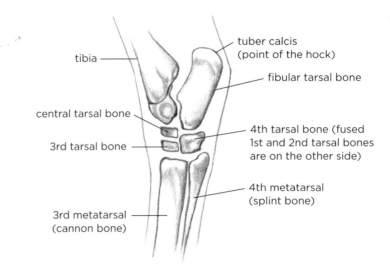

tibia

tuber calcis
(point of the hock)

fibular tarsal bone

central tarsal bone

4th tarsal bone (fused
1st and 2nd tarsal bones
are on the other side)

3rd tarsal bone

4th metatarsal
(splint bone)

3rd metatarsal
(cannon bone)

▶ The bones of the equine hock correspond to the bones of the human ankle joint.

KNEES AND HOCKS

The horse's front leg is like the human arm, with the equine "knee" corresponding to the human wrist and having the same seven bones in identical arrangement: six little flat bones in a double row, with the seventh bone, the accessory carpal bone, standing out at the back of the horse's knee, as does the small prominence at the back of the human wrist on the inner side.

The horse's hind leg compares to the human leg, with the hock joint corresponding to the human ankle and having the same seven bones. The point of the hock is similar to the human heel; both have an Achilles tendon. The strong muscle above the hock (in the gaskin area) is similar to the human calf muscle.

LOWER LEG

The cannon bone, front and rear (below the horse's knee or hock), corresponds to the human middle finger or toe, and the fetlock joint is equivalent to the middle knuckle on that finger or toe. The horse's hoof is like the tip of our middle finger, if it were encased in fingernail. The horse's hoof wall grows down from the coronary band in the same way our fingernails grow.

A human has five fingers and toes, but the horse has only one central "finger" and two reduced digits on either side of it. When comparing the horse's lower front leg to the human hand, we see that the horse's thumb and little finger have disappeared. The bones above the ring and index finger have shrunk in size to become the narrow splint bones that go partway down the cannon bone, leaving the enlarged middle bone (cannon bone) to bear the horse's weight. The knee joint is partially supported by these small splint bones, but the

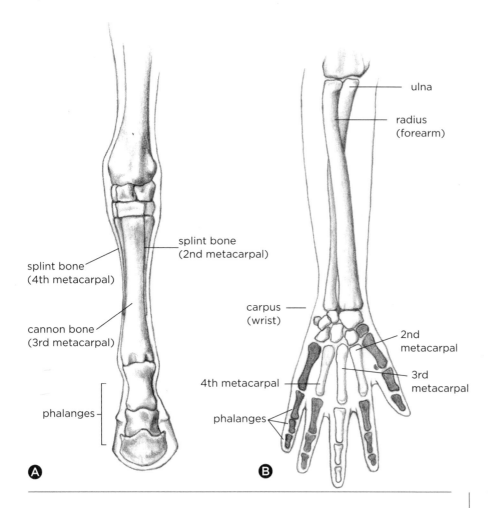

splint bone
(2nd metacarpal)

splint bone
(4th metacarpal)

cannon bone
(3rd metacarpal)

phalanges

A

ulna

radius
(forearm)

carpus
(wrist)

4th metacarpal

2nd
metacarpal

3rd
metacarpal

phalanges

B

◀ The bones of the horse's front leg (A) correspond to the human forearm and hand (B). The shaded bones in the human hand no longer have counterparts in the horse.

large, strong cannon bone (third metacarpal) is the main support structure. In the hind leg, the cannon bone (third metatarsal) compares with the human middle toe, with the hock joint also partially supported by the smaller bones (splint bones) alongside it.

CHEST SHAPE

The rib cages of horse and human have similar bones, although the chest shape is different. The thorax (chest) of the horse is flatter from side to side, and the shoulder blades move back and forth along its sides. The human chest is flatter from front to back, and our shoulder blades move at the back of our rib cage. The horse's chest is much deeper from breastbone to spine, and the horse has much greater lung capacity and therefore greater wind, or breathing capacity, and endurance than a human.

NECK AND HEAD

The horse's neck is longer and more mobile than the human neck but has the same seven bones. The horse's heavy head allows him to use his neck as a pendulum, swinging it up and down or to the side to shift his balance, which he can do quickly when he stops or changes direction. His long neck also helps him reach the ground when grazing. In his natural habitat, as a prey animal always looking for predators, the horse can turn his head quickly to view a large area.

The horse's long neck enhances his speed when galloping. When galloping swiftly, he carries his head as far forward as possible, creating a fixed point from which the neck muscle — rapidly contracting and relaxing in time with the front leg movement — can assist the muscles of the legs in reaching farther forward, generating speed. Even though the hind legs, with their large, strong muscles, generate much of the horse's propelling power, the front legs help pull the body forward at all gaits. Thus, the long-necked horse has a slight speed advantage over a short-necked horse (see chapter 3).

▼ The equine skeleton, side view.

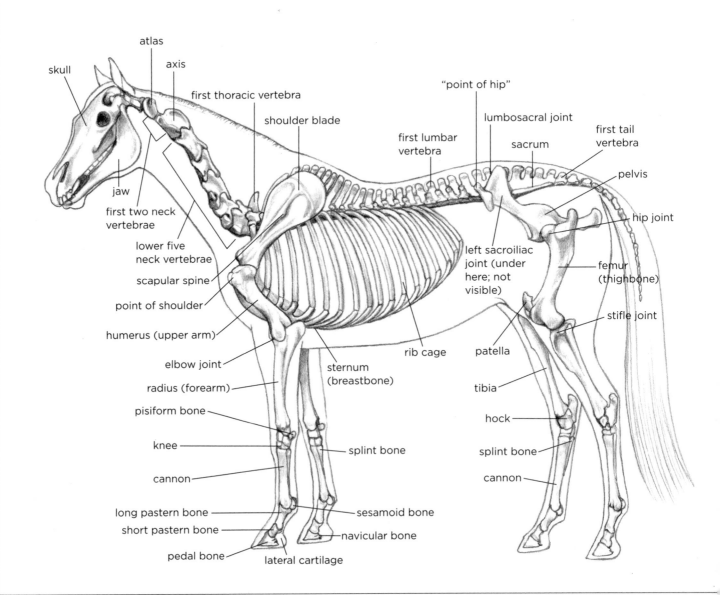

Basics of the Equine Skeleton

The horse's skeleton includes about 205 bones; some references list 210. The horse has roughly 54 vertebrae (give or take a few depending on the number of tailbones), 36 ribs, 40 bones in the front legs, 40 bones in the back legs, 34 bones in the skull, and 1 breastbone. Some of the long bones support and protect the chest cavity (ribs), and others support and move the horse (legs). Block-shaped bones of knee and hock help to absorb concussion. Bones are held together at joints by strong bands of tissue called *ligaments*, which are discussed later in this chapter.

BONE STRUCTURE MATTERS

The horse's bone structure is determined principally by genetics and influenced somewhat by nutrition. Although improper nutrition when a horse is young and growing can damage an inherently well-conformed skeletal structure, adequate nutrition can't do much to improve a structure that is inherently poor.

Likewise, no amount of muscle conditioning to try to enhance a horse's ability or appearance can change his basic conformation, although some faults may be disguised somewhat by good muscle development or fat covering. Some leg deformities in foals can be helped with surgery or corrective trimming of hooves while the leg bones are still growing, but for the most part a horse's basic structure is present at birth and cannot be changed. The skeletal structure must be carefully evaluated when selecting or judging a horse.

The conformation of any animal depends on the shape and character of the vertebral column. The horse's backbone ties the entire skeleton together, and all other structures of the animal attach to the spine. As an early horseman said when discussing horse breeding, if a person could breed the perfect spine, he could be certain of breeding the perfect horse.

TYPES OF VERTEBRAE

The vertebrae vary in shape according to their position in the spine. There are 7 neck bones (cervical vertebrae), 18 bones in the back (thoracic vertebrae, sometimes called the *dorsal vertebrae*, the first 9 of which make up the withers), 6 bones in the loin area (lumbar vertebrae), 5 fused bones in the sacrum (the area of the rump, between the point of the croup and the tail head), and 15 to 20 small tail bones. The different parts of the horse's back can vary in length among individuals, depending on the shape of certain vertebrae; horses have short necks or long necks, long backs or short ones. Arabians often

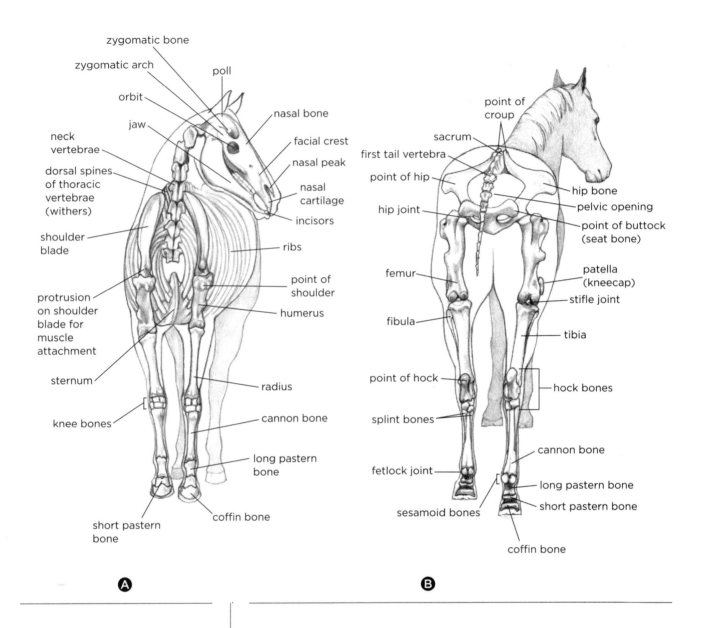

zygomatic bone

zygomatic arch

poll

orbit

jaw

nasal bone

facial crest

nasal peak

nasal cartilage

incisors

neck vertebrae

dorsal spines of thoracic vertebrae (withers)

shoulder blade

protrusion on shoulder blade for muscle attachment

sternum

ribs

point of shoulder

humerus

radius

cannon bone

knee bones

long pastern bone

short pastern bone

coffin bone

point of croup

sacrum

first tail vertebra

point of hip

hip joint

point of hock

splint bones

fetlock joint

sesamoid bones

femur

fibula

hip bone

pelvic opening

point of buttock (seat bone)

patella (kneecap)

stifle joint

tibia

hock bones

cannon bone

long pastern bone

short pastern bone

coffin bone

A

B

⬢ The equine skeleton A. Front view B. Rear view

have one less lumbar vertebrae than other horses in the loin area.

The backbone protects the spinal cord (the cable of nerves that links the brain to all parts of the body), and the main nerves emerge between each of the vertebrae. The bones lying end to end form a tunnel for the spinal cord. The cartilage disks between the bones not only cushion the bones but keep them from pinching the nerves that branch out from the spinal cord. The vertebrae also contain bone marrow (the core of all the larger bones), which plays a part in the horse's blood production.

The ribs attach to the thoracic vertebrae. The pelvic bones are attached to the spine in the area between the lumbar vertebrae and the sacrum (at the lumbosacral joint), creating an attachment for the hind legs. Muscular development of loins and hindquarters depends a great deal on the conformation of the spine.

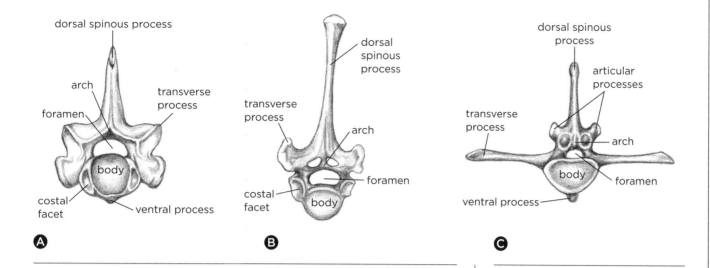

PELVIS

The hind legs are attached to the spine by means of the pelvis, which is actually a bony girdle made up of several fused bones. Each side of the pelvis is a flat semicircle made up of the ilium (haunch bone, which at its top joins the spine at the iliosacral joint), the ischium (seat bone, whose rearmost part forms the point of the buttock), and the pubis, the smaller bone on the bottom that forms the lower edge of the circle. These six bones (three on each side) are so firmly fused together by early adulthood that they seem to be one large bone.

The pelvis has several projections to which various large muscles attach, giving the hindquarters their shape. The muscles of the loins attach here. The bony girdle is not upright, but slanted, and the angle varies with the breed and the individual horse. The degree of angulation influences the shape of the rump and the general conformation of the hind leg. (See chapter 11 for a discussion of body angles.)

SPINAL FLEXION

In a horse, movement between the vertebrae along the back is quite limited, except in the neck. In the region of the back (thoracic vertebrae), there is little movement. There is some flexibility in the lumbar region (at the loins), with some up-and-down and side-to-side motion, but not nearly as much motion as in the dog, for example. The backbone of smaller mammals (such as cats, dogs, and rabbits) is much more flexible than that of a horse.

The limited amount of flexibility in the equine spine diminishes further as a horse grows older, because some of the lumbar vertebrae tend to fuse together. The horse's spine is designed for rigidity and gives a stable point of reference and leverage for the powerful thrust of the hindquarters, allowing that force to be transmitted into forward movement.

Three joints in the spine between the vertebrae allow extensive up-and-down movement. The occipitoatloid joint between the head and neck allows the horse to flex at the poll behind the ears to carry his nose straight forward or closer to his chest. The cervicothoracic joint between the neck and thoracic vertebrae of the chest permits the horse to lower his head to graze or raise it higher to look for danger in the distance. The lumbosacral joint joins the last loin (lumbar) vertebra and the sacrum.

The lumbosacral joint allows the horse's pelvis and hindquarters to rotate forward so his hind legs can reach far beneath his belly when galloping, giving him a much longer stride. This enables him to create a strong push-off when jumping. Considering how stiff the backbone is, this is a remarkable hinge, enabling the horse to tuck his hindquarters underneath himself for greater agility and balance going down a steep hill or to "collect" himself, with more weight carried by his hind legs.

NECK VERTEBRAE

Viewing the neck from the side, the neck bones do not go in a straight line, but follow an S-shaped curve, with a dip at the base (see illustration on page 43). The neck bones straighten when the horse lowers his head to graze and when he stretches his neck to its full length while galloping at top speed.

Just ahead of the shoulder, the neck is primarily thick muscle, with the bones at the lower portion. The horse is able to support his heavy head by means of the nuchal ligament, a thick, fibrous double ligament that stretches from the bones of the withers to the back of the skull; there is one ligament on either side of the head. From this strong brace, flat bands run down to the neck bones to help the muscles of the neck support the head. Without this brace, the muscles would have to be much thicker and stronger, making the horse less balanced and a lot less agile.

SHAPE OF THE VERTEBRAE

Each vertebra in the spine has transverse processes (bony projections, like wings, that stick out to the side) and a dorsal spinous process (a projection that sticks out at the top). The dorsal spinous processes are short in the neck bones and along the back where the rider sits, but the 6 to 10 vertebrae that make up the withers have dorsal spinous processes that gradually increase to about 6 inches in height and then diminish. This forms the characteristic curved, raised ridge of the withers and is where the muscles that hold the shoulder blade in place attach. The transverse (lateral) processes, or side wings, of the lumbar vertebrae (in the loin area) are wide to create an attachment for the large muscles of the back and quarters, which power the horse's actions as he jumps or gallops.

HOW THE LIMBS ATTACH TO THE BACKBONE

The horse's skeleton is an example of mechanical perfection, exemplifying basic principles of leverage and physics. The shock-absorbing characteristics and muscular suspension of the front quarters are a marvelous design. The shoulders of the horse are not attached via bones to the spine; instead, the body is suspended between the shoulders and supported by springy muscle attachments that are ideal for minimizing concussion.

The hind legs, by contrast, are firmly and directly attached to the spine at the pelvis. This enables the horse to have a perfect union of hind legs and body for creating maximum power and forward propulsion when running and jumping. Leverage and thrust from the hind legs are maximized by this direct connection.

In this arrangement, however, the hind legs must be properly constructed to absorb concussion impact, including appropriate angles in the hocks and stifles and a concave sole in the hind foot that can flatten and give when the foot bears weight. Because the pelvis is attached to the spine at the sacrum, which is capable of only limited movement, any concussion not absorbed by the hind leg itself is transmitted to the disks between the vertebrae. If these have already suffered jarring and overcompression or have become fused due to concussion (and subsequent inflammation and calcification), any buffering effect they once offered will be eliminated. Therefore, poor hind leg structure (resulting in excessive concussion in the hind limbs) can lead to a painful spine.

How Bones and Muscles Work Together

To evaluate the horse's conformation we must look individually at the various parts and consider how these parts work together, enabling the horse to function and perform his job. Apart from the body cavities that contain internal organs, the rest of the horse consists of bones, muscles, joints, tendons (which attach muscles to bones), and ligaments (which hold bones together at various joints).

Muscles cover the bones. Muscles and fat give the horse his external contour; they enable him to have more strength and endurance

Thorax and Abdomen

The horse's body consists primarily of thorax and abdomen: two separate cavities that are suspended from the backbone. The abdomen takes up the largest space, with the thorax, or chest cavity, ahead of it. The thorax lies within the front portion of the rib cage and contains the heart and lungs. The diaphragm (a large partition of muscle) separates the thorax from the abdomen. The abdomen contains many of the body's organs: stomach, intestines, liver, kidneys, and spleen, among others.

Bone Types

There are two kinds of bones: round ones that contain marrow in their centers and flat ones that do not. The long bones of the legs that support the horse's weight are considered round bones and have a joint at each end. Flat bones (like the ribs) and bones of irregular shape have a hard outer layer and a softer interior.

when he is fit and in shape and can add to or detract from his overall appearance. The bones underneath must be structurally correct, however, for the horse to perform at his best.

⊶◯ *Conformation Close-up*

Muscle and fitness alone cannot compensate for structural defects like an upright shoulder, a too-short neck or hindquarter, or a back that's too long.

MUSCLES MOVE THE BONES

Muscles are attached to bones by tendons at strategic locations, and they move the bones by contracting and relaxing. The bones are connected to one another by joints, which extend (open) or flex (close) in response to the movement of muscles.

For example, the two prominent muscles in the shoulder area — the biceps and the triceps — open and close the elbow joint by pulling on the bones at different positions. When the biceps contracts, it flexes the elbow joint and pulls the arm bone forward and upward, lifting the horse's front foot from the ground. The triceps has the opposite effect. When it contracts, it extends the elbow and sends the foot back down to the ground. The two muscles work together to create smooth action, without jerking the leg or putting strain on the joints. Both muscles contract simultaneously, but one is more dominant than the other during specific phases of the horse's stride. All of the muscles that move bones must work in perfect synchronization or the joints won't move smoothly and will be under stress, and bones will be at risk of being broken.

JOINTS AND THEIR ANGLES

Joints are the junctions between bones that enable one bone to move in relationship to another. There are three types of joints within the body: movable joints (in which the bones are joined together with ligaments and the moving parts are lubricated with synovial fluid contained within the joint capsules), slightly movable joints (in which the bones are bound together by cartilage and have limited movement, such as between the vertebrae), and immovable joints (such as points where bones of the skull meet, fusing together to create a solid structure).

The movable joints in the legs enable the horse to bend and lift his legs, and help to absorb the concussion created by the impact of feet hitting the ground. The joints between the leg bones are created by the ends of the bones, each covered with a protective layer of smooth, tough cartilage to make a frictionless gliding surface. The surface is made even smoother and slicker by the synovial fluid secreted by the inner lining of the joint capsule. The fluid provides perfect lubrication for the joint and works as a greased ball bearing does, protecting the bone surfaces from wear and tear. Because of the demands of movement, however, movable joints are the ones most likely to be injured by uneven stresses caused by improper angles and hard work.

The joint is secured by ligaments attached to both bones and is stabilized by the fibrous joint capsule that surrounds it. The ligaments connect the bones firmly so that they move only in certain ways. The basic conformation of the horse determines the long-term strength and durable service of the leg joints (stifles, hocks, elbows, knees, fetlock joints); ideally, it allows the leg bones to move continually without overstraining the joint.

The angle at which certain bones in the body connect can vary greatly from one horse to another. This affects the horse's conformation and athletic power, speed, and agility. The angle between femur and tibia in the stifle joint of the hind leg, for instance, may range anywhere from 100 to 140 degrees, depending on the horse.

If the angle is closer to 140 degrees, the horse will have a straight stifle and usually a straight hock, making him *post-legged* (hind leg too straight; when viewed from the side, the hock is nearly under the stifle instead of being directly under the buttocks). This poor conformation hinders athletic ability and tends to pull the patella out of place, locking the stifle joint.

If the angle is closer to 100 degrees, the stifle and hock joint are overbent, creating a condition called *sickle hocks:* there is too much curve at the hock joint, putting the lower leg at an angle, with the feet

Balance Is Key

A horse with good conformation exerts balanced stress on the leg joints. With proper leg angles and equal weight bearing on the various parts, the stresses on joints are minimized, connecting tendons stay strong, lubricating sacs function properly, and joints stay sound and healthy. Conversely, the joints of a horse with poor conformation undergo uneven stress, which can create more pull (of ligament or tendon on bone) on one side of the joint than the other, for example, and in turn may prompt joint problems if he is worked hard. In such a horse, there is risk for pulled tendons and ligaments and more wear on joint surfaces.

A crooked leg may eventually cause inflammation in certain joints or a tearing away of the ligament attachment. With even a minor tear or disruption, the resulting inflammation may lead to lameness and arthritis (inflammation of a joint) and a number of other serious problems. If there is excessive stress on a joint capsule, it may produce too much synovial fluid, causing joint swelling, or it may be unable to prevent friction between the moving parts, resulting in painful wearing of the bone ends. An improper angle between the bones will make the horse less efficient, hampering his ability as an athlete.

too far underneath the body. Ideal angulation is somewhere between the two extremes and can vary slightly, depending on what the horse is used for. A moderate angle (at neither extreme) enables the horse to be a better athlete, and exerts less stress on the joints, reducing the risk of injury and unsoundness (see chapter 11 for more on body angles).

🔍 *Conformation Close-up*

In an individual horse, angles tend to be similar. A horse with straight stifles usually has straight hocks, and a horse with bent hocks (curved, sickle hocks) usually has similarly angled stifles.

MECHANICS OF THE FRONT LEG

In the front leg, the shoulder blade is a flat bone that joins the humerus, or upper leg bone. The shoulder blade is divided lengthwise by a ridge of bone known as the *spine of the scapula*. On either side of this ridge, there is a deep depression to which the shoulder muscles are attached. The size and development of these muscles determine whether the horse has a light, flat shoulder or a heavy, bulging (loaded) shoulder.

The lower end of the humerus forms a joint with the upper end of the fused radius and ulna: the elbow. The back part of the humerus has two pronged surfaces for joining the radius and ulna, and between these two surfaces is the olecranon fossa, a deep groove. When weight is placed on the foreleg, the olecranon process (the free portion of the ulna) enters the olecranon fossa and completely locks the joint, providing exceptional stability to the leg. The elbow joint can move only in a straight line, with the rest of the leg (see chapter 7).

When the foot bears weight, therefore, the elbow and front leg become rigid, giving dependable support for the horse. When the foot is lifted from the ground with knee bent (with the back of the cannon parallel to the back of the forearm), the elbow joint is unlocked and becomes capable of a wide range (about 100 degrees) of backward and forward motion. The elbow can only move when the knee is bent.

Like the elbow, the knee can only flex in one direction. The ligaments of the knee and the muscles and tendons of the foreleg keep the knee from advancing forward beyond a perpendicular position.

MECHANICS OF THE HIND LEG

The hind leg is attached to the spine at the pelvis. The pelvis consists of two bony semicircles, one on each side of the spine, that fuse together to form a complete bony circle. A joint cavity on either side creates a socket for the head of the femur, or thighbone.

The stifle is the largest joint in the horse's body. Comparable to the human knee, it consists of the lower end of the femur, the upper end of the tibia, and the patella, or kneecap. The stifle joint keeps the leg rigid when the foot is on the ground bearing weight. Due to the arrangement of muscles and tendons, the hock cannot bend when the stifle is straight (extended), nor can the stifle bend when the hock joint is extended. The two joints must work in unison. This configuration, along with the locking elbow joint and support of the head from the neck's large ligament, makes it possible for a horse to sleep while standing up.

LIGAMENTS

Ligaments are the strong bands of connective tissues that hold bones together at joints. They support and strengthen the joints. Many joints have collateral ligaments, or ligaments on each side, to hold the bones together. A few joints, such as the hip and stifle, have intra-articular ligaments, that is, ligaments inside the joint itself. Some ligaments are long, like those running along the neck or back, and some are short, like those between each vertebra. Some are cords, such as in the lower legs, and some are complex structures, such as the one that runs down the crest of the neck, fanning out in sections to attach to the neck vertebrae below it. Other ligaments are sheets of tissue that wrap around certain joints.

In the horse's front legs are check ligaments, which help connect a bone to a tendon. For example, the inferior and superior check ligaments prevent bending of the knee when the horse sleeps while standing up. An annular, or ring-shaped, ligament goes across or around a joint to hold the nearby tendons close to the joint; the back of the fetlock joint has such a ligament.

TENDONS

Tendons are bands of dense, white, fibrous connective tissue at the ends of muscles that connect the muscle to the nearby bone. These strong cords create movement by transmitting the muscle contraction into a pull on the bone. Some tendons attach to more than one

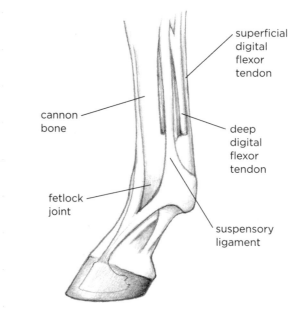

▲ Ligaments and tendons of the front leg.

The Tendon Sheath

If a tendon passes over a joint, a tendon sheath that produces a lubricating fluid protects the tendon from friction wear. In this way, a tendon sheath is similar to a joint capsule.

bone and can thus act on several joints at once with an additional muscle contraction.

Tendons are made of long fibers and are stronger than muscles but less elastic. The thicker and shorter the tendon, the stronger it is. Long tendons are weaker, due to the increased effect of leverage. A long cannon bone and its lengthy tendon has less strength than a shorter one, for instance, because the longer tendon has to move a greater weight or withstand a greater force over more distance.

MUSCLES

The horse has more than seven hundred skeletal muscles, which contribute more than one-third of his body weight. Muscles are bundles of elastic fibers. The muscles that move various bones are usually shaped like bands, with ends that taper into tendons. Most muscle ends attach to bones, but some attach to other muscles or to the skin.

In addition to creating movement, muscles can limit or prevent movement in a different direction. For instance, the muscles that pull the forearm (top of the front leg) in toward the body also restrain it from being pulled too far out from the body.

Most of the muscles that enable the horse to move are arranged in pairs, with one on either side of the body or leg bone. When one contracts, the other relaxes. This is called *reciprocal muscle action*. This paired arrangement enables the bone to move in opposite directions, such as a leg moving both forward and back, and also keeps the action smooth rather than jerky and irregular. The muscles on each side of the bone regulate and maintain the proper tension or relaxation for precise movement.

The horse's neck has twenty-four pairs of muscles responsible for arching, bending, and straightening the neck and lifting, lowering, and rotating the head. Muscles are anchored to vertebrae at the withers, which serve as a leverage point for neck, shoulder, and back movement. Muscles at the front of the chest help move the front legs.

The ring of muscles encircling the chest to give attachment and support to the front legs is called the *shoulder girdle.* In the horse, the shoulder blade is not attached by bone to the body, so these strong muscles hold the shoulder blade in place and help absorb the concussion that travels up the leg each time a front foot hits the ground, reducing stress and impact on the backbone.

The shoulder girdle allows the shoulder blade to move back and forth, enabling the horse to extend his front legs much farther than would be possible if they were connected to bone joints. The more flexible muscle girdle also allows his body to move up and down, affecting the horse's center of gravity, and to shift a front leg toward or away from the body to aid in sudden changes of direction or tight turns. At a fast gallop, for instance, the horse can lean into a turn with his legs while keeping his body and spine straight.

The muscles of the legs are extensors and flexors. The extensor muscles at the front of the forearm move the front leg forward, while the flexors at the back of the forearm flex the joints of the lower leg (knee, fetlock, and pastern joints). The knee has muscles that straighten it and muscles that bend it. Below the knee, all the muscles of the forearm extend downward as long tendons. There are no muscles below the knee. The same is true in cattle, deer, and other ungulates. The legs work on a leverage system. Because there are no muscles in the lower legs, there is less blood supply, which enables these animals to withstand cold weather and stand in snow with no risk of frostbite in their feet and lower legs. (For more information, see page 113).

The hindquarters contain the largest muscles of the body, providing the power and leverage to propel the horse forward or to rear or kick. Some of these muscles extend the joints of the hind leg, while others act to flex the joints. As in the front leg, the muscles above the hock taper into tendons that extend down the leg to activate the lower leg joints.

Did You Know?

The muscles of a horse and their shape and strength depend partly on the way the bones are formed (inherited conformation) and partly on how fit the horse is. The overall appearance of the horse is a combination of his bone and muscle structure.

3

Head and Neck Conformation

A HORSE'S HEAD IMMEDIATELY attracts the eye. His graceful neck also garners attention. It's not surprising, then, that when judging a horse, a horseman looks at the head and neck first. A well-formed head with defined features and a proportional neck enhance a horse's appearance; more important, they contribute to his balance, athletic ability, and a rider's ability to communicate with him through the bit.

Head and neck conformation determines how a horse carries and uses his head for balance. It is a major factor in a horse's level of agility and athleticism and also affects how well he can respond to a bit.

The Head

The head of the horse is large and heavy, weighing approximately 40 pounds, on average. The horse uses his head as a pendulum, raising and lowering it to counterbalance the action of his hindquarters, to maintain and regain balance, and to help adjust speed or direction. This significantly increases his agility, enabling him to move with great precision at any speed and to have superb control of his legs.

HEAD LENGTH

One of the hallmarks of good conformation is balance and proportion. For best physical balance and maneuverability, a horse's head should complement his neck in size, weight, and length, and it should be proportionate to the horse's overall size and conformation (see page 38 for a discussion of neck conformation).

Measured from poll to top lip, the head should not be longer than the neck, which is measured from just behind the ears to the point at which it joins the withers. The horse's head should be long enough to accommodate large nasal passages and strong teeth. Some horses with very short or small heads, like miniature horses, have dental problems because their teeth are full-sized but their heads are not.

Head length varies somewhat with the breed and size of the horse. Thoroughbreds, for example, have longer heads than do Arabians or Quarter Horses.

Coarse or Heavy Head

A *coarse* head usually suggests a general coarseness or lack of refinement in other parts of the body. A certain amount of refinement is desirable in a riding animal, for it enables him to be quick and agile, whereas a draft horse needs weight, power, and strength for slow work and pulling, not speed and agility. Some aspects of conformation that are desirable in a riding animal are not advantageous in a draft animal, and vice versa. (See chapter 15 to learn how to evaluate a horse for a specific job or need.)

Because the head and neck counterbalance the body for instant changes of direction, a horse with a heavy head and long neck generally won't have the precise balance that a horse with a lighter head and long neck might have; the weight of his heavy head won't allow him to move with enough coordination for proper strength or balance.

A coarse or heavy head requires a heavier, shorter neck to carry it; however, a short, wide, or heavy-crested neck is not very flexible and hinders athletic ability. A horse with a heavy head and neck is also

usually heavy bodied, generally better suited for draft work than for agility under saddle.

⬛ Head and neck should always be in proper balance and proportion with the rest of the body.

The Too-Large Head

The size and length of the head must be proportional to neck length and body size. A horse with a head too large for his body will travel too heavily in front. A large head on a long neck will make him clumsy and difficult to collect, and he will lean heavily on the bit. Such a horse usually does not have the balance and agility needed to be a good athlete. A young horse with a too-large head may "grow into" his head, but it also may be an indication that when he matures he will have a head that is too coarse and too large.

The Too-Small Head

Because the horse uses his head as a counterweight for balance, it should not be small. A horse with a head that is small and light compared to the length of his neck and body may lose agility and is more apt to bounce when performing quick stops and to have some wasted motion during precision movements. If a young horse has a very small head, this may be an indication that he will mature to a small size and not grow well.

The Nuchal Ligament

The ligamentum nuche, the broad nuchal ligament under the mane at the top of the equine neck, stretches from the bones at the base of the skull to the bones of the withers and serves as a strong brace. From this big cord, comparable to a double rope, flat bands extend down to the neck vertebrae beneath it, helping the muscles support the heavy head.

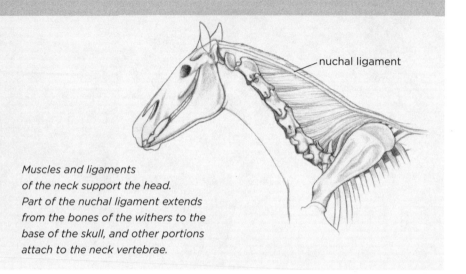

nuchal ligament

Muscles and ligaments of the neck support the head. Part of the nuchal ligament extends from the bones of the withers to the base of the skull, and other portions attach to the neck vertebrae.

PROFILE

The appeal of the head is greatly influenced by its profile, whether straight, concave, or convex. A slight dish, or concave profile, below the eyes is favored by Arabian breeders. A dished face is often accentuated in Arabian horses by a *jibbah*, a slightly bulging forehead. An extremely dished face may result in detrimental narrowing of the air passages, however.

A straight profile is acceptable in most breeds. A convex profile (Roman nose, bulging outward from the eyes down) generally is not preferred, particularly in a riding horse, because it can interfere with good vision. A Roman nose is common in draft breeds, and a convex profile may suggest cold blood somewhere in his ancestry. (See chapter 15 for more on the bloods.)

Even though a pretty head is not a necessity for the equine athlete, coarseness should be avoided. "You don't ride the head," as the old saying goes, but a head that is too coarse can interfere with balance and the horse's ability to collect and move with agility. Communication

▼ Head profiles. **A. Straight. B. Concave ("dished"). C. Convex ("Roman nose").**

A

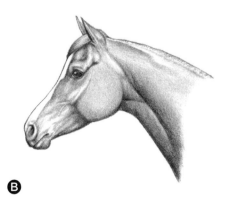

B

C

between horse and rider through the bit is enhanced when the head (from poll to mouth) is somewhat fine and mobile.

FOREHEAD WIDTH

A wide forehead is desirable because eyes set wide apart allow for better side vision. Horsemen have always believed that a wide forehead is an indication of intelligence because, presumably, a broad, flat forehead allowed more room for the brain. Sinus cavities, tear ducts, and air passages are all housed by the skull, but much of the space behind the forehead is actually devoted to sinus cavities, not the brain. The brain is located deep in the skull between the bases of the ears. A wide forehead also is often indicative of hot blood from the Arab — a breed well known for intelligence and a user-friendly, people-oriented personality. Conversely, a narrow forehead is often thought to correlate with cold blood, which traditionally is less intelligent and less tractable in disposition.

If the head is wide, it allows for a generous, roomy throatlatch, with more space to accommodate windpipe and jugular veins. The poll should be well defined, extending up as a definite prominence, contributing to the size of the brain cavity. A wide poll is typical with a wide forehead, with the base of the ears far apart rather than close together. A narrow poll and forehead are more typical of a donkey than of a horse.

◄◯ *Conformation Close-up*

Horsemen usually prefer an animal with eyes set wide apart, at the corners of a wide forehead, for best vision. Horses in careers that require good forward vision may do a little better, however, if the forehead is narrower and eyes are somewhat closer together. When selecting a horse for racing, hunting, or jumping, some horsemen prefer a slightly narrower forehead with eyes not so widely spaced.

THE EYES

The eyes should be large (round and prominent, but not bulging) and dark colored, ideally. In some horses, part of the iris is lacking color or the whole iris may be colorless; this is called *walleye*. A colorless or "blue" eye with no pigment, which is sometimes seen if a horse has a white face marking around the eye, is more sensitive to light and prone to sun damage.

Large eyes, set wide apart, are often thought to denote intelligence and tractability, whereas so-called pig eyes may indicate stubbornness and a less desirable disposition. A *pig eye* is small, set back in the head

Beauty

Beauty is important only if it enhances a horse's ability to handle himself as an athlete. The head doesn't need to be beautiful. It does need to be well balanced and functional (not too large or coarse) because it plays an important role in the horse's overall balance when he's moving. The face should not be too narrow, because narrowing of the nasal bones can interfere with flow of air when the horse is breathing hard. The muzzle should not be too small, or the air passages will be compromised and the horse will be more likely to have mismatched jaws and teeth.

Did You Know?

Eye size is consistent in horses; it's the bone structure surrounding the eye that gives the appearance of large or small eyes.

(recessed as opposed to being prominent), and often accompanied by thick eyelashes. A horse with pig eyes has a narrower field of vision and may not see as well as a horse with larger eyes. Horses with pig eyes may be nervous and unpredictable or have bad temperaments, simply because they don't see well. A horse with a narrow face and small eyes (especially if the eyes are set high on the skull) may be a poor choice; most horsemen prefer a horse with large eyes, set wider and lower. Looking at the horse's head from the side, there should be a lot of distance between the base of the ear and the outside corner of the eye; the greater the distance, the larger the brain cavity.

Normally, when looking at a horse's eye, we see only the *iris* — the colored part of the eye. The *sclera* — the white of the eye — doesn't show, except in the Appaloosa breed, unless the horse rolls his eyes. In the foal, the pupil of the eye is nearly round or oval, but in the adult horse it is more oblong and horizontal. The horse has built-in sunglasses that consist of the corpora negra, several tiny round black objects hanging down from the upper edge of the pupil, to keep out some of the bright light. These make a tiny treelike pattern in the horse's pupil. You can see these pealike bodies suspended from the upper edge of the margin of the pupil if you look carefully at the eye in good light.

Just above each eye, between the eye and ear, there is an indentation. When the horse is chewing, this area appears to alternately bulge outward and sink inward. This dent is part of a fat-filled cavity that lies behind the eye as a cushion. If the eye is bumped, it is pushed back into this cavity instead of bursting. As the horse ages, these hollows above the eye become less fat filled and more pronounced.

The upper eyelids should have dense tufts of eyelashes to keep sweat and dust from getting into the eyes. The lower lashes are usually thinner but longer; they keep dust and foreign matter from blowing up into the eye. A third eyelid is attached to the inside corner of the eye. Whenever a fly, a piece of dirt, or some other foreign object touches the eye surface, the eye automatically withdraws into the fatty cavity behind it, and the third eyelid membrane then quickly wipes over the front of the eyeball, like a windshield wiper, to remove it.

How a Horse Sees

A horse's vision is quite different from ours. Because his eyes are set wide apart at the sides of his head, he seldom sees an object with both eyes at once. He sees a different picture with each eye and can watch different things on either side of him simultaneously. He can focus both eyes on something in front of him, but it takes more effort for him to do so. Because of the width of his muzzle, he cannot see anything directly in front of his nose.

He has two blind spots when standing squarely and facing forward: a small area directly behind him and a small area directly in front of him and extending about 4 feet below his muzzle. As he approaches an object, the horse must turn his head a little to one side if he wants to focus an eye on it. The range of vision of each eye is influenced by its position in the skull. In order to see directly behind him, he must move his head to one side. To see over his back, he must raise his head so his eye is above the level of his withers. Wide-angle vision may be a disadvantage when he tries to look down at the ground in front of him, but it's a tremendous asset when he scans for predators; he can see from any angle, sees a different view with each eye, and simultaneously sees what's on either side of him.

Faults to Avoid

Some horses have eyes that are not set properly; one is set at a different angle than the other (called a *gotch eye* by old-timers). This may not be immediately apparent when examining a horse, especially from the side. A horse with this problem may shy a lot or bump into things because he can't see normally. There are four common gotch eyeball positions.

ONE EYE POINTED OUT. One of the most common gotch eye positions is one eyeball pointed out (looking out to the side) more than the other. This hinders a horse's ability to focus properly on objects because the abnormal eye cannot shift to look forward. The horse will not see something as quickly on that side as he goes past it as he does on the normal side. A rock or tree, for instance, may not come into focus on his abnormal side until he is quite close to it, and he may suddenly dodge away or shy when he becomes aware of it. A horse with this problem may be skittish and possibly unsafe to ride.

ONE EYE TURNED DOWN. Another abnormal eye position is one eye turned downward. The horse is not as able to see things out to the side as things on the ground. He may be much too worried about rocks and ground-level objects on that side and not aware of obstacles out to the side. The eyeball is turned down, with a portion of sclera (the white of the eye) showing between the iris and the upper eyelid.

ONE EYE TURNED UP AND OUT. The opposite problem is a horse with one eyeball turned upward and outward, preventing him from seeing the ground on that side. His eyeball would be constantly rolled back and up, enabling him to see his rider, but not the area in front of him or where he is walking. This condition can make him "spooky" on his bad side. The white of his eye will be showing between his iris and the lower eyelid.

CROSSED EYES. A few horses are cross-eyed, which can interfere with proper vision. The horse may be uncertain of his footing and may not want to cross a bridge or step over a log or any other obstacle that would normally offer little challenge. He constantly sees double when trying to focus on something in front of him, until he turns his head to one side.

THE EARS

The ears should be set just below the level of the poll at the top of the head, in a position where they can be rotated forward and backward to catch all sounds from the greatest possible area. Active ears are a sign of intelligence, alertness, and interest in what is going on around him; they can also be a sign of nervousness, however.

Many horsemen prefer finely formed, small- to medium-sized ears, but ear size has no bearing on a horse's ability. In fact, large ears can actually help dissipate heat through the network of blood vessels close to the skin.

Ears that are too large or too small may make the horse's head seem too small or large in comparison. Carefully evaluate the relative size of the ears and the head to get a true sense of head size. Otherwise, ear size is not an important factor in overall conformation and is not considered a fault.

THE JAWS AND TEETH

The lower jaw should be clearly defined, and the space between the two sides of the lower jaw (the deep groove between them, underneath the head) should be wide, with adequate room for the larynx and the muscle attachments. Old-timers used to say that a man should be able to put his closed fist between the two halves of the jaw at the throat beneath the larynx. To check the width, make a fist and place it fingers up, with the back of the hand facing the neck, under the horse's throatlatch, then slide it forward between the two jawbones. If there is room to accommodate all four knuckles of a man's average-sized hand (at least 3 inches), this is considered a good width.

 Conformation Close-up

A wide space between the upper ends of the lower jaw is regarded favorably because it allows enough room for a large, unconstricted windpipe, giving the horse adequate wind and endurance. Width and roominess between the two sides of the lower jaw at this spot depend partly on the way the horse's head is set on his neck.

The angle at the throat should not be sharp and cramped but gradual and arched, so when flexing at the poll (bringing his head and neck into good working position for collection and balance) the horse's airway isn't constricted. For proper neck flexion, there also should be some space between the large first vertebra of the neck and the cheekbone.

🔺 Make a fist and slide it forward between the jawbones to check the width of the lower jaw.

The cheek (jowl) should not be too large and heavy. A large jowl gives the head a false appearance of being short and adds a lot of weight to the head. It also reduces the horse's ability to flex at the poll to bring his head and neck into proper position for collection and for balancing himself during various movements. Heavy jowls can hinder the horse's breathing when he is working hard and may prevent proper position of the tongue when eating, drinking, and swallowing.

The cheekbones should be well constructed because they support the molars, which are essential for chewing. The cheekbones influence the shape of the head; a horse should not be too narrow through the cheeks.

In profile view, the horse's molars lie along the line that starts below the upper corner of the horse's eye and ends about an inch above the corner of his mouth. The bone structure supporting the line of molars should be broad and substantial, giving plenty of width to the horse's cheekbones, which should appear prominent and well sculpted.

There should be no mismatch in length of upper and lower jaw. Top and bottom teeth should meet evenly. A horse with an overbite (*parrot mouth*) or an undershot jaw (*sow mouth, monkey mouth*) will have difficulty eating, and it will be a chore for him to consume enough food to satisfy his energy needs, especially if he is worked hard in an athletic career. A serious mismatch between top and bottom teeth makes it difficult for the horse to bite off grasses when grazing and impossible for him to chew food properly. He will develop dental problems due to the misalignment, specifically hooks that form on the first and last molars when they are not worn evenly by the opposite tooth; these hooks can hinder proper movement of his jaws, which in turn can interfere with positioning of his head, affecting his athletic performance.

THE MOUTH AND MUZZLE

The horse's mouth should allow for proper eating and proper use of a bit. The mouth should not be too deep when measured from the front of the incisors to the corner of the mouth or too shallow. (A deep mouth extends beyond the narrowest part of the chin; a shallow mouth ends below that narrow chin groove.) The muzzle should be smooth and proportionate in size to the head, not too coarse or too tiny. A too-small muzzle might suggest inadequate width of nostrils and air passages and improper jaw alignment.

Because the horse can't see the end of his nose, the whiskers on his chin serve as feelers. He can feel the ground, the side of his stall, the water level when he lowers his head to drink, or the bottom of his manger without bumping his chin. Because whiskers serve an important purpose, they shouldn't be trimmed when grooming.

His nose and lips are soft, sensitive, and very flexible. The horse uses his flexible upper lip and muzzle for sorting his feed, pushing away sticks or weeds as he grazes. He can pick up wisps of hay or kernels of grain with his lips and can usually keep from getting dirt, small rocks, or other foreign objects into his mouth.

THE NOSTRILS

Unlike humans, horses cannot breathe through their mouths very easily, because the soft palate at the roof of the mouth tends to drop down, obstructing the air passage. Therefore, the horse must be able to inhale and exhale great drafts of air through his nostrils when running hard. The opening of the nostrils should be very wide as well as thin and elastic to allow for maximum expansion. A horse with small, narrow nostrils or thick-walled nostrils cannot expand them enough for adequate air intake when exerting strenuously.

Draft horses tend to have small nostrils since they originated in cold climates (a small nostril was advantageous for protecting the lungs from too much cold air) and do not need substantial airflow to do slow, steady work. The *false pouch*, a chamber just inside the nostrils, protects the air aperture higher up and also warms the air before it is drawn into the lungs. The false pouch also enables the horse to snort or whistle; he blows air through the pouch, making it vibrate loudly.

THE THROATLATCH

There should be an open-looking area just behind the jowl and a clean-looking *throatlatch* rather than a heavy, meaty bulge of muscle where the jaws join the neck. A good throatlatch does not have excess fat or muscling; it gives the windpipe more room and allows greater range of motion of the head and neck. The esophagus, windpipe, blood supply, and nerves all pass through the throatlatch. If this area is too thick, these passageways are constricted when the horse tucks his head.

The throatlatch should not be thick and bulky, but it should be wide. A horse with a narrow throatlatch often has narrow jaws, as well. A narrow throatlatch can constrict the airway and make him more prone to respiratory problems. It may also cause restricted upper airways or air turbulence, due to impairment of the nerve that opens the larynx, which can cause *roaring*, a loud raspy sound made each time the horse inhales when he gallops.

Conformation Close-up

If there is not enough room at the throatlatch, there won't be enough arch in the neck. The top neck bones (behind the skull) come from below the ears rather than from behind them, making the horse hammer-headed and ewe-necked, like a donkey.

The Neck

The neck of a riding horse should be of reasonable length and never too short. The neck is the vital link between head and shoulders; the horse must be able to swing his head up and down to shift his weight and maintain balance with each stride. There must be sufficient length for effective balance.

The ideal neck has a long upper curve in the bones just behind the head and a shallow lower curve in the bones that join the withers. This results in greater arch in the neck and provides a proper head/neck joint so the horse can easily flex at the poll and give to the bit. All the muscles are in proper proportion and can develop adequately, with none becoming overdeveloped. Such a neck promotes balance and flexibility. The horse can use his head and neck to good advantage to counterbalance the rest of his body actions.

The muscles help determine the shape of the neck, even though bone structure has the most influence on the neck's appearance. The same bone structure will look different if a horse has well-developed neck muscles or poorly developed muscles, or when a thin horse has very little flesh and muscling on the neck.

The Mitbah

The Bedouin, nomadic tribes who relied on good horses and selectively bred the "hot bloods" that influence all breeds of light horses today, called the spot where the horse's head and neck meet at the throatlatch the *mitbah*. This area must be well defined, clean-cut, and lengthy to allow plenty of room for the windpipe when the head is pulled toward the chest or when the neck is arched in collection.

A neck with no mitbah has no suppleness; the horse is apt to pull on the bit rather than yield. A short, stiff neck makes for a less agile horse. A horse that would "choke down" when restrained by the bit and a horse with a neck so short and stiff that it had no length of mitbah were undesirable to Bedouins and are to anyone who needs an athletic horse.

Ideal Head and Neck Conformation

The most ideal head carriage, according to old-timers, is a head higher than the withers, with a gentle arch in the neck, and a head profile that has a gentle slope of about 45 degrees. If the nose sticks out too far in front (head too horizontal) or tucks down too low (head vertical, or even past vertical, with chin tucked toward the chest), the horse's freedom of action is reduced and his field of vision — especially his ability to see the ground in front of him — is impaired. If his nose is too high or if he is overbent, he will not be properly controlled by the bit.

The muscles of the neck help pull the shoulders and front legs forward at each stride. The neck muscles can contract and extend about two-thirds of their actual length. Thus, a short-necked horse with a short upright shoulder will have a short stride. If the neck muscles are poorly developed or too short, the horse will not be able to run as fast or as far as a horse with strong neck muscles of proper length.

NECK LENGTH

The length of a horse's neck and its conformation dictates how he uses his head to shift his center of gravity and maintain his balance, not only at various gaits but also throughout various actions and maneuvers, particularly in emergencies, such as slippery footing or to dodge an obstacle at fast speeds.

Measured from poll to withers, the neck of a riding horse should be proportional to the rest of his body: about one-third of the horse's overall length. It should be fairly long and slender, slightly arched along its topline, and relatively straight on its underside.

The horse can more fully collect himself or extend himself for longer strides by using his head and neck. Optimal neck length contributes to a horse's agility, allowing him freer movement and better head position for ideal balance in all of his athletic endeavors. Anything other than optimal neck length can be problematic.

The Too-Short Neck

A neck that is exceptionally short and thick is usually a hindrance to balance and good action in a riding horse, for the neck is less able to move freely and quickly. The horse has less precise use of his head and neck during athletic movements and is more prone to stumbling and clumsiness. A short neck is often thick, which makes it heavy and less supple. It adds more weight to the forehand, reducing agility. A short, thick neck and a thick throatlatch limit flexion at the poll and inhibit side-to-side mobility. The ability to flex and bend is crucial for proper balance and collection.

A short neck is generally accompanied by a short, upright shoulder. Because the neck muscles help pull the shoulder and front leg forward, a short neck means a shorter stride. A short, thick "bull neck" interferes with movement, balance, speed, and agility, especially when carrying a rider. The horse with a short neck may have a quick burst of speed, but because his stride is so much shorter, he must move his legs much faster than a longer-striding horse, with the higher frequency contributing to stress on his legs and body.

The Too-Long Neck

If the neck is more than one and a half times the length of the horse's back (from withers to croup), it is too long. Another way to measure this is to look at the length of the neck (from poll to peak of the withers) in relationship to the rest of the topline (from peak of the withers to tail). A neck that exceeds the length of the rest of the topline is excessively long. This places the horse at a disadvantage for agility and balance because the horse's center of balance is too far forward.

A very long neck is usually less flexible than one of average length. Because the horse has only seven vertebrae in his neck, regardless of whether that neck is long or short, a longer neck has greater distance between each joint and has less flexibility than a short neck. In the shorter neck, the joints are closer together and the neck is more flexible for its length.

A horse with a too-long neck may have trouble responding properly to the bridle (not collecting adequately) and may not travel straight. A very long, slender neck can also be associated with malformation

▼ Neck length (A) should be one-third of the horse's total length (B), one and a half times the length of the head (C), and the same length as the front legs (A). For athletic ability, neck length can be the same as but should not exceed the length of the rest of the topline. The neck is measured from the poll to the peak of the withers.

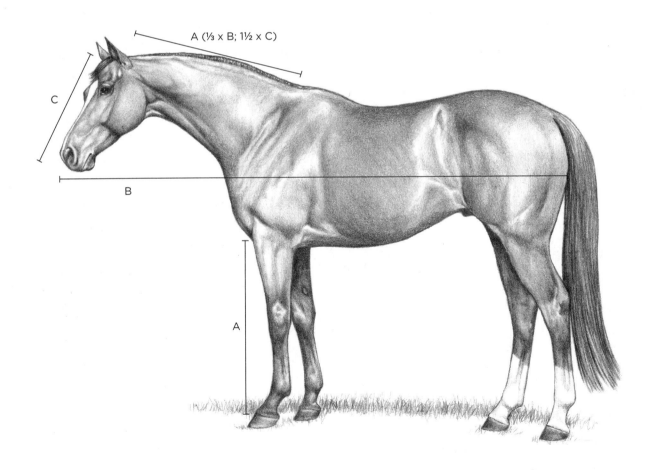

A (⅓ x B; 1½ x C)

C

B

A

of the neck vertebrae; a narrowing of the spinal canal may press on the spinal cord, resulting in central nervous system disability and lack of coordination (*wobbler syndrome*). A long, slender neck is also accompanied by a narrow throatlatch and resulting impairment of the airways.

The muscles of a too-long neck may be underdeveloped, and the horse may tire too quickly when working hard. When he tires, he may drop his head, putting too much weight on his forehand, and his stride will become weaker and uneven because it is no longer being aided by the neck muscles. A horse with an overly long neck has more difficulty developing those muscles. He may also be more likely to suffer partial dislocation of the vertebrae.

HEAD/NECK ANGLE

One of the most important aspects of general conformation is the angle at which the head and neck meet. This is determined by the top two vertebrae.

The *atlas* — the first large vertebra of the neck, which forms the joint between neck and head — lies directly behind the poll and forms a curved ridge that can be easily observed in most horses. The atlas slips over the *axis*, the second neck vertebra, hinging to it in such a way that the horse can nod his head up and down without moving the rest of his body; this enables him to flex at the poll and make a tight bend in his neck, bringing his chin down toward his chest. Neck flexibility makes it easier for the rider to teach the horse to give to the bit and flex at the poll.

The configuration of the atlas and axis enables the horse to swing his head from side to side, helping him shift his balance while traveling and allowing him to turn his head to the side to get better focus on something he is looking at. After the atlas and axis, the rest of the vertebrae dip down toward the jugular furrow at the bottom of the neck and stay low in the neck until they get close to the shoulder,

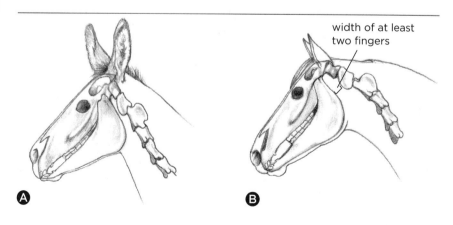

▶ The angle at which the head and neck meet depends on the curve, or lack of it, of the neck vertebrae. **A.** Neck vertebrae in the donkey are relatively upright. **B.** In the horse, there should be room for the width of at least two fingers between the jawbone and the first neck bone.

width of at least two fingers

Ⓐ

Ⓑ

where they rise to join the thoracic vertebrae at about the level of the shoulder joint.

The head should be set on the neck at such an angle that the horse can flex at the poll to collect himself when traveling and changing direction, while maintaining proper balance. If the jowls are too large or the throatlatch is too thick, the neck cannot arch properly, making it impossible for him to flex at the poll.

🔍 Conformation Close-up

The neck of a well-proportioned horse is well arched (convex rather than straight or concave topline), with a flat, level area just behind the ears where the skull attaches to the first vertebra. The length of neck usually can easily be determined by the way the horse carries his head and how the neck joins the withers. If these joints are graceful and proper, the neck is the right length. If they are abrupt, the neck is probably too short. If they are loose looking rather than smooth, with the head improperly attached to the atlas vertebra, the neck may be too long. If the neck fits properly onto well-sloped shoulders, it will be in balance with the rest of the horse.

For adequate room to flex at the poll and for sufficient airway, there should be some space between the atlas and the cheekbone. You should be able to place at least two fingers between the top of the round jawbone (cheekbone) and the first neck vertebra, at the top of the neck.

A Too-Abrupt Angle

If the angle at which the head meets the neck is too abrupt, forming a right angle instead of a curve, the lower line of the neck may be too fleshy and the neck will meet the throat at a low level, which tends to constrict the windpipe. This condition is sometimes associated with compression of the larynx when the horse is doing a fast gallop, which hinders his ability to breathe and hence his speed. If his throatlatch and airways are cramped, restricting the flow of air, he may also resist flexing at the poll; and instead of collecting properly, he may brace his neck and back, which makes him difficult to train.

This abrupt head/neck configuration is often found in horses with a short, thick neck and an upright shoulder. Old-timers called this acute angle of head and neck *cock-throttled*. If the head/neck angle is also accompanied by lack of curvature in the neck bones just behind the neck, the angle is even more abrupt and the horse is considered *hammer-headed*.

⏥ A short, thick neck was called *cock-throttled* because the abrupt angle could impede the airway.

NECK/SHOULDER ANGLE

The way the neck is set on at the shoulders is just as important as the way the head is set onto the neck. The juncture of the neck and shoulder affects the shape of the neck. The neck should emerge from the shoulders fairly high, with a distinct breast area below it. If the neck is set too low (like that of a zebra or Przewalski's horse, whose neck starts so low it appears to be coming from between the front legs), with no visible breast below it, the neck is almost as deep (thick from top to bottom) as the body. The horse will have limited flexibility. The ideal neck of a riding horse reaches out from the body with a well-defined shape.

The way the neck is set on the shoulders is important for proper balance. Viewed from the side, there should be a smooth transition from shoulder to neck, with neck set neither too high nor too low. If the neck is so low set that the horse has hardly any "chest" (breast) below the base of his neck (with the neck set rather horizontally), he will always seem to be leaning too far forward, traveling heavy in front, and will be difficult to collect; he has poor balance and impaired agility. The base of the neck (its departure from the chest) should be level with the point of the shoulder or higher. If the head and neck are carried too low, shoulder action is restricted; the forelegs can't be raised high enough or forward enough for a good stride, which reduces the horse's speed and jumping ability.

◖⃝ *Conformation Close-up*

At the base of the neck, at its bottom surface where it blends into the shoulder, the jugular furrow between the windpipe and the muscles above it should be distinct. This provides plenty of room for the windpipe to expand when the horse is breathing hard and for the jugular vein to carry a large volume of blood without being inhibited by pressure from the muscled area.

NECK SHAPE

The shape of a horse's neck (and its bone structure) is actually more important than its length in terms of athletic ability. There are seven neck vertebra. Each has a different size and shape, and the joints between them cause the bones to fit together in an S-shape. The column of vertebrae that comprise the neck bones does not follow the curve or line of the neck (which is made up primarily of a large mass of muscles) but instead forms two curves.

There is a small curve at the top, just behind the head (creating the crest), and a larger curve at the bottom of the neck where the last neck

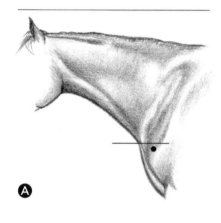

Ⓐ

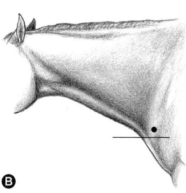

Ⓑ

▲ A. Normal neck; the base of the neck is level with the point of the shoulder or higher. **B.** Neck set on too low, below the point of the shoulder; there is hardly any breast area below the neck. (*Note:* ● = point of shoulder.)

vertebra forms a joint with the first long-spine vertebra of the withers (between the shoulders). The shape, length, and range of motion of the neck — whether the horse has a "ewe neck," "swan neck," "bull neck," or a normally curved neck — depend largely on the proportions of the S-curve of the vertebrae.

The most important aspect of neck shape is the lower curve in the S. If that lower curve is short and shallow (so the base of the neck attaches high on the chest rather than low toward the breast), maneuverability, flexion, and collection will come naturally. It will be easier to carry his head and neck properly. Straightening out that lower curve (as the horse must do to collect himself) is much easier for the horse with a curve that is already short and shallow.

Even if the neck is the proper length for good balance, it may have structural features that make it more difficult for the horse to achieve perfect mobility and balance, especially when carrying a rider. Some types of neck conformation make it more difficult to

▼ The shape of the S-curve dictates the shape of the neck. **A.** A normal, or "ideal," neck has a shallow lower curve and is situated high relative to the shoulder; there is a long upper "turnover" behind the head. **B.** A thick ewe neck has a wide and deep lower curve, but the upper curve is short, making the horse hammer headed. **C.** Ewe neck with wide, deep lower curve but a long upper curve. **D.** Straight neck; neither the upper nor the lower curve of the S is very deep.

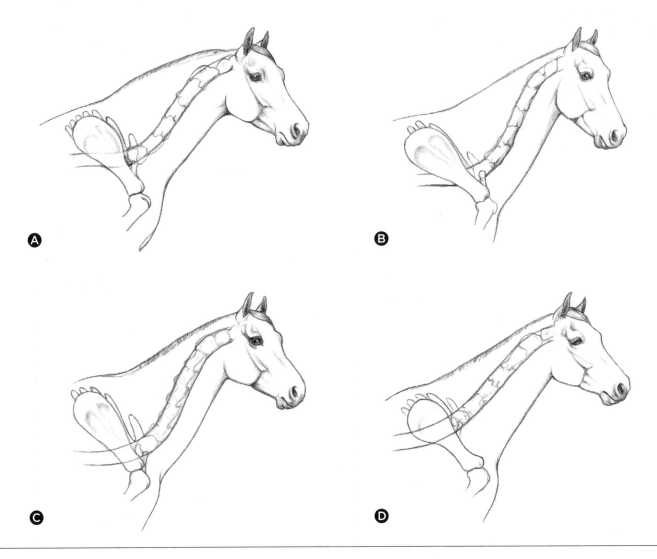

A   **B**   **C**   **D**

train and "collect" the horse, resulting in challenge when trying to create good communication through the bit.

A horse whose neck is too low at its base carries his head too high; it's hard for the horse to lower his head or flex his neck when the thickest part of the neck is along the lower curve of the S. If the lower curve is excessively large and deep, attaching low on the chest, the horse will be ewe-necked, even if the head is set on the neck at a good angle. Thus, in a ewe-necked horse, the widest part of his neck is lower than the midpoint of the shoulder. By contrast, the widest part of the neck on a horse with a properly arched neck (with a flat, shallow lower curve, coming higher out of the shoulder area) is higher, with better potential for efficient muscle development and maneuverability.

The upper curve of the S determines how the head sets onto the neck. A short upper curve creates an abrupt attachment and acute angle at the throatlatch (known as hammer-headed) and the head is often carried too high, with limited flexion at the poll. A medium to long upper curve creates a better angle at the throatlatch, enabling the horse to flex more effectively at the poll.

Ewe Neck

The ewe-necked horse has an "upside down" neck; the topline is concave rather than arched, and the head usually forms a right angle to the neck at the throat instead of a curved arch. There is a downward dip in the neck, ahead of the withers, and the muscles at the bottom surface of the neck are thicker. This neck structure makes it almost impossible for the horse to stretch his head and neck out and down or to flex at the poll.

If the lower curve of the S is too deep and wide (no matter what the size and shape of the upper curve), the horse has a ewe neck, with a hollow ahead of the withers. Many horses with this neck configuration also have an upright shoulder; the upright shoulder and the long lower curve of the neck tend to go together.

The ewe-necked horse has trouble forming a proper bend in his neck for flexing at the poll and "giving" to the bit. It is harder for him to flatten out the lower curve for proper flexion. Thus, it is more difficult for a rider to collect him and shift weight more to his hindquarters. This type of horse travels heavy in front, especially when carrying a rider, making him less agile, clumsier, and more prone to stumbling. If the horse raises his head much above his withers, it becomes even harder for him to give to the bit, due to the "upside down" curve of his neck.

"Stargazers"

It is difficult for the ewe-necked horse to lower his head and neck, raise his back, and lower his hindquarters for good collection and impulsion. The horse usually carries his head high especially under saddle, with his nose stuck out in front (or perhaps flipped up in the air) instead of tucked in, making communication through the bit a challenge. As the rider tries to control the horse with the bit, he may poke his nose up even higher to avoid the bit contact, which can make him dangerous to ride because he braces himself against the bit. With his head and nose in the air, he also can't see where he's going and is more apt to trip or stumble.

The ewe-necked horse tends to throw his head in the air because he can't respond to the bit by flexing at the poll.

A short ewe neck tends to be thick, making the condition less obvious than in a horse with a longer neck. The short-necked horse has a short upper curve behind the head, creating a thick, relatively inflexible juncture between head and neck. Due to the inflexibility of the head-neck juncture, many of these horses are difficult for the average rider to train and collect, and they easily become hard-mouthed.

A long ewe neck has a longer upper curve behind the head that creates a small crest at the top of the neck, but the basic neck structure is concave rather than convex. The dip in front of the withers makes a "kink" in the neck when the rider asks him to flex. It is easier to try to collect this type of horse when his head is carried relatively low rather than too high. As he raises his head, the "kink" in the neck is accentuated, tightening all the neck, shoulder, back, loin, and hindquarter muscles, resulting in stiffness and an inefficient way of traveling.

A ewe-necked horse, whether his neck is short or long, may develop the habit of throwing his head in the air to avoid bit pressure, because it's hard for him to flex at the poll and bring his nose toward vertical. If the rider tries too insistently to make him give to the bit and flex, the horse may respond by throwing his head in the air. The ewe-necked horse can easily throw his head up in the rider's face if the rider overuses the bit, which can make for a sore forehead or even a broken nose.

Raising his head in the air also makes it easy for the horse to slide the bit back against his molars (taking the bit into his teeth), leaving the rider with no control. If the horse takes the bit and bolts with his head in the air, he is truly dangerous to ride, because he also can't see where he's going. The rider has no control over the horse unless he can get his head back down into a more flexed position.

It takes a lot of work to develop a good mouth and flexibility in a ewe-necked horse and is sometimes impossible. His conformation makes it difficult for him to flex his neck adequately for proper balancing, and he has a harder time "giving" to the bit and keeping a "soft" mouth.

⊸○ *Conformation Close-up*

A ewe-necked horse with high head carriage and his nose poked out in front is unable to make smooth transitions from one gait to another. He moves in a disjointed manner, with poor synchronization between his front end and his hindquarters. With his head raised and nose forward, he cannot "round" (elevate) his back; instead, his back is hollowed, which is less efficient for carrying weight. Loins and back muscles easily become tired or sore. If you want an athletic horse, it is much better to select one with appropriate neck structure.

Swan Neck

This term also describes a neck with an improperly curved topline, though it is not as obvious as the ewe neck. With a swan neck, the top third arches nicely and the head/neck joint is fairly normal with a good throatlatch, but the bottom third, nearest the withers and shoulders, is concave like a ewe neck. This type of neck is often set too low on the chest, with the base below the point of the shoulder. The withers may be quite prominent, with a dip in the neck ahead of the withers, creating the same kink in the neck as in a ewe-necked horse.

Like the ewe neck, swan neck conformation inhibits proper flexion. The horse tends to carry his head too high and to respond to overuse of the bit by throwing his nose in the air and becoming "rubbernecked," evading effective contact and control. If a horse has a long swan neck, he may lean on the bit and tuck his nose to his chest, traveling behind the bit, rather than elevating his back and collecting properly.

Straight Neck

Some horses have no arch in the neck. There is no concavity or convexity to the top or bottom line of the neck; the top and/or bottom lines are perfectly straight. Some horses have a nice upward curve on the bottom of the neck, but a straight topline with no crest at all.

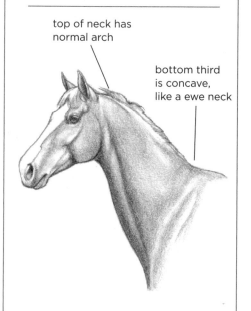

top of neck has normal arch

bottom third is concave, like a ewe neck

⏶ Example of swan neck. The head is usually carried too high and demonstrates improper flexion; the horse is more difficult to train and collect as a result.

Some necks are so straight, top and bottom, that there is no visible throatlatch; the neck looks like a long, slim version of a zebra neck. A horse with a straight neck is limited in ability to flex and balance properly (see illustration on page 43).

Heavy Crest

The horse with a short, beefy neck and a thick, heavy crest also lacks flexibility and will have poor balance. Some horses that are easy keepers, like some Morgans, draft horses, and ponies, develop a high, thick crest due to fat deposits above the nuchal ligament. A horse that displays this fat deposit in the neck may have a sluggish metabolism and may stay fat on very little feed; he also may be more prone to founder, especially when allowed to eat continually at pasture.

Stallions typically have a thicker, heavier crest than mares, but the crest should not be too heavy or the horse will have a coarse appearance and be too heavy in front for agility. A stallion should have a strong, masculine neck with good muscling: well arched, with some crest. A mare with a coarse neck and heavy crest is also a poor athlete and may have poor reproductive performance if used as a broodmare. A heavy crest in a mare is generally a sign of hormone imbalance and poor fertility.

For their size, ponies tend to have thicker necks than horses, but a pony with a heavy crest should be avoided. A thick, crested neck will make the pony less agile and also less controllable for young riders. It's easy for the pony to get into the habit of pulling on the bit and becoming hardmouthed.

A neck that is too thick is often too short as well. Sometimes, however, the neck will appear too short because the horse has a short, upright shoulder; there is no length of shoulder extending down past the bottom line of the neck. The neck may actually be of fairly good length, but the lack of shoulder makes it appear short and coarse. Even though neck conformation may be appropriate, the short upright shoulder will inhibit the horse's action, so this type of conformation should also be avoided.

Did You Know?

A thick, heavy neck and large head are advantageous for a draft horse, especially when starting to pull a heavy load. He has plenty of neck muscle to help move the shoulders, and both assist him as he leans into his harness to pull. A long neck and large head would be a disadvantage for balance as the horse leans forward.

The Teeth

GOOD TEETH ARE CRITICAL for equine health and longevity. Horses, whether working hard or working in a nonathletic career such as a broodmare, must be able to eat efficiently and chew feed properly for maximum nutritional benefit. A horse with a painful mouth may not eat enough and may lose weight. No horse can stay in good condition if eating is hindered or if he gets only part of the nutrition from his feed.

Teeth also affect a horse's attitude and performance. He may resent the use of a bit, toss his head, or travel with his head and neck crooked. To have a willing, athletic horse, bit communication must be as close to perfect

A horse's teeth and jaw length affect the way he eats and consequently his body condition and athletic performance. The teeth also play an important role in how a horse responds to a bit and carries his head and neck when performing athletic maneuvers.

as possible, so make sure the mouth is free of problems. The teeth and how they erupt from the jawbone will have a significant effect on how well or how poorly the horse performs.

Examining the mouth and teeth is an essential part of any horse evaluation. If you know what to look for, teeth can give a fairly accurate estimation of a horse's age and can tell you whether he will stay healthy and fit. A horse will last only as long as his teeth, because when his teeth wear out or fall out he can no longer eat. He may be only 18 years old, but if his teeth have aged prematurely due to genetics, poor feeding practices, or improper dental work that has rasped away too much of the wearing surfaces, he may have teeth like a 28-year-old horse. Poor management, neglect, or improper work on the teeth can subtract years from his life. Good teeth are just as important as good feet and legs for future performance.

Anatomy

The horse's teeth are divided into two sections: front teeth and back teeth. *Incisors* are in front and are easily seen when the horse opens his mouth. He uses incisors for biting off grass. The back teeth, or *cheek teeth*, are molars and premolars. The latter are more forward, in front of the molars. Cheek teeth are situated tightly against one another, in a line called the *dental arcade*, to provide a solid surface for grinding the food. A large *interdental space* divides the incisors and the cheek teeth; this is where the bit rests. All male horses and a few females have canine teeth; in females, the canine teeth are smaller. These rounder, sharper "tusks," or *tushes*, are located a short distance behind the incisors in the interdental space. *Wolf teeth* are found right next to the first premolar, at the back of this open space.

Because the horse is basically a roughage eater who consumes many pounds of forage daily, good teeth are crucial for breaking down the fibrous food he eats. The way a horse's teeth develop is one reason why horses sometimes have tooth problems or a poor mouth for responding to a bit. If a horse has even one bad tooth, uneven wear on the opposite tooth results. This can create hooks or sharp edges, and he may suffer pain that interferes with proper chewing.

HOW THE TEETH GROW

Teeth of young humans and other carnivores grow rapidly; once the permanent teeth come in fully, growth ceases. The horse's permanent teeth continue to slowly erupt out of the gum line throughout the animal's life. Because teeth are worn down by the grinding action of eating, the horse's teeth are gradually pushed up through the jawbone to

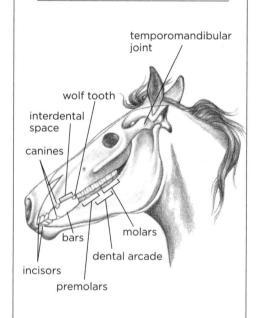

temporomandibular joint

wolf tooth

interdental space

canines

bars

molars

dental arcade

incisors

premolars

▲ Cross-section of horse's head showing the jaw structure and various teeth.

compensate. A horse's teeth are very long to begin with, and in a young horse, most of the tooth is still embedded in the jaw; only the top portion is visible. Each tooth slowly pushes up as the horse ages. The horse chews by using a circular motion with his lower jaw, grinding the feed as the lower teeth slide past the upper teeth. Because grass and other roughages are somewhat abrasive, over time they wear down the teeth.

The equine tooth has a long crown or shaft (extending nearly 4 inches into the jawbone) and a short root (in contrast to human teeth, in which the crown only goes to the gum line). Only the topmost portion of the equine crown protrudes from the gum; about ¼ inch of the long tooth is the root, deep in the jaw. The visible part of the tooth is called the *clinical crown*, and the part still embedded in the jaw is called the *reserve crown*, or the body of the tooth.

As the horse grows older, the top of the crown wears down, followed by the neck of the reserve crown, and last the root. A very old horse may end up with short stubs that eventually fall out. A 4-year-old horse may have barely half of the tooth protruding — the rest is still in the jawbone and not yet visible — whereas a 25- to 35-year-old horse may have only about ½ inch left, and most of that may be visible in the mouth. All that's holding it might be ½ inch of root (still in the bone), until it finally falls out.

Judging Age

The horse's teeth have a rough surface so that when the upper and lower molars meet in their sideways motion, the action is like a grindstone, pulverizing the grass or hay into more easily digested particles. The grinding surface must stay rough or the constant wear will grind it smooth, making it less effective. The horse's teeth are made of pulp, dentin, and enamel, each of which varies in hardness and wears away at different rates to keep the surface abrasive. As the upper and lower teeth work against each other to grind the food, the softer dentin wears down and makes shallow spots, while the hard enamel remains in protruding ridges.

Different areas of the tooth wear away at different stages in the horse's life. It is this rate of wear that enables the horseman to "read" a horse's age by assessing the teeth. And in the young horse, the age can readily be determined by which teeth are present.

BABY TEETH

A foal's *milk teeth*, or baby teeth, emerge soon after birth; sometimes the two front teeth are already present at birth. The temporary milk teeth are smaller, whiter, and smoother than the larger, more yellow

| 3 | 6 | 12 | 18 | 24 |

▲ Cross-sections of an incisor at different ages (age in years).

permanent teeth that replace them. The milk teeth are also easy to recognize because they have a slight indentation at the gum line.

The first baby teeth to appear are the central incisors and first set of premolars. By the end of the second week of life, the next two sets of premolars appear. The second set of incisors usually comes in at 4 to 6 weeks of age, and the third set appears between 6 and 9 months of age. By the time a horse is a year old, he typically has all 12 temporary incisors, 6 on top and 6 on the bottom, along with 12 permanent premolars. He also has 4 of his permanent molars; they have come in farther back in the mouth, behind the premolars. By the time he is 2 years old, all of his milk teeth are fully erupted and the incisors are all touching and beginning to show wear, especially the central incisors, which have been fully erupted the longest. Because they appear at different times, the later-erupting teeth do not meet until they have grown in fully.

PROBLEMS WITH CAPS

The milk teeth are shed in the order they emerge. They have short roots and are usually pushed out easily by the erupting permanent teeth that replace them. For a while, the baby tooth remains stuck on the erupting permanent tooth as a *cap*. Caps should only be removed if they stay on too long and cause problems. If just part of the cap comes off, the remaining fragment may irritate the mouth. If a cap

Look Closely

The temporary incisors are all present at age 2 and the permanent incisors are all present and at the same height by age 5. Between ages 2 and 5, some of the temporary teeth will be emerging and some of the permanent teeth will be coming in or growing up to the level of the others. But at ages 2 and 5, the mouth is "level," and a horseman might occasionally mistake a 2-year-old for a 5-year-old if he doesn't look closely to determine the difference between baby teeth and permanent teeth. The baby teeth are smaller and whiter.

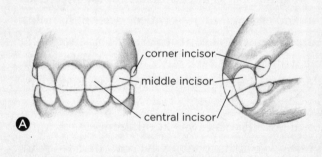
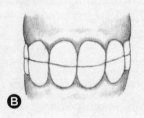

corner incisor
middle incisor
central incisor

Temporary teeth. **A.** One year old (complete set of baby teeth): The upper and lower milk teeth incisors have erupted but not all of them are touching. **B.** Two years old: All the milk teeth are fully erupted and touching (in wear). At this age, a 2-year-old might be mistaken for a 5-year-old.

comes off unevenly, it may lead to "step mouth." Sometimes a baby tooth breaks and lodges in the gum or loosens but does not come out, trapping (impacting) the permanent tooth in the jawbone. The lower jaw may be too narrow and the permanent cheek teeth don't have enough room to push up through the gum. In this situation, the horse develops an enlargement or knot on the lower jawbone. These "tooth bumps" are common in horses between ages 2 and 4, as the jawbone remodels to make way for teeth that are trying to come through the gum but cannot. Once the offending cap is removed — it can be extracted with forceps — or works loose on its own, the trapped molar can then erupt; the lump on the lower jaw then disappears as the bone again remodels itself.

In most instances, caps should be left alone because they are there to protect the permanent tooth as it emerges; the caps usually come off on their own when the permanent teeth have fully erupted. Removing a cap too soon exposes the permanent tooth and subjects it to premature wear, before its surface is fully developed and strong. The erupting tooth is also vulnerable to decay and needs protection. If a cap is rasped off instead of coming off in one piece, shards of the baby tooth may be left hanging onto the permanent tooth, creating sharp edges that may injure the horse's tongue.

Caps that remain too long can cause chewing problems. Young horses kept in stalls and fed soft feeds tend to retain their caps more frequently than horses eating natural feeds at pasture; the more abrasive roughages produce more normal wear and grinding, which helps the caps come off when the time is right. If a young horse does not shed caps correctly due to his abnormal eating conditions, they may come off unevenly or come off one side of the mouth before the other. This can lead to development of step mouth, an abrupt change in the height of the teeth at some portion of the dental arcade because of uneven pressure and wear.

PERMANENT TEETH

The first permanent molars appear at the back of the mouth behind the baby teeth, coming in at 9 to 12 months of age. The second set comes in to replace baby teeth at about 2 to 2.5 years of age. Baby teeth are generally shed in fall; these temporary teeth are typically

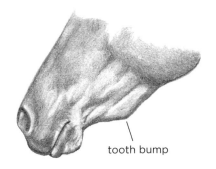

tooth bump

◀ Tooth bumps in a young horse.

Wolf Teeth

Some horses develop another set of premolars, both top and bottom, but sometimes only on top, just in front of the cheek teeth, called *wolf teeth*. Wolf teeth are usually small, with short roots — carryovers of teeth that were much larger in the early ancestors of the horse but that are no longer necessary to him today.

The first set of wolf teeth may appear at about 5 or 6 months of age. In some horses they don't appear until the horse is about 2 years old. In some individuals, they are present but do not come up through the gums. Their presence may make it painful for the horse to wear a bridle because the bit puts pressure on the tooth beneath the gum.

The first wolf teeth are often shed about the same time as the temporary first molars. Wolf teeth can be easily removed by a veterinarian or equine dentist if they interfere with the use of a bit.

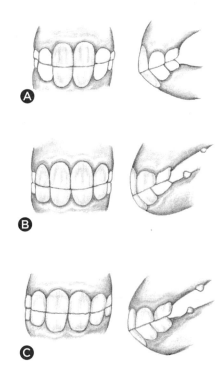

Permanent teeth. **A.** Three years old: The central baby incisors have been shed and replaced by permanent teeth (larger and darker than temporary teeth). **B.** Four years old: The central and middle incisors are permanent but the corner baby teeth have not yet been shed. The canine teeth have erupted. **C.** Five years old: The permanent corner teeth are in place; all the permanent incisors are in.

replaced by permanent teeth in the same order the baby teeth appeared, starting with the central incisors.

The two permanent central incisors are fully erupted by the time the horse is 3 years old. The two middle incisors, the laterals, located between the central and the corner tooth on each side, push out the baby teeth at about age 3.5 and are fully erupted by age 4. The corner incisors erupt at age 4.5 and are fully in use by age 5. By this time, the horse also has a complete set of 24 permanent cheek teeth (premolars and molars).

All the baby teeth are replaced by the time the horse is 4.5 years old. At that time he will have at least 36 teeth. He will have 12 incisors (6 on top, 6 on the bottom) and 24 cheek teeth (6 to a side, top and bottom). In addition, he may have as many as 4 wolf teeth and 4 canine teeth (or tushes). If canine teeth come in, they emerge behind the incisors at about 4 years of age.

EVALUATING AGE BY WEAR AND SHAPE

After the horse is 5 years old and all the permanent teeth are in, the way to determine age is by the amount of wear and the shape and slope of the incisors. In an older horse, another clue is the position and length of a groove that appears in the upper corner incisors. The most obvious teeth in the mouth to look at are the front incisors, which horsemen use to determine age.

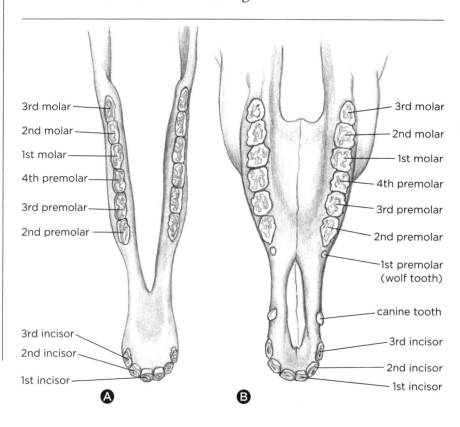

Teeth of a 4.5-year-old horse. **A.** Lower jaw. **B.** Upper jaw.

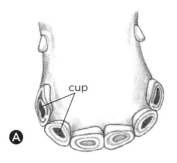

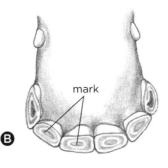

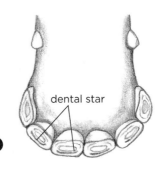

In a young horse, there are indentations known as cups in the center of the grinding surface (the "table") of the tooth. The cups are usually darker colored than the rest of the tooth surface. Surrounding the cup is a ring of enamel. As the horse grows older and the tooth wears, the cups gradually disappear. These dark spots in the center of the grinding surface can give a good clue to the age of the horse from about age 3 to 9, looking at the lower incisors.

In the lower incisors, the cups disappear from the central incisors at about age 6, are gone from the middle, or lateral, incisors by about age 7, and from the corner incisors when the horse is 8. The cups in the upper incisors are gone a bit later; disappearing from the upper central incisors by age 9, from the middle incisors by age 10, and the corner teeth by the time the horse is 11. The horse is then "smooth mouthed." The changes are gradual and may not be the same for every horse. Tooth wear can vary, depending on his health and diet, how he is fed, and how abrasive the feed is.

Up-and-down rough ridges on the outside of the incisors can be another indication of age. These ridges start forming on the central incisors at 10 years of age and then form on the middle teeth and last on the corners. The corner incisors are ridged by the time the horse is 14 to 16 years old.

Teeth also change shape as the horse gets older. When they first come in, the permanent teeth have oval surfaces. By age 12, the chewing surface of the central incisors has become round instead of oval. By age 17, all the incisors have round surfaces. By age 18, the central incisors are more triangular than round. By the time the horse is 23, all the incisors have become triangular. After that, especially from age 24 to 29, the grinding surfaces again become oval.

It is easy to tell the difference between the oval-surfaced tooth of a 6-year-old and that of a 24-year-old; the young horse's teeth are broad across the front and narrower from front to back. The old horse's teeth elongate in toward the back of the mouth instead, long from front to back and narrow from side to side (see illustration, page 51).

◭ **A.** Six years old: Permanent incisors are showing wear; between age 6 and 7, the cups of the central incisors disappear in the lower jaw. **B.** Seven years old: Between ages 7 and 8, the cups of the middle (lateral) incisors disappear (lower jaw). **C.** Eight years old: Between ages 8 and 9, the cups of the corner incisors disappear (lower jaw).

Did You Know?

The gum line also changes with age. In a young horse, the gum line is fairly straight across the tooth. In an older horse, the gum line sags down in an irregular scallop effect, exposing more of the middle shaft of the tooth.

Why the Incisors Change Shape

The young horse's teeth are largely still embedded in the jaw. Because the jawbone is not as wide as the mouth, the lower incisors erupt at an angle. The shafts of the incisors, which are packed together in a rough fan shape, have different dimensions at the top than they do at the bottom at their bone sockets. Because there is more distance across the top of the "fan" than in the bottom inside the lower jaw, the teeth are much wider at the top. They narrow, with more front-to-back dimension, toward the bottom. As the teeth are pushed out and worn away, the grinding surface gradually changes shape as it moves down the shaft of the tooth. The shape of the grinding surface is usually an accurate indication of the horse's age.

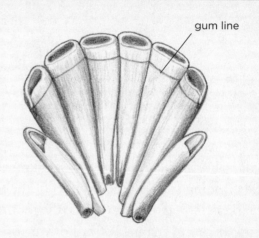

Inside view of the mouth in a 6-year-old with flesh and gums removed to show the curve of the shafts of the teeth and how they are embedded in the jaw at that age. Notice how much tooth is left to erupt as the horse ages.

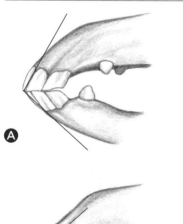

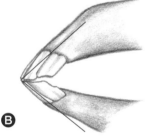

▲ As the horse ages the incisors protrude forward. **A.** Angle of teeth at age 10. **B.** Angle of teeth at age 20.

The young horse's teeth are also shorter and almost straight up and down when viewed from the side, meeting at almost a right angle. An older horse's teeth are longer and protrude forward at an acute angle. The older the horse, the more his incisors slant forward, coming together in a point, like the beak of a bird. This makes the teeth less effective for biting off grass. The horse's teeth usually become quite long by his late teens and into his 20s, but may then become shorter again as he gets very old and the teeth wear away more completely.

The upper corner incisors tend to develop irregularities or hooks on their back outside surface, which change with age. A hook usually starts to appear at age 8 or 9 and is fairly pronounced by age 12. If you observe a hook on the corner tooth, you can be quite sure the horse is older than 7. In the horse's teen years this hook starts to wear off, due to changing angulation of the incisors and different wear points than the teeth had earlier. By the time the horse is 16, the hook on the corner incisors of the upper teeth is usually gone again.

The wear and length of the incisors can vary greatly from one horse to another, however, depending on how much use they've had. A horse that has been eating hay and grain all his life rather than biting off grasses may show less wear on longer front teeth. A horse fed or pastured on sandy soil will wear his teeth faster because of occasional bits of sand he chews with his feed. A 6-year-old horse that has been eating short grass in sandy soil, for instance, may exhibit an 8-year-old mouth.

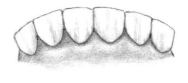

A. Front view of a 5-year-old with the gum line fairly straight across the teeth. **B.** Front view of a 20-year-old, showing how the gum line has become scalloped (sagging down at the base of each tooth).

A horse with a severe overbite or underbite will not have much wear. A horse that chews wood or cribs will wear his incisors more rapidly than other horses; some cribbers wear the incisors down to the gums. All these factors can make age determination more challenging.

GALVAYNE'S GROOVE

At about age 10, a groove usually appears at the gum line of the upper corner incisors. It becomes easier to see as the horse gets older, becoming yellow-brown and extending down the tooth. By the time the horse is 20, Galvayne's groove extends from the gum clear to the grinding surface of the tooth. Then it starts to disappear at the top (from the gum line), and as the tooth continues to erupt, this groove moves down the tooth and wears away by the time the horse is 30.

Dental Problems

If the jaws are not in proper alignment as teeth gradually erupt through the gum to compensate for wear, that wear may be uneven. The most common problems occur because the horse's upper jaw is normally wider than his lower jaw, often causing uneven wear of the teeth. This problem is accentuated if the upper and lower jaws are not the same length. If the lower jaw is too short, upper teeth protrude farther forward, a condition known as *parrot mouth*. If the lower jaw is too long, the lower teeth protrude forward, known as *sow mouth* or *monkey mouth*. Look for these conditions when evaluating a horse's conformation. A mismatch of more than ½ inch in jaw length

A. At about age 12, the incisors are slanting more forward and Galvayne's groove has appeared at the gum line on the upper corner incisor. The wearing surface of the central incisors are becoming more round than oval. **B.** At about age 15, the teeth are becoming longer and more slanted. Galvayne's groove is halfway down the corner incisor. The middle incisors are becoming rounder.
C. About age 22, the teeth are more slanted. Galvayne's groove is disappearing from the top half of the corner incisor, and by age 30 it will be gone. The central and middle incisors have become triangular by age 22; from age 23 to 29 they will go back to oval shape, but elongating in toward the back of the mouth rather than being long from side to side.

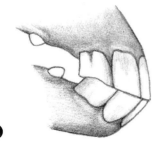

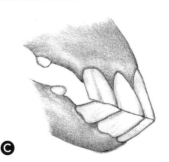

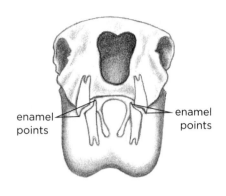

enamel points — enamel points

△ The upper jaw is wider than the lower jaw, and sometimes this creates hooks and ridges on the outside edge of the upper teeth and on the inside edge of the lower teeth.

is a serious conformation fault and should be avoided when selecting a horse for work or for breeding, because jaw length is hereditary.

The wearing surface, or table, of the tooth has a patterned surface, an interweaving of hard enamel and softer material called *dentin*. These materials wear away at different rates, as we already learned, providing clues in determining a horse's age. In order for teeth to grind the feed adequately, the top and bottom teeth must have good enamel-to-enamel contact.

Teeth that do not meet properly, due to malocclusion or loss of a tooth, prevent the harder enamel portions from making contact and will instead interact with the softer parts of the opposing tooth. This can wear portions of that tooth much more rapidly than normal, and it will become malformed. This can accentuate the original mouth problem.

Loss of a tooth can cause serious trouble; the opposing tooth has nothing to grind against and continues to grow. Unless it is cut off or periodically floated, the tooth may grow so long that it punctures the opposite jawbone. If the first premolars grow quickly, they can cause mouth damage, too. Regular floating can correct the condition, but in severe cases, the top of the teeth must be clipped.

Helpful Verse

To tell the age of any horse, inspect the lower jaw of course.
The six front teeth the truth will tell; now learn this lesson very well.
The middle nippers you behold before the colt is 2 weeks old.
Before 8 weeks two more will come; 8 months the corners cut
    the gums.
The dark cups nearly disappear from middle two in just 1 year.
In 2 years, from the second pair; in 3 the corners too are bare.
At 2 the middle nippers drop; at 3 the second pair can't stop.
When 4 years old the third pair goes; at 5 a full new set he shows.
The deep black spots will pass from view; at 6 years from the
    middle two.
The second pair at 7 years; at 8 each spot the corner clears
From middle nippers, upper jaw; at 9 the black spots will withdraw.
The second pair at 10 is white; 11 finds the corners bright.
As time goes on the horsemen know, the oval teeth three-sided grow.
The old horse has more woe than get; you only keep him for a pet.

O. R. Gleason, "To Tell the Age of Horses" (1882), as modified by Dale Jeffrey, *Horse Dentistry: The Theory and Practice of Equine Dental Maintenance* (Norfolk, NE: World Wide Equine, 1980), 78.

Signs of Trouble

A common sign of tooth trouble is difficulty chewing. The horse may turn his head sideways, or briefly stop chewing and begin again, or rub his head or jaw on a feed trough or some other surface while chewing. He may sling his head in a nodding fashion or swallow feed without chewing it, which may lead to indigestion or impaction colic. He may drop wads of partially chewed feed out of his mouth, known as *quidding*, or pass whole grains in manure.

Other clues to a dental problem include eating slower than he used to or losing weight in spite of good feed. He may dribble feed out of his mouth, especially if he can only work his jaw up and down rather than in normal side-to-side and circular motion. You may notice drooling, blood-tinged mucus in the mouth, foul-smelling breath, nasal discharge, pain or swelling of jaw or face, lack of desire to eat, reluctance to accept a bit, and head shaking while being ridden. Any of these signs mean your horse needs the assistance of an equine dentist.

Conformation Close-up

When evaluating a horse for possible purchase, always check the teeth with the help of a veterinarian or an equine dentist. Some dental conditions can have subtle or serious adverse effects on a horse's performance. If you decide to purchase a horse with dental problems, understand that the horse will need periodic, corrective dental work for the rest of his life. The goal of equine dentistry is to enable the horse to have free movement of the upper and lower jaws for smooth grinding action and normal head movement.

UNEVEN WEAR

Ideally, the rate of tooth growth is matched by an equal amount of wear. When the horse is eating, the lower jaw moves back and forth in a circular motion, grinding the feed between the upper and lower teeth. As long as there is full side-to-side movement of the jaw, normal teeth will wear evenly.

If the upper and lower rows, or *arcades*, of teeth are not in perfect opposition, or if full sideways motion is hampered, uneven wear will create sharp points, usually on the inside of the lower cheek teeth and on the outside of the upper cheek teeth. Because the upper cheek teeth are slightly farther apart than the lower ones, the outside edge of the upper teeth and the inside edge of the lower teeth do not contact the opposite teeth unless there is full sideways motion. As a result, the outside edge of the upper teeth and inside edge of the lower teeth may not wear away like the rest of the surface and may create sharp ridges.

Malocclusion, missing teeth, or abnormal chewing patterns due to disruption of proper side-to-side motion can result in a dominant

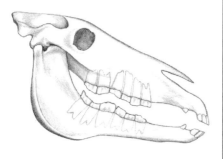

tooth: one that grows longer than the others because it is not worn down adequately. A dominant tooth may wear its opposing tooth excessively, perhaps into the gum line, or drive food into an empty socket left by a missing tooth, where it may cause infection. If several teeth become dominant, they may create a dental arcade that has high and low sections, a condition called *wave mouth*. A dominant tooth or teeth will need periodic correction (rasping) for the rest of the horse's life.

In order to be properly digested, feed must be chewed correctly. As it goes through the mouth, it turns in two circles before it is swallowed. It goes one way on one side of the cheek and on the other side it turns in the opposite direction, working its way back through the cheek teeth until it is fully ground — similar to the action of a mortar and pestle. The jaws move in a circular motion for most efficient grinding. If the jaws are hindered in their sideways movement by hooks and edges on the cheek teeth, the horse no longer has adequate back-and-forth grinding motion and can only chew up and down by opening and shutting his mouth on the feed. This may break it up a little but does not grind it. A horse with a painful mouth may not eat enough food and may lose weight. Even if he is able to eat and cleans up all his feed, he may still lose weight because he can't chew the food sufficiently for thorough digestion and thus won't receive maximum nutrition from it.

MALOCCLUSION

Many tooth problems are the result of malocclusion, when the upper and lower teeth do not meet properly. The most common malocclusions are parrot mouth, or overbite, and sow mouth, or underbite. Horses with untreated malocclusion may develop ridges and ledges on teeth that interfere with grinding food. The sharp edges may lacerate the tongue and sides of the mouth. Cuts along the tongue or inner surfaces of the mouth may become so large a person could put a thumb into them. Deep pockets may develop abscesses.

Because of mismatched incisors, the horse with parrot mouth or sow mouth has a hard time biting off grass when grazing, and his cheek teeth will develop sharp hooks because they do not wear properly. The overlapping tooth grows too long because it has nothing to grind against to wear it off, and this creates a hook, an elongated portion on the unworn edge. With parrot mouth, the unopposed portion of the first upper cheek teeth and the last lower cheek teeth grow too long, creating hooks, making it difficult for the horse to chew his feed.

Because the horse has 4.5 inches of tooth to erupt during his lifetime, these hooks can become quite long, sometimes so long that they puncture the opposite gum and create abscesses, or even penetrate the opposite jawbone. The hooks can be filed off with a dental rasp or cut with nippers or shears by an equine dentist or a veterinarian.

If malocclusion forces abnormal wear on the incisors, the unevenness may interfere with the normal sideways chewing motion of the jaws. If incisors become too long, they may prevent normal grinding of the cheek teeth. Small changes in the incisors can often have large adverse effects on the grinding teeth, so all the teeth need to be in proper alignment and wear evenly.

Hooks created by malocclusion on the cheek teeth at the back of the mouth and at the front of the dental arcade can interfere with the natural movement of the jawbone, keeping the lower jaw from sliding forward and back when the horse raises or lowers his head. This can cause pain in the temporomandibular joint near the top of his head. It may also inhibit normal flexion and hinder his ability to perform or respond properly to training (see page 64).

◀─◯ *Conformation Close-up*

A horse with a severe malocclusion should be avoided, even if he has a lot of athletic ability and good conformation in all other aspects; eating and athletic performance will always be problematic unless the horse has constant dental care. Although he may eat reasonably well when young, problems will increase as he ages. Horses with poor jaw conformation should never be used for breeding, since they will likely pass on these problems to their offspring.

Parrot Mouth

In a horse with parrot mouth, the top teeth are forward of the lower teeth, usually only slightly, but sometimes as much as several inches. The lower jaw is shorter than the upper one, like the mismatched beak of a parrot. This is an inherited condition, present from the time the horse is born. It occurs in all breeds but is seen more frequently in certain bloodlines.

Any degree of misalignment more than half the width of a tooth is defined as parrot mouth, a condition traditionally considered an unsoundness, since the horse will have a hard time eating and may not be able to keep up his energy and weight. In extreme cases, the last lower molar protrudes up behind the last upper molar. If the condition is obvious in a young horse, it usually gets worse as he

Floating

If there are sharp edges on teeth, these can be rasped off. Filing the teeth smooth is called *floating*; the dental rasp is called a *float*, from an old English term. A float was the tool used to file or grind plaster or concrete. The horse's teeth are floated to make them smooth and symmetrical. The chewing surface itself should not be rasped — just the rough and uneven edges and hooks. Most horses tolerate this procedure because it is not painful if done properly. Nerves in equine teeth are deep, far below the grinding surface. The exposed crown of the permanent tooth has no nerve structure.

Teeth can be floated by hand the traditional way, or with modern power tools. The latter should only be used by an experienced equine dentist or by a veterinarian who also practices dentistry. Power tools can take off too much tooth too quickly, or injure the soft tissues of the mouth, if they are not used with care.

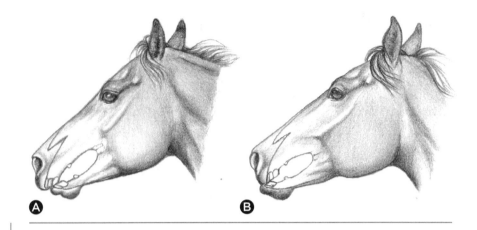

A mismatch in jaw length (malocclusion) may be obvious by looking at the muzzle, but mild cases can't be detected unless you look into the horse's mouth and examine the teeth. Both of these conditions are inherited conformation faults. **A.** Parrot mouth (overbite). **B.** Sow mouth (underbite).

grows up; while the horse's jaws are still growing, the mismatch may become greater and greater.

Sow Mouth

In a horse with sow mouth, also called monkey mouth or bulldog mouth, the bottom teeth are more forward than the top; the lower jaw protrudes farther forward than the upper jaw. In a severe case, the bottom incisors protrude up past the top ones, and the last upper molar protrudes down behind the last lower molar. Sow mouth is not as common as parrot mouth, but is just as serious, and also an inherited condition.

Conformation Close-up

Because of the uneven tooth wear in a horse with parrot mouth or sow mouth, it may be difficult or impossible to tell his age by his teeth. Take this into consideration when examining a horse to purchase.

Shear Mouth

Another dental abnormality found in some horses is an exceptionally narrow lower jaw. The molars do not meet squarely. Grinding action eventually wears the teeth off at an angle, making the grinding surfaces steeper and steeper rather then level. Eventually the teeth slide past one another. This condition is called *shear mouth*. If this problem is discovered early enough, before the teeth surfaces become extremely slanted, regular dental care can maintain more normal grinding surfaces.

Teeth and Feeding Practices

The incidence of mouth problems in a horse depend primarily on the conformation of his jaw and partly on the type of food he eats and how he feeds. Horses have fewer teeth problems if they are on pasture most of their lives rather than eating hay, grain, or pellets. Horses pull hay into the mouth rather than bite it off, and the incisors get minimal wear. The incisors may grow too long, making it impossible for the cheek teeth to meet and grind the food. Feeding grain or pellets and very little roughage can create even more problems; these feeds need less grinding and the cheek teeth may not wear properly.

Horses kept in stalls and fed hay and grain rather than being allowed to graze at pasture also tend to have more dental problems due to the position in which they eat. The horse in a stall is often fed in a manger or feed tub up off the ground, or he eats his hay from a net hung in his stall or doorway. His jaw and teeth are designed to meet most perfectly when his head is low, in grazing position. The lower jaw has some backward and forward movement and is in a slightly different position when his head is up rather than pointed down toward the ground (see page 64). A horse that spends his life eating from a manger or hay net rather than lowered to ground level does not wear his teeth properly and can develop serious dental problems.

A horse also needs the wide side-to-side circular grinding action of chewing roughages, rather than the more limited motion needed when chewing grain or pellets, to wear cheek teeth evenly and keep the edges smooth. With limited grinding movement, the horse develops sharp hooks and ledges on the inside portion of the lower teeth and the outside of the upper teeth, which limit the side-to-side jaw action even more.

Teeth and Performance

Teeth can affect a horse's performance in several ways. A problem with mouth or teeth can greatly affect a horse's performance or willingness to work. If he is uncomfortable, he may not give his best effort when asked to perform. He may cock his head to one side in an effort to avoid pain from the bit, or hold his head stiffly. This affects his freedom of movement and balance and he may travel with a stiff gait, with more risk of leg injury due to his poor way of traveling. If the head is not held correctly, the rest of his body will be off balance.

MOVEMENT OF THE MOUTH AND JAW

One of the most common and least frequently diagnosed performance problems is teeth that hinder free movement of the mouth

Did You Know?

Wave mouth often develops when a horse is fed in a stall with his head too high. The grinding surface of the cheek teeth becomes uneven, developing an undulating "wave" instead of maintaining a level plane. The dental arcade may be high or low in the front. The surface of the teeth may undulate several times from front to back.

and jaw. When the lower jaw cannot slide properly, the horse's agility and speed are reduced, along with his willingness to perform what the rider asks, because he can't get his head into proper position.

MOVEMENT OF THE HEAD AND NECK

Some performance and behavioral problems encountered in horses, such as head slinging, refusal or reluctance to respond to riders' cues, and mouth gaping open, are due to mouth problems. Even a horse being ridden without a bit in a bitless bridle or hackamore may open his mouth (if he has poor teeth) when asked to halt or do something that requires flexing at the poll. For a horse to flex at the poll, the lower jaw must be able to slide forward. If the horse has hooks on his cheek teeth that inhibit normal movement of the jaws, the opposing tooth catches on the hook and the jaw cannot slide forward or back freely; it is locked in place. If jaw movement is limited, the horse must open his jaws wider than the hooks that are blocking the movement. This is the only way he can create enough room to allow his jaw to slide so he can flex at the poll.

To understand this more fully, raise and lower your own head. If you raise your chin up and arch your head and neck backward, your lower jaw slides back. If you put your head downward (chin to chest), your lower jaw moves forward. It's the same with a horse. In order to easily change his head and neck position, his lower jaw must be able to move.

Trying to force him to perform, putting a tie-down on him to keep his head down, or a noseband to keep his mouth shut, will only make it harder for him to perform and create more mouth pain. If hooks in the back of the mouth lock the mouth in position so the jaw can't slide, this creates pain in the temporomandibular joint, the hinge between the top and bottom jaw, located a short distance below his ear and above his eye. This may make him resist certain actions, and he must open his mouth to avoid this pain. The horse cannot flex effectively or willingly unless he has no restricting hooks in his mouth.

The ability to hold a bit in his mouth without discomfort is critical for any horse that wears a bridle. The bit is one of the important ways a rider communicates with the horse. The horse's actions and athletic ability all depend on proper head and neck angle and his ability to position his head correctly for flexion and balance. Horses that can't move their heads freely cannot perform. A bad mouth can affect a horse's actions just as adversely as any other unsoundness.

BREATHING

A horse with a mouth problem may also have problems breathing while running. If he "swallows his tongue" (wads it up behind the bit, blocking the windpipe), this can be a clue that he is having trouble with the bit. The tongue is not able to sit flat in the mouth and breathing is restricted. The horse may make a roaring or whistling noise while exerting, if the bit is putting pressure on the tongue and pushing it backward. Sometimes the canine teeth are too big and long, encroaching on the space where the tongue lies. The tongue must buckle upward. This problem can be resolved by removing the canine teeth. Many problems can be corrected by creating more space for the bit in front of the first upper and lower cheek teeth. "Rolling," or smoothing and curving, the front edge of the first cheek teeth to make room for the bit is called putting in a "bit seat."

The Importance of Regular Dental Care

A graduate student in veterinary medicine checked the teeth of more than 250 horses brought to a university clinic for treatment of other conditions and discovered that 15 percent had major dental problems. Many horses have serious dental problems that are not obvious to the horse owner because the teeth are so far back in the mouth.

It is vital for horses to receive regular dental examinations, so problems can be discovered early and corrected before they become serious. Young horses (ages 2 to 4 years, when teeth are changing and permanent teeth are erupting) and old horses (late teens and older) may need dental care twice a year. Horses in the prime of life (5 to 15 years) may need only a yearly checkup. A horse with a serious problem that needs regular correction will require more frequent care.

5

Chest Conformation

THE SHAPE OF A HORSE'S chest plays a significant role in his level of endurance and stamina. A horse that will do slow, steady work might not be hampered by chest conformation that limits lung capacity, but any horse that will do work requiring speed, power, or endurance needs as much room as possible for maximum lung expansion.

The horse's ribs form the outer surface of the chest and define the appearance of the horse's midsection or *barrel*, the area between the front legs and hindquarters.

The shape of a horse's chest contributes to his lung capacity and therefore his endurance. When evaluating the chest, look for widely spaced ribs that extend outward and back from the spine and allow for maximum lung expansion.

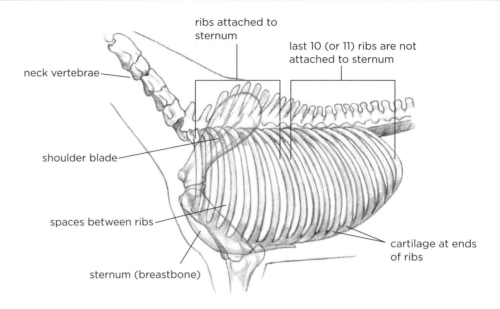

ribs attached to
sternum

last 10 (or 11) ribs are not
attached to sternum

neck vertebrae

shoulder blade

spaces between ribs

cartilage at ends
of ribs

sternum (breastbone)

▶ **Skeletal components of the chest, side view.**

The rib cage serves as protection for the heart, lungs, arteries, and windpipe, and the shape of this housing can have a significant influence on the athletic ability and endurance of the horse. Shape and curvature of the ribs determine whether he has a well-rounded, deep barrel, with plenty of room for the heart and for lung expansion, or a narrow, flat-sided midsection. The ribs should be curved and project backward rather than straight down. There also should be relatively large spaces between the ribs to allow for greater movement and lung expansion when the horse takes a breath.

Anatomy

The thorax, or chest, is the front portion of the barrel of the horse. The chest cavity is formed by the flexible, curved rib bones, which are attached to the backbone vertebrae at the top. The ribs at the front of the chest are attached to the sternum, or breastbone, underneath. The sternum lies between the forelegs and consists of six to eight bony segments connected to one another by cartilage to create the floor of the thoracic cavity. The width of the breastbone partially determines the width of the horse's front end, and the distance between his front legs. When viewed from the front, the horse's chest, also called the *breast*, is defined as the area between the bottom end of the neck and the tops of the front legs.

Unlike the human chest, which is wide from side to side and shallow from backbone to breastbone, the horse's chest is an oval. It is long from backbone to breastbone and narrower from side to side. The ribs form the skeletal support for the sides of the chest. Just outside the ribs are the scapula, or shoulder blades. These attach to the humerus, the uppermost bone in the front leg, between the shoulder joint and the elbow joint. Viewed from the front, the horse's chest is positioned between these two arm bones.

RIBS

Most horses have 18 pairs of ribs, though some have 19 and a few have only 17. The number of ribs depends on the number of thoracic vertebrae because the ribs are attached to these vertebrae (see chapter 6 for more on back conformation). Some Arabians and Thoroughbreds have 19 pairs of ribs but compensate by having 5 lumbar vertebrae instead of 6. This conformation provides a shorter, stronger loin area, or *coupling*, the lumbar area of the spine. The extra rib gives a well ribbed-up appearance and depth of flank. The underline of the horse should rise gradually toward the hindquarters, not up sharply toward the flank.

Rib Attachments

The first rib is the shortest and angles slightly forward from its vertebral attachment. The second rib is vertical. The remainder, however, should slope backward rather than straight down. The first 6 or 7 thoracic vertebrae are located behind the shoulder blade. The first 10 thoracic vertebrae have the tallest dorsal spinous processes, which create the withers. The first few ribs are not visible because they are underneath the shoulder blades.

The first 9 rib pairs provide attachment sites for the muscles that activate the shoulders. The first 8 pairs of ribs, the *sternal ribs*, are attached at their bottom end to the sternum with cartilage. The last 10 or 11 pairs of ribs are attached only to the backbone and not to the sternum. At the backbone, the thoracic vertebrae form joints with the ribs; each vertebra has four joint surfaces (two on each side) that form half a socket; the other half of the socket is on the adjoining vertebrae. The rib hooks into this socket.

The last 11 pairs of ribs (or 10 or 9, depending on the horse and his total number of ribs) are linked together at the bottom by only a band of cartilage and thus have greater mobility. Those last ribs allow for maximum chest expansion when the horse breathes, rotating into their widest position. The last one or two pairs are often called *floating ribs* because the bottom end may not be attached to the adjacent ribs.

"Well Ribbed Up"

It is important that the ribs extend well back along the abdomen, to allow for maximum chest expansion and lung room. Arabians and

close coupling; very little space between the last rib and the angle of the hindquarters

ribs extend well back, making the horse deep through the flank

⬥ For optimal lung capacity, the rib cage should extend back deeply, with little space between the last rib and the angle of the hindquarters.

horses with Arabian blood such as Thoroughbreds, which may have the extra pair of ribs, often have great lung room and exceptional endurance, due in part to the extra ribs.

For a horse to be well ribbed up, the thoracic vertebrae that carry the ribs should extend back toward the pelvis, leaving no slackness between the last rib and the hip and very little space between the rib and the angle of the hindquarter. The horse with well-sprung ribs that curve out and project backward has a round barrel and a short loin (short back).

MUSCLES OF THE CHEST

There are many muscles in front of the chest, some of which are neck or shoulder muscles. Many of the muscles associated with the neck and front legs are attached to the ribs. The pectoral, or breast, muscles are large, paired muscles that form the inverted V shape at the front of the chest, at the top of and above the front legs. They define the shape and width of the horse's front end and play a key role in front leg movement.

Viewed from the front, the chest should be well defined rather than blending into the neck. Even if the horse has thick muscling, the actual width of the chest is defined by its bone structure. Width of the breast is measured from shoulder to shoulder, at the points of the shoulders. The breast should be wide, with a relatively wide gap between the front legs, but not too wide or the horse will have less agility and speed; see illustrations on page 78 and 79. (For more on front leg conformation, see chapter 7.)

Chest Attachments

The chest is not rigidly attached to the front legs but is suspended between them, supported between the shoulder blades by muscles. The primary muscle attachments are at the bottom of the rib cage and suspend the chest from the sides of the forelegs. This is an ideal arrangement for minimizing concussion to the body. Muscular attachments have more give and elasticity than bony attachments and can absorb much of the shock that would otherwise be transmitted directly to the body through the feet and legs. This suspension arrangement also minimizes jarring of the heart and lungs, the principal organs within the chest cavity.

CHEST SHAPE

The shape of the rib cage can vary greatly among individual horses. It may be wide or narrow, deep or shallow. When viewed from the front, the horse's chest should be wider at the bottom than at the top. The shoulder blades should be much closer together at their tops, toward the withers, than at the points of the shoulders, where the front legs attach. If the shoulder blades are too wide apart at the top, the horse will have broad, low withers and a rolling gait with considerable side-to-side motion. This type of conformation is common in draft horses (and in some ponies and warmbloods, or other horses with "cold" blood in their ancestry; see chapter 15) but should be avoided in a riding horse. The rolling gait is not only uncomfortable to the rider but also compromises agility.

Even though old-timers talked about chest shape in terms of room available for heart and lungs, the most important aspect of chest conformation is room for lung expansion. Of course, the heart also needs room to work efficiently as a pump. A horse's body weight is 1/8 blood, or 125 pounds (15.5 gallons) in a 1000-pound horse. The heart pumps about a quart of blood at each beat, at a rate of about

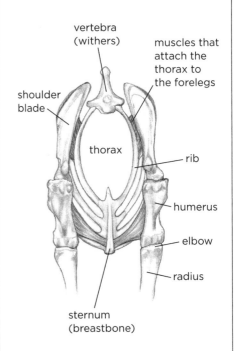

△ The horse's thorax is suspended between the forelegs by muscle attachments.

32 beats per minute at rest and 60 beats per minute or more during hard work. If a horse is working during part of the day, his heart will beat more than 48,000 times and pump the equivalent of 12,000 gallons of blood.

Lung expansion in the working horse requires more space than the heart and its big blood vessels. If a horse has a wide rib cage with maximum room, his diaphragm will be larger. This muscular wall separates the chest cavity from the abdomen; it helps pull air into the lungs and push it out with a bellows-like action. The wider the rib cage, the more effective the diaphragm will be and the more room for the lungs to expand when the horse inhales.

─◯ Conformation Close-up

When judging the shape of a horse's rib cage, look for depth and width. Evaluate him carefully from front and rear as well as from the side. Note whether he is well ribbed up toward the back of the abdomen. His rib cage can give clues about his capacity for endurance and his potential as an athlete.

▶ **A.** A horse with well-sprung ribs that curve outward and project backward has a round barrel and a short loin. **B.** A slab-sided horse. Flat ribs project straight down instead of back, with a narrow rib cage. The loin is long, with a wider space between the hip and last rib.

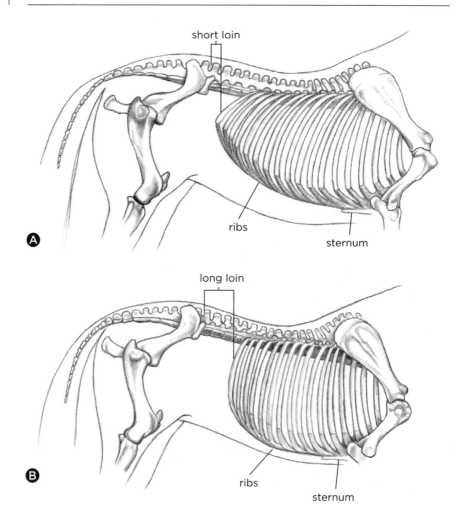

Well-Sprung Ribs

The greater the degree of rib curvature, the greater the "spring of rib" in traditional horsemen's terms. A horse with good "spring of rib" is preferred, because a horse with a well-rounded chest usually has more endurance and is a better "doer." A horse with well-sprung ribs that project backward also has a long, deep underline and a shorter back and loin, which contribute to a stronger back (see page 88). The loin is the muscular portion of the back behind the saddle area, from the last rib to the point of the croup, the highest part of the rump.

Slab-Sided Ribs

If the ribs are flat, short, upright, and straight rather than sloping backward, the horse is said to be *slab-sided*. Because the ribs go straight down instead of outward and back, there is less room for lung expansion.

A horse with short rear ribs has less depth at the flank than a horse that is well ribbed up. The *flank* area is just ahead of the sheath or udder and includes the lower line of his abdomen at the rear. A horse

⚠ A "herring-gutted" or "wasp-waisted" (also called "hound-gutted") horse with shallow flanks tucked up like a greyhound (ribs not placed far enough back) often lacks stamina and does not hold up well during strenuous work.

Speed and Stamina

Both the sprinter, who is fast over short distances, and the stayer, who runs swiftly over a long course, need a large barrel, but the stayer generally has less muscle bulk on his body and longer, leaner muscles. A horse with heavy muscles may have a faster take-off and more power for a short sprint, but he also tires more quickly because he has more body bulk to carry.

Staying power and endurance depend on the fitness of muscles and lungs. Even more important than muscle fitness is ample space within the chest for lungs to expand to full capacity during strenuous exertion. A horse with limited chest room will have limited stamina and will run out of gas before the end of a long race or a long ride, no matter the strength of his muscles.

that is shallow through the flank generally has less-developed abdominal muscles and less stamina. A slab-sided horse also has a longer, weaker loin and cannot carry as much weight.

Chest Shape and Stamina

Chest shape determines stamina. Even though the ribs at the back of the thorax can rotate with each inhalation to create more room for lung expansion, the shape of the rib cage dictates how much extra room can be created by this expansion. The shape of the chest is determined not only by the angle of the ribs and degree of rib curvature but also depends on the part of the rib at which the curvature is most pronounced. A wide chest is favored by horsemen.

Spacing between each rib is also important. When the ribs are well separated, the chest walls present a larger surface from front to back; there is greater capacity for the chest to expand when the ribs rotate forward with each breath as the horse draws air into the lungs. Each movable part of the chest should have as much space as possible for this expansion. Large spaces between the ribs aid this movement and give more room for muscle attachments. These muscles help expand the chest as the horse takes in air.

BARREL CHEST AND DEEP CHEST

There are two types of efficient chest conformation: the round, barrel chest and the wide, deep chest. Horsemen tend to prefer the wide, deep chest, because the barrel-chested horse often appears to have too much "daylight" under him; his length of leg is greater than his depth of chest. If his legs are too long for the depth of his body, this decreases his agility and balance. In terms of actual efficiency and endurance, though, a barrel chest with the proper proportions can provide just as much lung room as a deep chest.

▶ Cross-section of a barrel chest (A) and a deep chest (B), as viewed from the front.

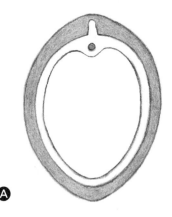

A barrel-chested horse generally has good stamina. If a horse seems shallow in the chest from a side view, without much depth through the girth, take a closer look from another angle. He may make up in width what he lacks in depth. Looking at him from the front or rear, you can tell whether he has adequate chest room. The ribs should be wide enough to be apparent from a front view, visible behind the front quarters. From a rear view, ribs should be slightly wider than the hindquarters. If the horse has wide, powerful hindquarters, the rib cage may be the same width as the hindquarters. This round barrel should also be symmetrical, with the same shape apparent on both sides of the horse.

Ribs of only moderate length, projecting downward rather than toward the rear, and lacking curvature, may give the illusion of depth and adequate lung room when a horse is viewed from the side; however, in reality the sides of the ribs are flat. They cannot rotate outward very much; the capacity of the chest is limited. The more the thorax departs from a cylindrical, round shape, the less its total volume.

The horse should be wedge-shaped, with the chest narrower at the front and wider at the back. This makes him more streamlined and agile, with better body balance. The widest part of the rib cage should be behind the girth. The barrel is thus wider behind the rider's leg than at the girth. The greatest roundness is in back of the girth and fullest at the floating ribs toward the rear, allowing for a very wide, strong diaphragm.

A tapered barrel is not only more comfortable for the rider because it is less wide at the girth than at the rear of rib cage, but also provides the greatest expansion potential in the lung area. This shape also gives a larger area for muscle attachment to the body and range of motion for shoulder, leg, and neck muscles and helps the saddle stay in proper place at the center of the back; it keeps the cinch or girth in proper position. It's easier for the rider to stay in correct balance with the horse because the saddle isn't slipping forward, backward, or to the sides.

The tapered barrel helps keep the saddle from sliding back when the horse is going uphill, and from turning when the rider mounts. If a horse has the same roundness from front to rear (too round at the girth area), the saddle will turn.

⚲ *Conformation Close-up*

The last rib (toward the flank) should be sprung outward and slanted to the rear. This gives sufficient room for strong loin muscles between the last rib and the hip bone and croup, while still maintaining a short coupling.

Did You Know?

If the curve of the ribs isn't apparent when you stand directly in front of a horse, he won't have much endurance, especially if he is shallow through the chest and narrow. But if his chest is wide and easy to see (nearly cylindrical in shape), his stamina may be surprisingly good, even if he is shallow through the chest, for what was lost in height or depth of chest was gained in width and still allows adequate space for lung expansion.

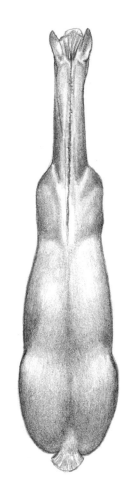

⬤ The horse should be wedge-shaped: narrower in front and wider behind.

Heart Girth

Many old-timers measured the girth when judging conformation to determine whether or not the horse had enough chest capacity. The rule of thumb was that for adequate lung function, a 16-hand horse should have a girth measurement of at least 6 feet (72 inches) in circumference. Most good athletes have an even larger circumference, which gives them stamina for strenuous work. A taller horse should have greater circumference, proportionately. Each additional inch greater than the minimum will increase the percentage of space available for air intake. Some horsemen go so far as to say that a 14.2-hand horse should have at least 6 feet (72 inches) of chest circumference. The heart girth measurement should always be greater than the horse's height. If you compare two horses of equal height, the horse with the greater chest capacity (heart girth) will almost always have better endurance than the one with less chest room. Girth measurement also can provide a rough indication of a horse's weight.

Problematic Chest Conformation

A chest that is too narrow or too wide is considered poor conformation. Either extreme hinders a horse's athletic ability, so give this careful consideration when evaluating a horse.

NARROW CHEST

A narrow-chested horse may be too narrow in front, with a narrow breast and not enough room between his front shoulders. A horse with a narrow front may also lack adequate thickness and development of the shoulders. A horse's ability to carry weight is affected by the width of his front end.

A really narrow horse may have a harder time carrying a rider's weight; he has less base of support for the saddle and rider due to the relatively narrow back muscles; unless the horse has good withers, the saddle may slip to one side. If the horse is too narrow, the rider may also have less leg contact with the horse's body. The rider's legs would hang down without being able to "close" readily on the horse to give leg signals.

A horse should not be too narrow in the chest or in his front end (breast). If he is too narrow in his front quarters, the front legs may be too close together where they depart from the body. The old-timer's expression for this fault was "both legs out of the same hole." If the chest is too narrow, the forelegs may be too close together all the way down (though straight) or may angle outward on the way down and be base wide (see chapter 7).

Estimated Weight Based on Girth Measurements*							
PONIES				**HORSES**			
Girth		Weight		Girth		Weight	
in.	(cm.)	lb.	(kg.)	in.	(cm.)	lb.	(kg.)
40	(101)	100	(45)	55	(140)	538	(240)
42.5	(108)	172	(77)	57.5	(146)	613	(274)
45	(114)	235	(104)	60	(152)	688	(307)
47.5	(120)	296	(132)	62.5	(159)	776	(346)
50	(127)	368	(164)	65	(165)	851	(380)
52.5	(133)	430	(192)	67.5	(171)	926	(414)
55	(140)	502	(234)	70	(178)	1014	(453)
57.5	(146)	562	(252)	72.5	(184)	1090	(486)
				75	(190)	1165	(520)
				77.5	(199)	1278	(570)
				80	(203)	1328	(593)
				82.5	(206)	1369	(611)

* Body builds can vary significantly between breeds and types of horses; therefore, these weights are only estimates.

If he is too narrow he also may have turned-in elbows and a twist to the front legs, causing his front feet to toe out (see chapter 7). The splay-footed stance makes him wing his feet inward when he travels, increasing the chances of striking the other leg. The horse that is too narrow in his chest and front end may also "plait" as he travels; the front feet practically cross over one another and land directly in front of each other (like walking a tightrope instead of having the tracks in two lines).

A narrow horse is often tucked up at the flank instead of well ribbed up and deep in the flank, and often too long in the back with a weak loin. There is usually more than a hand's width of space between the last rib and point of the hip. Horses with this conformation not only have a weak loin, but generally less strength in their abdominal muscles, as well; it is harder for them to flex properly (to lower the hindquarters to bring the hind legs farther underneath the body) and round the back for good weight carrying. A narrow horse is usually harder to condition for strenuous work.

TOO-WIDE CHEST

Occasionally, a horse has the opposite problem — such a wide rib cage (extreme barrel chest) that upper-arm movement between shoulder blade and elbow is restricted. The wide ribs hinder the backward sweep of the upper arm. A very round rib cage may also spread the rider's legs apart uncomfortably at the hips and pelvis, and put more stress on the rider's knees. Sometimes a narrower rib cage

Ideal Chest Conformation

The ideal chest has ribs that extend well outward and back from the spine, giving the horse a strong back for carrying weight and enough rib curvature for adequate lung capacity. The first ribs (under the shoulders) should be proportional with minimal curvature so they don't inhibit rotation of the shoulder and upper-arm bone.

Large spaces between the ribs allow for maximum chest expansion, and long ribs can give more curvature than short ones. The better the ribs and chest are formed, the greater the area available for proper attachment of shoulder, leg, and neck muscles, for this is where those muscles unite with the body.

is easier on the rider, especially if the horse is being used in an activity that requires many hours in the saddle. In most cases, however, a wide rib cage is an advantage rather than a disadvantage, particularly as it pertains to the horse's endurance and abilities.

There should be sufficient width between the front legs, yet the front of the horse should not be too wide and heavy. Width of chest cavity (thorax, rib cage) and width of breast are two entirely different things. A horse can have a wide rib cage (a good quality) without being too wide in the breast.

Too-Wide Breast

A wide breast is a disadvantage to any riding horse or race horse, because excessive width in front cuts down on speed and agility. Horses should always be wider at the hindquarters than in front. He needs strength of loin and quarters, and it is best if his center of gravity is not so far forward. He will have much freer action in his front legs and more agility if his weight is balanced farther back. A wide breast creates a rolling gait that is uncomfortable for the rider and more stressful for the horse, with more impact force on each front leg at every stride.

The sternum varies a great deal in length and width in different horses. If the sternum is too wide (and the pectoral muscles are bulky) there will be a lot of width between the forearms.

The draft horse tends to have a wider front than a riding horse. This can be an advantage for the draft horse, giving him a wider shoulder area to lean into a collar. He depends on slow strength and pulling power to do his work. In a riding horse, however, this much

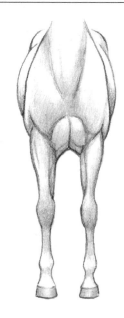 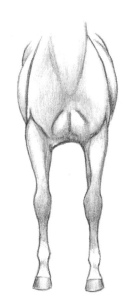

▶ Chest of average width (A) and chest too wide (B).

Ⓐ　　Ⓑ

width is a hindrance to speed and agility. He needs good balance and maneuverability while working at speed.

Quarter Horse breeders like a relatively wide breast because it gives room for more muscling (more power), but if the horse's breast is too wide, he has a rolling gait and may paddle outward with his front feet. This cuts down on efficiency of motion, hindering speed and agility even more. He will have more trouble moving his legs freely at fast gaits. Anything that hinders free, straightforward leg action will hinder speed and surefootedness.

IMPROPER CHEST MUSCLING

If the breastbone is too wide, and the pectoral (breast) muscles too bulky, the horse will be too wide and heavy in front for great speed or maneuverability. From the front, the pectoral muscles should form an inverted V shape between the tops of the front legs. If a horse does not have adequate muscling, there will be a flat space here instead of the inverted V.

When looking at the horse from the side, the pectoral (breast) muscles should be visible as a slight bulge in front, but not too much. A horse should not have so much pectoral muscle mass that it protrudes (pigeon breast; see chapter 7), or he may also be "camped under" in front (feet positioned too far back, rather than the front legs being perfectly straight up and down).

The shape of a horse's rib cage and front end can tell you a lot about his stamina and agility, and also give clues about the angles and conformation of his front legs. Thus, the chest should always be carefully evaluated when judging a horse.

◀ Exaggerations: "bulldog" chest (A) and too-narrow front (B).

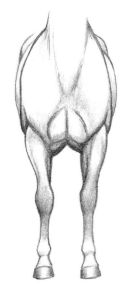

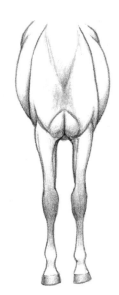

Back Conformation

BACK INJURIES, WHICH MAY involve bone, soft tissues, or both, are more common in horses than we realize. Horse's backs, including the bones, joints, and connective tissues, must withstand a lot of stress when at work, both under saddle and while driven, because the backbone transmits the force and driving power from the hind legs. When carrying a rider, the horse may have to support additional weight of up to 25 percent of his own body weight.

A good back is of medium length and bridges the span between the shoulders and the hindquarters with strength and flexibility. It has well-conformed withers in front and a short, strong loin behind for maximum support while carrying a rider during athletic maneuvers.

Ideal Back Conformation

A well-proportioned back is of medium length, neither too short nor too long. It is relatively flat (rather than too sloped), well muscled (without the spine showing prominently or thickly padded with fat on either side of the backbone), and wide enough for a comfortable saddle fit for horse and rider.

Because the spine is one of the last parts of the skeletal structure to mature, hard use and training when a horse is young can cause problems. The backbone may not develop fully until age 5, 6, or 7 in some horses; back problems may manifest as poor performance or be mistaken for leg lameness or a behavioral problem.

It is important to learn how to recognize good back conformation. A good back is strong and contributes to a horse's overall soundness; it supports a saddle properly and a rider comfortably. A poorly built back or one that is too long for balance hinders athletic ability and durability and increases stress on the horse's legs.

Evolution of the Equine Spine

The ancestors of the modern horse were smaller and had a more flexible backbone. They lived in forests, eating leaves, and could bend and twist to maneuver around underbrush and trees when fleeing from predators. By contrast, the modern horse is designed for swift flight in straight lines. His more recent ancestors adapted to running swiftly over the prairies. Modern horses developed withers as a firm anchor for neck and shoulders, and a shorter, straighter span of lumbar vertebrae for stabilizing the coupling between hind legs and backbone. This evolution was essential for straight-line running, which was crucial for survival in wide-open spaces.

After the horse's back became less arched and more stable, his legs became longer, enabling him to run faster. As evolution continues, the horse's back is becoming even more rigid and less flexible, especially in the lumbar area, to give a more solid pivot point for the hindquarters and to minimize the stress and inflammation that sometimes occurs between those vertebral joints. When examined after death, the spines of most horses are found to have bony fusions between the transverse processes (side wings) of the last several lumbar vertebrae. In a foal, there is a little movement between some of these vertebrae, but as the horse matures and ages the area becomes fused in many individuals.

Occasionally, extra stresses on the back — from too much flexion during athletic activity, for example — create contact between portions of adjacent vertebrae that are not supposed to touch, as in the lumbar region. This contact can pinch and tear the soft tissues between vertebrae or bruise or even fracture some of the bony processes. As they heal, they may fuse together. Jumpers and racehorses very commonly develop fusion, as do many other horses.

How the Spine Moves

In growing horses, there is both side-to-side and up-and-down movement of the spine, but mature horses have little flexibility in the spine. Almost all flexion in the horse's back comes in the loin area, right behind the saddle; there is also a little movement between the first, second, and third lumbar vertebrae.

The lumbosacral joint between the last lumbar bone and the sacrum is the primary area of flexion. The front half of the spine is rigid due to the stabilizing effect of the attached ribs, which limit side-to-side movement. The back part of the spine in the lumbar region is also rigid due to the articular processes on the vertebrae that help join them together and the fusion that often occurs. About the only place the vertebrae can rotate or bend from side to side is the saddle region, making it the weakest part of the horse's back because it lacks natural rigidity. This area is vulnerable to injury when a rider bangs down hard in the saddle or sits with weight too far back rather than carried forward over the stronger area just behind the withers.

Withers

The withers consist of the tallest thoracic (sometimes called *dorsal*) vertebrae, which begin at the base of the neck. The thoracic vertebrae, on average, consist of 18 bones (some horses have 17 or 19) that form the section of the spine between the neck and the lumbar vertebrae. The heights of the dorsal spinous processes on the first 9 or 10 of these thoracic vertebrae determine the height of the withers (see chapter 2). The first two thoracic vertebrae, where the neck ends and the back begins, have short spinous processes. The spines of the third through fifth thoracic vertebrae gradually increase in height, and the sixth through ninth vertebrae gradually become shorter again. For the rest of the thoracic and lumbar vertebrae, the heights of the upright spines of the back vertebrae remain consistently short along the length of the back.

Beginning where the neck ends, the withers should create a prominent upward curve. They should be covered with muscle, not too "sharp" but well defined, then widening so there is plenty of muscle covering the shoulder and back. The withers should be long from front to back, tapered smoothly into the neck and sloping smoothly into the back, with no dents or bumps. The rear part of the withers should provide a secure base for a saddle.

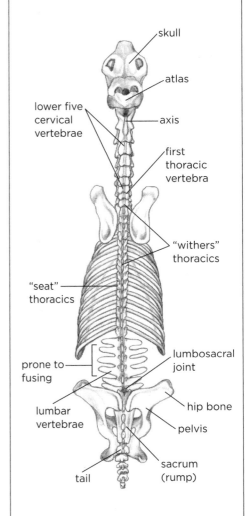

▲ **Backbone, top view.**

skull

atlas

lower five cervical vertebrae

axis

first thoracic vertebra

"withers" thoracics

"seat" thoracics

lumbosacral joint

prone to fusing

hip bone

lumbar vertebrae

pelvis

tail

sacrum (rump)

The withers serve as the anchor for muscles and the leverage point for the front of the back. The lumbosacral joint (at the point of the croup, between the lumbar vertebrae and the sacrum) serves as the anchor and leverage point for muscles at the rear of the back and a flex point for the hindquarters.

When the lumbosacral joint flexes, the rump angles down as the horse tightens his loins and raises his back. The elastic ligaments and long, strong muscles from neck to tail create a continuous band of support for the back, attached to various vertebrae. A pull on either end of this specialized support system (from the neck or the hindquarters) acts to raise the center of the back, making it stronger and capable of carrying the weight of a rider. As in a suspension bridge, this unique series of interconnected "cables" attached to the vertebrae holds up the back.

The withers should be well defined and of moderate height. This type of withers conformation maximizes the horse's athletic ability and is the easiest to fit to a saddle with the fewest problems. Withers and croup of the same height give a horse the best balance and the least strain on his front and rear quarters (see chapter 10).

FUNCTION OF THE WITHERS

The withers are a crucial part of the horse's overall conformation. They form the attachment point for the muscles and ligaments that extend the head and neck, and the muscles that bring the shoulder forward, elevate the shoulder, lengthen the back, and rotate the ribs to provide maximum expansion of the rib cage when the horse is breathing. A well-built horse has well-defined withers. A horse lacking adequate withers does not have proper bone structure for a good shoulder or athletic action; he also has difficulty holding a saddle.

The withers serve as an attachment and anchor for the strong nuchal ligament that begins at the top of the horse's head and poll and runs down the top of the neck to the withers; this elastic ligament helps support the horse's head in a raised position without exertion. The muscles that raise the head and neck and move it from side to side are also connected to the withers. The freedom of movement and strength of these muscles is increased dramatically when the withers are high rather than low, because they create a longer lever and allow for greater, more effective contraction.

The withers serve as an anchor for the muscles that attach the shoulder blade to the body. Without well-formed withers, it is almost impossible to have a well laid-back shoulder. The set and angle of the shoulder blade depends on the position of the withers (whether the withers are forward or extend well back), and the position of the withers in turn depends on the height of the spinal bones.

As discussed in chapter 5, a horse's rib cage is suspended between the forelegs by muscles holding the shoulder blade to the backbone, withers, and ribs. The height of the withers depends in part on the height of the dorsal spines of the vertebrae and on the way the thorax is suspended between the front legs and shoulder blades.

The withers play an important role in the horse's athletic ability and future soundness. For proper shoulder action and good head carriage, they should have plenty of length from front to back. Withers that are too short in height are often too short in length as well. In these horses the neck is often too thick and coarse. Withers should be properly shaped and covered with muscle at the sides, rather than thin and bony. Adequate muscle covering over the bones provides some padding so a saddle will be less apt to irritate the skin and make sores.

HIGH WITHERS

Well-defined, or high, withers are commonly seen with a well-sloped shoulder and provide good leverage for attached muscles of the neck and back. This makes it easier for the horse to collect himself and to "round" his back. He can extend his shoulder fully, which gives him a longer stride and more speed.

The tall spines of the vertebrae at the withers slant toward the rear, which helps them act like "tent pegs" that brace against the forward pull of the muscles and ligaments of the neck and hold them in place. The short vertebrae under the saddle area and the somewhat taller lumbar and sacral spines all serve as anchors for various muscles that support the horse's back. High withers, with well-attached neck muscles, create superior leverage for the horse to raise and lower his head and help keep his back strong.

When he lowers his head, the neck ligaments pull on the withers, which in turn pull on some connecting ligaments that raise the center of his back. Thus, a horse with good withers is more able to round his back for carrying weight. He is also more able to collect himself by using his neck and back muscles to "shorten" himself and bring his hindquarters more underneath his body. The exception would be a ewe-necked horse with poor muscle and ligament attachments between the neck and the withers (see page 44); he cannot raise his back very much by flexing and lowering his neck. For best athletic function, the horse needs a proper neck connection as well as good withers.

Length of Back

The back (from peak of the withers to point of the croup) should be about one-third of the body length, which is measured from the point of the shoulder to the point of the buttock. Back length is influenced by the number of vertebrae in the thoracic and lumbar regions. Most horses have six lumbar vertebrae, but some (especially horses with Arabian ancestry) have only five. Most of those have an extra thoracic vertebrae (19 instead of 18), which gives them one more set of ribs. This can be an advantage, because the lumbar section needs to be short and strong (and some of the vertebrae fuse together). Having 19 thoracic vertebrae gives that section a larger rib cage and more lung room.

The horse's back is relatively inflexible. If the back is too short in the saddle and loin area, much of the propulsion and concussion

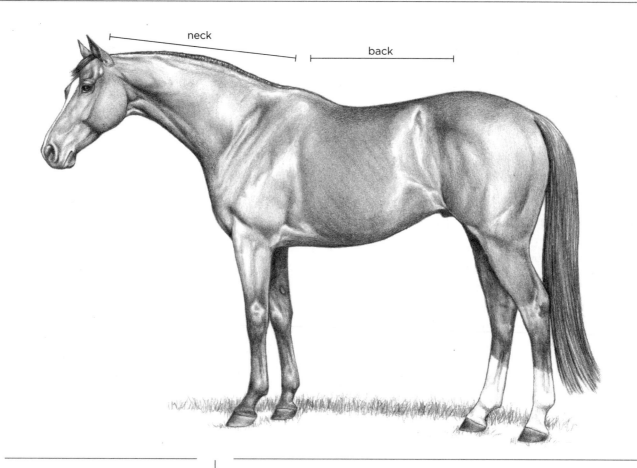

neck

back

▲ Good topline contour: long neck and proportional back.

from the hind legs is transmitted directly to the rider's seat, resulting in a jarring ride. A slightly longer back is more conducive to a comfortable ride, for there is more movement and some buffering of the upward thrust from the hind legs.

─○ *Conformation Close-up*

The length of the back (between withers and hip) should be exactly the same length as the horse's shoulder area (the part of his body that is forward of the back) and the same length as his hip area (behind the lumbosacral joint near the croup). The horse's body should thus be one-third shoulder, one-third back, and one-third hip (see chapter 10). The proportions and ratio are determined by the bone patterns of the spine — the length of the thoracic area, lumbar area, and so on — and these remain the same from foalhood through maturity. This is one aspect of conformation that can be judged at an early age.

LENGTH OF TOPLINE

Most horses that are of average height (14.2 to 15.2 hands tall) are usually about 7 feet long from the top of the head (at the poll, between the ears) to the point of the buttocks. The horse's *neck* (from poll to the top of the withers) is slightly longer than the back. The *back* is considered to be the area between the withers and croup. The *croup* is the high point of the rump, the coupling between the last lumbar vertebra and the sacrum. As defined by most horsemen, the *topline* is measured from the withers to the tail.

In a well-conformed horse, the topline is shorter than the *underline*, the underside of the horse from elbows to stifle. With this type of conformation, the shoulder is well sloped, and the rider sits comfortably behind the front quarters, where he experiences less thrust and concussion from the front legs. The length of the individual vertebrae that make up the spine determine the length of the horse's topline. When the seven cervical vertebrae in the neck are long, the shoulders will be well sloped — laid back rather than steep and upright — to connect with the thoracic vertebrae at the withers. This also creates a nice long neck and a relatively short back. The slope of the shoulders and length of the withers help determine the "shortness" of the back. A long neck and short back provide the most desirable conformation in a riding horse, providing maximum maneuverability of head and neck for balance and a strong back for carrying weight.

If the seven cervical vertebrae are shorter than the average length, however, the neck will be short and the shoulders more upright, resulting in a too-long back. If a horse has a short neck and a long back, he tends to have a more upright shoulder, which gives him a shorter stride, rougher ride, and makes it harder to fit a saddle on his back. He will jar the rider more and have more pounding weight on his front legs because the rider may be sitting directly over them. Anything that increases concussion of the feet and legs may eventually lead to breakdown injuries.

⊸O *Conformation Close-up*

The horse's back should be carefully assessed from each side and from above to see if there is any crookedness in the topline or asymmetry from one side to the other. A slight asymmetry in the topline may not affect the horse's performance, but obvious crookedness will hinder the way he moves, perhaps creating an uneven stride or thwarting his ability to move straight forward without "drifting" off to the left or right as he travels. A back problem may make the horse uncomfortable to ride or adversely affect his performance, making it difficult for him to turn in one direction or take a certain lead. Thus when evaluating his topline, check it from above as well as from the side, to detect any deviations from smoothness and straightness.

Bird's-Eye View

If you are short and want a bird's-eye view of a tall horse, stand on a bale of hay or a fence directly behind the horse but out of kicking range so you are high enough to look down on the back. This perspective will help you see whether the back is straight and the muscling and structure symmetrical on both sides of it.

LOINS

The horse's *loin* is the muscular area of his back between the last rib and the point of the croup and hip joint. This area should be short and wide. Together, the loins of the two sides form a triangle (the apex pointing forward, starting at the lumbar vertebrae, and the base being the line at the croup between the two hip bones). Horsemen prefer a strong, short loin with no more than about three fingers' width between the last rib and the point of the hip. A horse that is "well ribbed up" (the last ribs extending far back and slanting backward rather than straight down) tends to have a short loin. A loin is considered long if it is more than a hand's width across. A horse with a strong loin shows a slightly convex contour on either side of the backbone in this area; a slack, concave area is a sign of inadequate muscling. A slack loin is always considered weak, especially if it is narrow and dips downward.

The lumbosacral joint, or coupling, is where the last lumbar vertebra in the loin area joins the front of the sacrum, the group of fused vertebrae that form the underlying structure beneath the rump. Most of the movement, or flexion, in a horse's spine occurs here, and it is the point at which the driving power of the hind legs transfers to forward propulsion. The horse must be able to flex here in order to bring his hind legs underneath himself. In many ways, the lumbosacral joint is the most important joint in determining whether a horse can move well.

A horse that is *close coupled*, with a short loin area, usually has strong, short muscles and can tense the spine more readily to raise and propel the front quarters and thus is more easily collected. As the back muscles stiffen his spine and the loin muscles contract to pull the hindquarters farther underneath himself, he can lift his front end.

There should be a firm, short coupling of pelvic bones where they attach to the spine. This creates the desirable slight arch over the loin area. The opposite is a loose, long coupling that makes a hollow, weak loin. When the coupling is in proper position in relation to the hips, it will be in a line between the hip bones, directly above the point of the hip.

The position of the coupling between the last lumbar vertebra and sacrum varies from horse to horse and may be a little more forward or back without too much problem; however, if it's too far back it may cause foaling problems in a mare. It also creates a weak coupling and too much length of loin. A horse with a long, weak coupling has difficulty getting his hindquarters and hocks underneath his body and

The Loin Triangle

To determine the area of the lumbosacral joint, draw an imaginary line across the horse's back from one point of the hip to the other, then feel the backbone in that area to find a slight, soft dip; the dip is the joint. Ideally, the lumbosacral joint should be as far forward as possible, on the imaginary line. This makes the loin short and the sacrum long, creating more leverage when the horse is performing athletic movements and flexing that joint. If it is too far in back of the line, the horse is probably too long in the loin and has a long, weak coupling.

The easiest way to see the loin area is to stand above the horse, looking at the triangle created by the hip points and the first lumbar vertebrae (just back of the ribs, where the thoracic vertebrae end and lumbar vertebrae begin). A long loin forms a long triangle (longer than it is wide), whereas a short loin forms a short, broad triangle. From above, you can also see the position of the lumbosacral joint.

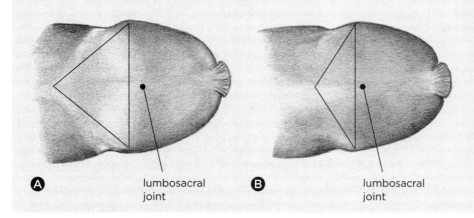

A. Long back and weak coupling (lumbosacral joint back too far), making a short rump and long loin. **B.** Short back and short loin. The lumbosacral joint is ideally located, creating a long sacrum (rump area) and a short lumbar span.

Ⓐ lumbosacral joint Ⓑ lumbosacral joint

tends to be more "strung out" behind, traveling heavily in front. He has less coordination and poor balance (he can't distribute the weight properly between his front and hindquarters), especially when trying to jump or go uphill or down. He can't position his hind legs underneath himself enough for good thrust; neither can he hold his balance when going downhill. A long loin and coupling reduces the thrust of the hindquarters when he is running and limits his ability to collect himself quickly and strongly. A long loin often makes a long back and a too-short hindquarter. A forward-positioned lumbosacral joint creates a shorter lumbar span (which is good, since it's the weakest part of a horse's back) and a longer hindquarter for more power and speed.

BENEFITS OF A SHORT, CLOSE-COUPLED BACK

The horse with a short back often has a stronger loin than a horse with a long back. The horse's loin should be well muscled and rise gently from last rib to croup and should never appear hollow, or the back will be weak. The loins must be strong, but never too long, or

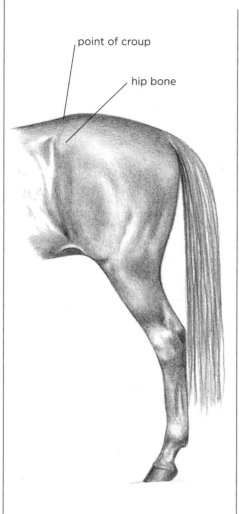

point of croup

hip bone

⬭ The point of the hip should be in line with, or just slightly ahead of, the point of the croup.

there will be too much gap between the angle of the haunch and the last rib, making the horse "slack coupled." A "close-coupled" animal has a stronger back, more agility, and is able to work longer without his back becoming tired.

Croup and Quarters

The *croup* is the highest point of the back or rump, behind the loins. This is the point where the ilium, or top of the pelvis, meets the sacrum, the spot where the hind leg joins the spine. Running down from the croup toward the horse's tail at the rear and toward the hips on either side are the *quarters*. When judging the hindquarters, the rump area should be assessed from all aspects: length, width, thickness, muscular development, and slope. Some people speak of croup and quarters together as though they are the same. Technically, however, the croup is the highest point, formed by the upper extremities of the pelvic bone. The croup should not be too prominent or high, but rounded and encircled by muscle, with a smooth contour. The croup should be the same height as the withers.

SHAPE OF PELVIS DETERMINES SHAPE OF RUMP

The size and angle of the pelvis influences the rump and hindquarters greatly, establishing the general conformation and angles of the hind leg (see chapter 8). The shape of the sacrum and the length of the ilium (top portion of pelvis) determine the height and shape of the croup and quarters. Variations in the croup among different horses will also create corresponding differences in the outline of the loins and quarters, along with the set-on of the tail.

If the dorsal spines of the sacrum are high, or if the ilium is high, the croup will be high, perhaps higher than the withers. With a high croup, the quarters usually slant down toward the tail, and if the rear end of the sacrum also dips, the tail connection will be low. An exceptionally high croup and sloping quarter creates a "goose rump" (see page 93). A level quarter is usually associated with a level sacrum and high tail carriage.

HEIGHT OF CROUP

Some horses have a croup that is higher than the withers. Most young horses are several inches higher at the croup when they are still growing, which is most noticeable in draft horse breeds and Quarter Horses. A few mature horses, however, are an inch or more higher at the croup than at the withers.

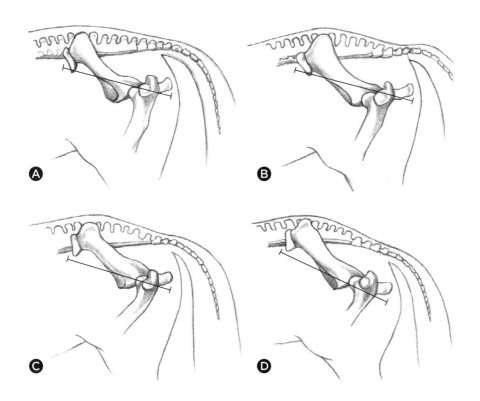

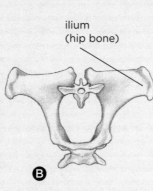

Pelvis and sacrum determine the shape of the rump. **A.** Slightly tipped-up sacrum makes a level rump, though the pelvis has a normal slope. **B.** Actual position of sacrum is the same as (A) but the point of the croup is higher. Pelvic slope is the same. **C.** Sacrum is straight, but its topline slants down and the tail is set lower; pelvic slope is the same as in (A) and (B). **D.** Pelvis and sacrum are both sloped downward, creating a lower tail set.

Anatomy of the Pelvis

There are three main projections from the pelvis: the haunch or hip bone (the external "wing" of the ilium), which forms the bony prominence that we call the hip; the seat bone, which juts out at the rear to create the point of the buttock; and the internal angle of the ilium, which joins the sacrum. The sacroiliac joint is the firm bony attachment at the spine that makes it possible for the power of the hind leg to be transmitted directly to the body via the backbone.

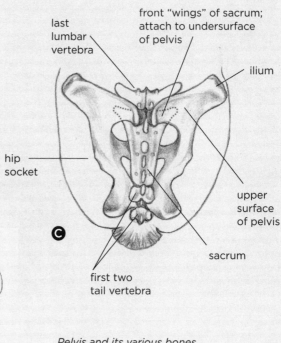

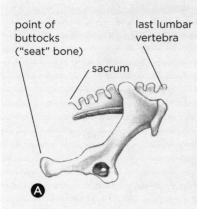

Pelvis and its various bones.
Side view (A), front view (B), top view (C).

Some horsemen feel this type of conformation makes for more speed and better jumping ability. Indeed, some individuals with this conformation have done well over jumps and at the racetrack. But the horse with a high croup and low withers gives the rider a feeling of always going downhill, and the saddle tends to slide forward onto the horse's neck.

To be an outstanding athlete, the horse with croup higher than the withers must have strong, well-developed, and well-constructed front legs in order to take the stress, especially when landing from a jump. There will be more strain on the front legs from the additional weight of the disproportionately tall hindquarters.

Many high-crouped horses jump well, so this type of conformation is not a disadvantage to the jumper. A horse with a high croup, however, is not necessarily superior to horses of normal conformation in which the croup is the same height as the withers. When selecting a horse for a particular sport or athletic career, it's usually safest to choose one with well-balanced conformation. There is usually less to go wrong in the long run.

▼ Pony with croup higher than withers.

withers

croup

LENGTH AND SLOPE OF QUARTERS

Ideally, the quarters should be neither too flat nor too sloping. Horsemen speak of a straight or level rump, as contrasted with a sloping rump, when describing whether the sacrum lies horizontally or is tipped slightly upward, as in the case of some Arabian horses with a very high tail placement, or is tipped downward, with sloping quarters: the classic goose rump.

The length of the quarters is measured from the point of the hip to the point of the buttock. The length of the pelvis (which is formed by the circular girdle made by the bones that create the hip and the buttocks) is very important to speed. A long pelvis is crucial for an athletic horse with a career that demands speed, but is not as important for a horse that does slow work (such as a draft horse).

The point of the hip should be in line with or just slightly ahead of the croup. Length of the quarters should be at least 30 percent of the length of the horse's body; 33 percent is ideal. Most horsemen consider a hindquarter of 30 to 33 percent to be "average" and a longer hindquarter (34 to 35 percent or more) to be better, especially for racing. Some Thoroughbreds have quarters 35 percent the length of their bodies. The quarters are too short if they are less than 30 percent of a horse's length. If the rump is too short, the horse won't have the muscling, balance, or power to be a proficient athlete. He does not have the proper angles for maximum pendulum motion of the hind legs.

A long quarter is always a good trait, for a long and fairly level rump gives more driving power to the hind legs, and also more weight-carrying ability. Some Thoroughbreds, many Arabians, and a few horses of other breeds tend to have long and level quarters, often with a high tail connection.

Flat, level quarters are usually associated with a flat pelvis; the topline of the horse is relatively flat all the way to the tail rather than

⬇ Don't be misled by tail carriage when evaluating sacrum and pelvis. **A.** Sacrum and tail are high but pelvis is somewhat sloped; high tail carriage can make the hindquarter appear more level than it is. **B.** A high tail tends to disguise a "goose rump" (sloped pelvis). **C.** Goose rump in which the tail is low (sacrum and pelvis are both sloped).

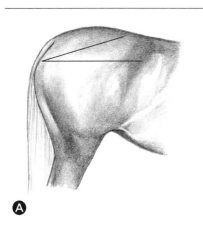

A

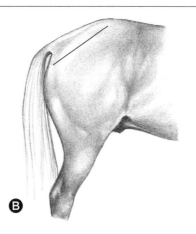

B

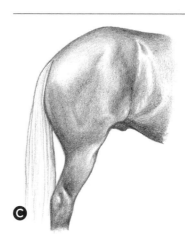

C

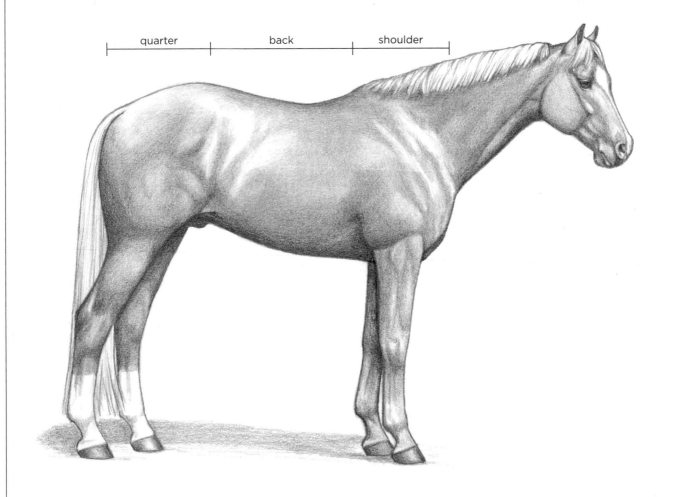

quarter | back | shoulder

Short quarters make the horse's back and front end look longer.

sloping off over the hips. The pelvis is long and may be somewhat tipped upward. As far as athletic ability is concerned, this is not a serious fault, and can be an advantage rather than a hindrance. The flatness allows the horse to have a longer swing of the hind leg and is conducive to speed, if the quarters are long enough to allow good leverage and range of action. The horse with a level rump needs a long femur (thigh bone), however, to create enough stifle and hock angle so he does not experience slipping of the patella (and upward fixation of the kneecap).

When judging the levelness of the quarters and determining the slant of the pelvis, look closely at the relationship between slope of the pelvis and the slope of the sacrum: these are not always the same. The sacrum can be level even if the pelvis is tilted slightly downward as it should be (see page 91).

In many Arabians and Thoroughbreds with a level quarter, only the sacrum is actually level (making a flat topline) and the pelvis itself has just as much slope as in some horses with a so-called sloped or steep quarter. Always visualize the underlying structures, using the line from point of hip to point of buttocks as a guide. If the horse's pelvis has the proper angle and length, the horse will have the speed and power he needs, even if the rump itself is fairly slanted or somewhat steep.

A horse with a very high tail set can often give the mistaken impression of levelness even though his pelvis is sloped. The sacrum is short and tilted up (and tail set high) but the pelvis and its end section that forms the point of the buttock is slanted down, placing the buttock fairly low. The pelvis may be slightly sloped or very sloped, even though the top of the quarters seems level, due to position of the tail. The position of the hip joint (how far forward or back it is) also has an effect on the strength and structure of the hindquarter (see chapter 8).

It is the length of quarter, more than its slope, that is most important for a riding horse. In a goose-rumped horse with a too-short quarter, the pelvis itself is slanted too far downward and too short. This type of horse rarely has much speed because the attached muscles are shorter. The pelvis is the structure in the hindquarter that corresponds with the shoulder in the front end of the horse; the length and slope of each is always similar in an individual animal. A horse with a long, well-laid-back shoulder (more horizontal than upright) will also have a long and relatively level pelvis and quarter.

⭕ Conformation Close-up

Hook bones and *haunch bones* are old-timer's terms for the hips. The hip bones should be well covered with muscle. If a horse is thin, with little muscle or fat covering, these bones become quite prominent. When you are standing directly behind the horse and he is standing squarely, the two hip bones should be perfectly level and equally matched. There should be ample width of quarters between the hip bones, with the muscles well rounded.

The Tail

One of the least considered aspects of conformation is the tail, yet it is part of what gives the horseman an overall impression of balance or beauty and also plays a small role in his health and welfare. Tail connection and carriage are also considered breed characteristics for many breeds and must be judged accordingly when selecting a horse for show.

The Sacrum

The rearmost part of the back is the sacrum, the bone beneath the muscles of the horse's rump. Viewed from the top, the sacrum is located behind the lumbar (loin) area and is a triangular bone composed of five fused vertebrae. Its flattened front surface joins the last lumbar vertebra to form the lumbosacral joint. This is where the horse can bend at the loin to bring his hindquarters forward to get his hind legs underneath himself. The back of the sacrum forms a small round surface that connects with the first vertebra of the tail.

Tailbones can provide a clue to the strength of a horse's backbone, for the tail makes up the final bones in the spinal column. The horse's tail is a snake-like chain of bones covered with muscles, just like all the other vertebrae, and the bones are similar in many ways. The root of the tail has the only vertebrae that are exposed and "visible" from all sides. The tail, however, is much more mobile than the rest of the backbone because it is not encased in much flesh or muscle.

The size of the vertebrae in the root of the tail can be an indication of the sturdiness or fineness of the rest of the spine. A horse with a tailhead that is large in diameter probably has large, strong vertebrae in the rest of his body. A horse with a small diameter tail that is thin and whiplike at its root probably has smaller vertebrae and smaller, weaker layers of muscle surrounding his spinal column. Various parts of a horse tend to match, so the external vertebrae of the tail can provide you a clue about the internal bones of his back.

HEIGHT AND ATTACHMENT

In many breeds, the tail is ideally set high rather than low, with a strong attachment, and carried somewhat aloft when the horse is traveling, rather than drooping or dragging. The tail's attachment and carriage will often depend on slope of the quarters. If the tail is set low on a goose rump, it cannot be carried high and will instead hang between or against the buttocks.

The Arabian typically has the highest tail carriage, and the zebra and donkey the lowest. Most horse breeds have tail carriage somewhere in between these two extremes. As far as bushiness of tail, the Appaloosa has the thinnest and sparsest mane and tail hairs, while the draft horse generally has the thickest and waviest mane and tail. Exceptionally thick mane and tail, especially if wavy, is usually a clue that a horse has some cold blood in its ancestry.

Problematic Back Conformation

There is a direct correlation between back conformation and performance. Poor back conformation invariably results in performance problems, including lack of agility, soreness, lameness, and leg breakdowns. Conformation of the feet and legs is often checked more closely than that of the back; however, many horses can have good leg structure and bad backs that won't hold up well in strenuous competition. Train yourself to recognize the difference between good and bad back conformation. A horse with a poorly built back has just as much trouble as a horse with poor leg conformation; he won't stay sound. Stay alert for the following red flags.

HIGH, NARROW WITHERS

High, narrow withers are sometimes associated with deficient spring, or width, of the rib cage, resulting in a chest that is too narrow. A horse with high, sharp withers and a narrow body often lacks stamina; there is not enough chest capacity for adequate lung expansion.

Withers too sharp and high are easily bruised by a saddle if it rubs them at the top. It also may be difficult to fit a saddle if a high-withered horse has a dip in the back just behind the withers, because there is less muscling for the saddle to rest on. If the saddle slips back too far, it will shift the rider's weight back too far, hindering the horse's action and balance, and will not fit properly.

If withers are higher than the croup, the horse will be more apt to suffer strain and injury to the stifle joints because of this improper

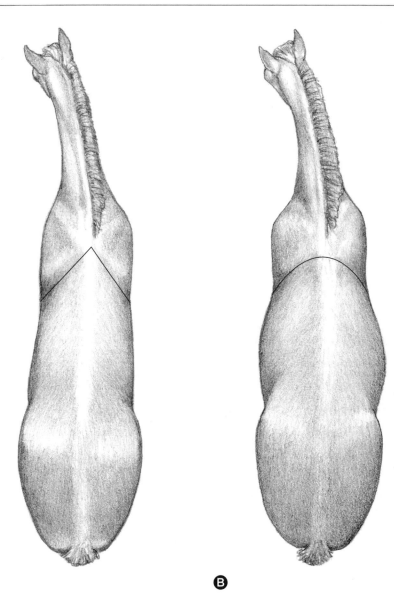

◀ Withers high and narrow versus wide withers. A slab-sided horse cannot carry weight as well as a wider horse with well-sprung ribs. **A.** A narrow horse with "peak roof" ribs. **B.** Normal width with well-sprung ribs.

Ⓐ   Ⓑ

Did You Know?

A young horse may appear to have low withers because the dorsal spinous processes of those vertebrae have not yet attained their full height (see page 196). In some slow-growing horses, the withers do not attain full height until the horse is 5 or 6 years old. Still, other horses are genetically predisposed to have low withers.

body balance. If withers are much lower than the croup, the horse is apt to suffer more strain on his front legs and stress on the lumbar area of his back.

TOO-LOW WITHERS

Low withers offer less attachment area for muscles that extend the head and neck and for muscles that activate the backbone; the horse is less able to raise (round) his back when his head is extended or lowered. Low, thick withers — a common fault in some breeds — are often accompanied by thick, overly muscled shoulders and a thick neck. A horse with low, thick withers and heavy shoulders also may have a wide front, with too much space between the forearms. All of these traits greatly impair a horse's agility and his ability to move the front legs properly. A low-withered horse generally has a short, upright shoulder and suffers more concussion in the front legs.

Flat, wide withers, with little distinction between the end of the neck the start of the withers, usually interfere with freedom of shoulder movement, restricting the range of motion in the front legs.

Low withers don't hold a saddle well. The round-backed, "mutton-withered" horse is difficult to fit with a saddle. You'll have trouble keeping the saddle in place; it slides backward when the horse goes uphill and forward over the neck when he goes downhill. It turns to the side (or turns under his belly) when you put weight in a stirrup to mount or lean your weight in one stirrup for balance when changing direction at fast speeds. If the saddle slides too far forward, it puts your weight forward, interfering with the horse's shoulder movement and stride, hindering his balance and increasing the concussion on the front legs.

GOOSE RUMP

Some horses have very high croups and sloping quarters, with a low tail connection. This conformation is known as *goose rump*. If not too pronounced, this is not a bad fault in itself, but the excessively goose-rumped horse often has improper leg angles and poor hind leg conformation.

The goose-rumped horse has a sharply sloping rump; the croup is much higher than the buttocks. The line from the coupling (at hips and croup) slopes off abruptly, the tail head is usually low, and the point of the buttocks is very low, almost as low as the flank. The steep slant of the pelvis lowers the point of the buttocks, bringing it closer to the ground, and thus shortens the muscle area between the point of the buttocks and the gaskin, making the hindquarter less strong.

This type of hindquarter does not have the proper angle to give the hind legs adequate swing and power, and the leverage action of the hind leg is lost. It also inhibits the stifle from moving the hind leg and, thus, the body forward with power and speed.

The hindquarter of the goose-rumped horse does not have the proper shape or muscling for speed or endurance. He is often clumsy because the angle of the hindquarter hinders the quickness of his foot leaving the ground at each stride. The goose-rumped horse is also more prone to hindquarter injury at the lumbosacral joint and stifle (which is set too low) than a horse with proper hindquarter conformation. Because of the rump's severe slope, all of the joints of the hind leg may be too low in relation to the joints of the front leg.

A horse with a steep slope from croup to buttocks usually has short quarters, which reduces the range of motion and stride in the hind legs. A steep pelvis shortens the backward swing of the hind leg because of the reduced action of the hip joint, resulting in less thrust in the hind legs. There also is less area for muscle attachment, which reduces the horse's potential for power and speed. It is more difficult for the horse to get his hind legs underneath him properly for good collection, making his loin muscles work harder and his back more prone to fatigue and injury. The horse with a goose rump and steeply angled pelvis is often "cat hammed," with insufficient muscling on his inner thighs.

A draft horse is not so adversely affected by goose rump, however, because it does not hinder short, slow steps and pulling power.

HIGH TAIL HEAD/TIPPED-UP PELVIS

An extremely high tail head is the opposite of goose rump. In this type of conformation, the tail head may be the same height or higher than the point of the croup. A level rump does not hinder athletic ability because there is no loss of power in the driving angle of the hind legs, and it enables the horse to have a long stride. If the tail set is too high, however, the pelvis may be tipped up too much. In such a case, there may be more strain on the lumbosacral joint.

If the pelvis is tipped up too much, with an exceptionally high tail set, the horse may have difficulty getting his hind legs properly underneath his body and he may travel more stiffly, unable to round his back adequately. He may travel with his back down and his head up too high.

There is a difference between the slope of the rump and the angle from croup to buttocks. Sometimes the tail is set high, even though the point of the buttocks is much lower. The high tail set makes the

Foaling Trouble

A tipped-up hind end is most problematic for a broodmare. During birth, the foal must pass up from the uterus through the pelvis in an arc. If the mare has a high tail set and tipped-up pelvis, the foal's front feet may hit the top of the birth canal rather than making the bend up over the pelvis. Because of the angle of her pelvis, such a broodmare may have greater difficulty foaling.

angle seem flatter than it actually is. A horse with a goose rump may have a tail connection that is relatively high, making the actual rump area quite short. Due to the shifting position of the backbone, over time a swaybacked horse may develop a more level rump and tipped-up pelvis.

SHORT QUARTERS

A horse with short quarters often has a too-steep angle (goose rump), which gives less length for muscle attachments for the thighs. This can hinder the horse's potential for speed or for jumping. If quarters are too short, the point of the croup is often located behind the point of the hips instead of directly above it, creating a long, weak loin and weak coupling. A horse with short quarters has less muscular leverage for collection. The hind leg may also be sickle hocked, with hind feet set too far under the body (see chapter 8).

APPLE RUMP

The "apple rump" (short and round, with a low-set tail that resembles the position of the stem of an apple), like some goose rumps, is also too short in the pelvis. Speed requires a reasonably long and level pelvis, while power (at slow speeds) can be enhanced by a steeper pelvis. Thus, the draft horse often has a more sloping quarter than a good riding horse.

TOO-LONG BACK

A long back (more than one-third his body length) will be weak, unless it is exceptionally strong over the loin. A horse with a long back cannot "round" his back upward as readily for collecting himself and carrying the weight of a rider. Because of his inability to carry himself and a rider with proper agility at fast gaits, the horse will usually have a sore back and sore legs. There may be excessive swing in the back, which can lead to limb interference, especially cross-firing (hitting the opposite front and hind feet together) at fast gaits. The horse tends to carry himself with his back dipped down (like a hammock) rather than arched up like a bridge. If the horse carries a rider in the dipped-down position, the back is more susceptible to strain and injury.

A too-long back hinders agility and durability, putting too much stress and strain on the legs. A long back is also a hindrance to athletic lateral, or sideways, movement when the horse is performing intricate maneuvers. A long back can also inhibit speed, for it is harder for the horse to stiffen and straighten his spine to provide more leverage thrust to the hind legs. A too-long back does not enable the thrust from the hind legs to be transmitted directly through the spine. Because the long back is not sufficiently rigid, there tends to be some buckling in the lumbar area, which may also lead to stress and inflammation between the bones.

⟶◯ *Conformation Close-up*

When trying to determine the length of a horse's back, focus on the back itself and don't be misled by the length of the quarters. Some horses have a short quarter, which will make the back look short, and some have a very long, flat quarter, which may give the erroneous impression that the back is long.

A long-backed horse can't go uphill or downhill with agility and coordination. There is more strain on the legs and loss of speed due to incoordination. When trying to make fast time on an endurance ride or to outrun a cow down a mountainside, the long-backed horse is at a serious disadvantage when going downhill. He also cannot collect himself properly for quick starts, stops, or fast turns, and cannot change direction efficiently when playing polo or competing in any sport that requires agility.

When doing dressage movements or trotting, a long-backed horse cannot round his back to carry the rider's weight properly; it is easier for him to hollow his back and stick his head in the air. Many horses suffer back problems (and subsequent leg problems) due to being too long in the back. If a horse with a long back puts his head up and nose out, the back hollows. He can't round his back and can't collect himself. He may be able to run swiftly, but he can't stop and turn efficiently.

TOO-SHORT BACK

Occasionally, you see a horse with a back that is too short, with a very constricted loin area. If the horse's back is less than one-third the length of his body, his ability to flex and bend is limited. A horse needs a few inches of loin area between the rear of the saddle and the croup — enabling him to flex his back a little when galloping and to be able to take longer strides with his hind legs. A too-short back can be a hindrance to speed. If he is stiff and rigid in the back, this can make his strides short, stiff, and choppy. If his back is too short in relation to the length of his legs, he may also overreach or forge, striking his front feet with his hinds when traveling.

If the back is too short, most of the impact and jarring from the hind feet is transmitted directly to the seat of the rider in the saddle,

Breed for Performance

Breeding for halter-class conformation instead of for athletic ability is ruining almost every horse breed for athletic performance. Many people who use horses in athletic competition believe that halter classes at horse shows have drifted far away from their original purpose of judging a horse's conformation as it pertains to athletic ability and soundness; that is, to identify the horses most likely to stay sound and move best while doing their jobs.

Today, horses are often judged on how they look rather than on conformation compatible with performance. In some breeds, the horses bred for halter classes often look like "sausages on stilts," with upright shoulders, short hips, and a long body in between. A long back has become common in several breeds. Halter horses and many so-called pleasure horses are often disappointing in terms of their athletic ability and durability, mainly because of a too-long back.

and there is none of the flexibility or buffering effect that would be provided by a slightly longer back. Almost all of the spinal flexion of any horse (which is limited, at best) is in the junction between the last thoracic vertebra and the first lumbar vertebra (the start of the loin area), in the lumbosacral joint between the last lumbar vertebra and sacrum, and in the large intravertebral discs between the lumbar bones. If this area is too short, there is very little flexibility.

CONVEX BACK

A convex back is undesirable; any upward arch in the spine hinders the horse's action, shortens his stride, and gives a very uncomfortable ride with a jarring, rough, and lurching stride. There is little flexibility and elasticity in this type of back. An arched back tends to make the horse forge when he travels.

The only area where the back should arch is over the loin, indicating a strong coupling and good muscles; the muscles, not the backbone, should arch. If the spine is arched in a fixed position at the lumbosacral joint, the loin muscles are often less developed than they should be and muscles that activate and elevate the back are unable to contract efficiently. The horse tends to be stiff in the back, with less flexibility in side-to-side and up-and-down motion. The vertebrae may rub one another, making it painful for him to perform athletic actions. Because of the rigidity of his back, he will be less smooth to ride. It will be difficult for him to perform well in any activity that requires collection and equally difficult for him to jump. A thin, sharp, arched-up back is called a *roach back*.

SWAYBACK

The opposite problem is swayback, or hollow back: a pronounced dip between the withers and loin area. This type of back is usually too long and excessively flexible. A horse with a long, weak back often becomes swaybacked and also tends to have a too-high head carriage. Swayback can be a congenital problem or caused by insufficient calcium in the diet when the horse was young and growing. It also can result from old age, especially if a horse has been worked hard. Older mares often develop a sag in the back after carrying many foals. A horse with a too-long back may become swaybacked more readily because the ligaments of the back tend to become weak and sag.

A swayback is often a weak back. The horse has less ability to carry weight; any load tends to make the back dip down farther, and the strain and stress is on the ligaments of the back more than on the backbone itself. In order to carry weight well, the horse must be able to "round" (arch) his backbone a little, and he can't do that if the back dips too much to begin with. Swayback also makes it more difficult to fit a saddle. The saddle tends to "bridge" the back, making the most contact just behind the withers and in front of the loins rather than distributing the weight and pressure of the rider evenly along the back. A swayback puts the rider too far back behind the horse's center of gravity. This can interfere with the horse's balance while working, making it difficult for him to collect himself and travel well.

Swayback is also a detriment to speed. Much of the thrust and power of the hind legs is wasted because it can't be transferred effectively to the front end of the horse unless there is some rigidity in the spine. A swayback horse may tire easily and become sore from the extra stress and strain (see page 347 for a discussion of swayback in the senior horse).

Conformation Close-up

A horse with an abnormally high head carriage may appear sway-backed, as will a horse with abnormally short dorsal processes on the vertebra just behind the withers. For proper evaluation, look closely at the back and evaluate its length and structure.

Foreleg Conformation

CONFORMATION OF THE forelegs greatly affects a horse's athletic ability and soundness. Because the front end of the horse is heavier than the hind end, the forelegs bear about two-thirds of his weight and are subject to greater concussion. As a result, conformation faults in the front legs are more serious than faults in the hind legs, and many types of lameness are more common in the front legs. Forelegs influence a horse's stride, speed, and agility; properly conformed forelegs keep joints strong during athletic activities.

The front legs carry more weight than the hind legs, and for a long career without breakdowns they must be well conformed to withstand the stress of athletic movement and concussion at fast speeds. Front leg angles also contribute to a horse's level of speed and agility.

Ideal Foreleg Conformation

Ideal foreleg conformation consists of straight legs with sturdy bone structure, big flat knees, and deep, well-shaped fetlock joints that support the horse and enable swift, efficient action and sound durability.

Anatomy

A horse's front leg consists of bones, joints, and muscles that move the bones. Below the knee, there are no muscles, only long tendons controlled by the muscles above the knee in the forearm.

SCAPULA

The scapula, or shoulder blade, is a large, flat, triangular bone that attaches the front leg to the body and overlies the first six or seven ribs. A ridge, the scapular spine, extends along almost the complete outer surface of the scapula, from the top to near the bottom. The muscles that move the shoulder attach to bone on either side of the scapular spine. The scapula is connected to the body with muscles attached to a large depression on its inner side. The front leg does not connect directly to the spine but is attached by a system of ligaments, muscles, and tendons. The top of the scapula anchors a soft tissue sling that supports the front end of the horse's body.

▶ **A. Bones of the foreleg.**
B. Muscles of the foreleg.

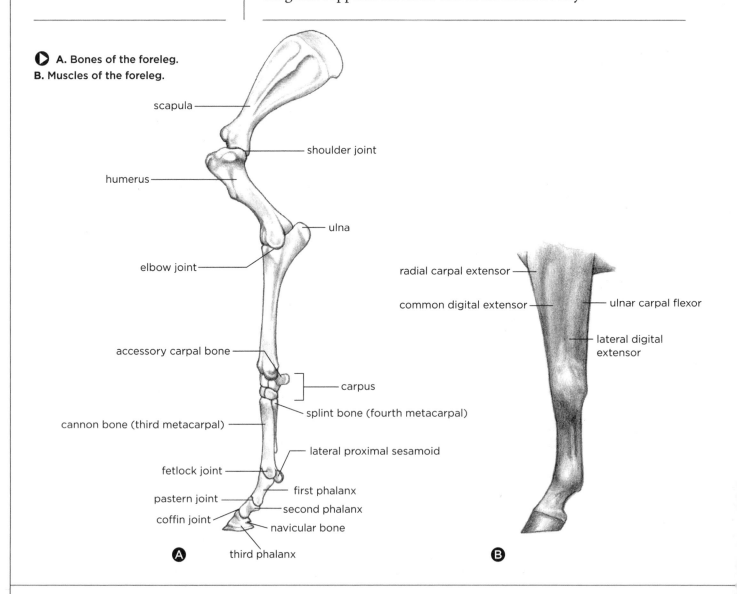

- scapula
- shoulder joint
- humerus
- ulna
- elbow joint
- accessory carpal bone
- carpus
- splint bone (fourth metacarpal)
- cannon bone (third metacarpal)
- lateral proximal sesamoid
- fetlock joint
- first phalanx
- pastern joint
- second phalanx
- coffin joint
- navicular bone
- third phalanx

A

- radial carpal extensor
- common digital extensor
- ulnar carpal flexor
- lateral digital extensor

B

HUMERUS

The humerus, or arm bone, connects shoulder to elbow. It is covered with heavy muscles and serves as a leverage point for muscles of the front leg that attach near the elbow. It is very strong, though shorter in length than the shoulder, and has many irregularities on its surface that serve as points of attachment for muscles.

The top of the humerus and the lower end of the shoulder blade come together in a ball-and-socket joint; it is the only joint in the front leg capable of side-to-side movement. It allows the humerus to swing forward and back to raise or lower the elbow; it also allows the front legs to rotate outward when a horse is thrusting his front end from side to side to herd a dodging cow, for example, or inward to cross over one another.

The bottom of the humerus connects with the elbow. Length and angle of the humerus can be determined by the outward appearance of the horse, from point of shoulder to elbow.

Length

The length and angle of the humerus influences the action and stride of the foreleg (see chapter 11) and determines how tightly the elbow and leg joints can flex and how far forward the entire leg can extend when the horse is moving. No matter its conformation — whether long and steep, long and level, short and steep, or short and level — the humerus plays a major role in how the horse moves his front legs.

If the humerus is long, it provides more leverage and consequently more strength and power to attached muscles. Length also increases the range of motion in the front leg, allowing for a greater arc at the elbow. A long humerus increases the mobility of the elbow, both outward, away from the body, and forward, when increasing stride length or tucking up the front legs to go over a jump. A long humerus is desirable if it is in proportion with the rest of the body, yet it should not be disproportionately long in comparison with the shoulder blade, because the shoulder muscles would be relatively short and restrict movement of the upper arm due to limited contraction.

The humerus is considered desirably long if its length is 50 to 60 percent of the length of the shoulder blade. If the humerus is of proper length, the elbow will be positioned beneath the front of the withers. The humerus is considered too long if it is more than 60 percent of the length of the shoulder blade. When the humerus is too long, the shoulder muscles are overtaxed, forward movement of the leg is diminished, and the horse's freedom of action is impaired, making him more apt to stumble.

If the humerus is too short, the horse will have a restricted, choppy stride. A short humerus increases concussion to the leg and is a detriment to lateral agility but not to forward impulsion, such as sprinting. Still, if he tries to maintain high speed for very long, the horse with a short humerus will likely tire. A short arm bone is also usually more horizontal, making its angle with the shoulder less than 90 degrees.

⊸○ *Conformation Close-up*

It is important to evaluate the whole horse and make sure that bone structure and joint formation is uniform and balanced for that particular animal. Occasionally, you see a horse that has mismatched bone structure, such as large knees and a too-fine cannon bone, or proper size arm and cannon bones and too-small knee bones ("calf-kneed"), or a heavy cannon bone under small hock bones. The joint cannot be in proper position when this type of mismatch occurs and puts more strain on certain parts of the joints. Mismatched bones will also make the leg crooked. Mismatches sometimes occur in offspring when large-boned horses are mated with small-boned horses. If some portions of the bone structure are inadequate, the horse probably won't stay sound, especially if some of the bones are too small for the body build of the horse.

Conformation

When the horse is standing squarely, the angle between the shoulder blade and the upper arm should be between 100 degrees and 120 degrees. To measure this angle, visualize the bones underneath the muscle, then measure down the center of the shoulder blade, using the center of the upper arm bone as the other angle line. An easier method is to use the point of the shoulder for reference, in which case the angle between the shoulder and humerus should be about 85 degrees (see chapter 11 for a detailed discussion of shoulder angle).

A long, well-sloped shoulder blade is generally accompanied by a fairly short and relatively upright humerus; an upright shoulder is usually paired with a longer and more horizontal humerus. If the humerus is too long and too horizontal, the horse "stands under himself"; that is, his front legs are back too far under his body and his breast sticks out in front. The front legs of a horse with well-sloped shoulders and a short, upright humerus, by contrast, are placed so far forward that it looks like he has no breast at all. If the angle of the

shoulder blade is too extreme (less than 45 degrees), the action of the horse's front leg will be somewhat stiff and stilted, even though he has a nice, long, sloping shoulder. Ideal front leg/shoulder conformation, therefore, is somewhere in between.

Although a horse with a long, sloping shoulder and relatively upright humerus has little breast, a side view should show the pectoral muscles protruding beyond the forearm. Pectoral muscles should also be heavy enough to create a well-defined, square appearance at the front of the chest when viewed from the side. If the front of the chest has little muscling or the point of the shoulder is too far forward, there may be no perceptible juncture between the bottom of the neck and the chest when viewed from the side. Instead, the underline of the neck blends into the shoulder and breast at a sharp, low angle, rather than having a discernible and separate region of chest/breast.

▲ With good length and angle of the humerus, the horse's elbow is directly below the front of the withers.

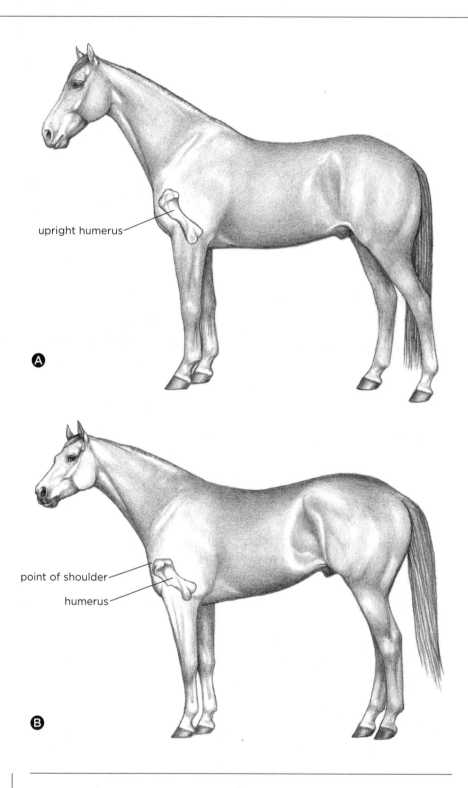

upright humerus

point of shoulder

humerus

▶ **A.** A long, upright humerus in a warmblood. **B.** A short, horizontal humerus in a stock horse or sprinter.

Ⓐ

Ⓑ

Faults

If the humerus is more vertical than horizontal, the angle of the upper arm will be wider than it should be. The angle should match the angle between pelvis and femur in the hindquarters and be neither too wide nor too narrow. If the humerus is too upright, the horse's motion will be restricted, and if the humerus is more horizontal than vertical, it can cramp the movement of the elbow and may also put the front legs too far back under the body. This latter arrangement is called *pigeon breast*, because the legs are back too far and the breast sticks out in front.

THE ELBOW

The elbow is the highest joint in the front leg that is not covered by thick muscles. It is located at the juncture of the humerus and the radius and ulna, which together make up the forearm. The tops of the radius and ulna form a smooth half-circle that fits the humerus. The portion of the ulna that protrudes at the back to form the point of the elbow is called the *olecranon process*. It helps hold the forearm in place and also serves as a leverage point to increase the power of the muscles that attach to it. The range of motion of the elbow is roughly 55 to 60 degrees.

Conformation

The elbow must rest squarely on top of the forearm and not turn in or out. The joint should be clear of the body and well defined. Viewed from behind, the olecranon process should be vertical. Viewed from the side, the point of the elbow should be in line with the front of the withers or at least ahead of the peak of the withers. The elbow should blend smoothly into the muscles of the forearm.

Faults

A horse that doesn't travel straight may have an elbow that is not straight. The elbow must be vertical in order for the front leg to be straight. An elbow turned in or out puts extra strain on the lower leg, especially the fetlock joint, which can lead to further problems and possible lameness or limb interference: one limb or foot may hit the other one, for example.

In-turned/Tied-in Elbow

In-turned elbows, sometimes called "tight" elbows or tied-in elbows, are too close to the body and twist the leg, making the horse toe out. Such a splay-footed horse tends to wing his front feet inward when the knee is flexed. The feet may cross over as the horse travels, putting one foot directly in front of the other, making him more likely to stumble. An in-turned elbow is often found when the breast or front of the chest is narrow.

The elbow is also cramped; there is restricted movement of the humerus because it angles too far into the body and does not allow the front leg to advance as far forward as it should, resulting in a shorter stride. The set of the elbow is partly determined by the pectoral muscles; if they attach low on the humerus, they hold in the elbow too tightly.

🔍 *Conformation Close-up*

To determine if the elbow has adequate space, try to fit two to four fingers between the elbow and the rib cage. If there is not enough space for two fingers, elbow tightness will restrict the horse's movement and hinder the forward and backward swing of the foreleg. If the elbow joint is "tied in" to the rib cage, the horse won't have a long stride no matter how well-sloped his shoulder might be.

Out-turned Elbow

Elbows that are turned out are usually associated with base-narrow conformation and pigeon-toed, or turned-in, feet. The out-turned elbow makes the legs too wide apart at the chest and too close together at the feet. This conformation also puts a twist on the leg that makes the horse throw his feet outward when the knee is flexed, known as *paddling*. Paddling is often most pronounced at a trot.

THE FOREARM

The forearm of the horse connects the elbow to the knee. It should be long, wide, thick, and well developed, and in perfect line with the knee and cannon bone when viewed from the front, back, and side. The bones of the forearm should be the same distance apart at the top, where the forearms emerge from the chest, as at the bottom, where the bones join the knee.

🔍 *Conformation Close-up*

The forearms should neither be too wide apart nor too close together. Excess width between the forearms, when the forelegs are set out to the sides of the chest, like a table, creates a clumsy, waddling gait with too much side-to-side motion and is undesirable in any riding horse. The rocking motion, which is often most obvious at the walk and trot, makes for less efficiency of movement and the expenditure of more effort over a long course; the horse will tire easily. The opposite extreme, the narrow chest with "legs coming out of the same hole," is poor conformation, for this also cuts down on speed and agility.

The radius is the principal bone in the forearm. The smaller ulna is situated behind the radius at the elbow and its lower part is fused to

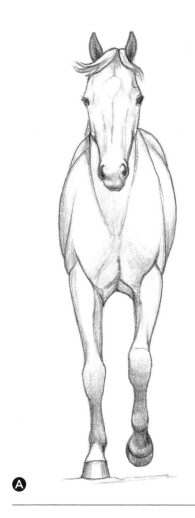

(A)

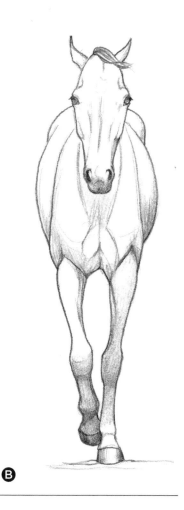

(B)

(C)

the radius. In a young horse, the ulna is bound tightly to the top of the radius by ligaments, which fuse into bone as the horse matures. The radius and ulna, when viewed from the side, determine the width and circumference of the forearm. Good width is desirable because these bones serve as attachments for the large triceps muscle at the top of the forearm and for the muscles that flex the leg.

Muscling

The muscles in the forearm contribute as much to a horse's speed and propulsion as the muscles of the hind leg: the front legs help pull the horse along. The arm muscles help drive the body forward, especially during the trot and gallop. Many of the shoulder muscles are attached to the upper part of the forearm. There is minimal fat in the forearm, so the muscles are easy to see.

Forearm muscles are larger at the top. The muscles at the front are extensors, which pull the lower leg forward. The muscles at the back of the forearm are flexors and bend the leg, flexing the joints. For best agility and endurance, the muscles should be smooth and long

▲ Forearm spacing: normal (A), narrow (B), wide (C). The too-narrow horse may interfere; the too-wide horse may paddle.

Did You Know?

The amount of forearm muscling gives a good indication of how much muscling a horse has on his body.

rather than bunched up and short. The bulk and development of the muscles at the top of the forearm are often quite large in the Quarter Horse, which is bred for a fast burst of speed, rather than for endurance. These muscles are also very large in draft horses but are quite large over the entire forearm rather than just at the top, and thus don't seem to bulge.

The heavy muscles at the top of the forearm become slimmer and taper into tendons toward the knee; there are no muscles below the knee. The lower leg is bone, tendons, and ligaments. The muscles of the forearm do all the work for the leg below the elbow and must be adequate for the task, especially in horses that have a lot of stress on the leg, such as jumpers. In such horses, the thick muscles at the top of the forearm should extend farther down the forearm toward the knee before tapering and becoming tendons.

Conformation

Viewed from the front, the muscles of the forearm should be well developed on the inner and outer leg, and the muscles at the top should form an inverted V between the front legs. A flat, weak muscle on the inner forearm does not provide sufficient support to the horse's body, which is suspended at the front between the shoulder blades, and puts greater burden on the muscling that attaches the body to the top of the shoulder.

The muscling of the inner forearm is also very important in determining the horse's aptitude for athletic lateral action of the leg, such as turning quickly, spinning around on his hind legs, dodging after a cow, or any other maneuvers that require good side-to-side action.

Length

For best leverage action and speed, the forearm should be relatively long and the cannon bone relatively short. A long forearm allows for longer muscles and shorter tendons, creating better leverage for moving the leg quickly, smoothly, and precisely. The longer the forearm, the greater the leverage power and range of motion. A short forearm might make more total movements in the same amount of time, but the strides would be shorter and the horse would have to work harder by moving his legs faster in order to maintain speed.

The combination of a long, powerful forearm and a short cannon results in more speed and agility and a longer stride. A long forearm with good muscling is also an advantage for jumping; the muscles help absorb concussion when landing. A long forearm and short cannon create less concussion on the lower leg bones and put less stress on the tendons. Short tendons suffer less strain than long ones. The muscles are more elastic than tendons and can handle stress better.

An athletic, well-balanced horse usually has a long shoulder blade and relatively short humerus, a long forearm, a relatively short cannon bone, and a long pastern. The longer the forearm, the shorter the cannon, and therefore the lower the knee. This conformation produces a stronger and more structurally stable front leg.

THE KNEE

The *carpus,* or equine knee, is a complex joint that consists of six small bones — the radial carpal bone, the intermediate carpal bone, the ulnar carpal bone, and the second, third, and fourth carpal bones (the first carpal bone is sometimes missing) — arranged in two rows between the radius and cannon bone. A somewhat larger bone called the *accessory carpal bone* (also called the *pisiform* or *trapezium*) projects backward from the inner knee.

The knee itself has three major joints within it: the radiocarpal joint between the radius and the upper row of little bones, the intercarpal joint between the upper row and the second row, and the carpometacarpal joint between the second row of bones and the cannon bone beneath them. In the last, there is very little movement between the small bones and the top of the cannon. All the little joints between the six small bones, as well as the lubricating sacs for the three major joints, are encased within a large joint capsule that encompasses the entire knee. Because the knee has no lateral movement, its action is synchronized with the elbow; both joints must move straight ahead. If a horse doesn't move his front legs straight, it may be because of some defect in one or both of these joints.

Conformation

The knee should be somewhat shield-shaped, with well-defined corners. It should be flat at the front, with no hint of roundness; as large as possible, front to back, to provide maximum bearing surfaces; and proportioned to the leg. Knees should face directly forward and should not angle toward or away from each other.

The front of the knee should be large, flat, and smooth to facilitate movement of the extensor tendons, which straighten the knee during each stride. The outer knee should look square. At the back, the knee should be wide enough to provide plenty of space for the flexor tendons that pass down the back of the cannon. A small, pinched-in knee crowds the bones, tendons, and joint cartilage and hinders free, smooth action.

Did You Know?

Very few "leggy" horses with long front cannons have much speed or stamina. Short forearms and long cannons produce higher knee action, which hinders speed.

The Knee as Shock Absorber

Because of the way the front leg is constructed, it forms a solid column when weight is placed on it. Poor or small knees can hinder weight-bearing capacity of the leg and increase the effects of concussion, whereas a well-constructed knee is an excellent shock absorber.

The small bones of the knee joint are arranged in two rows of overlapping bones between the forearm and cannon bone. They all have joints between them, allowing for some movement. They are surrounded by cartilage but "float" in a lubricating fluid within the cartilage casing. Because they can slide over one another to some extent, these small bones provide a lot of buffering protection for the major leg bones, minimizing the effects of concussive forces traveling up the leg.

The accessory carpal bone at the back of the knee should be large and well defined. This bone forms the leverage point and attachment for several of the muscles that bend the knee and for some of the important ligaments of the joint. The flexor tendon passes over it; the bone acts as a fulcrum for the tendon, which is attached to the lower leg at the splint bone. If the accessory carpal bone is too small or short, the knee will be weak and the joint less efficient.

Faults

The knee should be directly in line with forearm and cannon from all directions. If the knee is out of alignment, uneven weight distribution makes the horse more likely to suffer injury and strain on various parts of the leg, especially the fetlock joint. Such a fault generally affects both knees.

Calf Knees

If the cannon bone is set too far back under the knee, the horse is "calf-kneed" (*back at the knees*, also called *sheep knees*), a weak construction. The head of the cannon bone lies behind the line of the radius; from the side, the front of the foreleg looks concave at the knee or just below it. Looking at the standing horse from the side, the knee appears angled backward, with the muscle and tendon structure in a position similar to what it would be if he were traveling uphill.

Your eye can be fooled, however, if you look at the line of the tendons in back of the knee instead of the line of the cannon bone at the front. The back tendons may actually be fairly vertical, especially if they are somewhat tied in at the knee, but the cannon bone itself will slant backward at the knee. In a calf-kneed horse, the tendons take more stress, and the extra strain may injure the tendons.

Because there is increased concussion when the horse puts his foot on the ground, the calf-kneed horse has a jarring gait. He has decreased pulling power in his front legs, and there is less strength in the knee joint, especially at the back. If used in athletic activities, he is likely to damage the ligaments and tendons of the front leg.

Calf knees put great strain on the bones and ligaments within the joint. The calf-kneed horse usually cannot withstand hyperextension of the knee joint (pushing it toward the rear), which occurs each time the foot hits the ground when he runs on hard surfaces, lands from a jump, or comes to a quick stop at the end of a gallop. With this type of stress, the knee may eventually break down, resulting in carpal fractures. Compression fractures may occur on the front surfaces of the

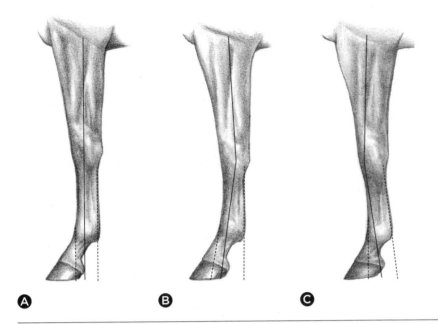

◀ **A.** Normal leg. **B.** Calf knee (back at the knee). **C.** Bucked knee (over at the knee).

knee bones, and bone chips may develop in the joint. The stress also extends to the tendons behind the knee and the check ligaments in the front leg. This type of horse rarely stays sound under hard use and should not be used in a strenuous sport.

Bucked Knees

Another deviation from ideal front leg structure is *bucked knees*, when the leg appears to be angled slightly forward at the knee. This is also called *over at the knees*, *goat knees*, or *sprung knees*. A slight bucked-knee conformation is found in many Thoroughbreds. This condition may be inherited or it can occur in a horse that has been overworked, with injury to the check ligament or too much stress on the structures at the back of the knee. Many foals have knees bent forward immediately after birth, but most straighten in a few weeks or months.

Because the knee joint is designed to bend forward, this construction is not as weak as calf knees, but perfectly straight front leg conformation is always preferred. The additional strain from bucked knees can make a horse more likely to suffer injury at the front of the fetlock joint and the back of the knee. The constant extra tension on the tendons behind the cannon bone and fetlock joint can injure the suspensory ligaments and sesamoid bones.

As the leg takes weight, it applies abnormal stress to the flexor tendons, increasing the risk for a bowed tendon. If bucked knees are the result of strain and overwork rather than genetics, the tendons behind the leg may be somewhat contracted, and the leg will not be as strong as if it were perfectly straight. The angle at which the deep digital flexor muscle attaches to the inferior check ligament is increased, putting more strain on that ligament. This muscle's purpose is to flex the joints of the lower foreleg, and the inferior check ligament originates just below the knee.

A severely buck-kneed horse stands with his front legs in the position of a horse traveling downhill, with tendons, knee joint, and muscles buckled forward. This abnormal position disrupts his balance when he is traveling and also makes him more prone to stumbling because the knees more easily "give" and buckle forward. The reduced flexibility of the knee shortens the horse's normal stride and increases the likelihood that he will trip and fall.

Bowlegged

A horse that is bowlegged, or "out at the knees" (carpal varus), has knee joints that deviate outward from a straight line when viewed from the front. This condition is often accompanied by base-narrow, pigeon-toed conformation (see page 136), which puts extra strain on the outer knee ligament, the inner portion of the knee bones, and the outer portion of the joint capsule. Bowlegged conformation is weak; a horse with this fault will not stay sound in an athletic career.

Knock-Knees

When viewed from the front, the knock-kneed horse appears to be "in at the knees" (carpal valgus), with knees too close together, or one or both knees rotated in toward the other. The lower leg may angle out in a splay-footed stance. If the knees are rotated in or severely knock-kneed, there is great strain on the legs; the knee joint and supportive ligaments are easily injured.

Mild knock-knees are not considered a fault, however. A recent study at Colorado State University of conformation and racing injuries showed that horses with mild carpal valgus held up better, without injury, than horses with perfectly straight front legs (T. M. Anderson, C. W. McIlwraith, P. Donay, "The role of musculoskeletal problems in racing Thoroughbreds," *Equine Veterinary Journal* 36 [2004]: 571–75.) A horse whose cannon bones slant slightly outward from the knee has decreased stress on the inner knee joint, the area most vulnerable to serious chip fractures (see page 283).

The strongest leg construction, with least risk for breakdown injury, seems to be a front leg that is slightly in at the knees and a hind leg that is slightly in at the hocks (see page 157). The weakest construction for both front and hind legs is bowlegs.

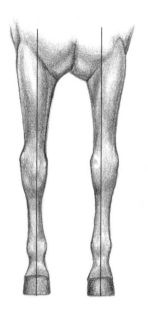

⏶ Bowlegged horse.

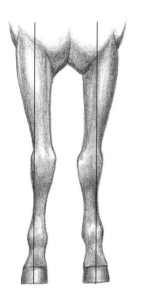

⏷ Knock-kneed horse.

Crookedness may be an inherited conformation trait, the result of a nutritional imbalance that causes improper bone growth when a horse is young, or the result of a traumatic injury to the growing ends of the long bones when a horse is young.

Other Knee Deviations

Another deviation from good leg conformation is *tied in at the knee*, which puts the flexor tendon too close to the cannon bone just behind and below the knee, inhibiting free movement. The cannon has a reduced diameter and decreased tendon area just below and in back of the knee, making the circumference smaller here than the measurement just above the fetlock joint.

This indentation usually means the tendons are too small and not as strong as they should be. The leverage ability of the muscles above the knee is decreased, for the tendons are pulling in against the back of the knee instead of exerting a straight pull down the back of the leg. Sometimes the tied-in appearance is due to an undersized accessory carpal bone, or trapezium — the small, irregular-shaped bone at the back of the knee over which the tendons glide. The too-small joint does not give adequate support to the leg and has more risk for injury.

Some horses have a cut-out-under-the-knee conformation. The knee joint and cannon bone do not join properly, and a depression just below the knee, in front of the cannon, is apparent. This makes the leg weaker and the tendons at the front of the joint work less smoothly.

THE CANNON BONE

The cannon is the principal lower leg bone and is located between the knee and the fetlock joint. Its job is to provide support. It has a small splint bone on each side of it, toward the back. The two splint bones travel partway down the cannon bone and terminate in small knobs. In the front leg, the cannon bone and splint bones are called the *metacarpals*; in the hind leg, they are called *metatarsals*. The cannon bone should be perfectly vertical when viewed from front, side, or rear. Viewed from the side, the line of the forelimb at the rear should be almost straight from elbow to fetlock, except for the outward bulge of the trapezium at the back of the knee.

Recall that the horse has muscles in the upper part of his leg but none in the lower leg. All the muscles of the forearm continue below the knee as long tendons, in front of and behind the cannon bone.

Sometimes a foal is born with noticeably crooked legs, such as knock-knees or knees bent forward. Some foals have "windswept" legs at birth; that is, one front or hind leg bends outward and the other bends inward. This is thought to be the result of lack of room in the uterus — the bend of the legs depends on how the foal was lying in the cramped space.

Many of these foals' legs straighten as they grow, but sometimes the crookedness does not resolve completely, leaving the horse with one or both legs a little less than straight. In some cases, corrective trimming may diminish the problems (see page 139).

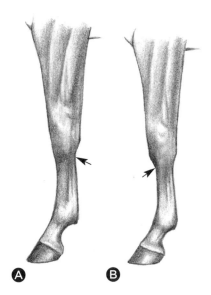

A. Tied in at the knee.
B. Cut out under the knee.

Support Structures behind the Cannon

At the back of the cannon bone are long tendons and ligaments that are clearly visible and easily felt in a thin-skinned horse. Outermost is the superficial flexor tendon. The deep flexor tendon is deeper in the leg. Closer to the bone is the main check ligament that goes from the back of the knee to the back of the deep flexor tendon about a third of the way down the cannon. The suspensory ligament runs down between the cannon bone and the deep flexor tendon.

There should be a well-defined groove between the back of the cannon bone and the front of the tendons, with the flexor tendons situated far enough behind the bone to be clearly visible. The tendons should be firm and tough and should feel like taut ropes when you palpate them with your fingers. They should be prominent, situated well away from the bone, and easily distinguishable from the suspensory ligament. The flexor tendons should be equidistant from the cannon from the knee to the fetlock joint (not tied in close to the knee), and the leg's circumference should be identical below the knee and above the fetlock joint.

How the Cannon Bone Moves

The muscles of the upper leg control the tendons and ligaments in, and the movement of, the lower leg. For instance, the extensor muscles at the front of the foreleg terminate to flat extensor tendons that pass over the knee. The tendons are protected by a tendon sheath and travel down the front of the cannon bone. The digital extensor tendon is joined at the fetlock joint by two branches of the suspensory ligament, a strong cord that comes from behind the fetlock joint. Contraction of the extensor muscles pulls on the extensor tendon, which straightens the lower leg joints.

The flexor muscles at the back of the forearm attach to tendons just above the knee that run down the back of the cannon bone as superficial and deep digital flexor tendons. They extend beyond the fetlock joint; one attaches to the sides of the pastern bone and the other to the underside of the coffin bone. They flex the lower leg, specifically, knee, fetlock, pasterns, and coffin joints. *Check ligaments*, which run from bone to tendon rather than from bone to bone like most ligaments, limit the action of the tendon to prevent overstretching. Two check ligaments in the lower leg (superior check ligament and inferior check ligament) link the back of the radius and the back of the cannon bone to the superficial digital flexor tendon and the deep digital flexor tendon. The suspensory ligament of the fetlock joint runs down the leg next to the cannon bone, underneath the other tendons and ligaments.

All the power generated by the muscles above the knee is expressed by the action of the cannon bone. If there is any defect in the lower leg, the energy put forth by the upper leg won't be used efficiently. No matter how strong his muscles are or how good his lungs and endurance capacity, if his cannon bones and their accompanying tendons are not up to the task, he will not be a successful athlete and hard work will cause breakdown injuries in the lower legs.

Length

Short front cannon bones and long rear cannon bones are ideal. In the hind leg, the cannon should come up to the level of the chestnut on the inner foreleg.

The front leg, from elbow down, is a rigid structure when it bears weight, and it needs a short, strong cannon bone, with short, strong tendons and a solid knee. The knee is the pulley over which the tendons pass. Muscles of the upper leg are levers that act on the tendons of the lower leg. Thus, a short cannon bone and short tendons create the most efficient movement and also reduce the weight of the lower limb that must be moved.

If the front cannon bone is too long, it lessens the mechanical advantage of the leg structure: the muscle pull of the upper leg on the tendons of the heavy lower leg is less efficient. A long cannon and its associated tendons increase stress on the tendons, making them more likely to become injured when the horse is doing fast work, especially on boggy, steep, or uneven terrain. This also puts more stress on the knee joint, because a long lower leg is not as stable. The horse's leg muscles will tire more quickly under strenuous work because there is proportionally less muscle and more weight.

Conformation

The cannon bone should be perfectly straight and smooth, with no bumps or protrusions, and should align centrally under the knee. Any lump or prominence on the inner or outer surface of the bone indicates a bony thickening that is probably due to injury — such as hitting it with the opposite foot, or a blow — or concussion.

Diameter

When viewed from the side, the lower leg, including bone and tendons, should be wide, not narrow and round. The horseman's term for ideal distance from front to back of the lower leg is *flat bone* (describing the combination of bone and tendon), which gives the lower leg the appearance of more substance from front to back.

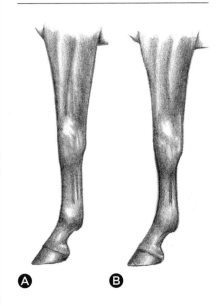

A **B**

⬤ Flat bone versus round bone. **A.** Flat bone with tendons set well back. **B.** Undesirable round bone; tendon too close to the cannon bone all the way down.

How Bone Is Described

Good bone describes a cannon that is short, strong, flat, and proportionate to the horse's size. No horse should be used for a strenuous career unless he has adequate bone, or he won't stay sound. The muscles need good solid bones to pull against, for efficiency of motion, strength, and speed.

Fine boned or *light boned* means the cannon bone offers insufficient support for the horse. The cannon bones are too small in diameter and the tendons may be too close to the bone, creating a very small circum-ference around the lower leg. If the cannons and pasterns are too light for the weight and size of the horse, the horse will likely suffer more concussion-related injuries, such as bucked shins, splints, and stress fractures. The tendons, ligaments, and muscles have less bone mass for their leverage effectiveness and the horse may have less power, speed, or stamina.

Coarse bone indicates a disproportionately large, clumsy cannon; if the bones are too large and coarse, the horse's speed and agility will be hindered.

The flexor tendons are ideally set well back of the cannon bone rather than right next to it. This position gives better leg action and more tendon strength. When the tendons are too close to the knee — or hock, in the hind legs — a common fault known as *tied in* is the consequence; friction and wear result, which can lead to lameness problems. The tendons are too small or too close right behind the knee, looking as though the cannon below the knee is squeezed and the tendons pulled in. This type of construction is weaker, and the small tied-in tendons lose much of their leverage advantage (see illustration A on page 119).

Undesirable *round bone* occurs when the cannon bone and tendon are too close together all the way down. This type of leg won't hold up as well as one with flat bone, with the tendon set back farther from the bone. In a horse with round bone there is always excessive friction between the moving parts.

Measuring Bone

For a long time, horsemen have evaluated "bone" when judging a horse's potential for athletic and weight-carrying ability. Circumference of bone is measured below the knee and includes the cannon bone as well as the tendons behind it. The horse with tendons set well back from the bone has more total circumference of limb than a horse with tendons too close to the knee or too close to the cannon bone all the way down the leg.

The average domestic riding horse should have about an 8-inch "bone" circumference per 1000 pounds of horse. A 1200-pound horse, for example, should have a 9.6-inch circumference below the knee for adequate support under his body and for durability of joints

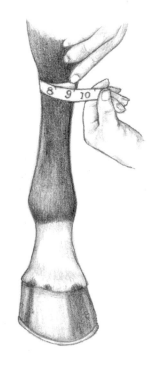

▲ Measuring circumference of cannon just below the knee to determine amount of bone a horse has.

and tendons. A horse with less than 7 inches of bone per 1000 pounds is considered too fine boned and is prone to injury.

Circumference is used to determine how much weight a horse can reasonably carry. In general, a horse with 8 inches of bone should be able to carry up to about 182 pounds of rider and tack; a horse with 9 inches of bone can carry up to 210 pounds; and a horse with still more bone can carry more weight and would be classed as a heavy-weight hunter or riding horse.

Obviously, a large horse needs large bones, but too little bone is a common problem in horses today. Leg muscles can only be as strong as the bones to which they attach. A horse whose bone structure is too fine in relation to body mass and weight has greater risk for structural injury to joints, tendons, ligaments, bones, and feet because concussion is proportionally increased. The repeated impact and jar on insufficient bone creates any number of soundness problems, like bucked shins, and strained tendons, ligaments, and joints. If you have a choice between a horse with adequate bone and too-fine bone, choose the one with adequate bone.

Bone strength is affected by the mineral content of bones as well as bone circumference; however; some fine-boned horses seem to have adequate bone strength. Keep in mind that small lightweight horses such as Arabians do not need as much bone as larger horses. Large bone on a small horse would make him clumsy. Bone diameter should be adequate for the horse's size.

Bones and Breeding

Over the past centuries, we've developed horses that are larger than their wild ancestors and relatives but without a corresponding increase in leg-bone mass. The average bone-to-body weight ratio of the wild equine is about twice that of the domestic light horse. The problem is most dramatic in larger horses. Many horses that are more than 16.2 hands tall and weigh more than 1300 pounds have only 5 inches of bone per 1000 pounds. A large, heavy horse rarely stays sound in a strenuous career, unless he has adequate, proportional bone. Even the draft horse is sometimes too large and heavy for his bone structure.

Horses we consider small today, such as Arabians that are less than 15 hands tall and weigh less than 1000 pounds, generally have bone circumference that is adequate or nearly adequate for their size; this was the "normal" size and weight of early wild and domestic horses until about 500 years ago, when humans started increasing their size by selective breeding. The Thoroughbred who stands several hands taller than his ancestors often has the same circumference of bone as did his much smaller forebears.

To make sure we select and breed horses with adequate bone support, we must be conscious of feet and legs, especially when breeding or selecting larger or heavier horses, such as Thoroughbreds, big warmbloods used for jumping and dressage, or heavily muscled Quarter Horses that are massive and stout, for a strenuous career. You don't want a horse too large for his bone structure. When evaluating a horse for breeding, athletic potential, and durability, carefully assess his legs, looking closely at bone size and strength.

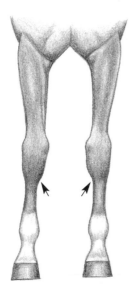

▲ Bench knees, with offset cannons set too far to the outside of the knee joints

Faults

The cannon bone should be under the center of the knee. Any deviation from this is considered a fault.

Offset Cannons/Bench Knees

If the forearm and cannon bone do not line up perfectly, such as if the forearm enters the knee more to the inside and the cannon bone meets the knee on the outside of the joint, a condition known as *offset cannons* or *bench knees* results. This forces the inner part of the cannon to bear more weight. The lower end of the forearm does not line up with the upper end of the cannon bone, putting uneven forces on the knee, which over time can make it change shape and become deformed.

With an offset cannon, there may be excessive movement between the cannon bone and the inner splint bone. In a well-conformed leg, the inner splint bone normally bears some of the weight and helps support the knee, but an offset cannon throws an abnormal amount of stress on it. This creates irritation and inflammation that can lead to the development of a *splint,* or bony enlargement, at the area of inflammation. This may occur anywhere along the splint bone but most often at the top, directly under the knee joint, especially in horses under 5 years of age, whose splint bones are not yet firmly attached to the cannon (see page 318 for more on splints).

A cannon bone offset to the outside of the knee may in some cases be caused by the unequal size and development of the several small knee bones that are situated in rows above the cannon. If the knee bones toward the inside of the knee are thicker than those on the outside of the joint, the knee joint will be "taller" on the inside and shorter on the outside, which forces the cannon bone to slant more toward the outside or be positioned more to the outside of the joint.

Offset cannon bones can also exert too much strain on the knee: the horse may not hold up under hard work. He may be more likely to suffer "popped knee"; the extra strain causes inflammation and swelling of the knee. There is also more stress on the outside surface of the entire lower leg, including the fetlock joint, pastern, and hoof.

A few horses show the opposite fault, with cannon bones set too far to the inside of the knee and the knees sticking out to the sides too much. This puts more stress on the outside part of the cannon bone, for it is then forced to bear most of the weight.

Rotated Cannon Bone

When viewed from the front, the leg should be perfectly straight, but sometimes, on one or both front legs, a horse will have a cannon bone that is rotated; it seems twisted in relation to the knee joint. It may be twisted outward or inward, making the horse toe out or in, though sometimes the fetlock joints, pasterns, and feet are relatively straight. If the cannon is rotated outward very much, it puts a lot of extra stress on the inside of the knee, or if rotated inward, the outside of the knee, as well as the lower joints of the leg.

THE FETLOCK JOINT

The horse's fetlock joints, between the cannon bone and long pastern bone, are hinge joints that can flex backward and extend forward. They help propel the horse as he travels and also play an important role in helping absorb the shock of impact when the foot lands on the ground. This joint provides the "give" that is necessary when the leg takes weight; the joint can hyperextend and sink down, dissipating the concussion. When the horse is standing, nearly two-thirds of his weight is on his front legs, pressing on the back of the fetlock joints where the lower end of the cannon meets the top of the long pastern bone.

Conformation

Fetlock joints, sometimes called *ankles*, should look broad from all angles. Just as in the knee, the fetlock joint should be relatively large, because a broad surface absorbs concussion better. The fetlock joints should be rounded a little at the front, but firm and flat on all sides. A fetlock joint that is too large or rounded may be a sign of overwork and damage. A horse that had physitis (enlargement or inflammation of growth plates at the ends of the long bones) as a youngster will have knobby fetlock joints. The joint should be perfectly straight, in line with a vertical cannon above and a straight pastern below it, when viewed from front and rear.

The fetlock joint should be wide from side to side to allow for supportive bearing surface where the bones at the lower end of cannon and upper end of pastern unite. Good width gives better strength and resistance to twisting actions. The joint should also be fairly deep from front to back to give support and leverage to the tendons that support and move the leg. The joint should not be too large from front to back, however, or it may force the back tendons out of plumb, creating a tied-in effect at the cannon bone. There should be no slanting inward of the tendon as it goes up the back of the cannon toward the knee.

The joint should be wide and smooth to give room for strong ligament attachments to support the bones, and enough room for the tendons to pass around and between the sesamoid bones. These two small bones (at the rear of the joint, on the sides) should stand out prominently, with the flexor tendons gliding over them. The pyramid-shaped sesamoid bones have a groove between them for the tendons. They act as a pulley, increasing the leverage effect of the tendons that go up the back of the leg from the foot to the knee (or hock, in the hind leg). The sesamoid bones at the back of the joint are joined together by fibrous connective tissue that creates a pulley at their rear for the flexor tendons; the two branches of the suspensory ligament terminate on the sesamoid bones.

With the other flexor tendons and the extensors at the front of the joint, the fetlock joint has three synovial membranes that act to lubricate the moving parts. Damage to any of these can create swelling. The most frequently damaged areas create *windpuffs*, permanent soft swellings toward the rear of the fetlock joint, due to the distension of these lubricating pouches.

◯ Conformation Close-up

Examination of the fetlock joints can provide clues about whether the horse has crooked legs and interferes when traveling. An open sore or a scar on the inside of the joint may mean that he strikes it with the opposite foot. Another clue as to whether the joint is straight is to pick up the foot and bend the fetlock joint completely. The space between the heels should be squarely in line with the tendons of the back of cannon; the foot should not be off to one side or the other.

Suspensory Structures

Fetlock joints must have strong suspension to prevent breakdown. The large suspensory ligament is a wide, thick band that attaches to the back of the knee and back of the cannon bone. It runs down toward the fetlock, where it divides into two branches and attaches to the outside of the sesamoid bones that support much of the weight of the cannon. A portion of these branches travels down each side of the pastern to merge with the large extensor tendon. This wraparound effect at the back of the fetlock joint supports the joint and helps keep it from dropping to the ground under a heavy load. The elasticity of the fetlock joint makes this part of the body into an efficient spring to buffer weight and impact.

The fetlock joint is under great stress even when the horse is in a normal standing position, so there is an elaborate system of muscles (above the knee only), tendons, and ligaments to hold everything in proper place. This unique system not only protects the joint when the horse is putting more stress on it during athletic activity, but also helps hold it in place (with no effort on the part of the horse) while the horse stands, including when sleeping while standing up.

The Ergot

The fetlock joint has a small horny structure located at the back, in the middle and slightly underneath, usually hidden by the fetlock hair. This is a normal part of the leg like the horny chestnut on the inside of the foreleg, but in some horses it grows and may need to be trimmed. If it gets too long, it can be injured or irritated by being bumped, as when the horse travels through rough terrain. This can cause irritation in the surrounding tissues similar to the pull of a hangnail. The ergot is an external remnant of a ligament at the back of the fetlock joint, which is thought to be part of an earlier structure when the horse's ancestor had several toes.

THE PASTERN

The pastern is the area between the fetlock joint and the top of the hoof and consists of two bones: the long pastern bone, or first phalanx, under the fetlock joint, and the short pastern bone, or second phalanx, that merges with the coffin bone, the third phalanx, inside the hoof. There is a joint between the two pastern bones, and though it has limited movement, it contributes to the total flexion and extension of the leg when the horse travels and helps increase the shock-absorbing capabilities of the pastern.

The length and slope of the pastern influence the soundness of the leg joints above it. Conformation of the pastern determines how well the leg can tolerate concussion and also contributes to the leg action of the horse, whether springy or plodding.

Conformation

Ideal front pastern slope — usually 47 to 55 degrees, depending on the individual horse — gives the horse sufficient leverage power and shock-absorbing ability to enable the leg to withstand hard use on firm surfaces and to maneuver through rough terrain with least effort. The horse will be more agile, more apt to hold up in a race or long ride through bad footing, and give his rider a smooth ride while doing it. He has more springiness of gait, whether at a walk or trot, or when running at top speed.

If the pastern slopes adequately, it transfers some of the weight to the tendons and their attached muscles in the upper leg, which have a

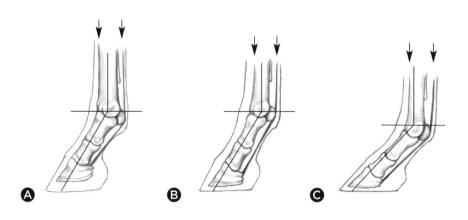

▶ Effect of pastern slope on the bones and tendons. **A.** Normal slope puts equal weight distribution on bones and tendons. **B.** Upright pastern puts too much stress on the bones of the leg (the bones must bear the greatest impact stress). **C.** Too-sloped pastern (coon footed) puts too much strain on the tendons.

degree of elasticity. If it is too upright, there is more concussion transmitted directly to the bones of the leg. If front pasterns slope properly, there is less risk for tendon strain and breakdown, sore shins, damaged knees, splints, or navicular disease. An overly steep (upright) pastern and foot makes it impossible for the weight to be transferred properly for adequate absorption of concussion within the coffin joint inside the foot; pressure is concentrated too much on the small navicular bone.

Excessive slope, however, will put too much pressure on the sesamoid bones at the back of the fetlock joint and on the navicular bone inside the foot. The weight of the horse will drive the fetlock joint down to the ground when galloping, particularly if he is worked hard or runs a long race; muscle fatigue leads to dropping of the fetlock joint. A long, sloped pastern is considered weak, because it allows the fetlock joint to descend too low when the horse is running, causing excessive strain on the suspensory ligament and potentially cracking or fracturing the sesamoid bones. A horse with a short, sloped pastern may be more likely to get by without injury.

If the muscles in the upper leg become fatigued, they no longer work in perfect synchronization; part of their job must be taken up by the tendons in the lower part of the leg. The normal suspensory apparatus that holds everything in place starts to work improperly and the leg does not have the support it needs. An overly long pastern with too much slope may also contribute to stretching/pulling injury to the back tendons behind the cannon bone, and in some cases may predispose a horse to bowed tendons.

At the other extreme, a steep pastern cannot act as a shock absorber; there is not enough give to the fetlock joint (it can't sink down as much as it should) when the foot hits the ground. The subsequent jarring makes the leg prone to concussion-related injuries.

The horse's entire body receives more pounding force, as does the rider. An upright pastern that is also too short is a real bone cracker. There is almost no spring or give, due to being upright, and the shortness accentuates this problem. A horse with this conformation is more likely to develop ringbone (arthritis and enlargement at the pastern joints) and other concussion-related leg problems.

Length

The length of pastern depends on the length of the first phalanx, which joins the short second phalanx near the hoof. The short pastern bone is only about 2 inches long, with half of it above the hoof and half of it within the hoof. It is joined to the coffin bone inside the foot. Lying behind these bones are the ligaments of the joints supporting them, and the flexor tendons.

When a front leg takes weight, the elbow joint is locked and the knee remains rigid. That leaves only the pastern and fetlock joint for shock absorbers. Thus, front pasterns must be somewhat long and sloped to allow the flexibility needed for this give and springiness. Front pastern length should be about one-half to three-fourths the length of the cannon. Proper length of the pastern is always relative to the length of the front leg, especially the cannon. The pastern and cannon of young horses (yearlings and 2-year-olds) may appear too long, partly because the horse has not yet attained full height (forearms are still growing) and his hoofs are also not full size yet (see chapter 12).

Faults

If pasterns are too long and sloping, they will be weak. If they are too short, the horse will have a choppy, jarring gait.

Too-Long Pastern

A long pastern is not necessarily weak if it has good bone, is well constructed, and the fetlock joint does not drop too low. But a long, weak pastern may break down if the horse is used hard. A too-long pastern (more than three-fourths the length of the cannon) may put too much strain on tendons and ligaments and too much stress on the sesamoid bones. A horse with excessively long, sloping pasterns will have a smooth gait but may be at risk for sesamoiditis (inflammation of the sesamoid bones), bowed tendons, and suspensory ligament injuries. The horse may also be at risk for developing arthritis due to extra stress on pastern and coffin joints, which results in ringbone (see page 331).

Conformation Close-up

A too-long pastern reduces a horse's potential for speed, especially sprinting, because it takes longer to "push off" at each step to get the foot off the ground. A rule of thumb that many horsemen use is that short pasterns are an advantage for propulsion needed for fast starts and pulling power, but that short pasterns must also slope enough to absorb concussion. A horse can usually manage fairly well with pasterns that are short and sloping or long and steep. But the opposite combinations (short and steep or long and sloping) can cause more trouble.

Too-Short Pastern

The pastern is considered too short if it is less than half the length of the cannon bone. This usually makes for a shortened stride length. A too-short pastern is almost always too upright, putting it nearly in a straight line with the cannon bone and forearm above it. This creates a pile-driving pounding action when the foot takes weight at speed.

A horse with short, upright pasterns is prone to all types of concussion-related front leg injuries, including chip fractures in the knees, strain injuries in the knees (including bucked knees), bucked shins, splints on the cannon bone, windpuffs at the fetlock joints (due to too much friction and jarring), ringbone, navicular syndrome, and fetlock joint arthritis (see page 322). Concussion that would otherwise be distributed across the entire foot (with a more sloping pastern that has more "give") is directed instead to the center of the foot in the navicular area.

The pastern joint between the long pastern bone and the short pastern bone beneath it has very little movement to begin with and minimal ability to absorb concussion. If the pastern is too short, the excessive pounding on the pastern joint will eventually cause inflammation and subsequent calcification of the joint; it becomes fused and solid. This makes the pastern less flexible, eliminating any movement the joint might have had. Concussion forces are increased, which can lead to ringbone in the pastern joint or in the joint between the short pastern bone and coffin bone within the hoof, or to sidebone (calcification of the cartilage along the side of the foot, just above the coronary band) in the foot or irritation and enlargement of the navicular bone.

The riding horse with short pasterns will always suffer more concussion injury than a horse with adequate length and slope, and if used hard will tend to be continually sore in the front legs due to accumulated injuries. By contrast, the draft horse usually performs

All about Impact

In the front legs, the impact of the feet hitting the ground at each step, known as *concussion*, is offset by many factors, including how the leg is constructed and how it travels. Poor conformation loads added stress on certain parts. The more nearly ideal the leg and joint conformation, the more uniformly the stresses of concussion are distributed so that no one part is affected more than the others.

Movement within the compound joints of the knee, the pumping action of the foot (with the plantar cushion acting as a shock-absorbing buffer), and the springy "give" of the fetlock joint, along with a properly sloped pastern, are the major shock-absorbing features of the front leg. The action of the pastern transfers some of the strain from the leg bones to tendons and hence to the more elastic muscles of the leg. The shoulder blade glides over the ribs, transferring any remaining concussion to the body.

If all the bones of the front leg were in a straight line (with no shoulder or pastern slope), concussion from each step would go directly from the ground to the shoulder and body. But with proper angles in the foot, pastern, and shoulder, most of the impact is dissipated on the journey up.

---

adequately with shorter and more upright pasterns because he travels at slower speeds and is using his legs for leverage in pulling.

Evaluating Foreleg Conformation

It is important to be able to judge how straight or crooked the leg is and assess how the leg structure will affect the horse's movement and future soundness. If the faults are slight and the horse can move in an efficient way, with unimpaired athletic ability and minimal concussion, the imperfections may not be worrisome. On the other hand, if one or both front legs deviate too much from ideal construction, athletic ability is likely to be diminished and lameness and injury are more probable.

STRAIGHTNESS AND SYMMETRY

Ideally, the front legs should appear balanced and straight, with proper bone length and proper angles at the joints so there is no undue stress on any one part of the leg. Both legs should bear weight equally; they should be perfectly straight when viewed from the front or the side, forming a 90-degree angle with the ground. Toes should point directly to the front, and the feet should be exactly the same distance apart as the distance between the forearms where they attach to the chest.

When looking at the horse head-on, an imaginary line dropped from the point of the shoulder should go directly down the center of the front leg, bisecting the forearm, knee, cannon, fetlock joint, pastern, and hoof. From the side, the leg from elbow to fetlock

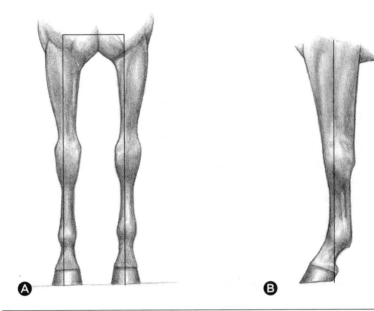

Front leg conformation. Front legs should be straight when viewed from the front (A) or from the side (B).

A B

joint should appear perpendicular to the ground and to the underline of the horse.

Viewed from the side, a line dropped from the front of the withers should go down the center of the front leg and barely touch the heel of the foot or be right behind it. From the fetlock joint up, if the line up the center of the front leg hits the middle of the withers, the front legs are set too far back under the horse and he probably has an upright shoulder.

Keep in mind that no two front legs are exactly alike and very few front legs have all the bones and joints facing perfectly forward. Even in an individual horse, there will be slight variations; the left leg probably won't match the right leg perfectly. The leg bones in one or both front legs may be slightly offset at the knee or fetlock joint, or rotated, or they may leave the joint at a slightly sideways angle instead of perfectly straight. Slight faults don't hinder athletic ability very much, as long as they are symmetrical and all leg parts face the same direction on each leg. The stresses will be somewhat evenly distributed this way, and the horse is more likely to stay sound.

Conformation Close-up

Crookedness that is apparent when viewed from the side, such as knees bucked forward or angled backward or pasterns that are too upright or too sloping, can produce stresses that create lameness and unsoundness. Asymmetries observed from the front that affect foot flight, such as bowed legs, knock-knees, or toes pointing inward or outward, may lead to limb interference and unsoundness.

Crooked Legs and Stress

If a leg is crooked, the weight it bears is distributed unevenly, and there is more pressure and strain on certain parts of a bone or joint, as well as increased tension on muscles, tendons, and ligaments. As the horse puts a foot down crookedly when traveling, the part that lands first takes all the weight that should have been shared by the entire bearing surface of the foot; additional overload occurs on upper parts of the leg and body. Bones may undergo constant stress on one side, and there may be too much stretch and strain on connective tissues on the other side; this may eventually lead to breakdown injury. When front legs are straight and move forward in straight lines, however, there is equal stress on all parts and no loss of energy from an inward or outward deviation of foot flight.

If a horse's feet wing inward when he walks, for instance, this may mean his leg bones are not straight, or are rotated outward at the knee, or have some other alignment deviation. When he travels fast, he may strike one hoof against the opposite fetlock joint or cannon bone. If he swings his feet inward or outward due to imperfections in the leg, the feet may not meet the ground evenly, and this will create more wear and tear on certain parts of the leg because of the added stress. The side that lands first will send more concussion up that side of the leg.

THE CHEST AND CROOKED LEGS

Front-leg crookedness often starts high in the leg, due to deviations at the shoulder and elbow joints. If the distance between the points of the shoulders and the distance between the elbows is approximately the same (creating an imaginary square box if you connect the lines), the horse will usually have straight front legs, with feet pointing forward. If the distance between his elbows is greater than that between his shoulder blades, the horse is *out at the elbows* and will have feet that toe inward. If the elbows are closer together than the distance between the shoulder blades, the horse will toe outward and his feet will move inward (coming too close together) when he travels (see page 135). A horse can have perfect leg construction in forearms, knees, cannons, and fetlocks, yet still toe in or out because of the misalignment of the humerus and the elbow.

If the box formed by the front of the chest/breast is not symmetrical, this is a clue that the horse is either not standing squarely or has a curved spine. If the box is slanted, indicating one shoulder or elbow is higher than the other, this may mean that the front legs are of differing lengths. If the points of the shoulders are not at the same level, for example, one humerus may be longer than the other. It's not uncommon to find a horse with front legs of different lengths, which

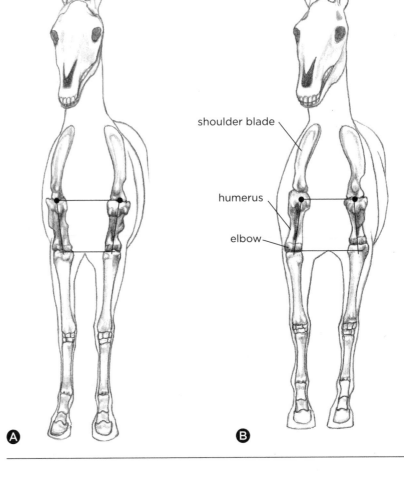

▶ Crookedness in the front legs often originates in the chest. The points of the shoulders and the elbow joints should form a perfectly square box. If the box is not square, the legs will not be straight. **A.** If the elbows are closer together than the shoulders ("in at the elbows"), the horse will toe out. **B.** If the elbows are farther apart ("out at the elbows") than the points of the shoulders, the horse will toe in.

Did You Know?

A foal or weanling may toe out slightly because the young horse is a bit narrow in the chest. Often, such youngsters become straighter as they fill out and the chest widens. Narrow-chested youngsters whose toes turn in, however, are less likely to straighten because chest width does not affect the toe-in stance.

creates an abnormal stride and gait. One foot angle will be steeper than the other, perhaps to the extreme point of clubfoot.

Conformation Faults

Horses with legs that are not straight cannot travel straight. At best, there is loss of efficiency, agility, and speed. At worst, the added strain leads to injury and unsoundness.

BASE WIDE

Base wide is an undesirable conformation in which the legs are farther apart at the feet than at the shoulders and forearms. The crookedness may start anywhere from the elbows on down to the fetlock joint (a turned-in elbow tends to make the leg turn outward). Base-wide structure is often observed in horses with narrow chests. Most base-wide horses are also splay footed, which causes the feet to wing inward as the legs move forward.

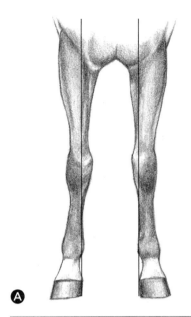
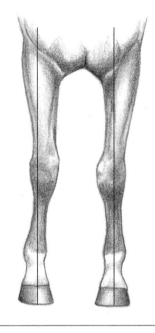

◀ A. Base wide and splay footed.
B. Base wide and pigeon-toed.

The inside of the limb is under greater stress in a horse that is base wide, especially if he is both base wide and splay footed. In the splay-footed horse, the toe on the weight-bearing leg points outward and the heels and fetlock joint are pointed inward. In these cases, the ligaments of the fetlock joints and pasterns are under constant strain. As a result, windpuffs, or swellings in the fetlock joint, are common; stress on the tendon sheaths and joint capsules causes them to fill with extra lubricating fluids, creating the swellings. Ringbone or sidebone may occur on the inside of the feet due to strain that causes inflammation and subsequent new bone growth. The inner aspect of the knee joint and cannon bone may suffer strain, making the horse more likely to develop splints on the inside of the leg. A few horses are base wide and pigeon-toed, which is very undesirable conformation that puts even more stress on the limbs.

Most splay-footed horses have crooked front legs that deviate outward from the chest area down. In other horses, the legs are relatively straight down to the fetlock joints and then begin to deviate outward; the leg is rotated at the fetlock joint. Regardless of the structure of the limb above it, the hoof of the splay-footed horse will be worn excessively on the inside because of the way it lands on the ground, always on the inside.

Splay-footed horses, whether they are base narrow or base wide, typically wing their feet to the inside and wear their feet excessively on the inside wall (they land hard on the inside of the foot rather than with the foot perfectly square and flat). There is also increased risk of

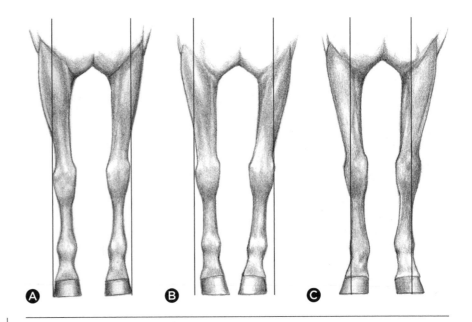

A. Base narrow. B. Base narrow and pigeon-toed. C. Base narrow and splay footed.

the foot hitting the opposite foreleg — especially at the fetlock joint, but sometimes at the coronary band or along the cannon and splint bone — and causing splints or even a fractured splint bone. The heels and fetlock joints are always at risk for being cut or bruised by the opposite foot because of their turned-in position. The opposite foot may even step on the heel, making the horse stumble or fall.

BASE NARROW

This undesirable conformation sets the horse's feet closer than the legs are at the chest and is seen most often in horses with large pectoral muscles and a wide breast. Base-narrow structure is often accompanied by pigeon-toed conformation.

Base-narrow, pigeon-toed conformation exerts strain on pasterns and fetlock joints, especially the ligaments on the outside of the legs, often leading to problems such as windpuffs in the fetlock joints, or ringbone or sidebone on the outside portion of the foot. The hoof will be worn excessively on the outside edge because the foot tends to land on the outside wall instead of squarely.

Base-narrow, pigeon-toed horses usually "paddle" with their front feet, swinging them outward as they travel. The pigeon-toed horse will usually paddle whether he is base narrow or base wide. Any deviation from straight action cuts down on the horse's speed, agility, and stamina. There is a lot of wasted motion as the lower leg and foot are flung to the outside at every stride.

A base-narrow, splay-footed conformation is weaker than a base-narrow and pigeon-toed conformation. Even greater strain is exerted

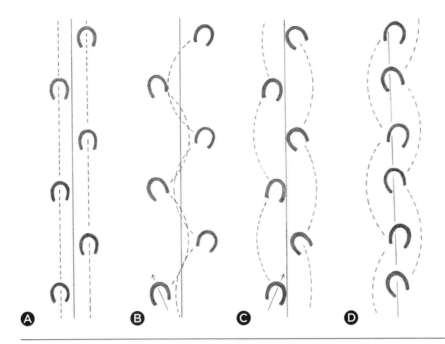

Leg conformation and foot flight. **A.** Straight legs and normal foot flight. **B.** Base wide, splay-footed horse winging inward. **C.** Base narrow, pigeon-toed horse paddling. **D.** Base narrow, splay-footed horse plaiting.

on the leg below the fetlock joint. Horses with this type of front leg conformation often go lame if they are worked hard. The feet of a splay-footed horse will usually wing inward as he moves, often causing limb interference, especially in the base-narrow horse whose feet are already closely placed.

The base-narrow, splay-footed horse may plait, or put one foot directly ahead of the other, so his tracks go forward in a single line, as if walking a bicycle track, rather than the normal double track. Less stability and poor balance result. If the advancing front foot strikes the leg in front of it, the horse may stumble.

Misalignment of any of the leg bones or joints in the front leg, including the elbow, knee, or fetlock, can cause the toe to point in or out. A splay-footed horse experiences excessive stress on the inner aspect of the leg, whether he is base wide or base narrow. A horse that is pigeon-toed has more strain on the outer aspect of the limb, whether he is base wide or base narrow. Some horses have relatively straight legs down to the fetlock joints and then toe in or out, but the stresses on the fetlock joint, pastern, and foot are still severe. Being splay-footed or pigeon-toed is the result, not the cause, of crooked structure and misalignment of the bones and joints higher up the leg.

TEST FOR STRAIGHTNESS

A simple test to tell if the front feet and legs are indeed straight is to pick up a front foot and flex the knee completely, bringing the heel of the foot clear up to touch the forearm or elbow. If the heels go toward the inside or outside of the elbow or forearm rather than remaining

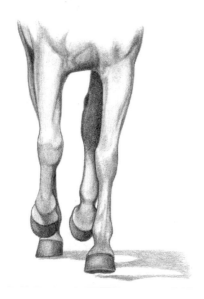

▲ **Properly constructed front legs.** When front legs are straight and move forward in straight lines, there is less stress on all parts.

centered, the horse's leg is not straight and you can predict that he will have crooked leg action, swinging his feet inward or outward when he travels. If the horse's cannon bone is directly under the forearm when the knee is bent, and the pastern and hoof stay straight when the fetlock joint is flexed, the leg is straight and will probably move straight.

If a horse has properly constructed front legs, he will pick up his feet squarely. The foot will be lifted from the ground at the heel, break over squarely at the center of the toe, carry the foot forward in a relatively straight line, and be set down again (landing heel first) with the toe pointing straight forward. If the leg is not straight, the foot will point slightly off to one side (splay footed or pigeon-toed) and the foot will neither pick up straight nor land squarely (see chapter 9).

You can easily tell whether there are any abnormalities in front leg conformation by watching a horse travel. Stand directly in front of him or directly behind him, to see if his feet are picked up straight and move forward in straight lines or crooked. Sometimes watching him move will help you detect a slight imperfection that you could not see while looking at him standing still. You can also get a clue by examining his feet. Pick up a front foot and see if his toe (or the toe of his shoe, if shod) is worn evenly or if there is more wear on one side or the other, indicating crooked breakover (the point where the hoof leaves the ground).

Most horses do not travel perfectly straight, and there is always some outward or inward movement during foot flight, because no horse has perfect leg conformation. Slight imperfections usually do not hinder a horse's athletic ability or make him unsound. Because no horse is perfect, it becomes a judgment call on how much imperfection can be tolerated, and this will depend largely on the career demands (see chapters 14 and 15) and on the structural integrity of the individual horse. Crooked foot flight should be evaluated carefully, especially if you want the horse to hold up for strenuous athletic activity. Aside from the appearance of the gait and whether he interferes, the most important consideration is how much strain and stress the crooked legs will cause.

◢◯ *Conformation Close-up*

Horses that travel straight do not need much space between their front legs because the legs will not strike each other, but you don't want a horse that travels too close in front. A simple test for brushing — when one leg slightly bumps the other — can tell you how close a horse's front legs travel.

Apply chalk to the inner side of each front hoof. After walking and trotting the horse, look at the legs to see if any of the chalk rubbed onto the inside of the fetlock joints or cannons. If there's evidence of brushing, you can pinpoint the portion of the hoof that's doing it by adding more chalk to the spot where the brush marks appeared and wiping the hoofs clean. Walk and trot the horse again, then look to see which part of the foot made contact with the chalk marks.

Corrective Trimming and Shoeing

When a horse toes in or out, an attempt is often made to correct the condition by trimming more off one side of the hoof or the other to put the foot in proper balance. Careful, modest, and frequent corrective trimming on a young foal can sometimes straighten a leg or minimize its crookedness as the bones grow. Once the bones have matured, however, there is no way to change their structure. No true correction can be made after the horse is a yearling. The optimum time to encourage proper growth of the leg is during the first 4 months of life.

Aggressive corrective trimming and shoeing may help the appearance of a crooked leg but also may hurt the horse. The foot can be leveled to help the horse travel a little straighter, but this correction must be done consistently with each trimming or shoeing. Excessive correction will simply put more strain on the bones and joints. The crooked-legged horse whose feet have been modified to look straight when he is standing squarely may still have some deviations in gait because of the way his bones are aligned, and he may not stay sound. It's better to try to balance the foot to match the leg structure so the limb will have its best chance for strength and durability, without adding extra stresses by trying to alter it too much.

A good farrier can keep the foot level and balanced, with proper support, to enhance and not interfere with leg movement. Shoes should promote ease of movement of the entire leg, rather than trying to change movement at the foot only. For a horse that interferes, for instance, the farrier will trim and shoe the foot so the foot flight begins straighter, which enables the horse to travel more normally and keeps him from hitting the opposite leg.

Caution

Corrective trimming and shoeing are usually done to improve a foot and make it more level, to balance it for proper breakover, or to try to make the foot and leg straighter. These adjustments should only be attempted by an experienced farrier.

8

Hindquarter Conformation

A HORSE'S HIND LEGS are typically less prone to lameness than the front legs because the hindquarters carry less weight and are subjected to less concussion and trauma. The hindquarters are the engine for the whole body, so they must be long and strong. Hindquarter conformation determines a horse's potential for speed and agility, and it can be a red flag for problems such as limb interference and locked stifles, as well as hock trouble such as spavin and curb.

The hindquarters play a role in how the horse travels at all gaits. Hind legs must be straight and well balanced to adequately distribute stress and concussion. Proper hind leg angles help prevent hock and stifle problems.

Because of their direct connection to the backbone, the hindquarters provide most of the horse's propelling power and the strength for proper collection. The groups of muscles in the hind legs are larger and more powerful than those in the front legs. The hind legs must be able to support the entire body weight at times and respond quickly when the horse "puts on the brakes" for stopping. Any horse that must stop and turn quickly needs strong, well-conformed hindquarters, as does a horse that travels up and down steep hills and over jumps.

Anatomy

The hindquarters comprises the croup and quarters, pelvis and hip, and buttocks and thigh — the upper part of the leg. The joints visible on the lower leg include the stifle, hock, fetlock, and pastern.

THE RUMP

The top of the hindquarter, from the croup (the highest point of the hindquarter) to the tail head, is generally called the *rump*. Although some horsemen call the entire topline of the hindquarter the croup, technically *croup* refers only to the top of the rump, the point where the lumbar vertebrae end and the sacrum begins. The muscle covering from croup to tail head, on either side of the backbone, is called the *quarter*. The term *hindquarter* refers to the entire hind end of the horse.

▼ **A. Bones of the hind leg.**
B. Muscles of the hind leg.

Shape

The shape of the rump is determined by the conformation of the pelvis and hips and the thick muscles that cover them. The pelvis comprises three fused bones that form a semicircle on their inner surface (see page 91). They connect to the corresponding bones on the other side to create a complete circular pelvic girdle through which the digestive tract (and birth canal in the mare) exits. The ilium, the largest of these fused bones, is attached to the backbone. The shape and length of the pelvis determines whether the horse has a level or sloped rump and how long it is.

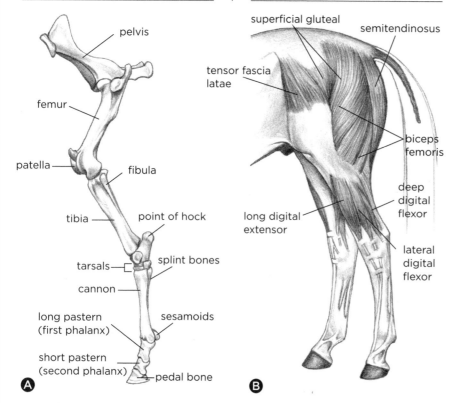

All of the major muscles of the hindquarters that propel the horse forward are attached to the pelvis. The longer the pelvic bones, the longer and more powerful the muscles. From behind, the hindquarters should look somewhat square, with the rump gently rounded and symmetrical. The width of the pelvis is not as important as its length in determining the power and strength of the hindquarters. Mares tend to have a wider pelvis to allow for foal delivery. Extreme width and bulky muscling are undesirable, for they hinder a horse's stamina.

A horse with narrow hindquarters lacks speed and power: his hind legs are too close together. The shape of the rump and hindquarters (the length and slant of the pelvis and the way it is attached to the backbone) plays a major role in how efficiently the horse converts muscle power into motion.

The size of the pelvis from top to bottom (that is, the depth of this circle of bones) can vary in individual horses. The deeper the pelvis, the more space and area of attachment there is for the biceps femoris muscle, which moves the hind leg forward and starts its thrust. Draft horses and sprinters do best with a deep pelvis that allows adequate room for powerful muscling.

⚲ Conformation Close-up

For best agility, balance, and smoothness of gait, the croup should be the same height as the withers. If the croup is higher than the withers, the hind legs are too long in proportion to the front legs, which can create problems with stride and forging (hitting the back of the front foot with the toe of the approaching hind foot). A high croup causes the saddle to slide forward over the withers. The long hind legs give the rider more thrust with each stride, resulting in a rougher ride.

Withers just slightly higher than the croup are considered an advantage for dressage. It enables the hindquarters to work better under the horse because it makes it easier for the horse to crouch down on his hindquarters and raise his front end for more extreme collection.

Slope

The topline of the hindquarters may be sloped or nearly level. A slight slope is generally considered the ideal topline conformation, but this varies somewhat with the breed. Arabian breeders prefer a level rump. Extremes in conformation lead to problems and should always be avoided.

The Croup

The croup is where the horse's hind leg joins the backbone at the lumbosacral joint, an area of only about 6 square inches. This is the highest joint in the hind leg. The thrust and power of the hindquarters is transmitted to the body through this small juncture. The height and placement of the croup play a significant role in the shape and alignment of the hind leg.

 *Conformation Close-up*

No matter the shape and angles of the hindquarter, there must be symmetry between the hindquarters and front end of the horse if the animal is to move in a desirable way with minimal risk of injury to legs and joints. Scrutinize the hind end and front end for correctness, but don't forget to evaluate the horse as a whole (see chapter 10). It is more important that front and hind conformation match than it is for the hindquarter to be perfect or the front end to be perfect. A mismatch in angles and basic form will create problems and risks for unsoundness.

HIPS

The hip joint resides deep beneath the muscles and is a few inches behind and lower than the point of the hip. While the front end of the horse is attached to the body only by muscles and connective tissues, the hind legs are connected at the hip joint. The head of the femur fits into the acetabulum, a cuplike socket formed by the bones of the pelvis. With this bony connection, the hind legs act directly on the spine, giving thrust and propulsion to the body.

The horse's front end and hind end should be in balance, with the hip joint no higher than the pivot point of the shoulder blade. The hip joint is located in front of and at the same level as the point of the buttock, the rearmost point of the hindquarter. A vertical line dropped from the hip joint (not the point of the hip) should pass through the tibia and the middle of the hoof if the horse is standing squarely. The distance from this line to one dropped from the patella (at the stifle joint) and another line dropped from the point of the buttock down the back of the hock and cannon should be exactly the same. This gives the end of the seat bone enough length for good muscle attachments, which are essential for the strength and power needed in cantering and galloping and for adequate swing of the hind leg.

The hindquarters should be reasonably wide at the hips. If the hind end of the horse is too narrow, the stifles won't be as large and strong as they should be, and the hocks and lower parts of the legs will be too close together. The lower legs need adequate room for the feet to make good contact with the ground for power and acceleration and to avoid limb interference.

Wide Hips

Sufficient width of hip is needed for good development and alignment of the hind leg. But if the hips are too wide, the legs may be too far apart at the top and the feet too close together. This results in a leg that is *base narrow*: it does not appear straight when viewed from behind. A base-narrow leg has less strength than a straight one and results in greater stress on the joints. Exceptionally wide hindquarters is not a fault in a draft horse unless the legs are exceptionally base narrow, for he needs great pulling/pushing power at slow speeds. This trait is not desirable in a riding horse; at fast gaits, the too-wide hindquarter is more of a detriment than a benefit.

Narrow Hips

A horse that is too narrow through the hips does not have enough room for muscling and won't have much driving power. The bone structure of the pelvis is crowded and improperly aligned, which always causes more stress and strain on joints in the leg.

Study the Shape

Viewing horses from the rear, you will recognize different shapes: apple, pear, and rectangle. Ideally, the hind end will be somewhat square or slightly pear-shaped. A pear-shaped hind end — one that is wider across the thighs than across the hips — is desired in horses that need a lot of muscle; the Quarter Horse is often widest at the thighs. By contrast, *rafter hips* are wide and flat, T-shaped when viewed from behind, with inadequate muscling at the thighs; this type of hip is often too wide. *Peaked hips* (mule hips) are A-shaped and also undesirable; the croup is much higher than the hips, creating a steep slope from the croup to each hip bone and a narrowness at the buttocks when viewed from above. Peaked hips are associated with inadequate muscling of the hindquarters.

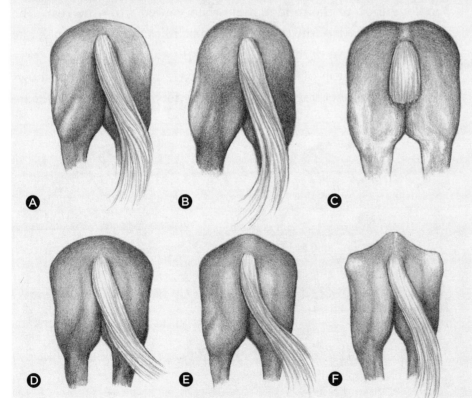

*Hindquarter shapes. **A.** Square (rectangular). **B.** Pear-shaped. **C.** Draft horse (apple rump). **D.** Rafter hips. **E.** Peaked hips (mule hips). **F.** Emaciated (inadequate muscle cover).*

THIGH

The thigh is the muscled area covering the femur. The adequacy of the muscling depends on the length of the femur and the angles of the hindquarters. The ideal angles create an equilateral triangle between the point of the hip, the point of the buttocks, and the stifle.

Length

Ideally, the femur and tibia are approximately the same length, resulting in a relatively low stifle. This allows room for longer thigh muscles, which enable the horse to generate great power and speed with a longer stride. If the femur is too short, the stifle is too high (sitting above the sheath on a male horse or the udder on a female) and the thigh muscles are too short for a long stride. Short femur/high stifle conformation is better suited for the short, quick strides of sprinting or for pulling (draft horse). If the femur is long, the stifle will be at the same level or slightly below the sheath or the udder.

Muscling

The thigh should be long (which suggests a long femur), well muscled, and deep. Viewed from the rear, the thigh should appear ample and thick so it can activate and give power to the femur, the largest and strongest leg bone.

The muscling of the inner thighs should be full, giving a square or oblong look to the hindquarter when viewed from the rear. The "hams," or back of the thighs, should be thick enough to touch one another for most of their length, until they abruptly split and curve inward to the top of the gaskin (see page 149). If daylight shows between the inner thighs when viewed from behind, the muscles are

▶ **A.** A horse with a high stifle has a somewhat triangular-shaped thigh area. **B.** A horse with a low stifle has a square thigh area.

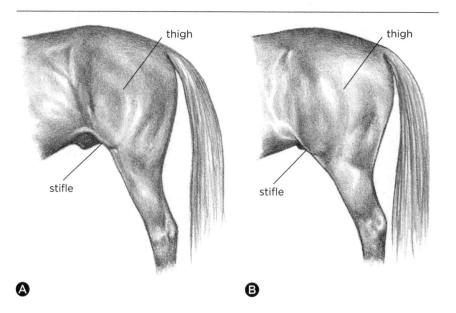

thigh

stifle

thigh

stifle

Ⓐ   Ⓑ

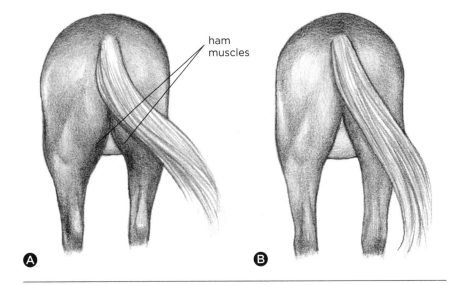

ham
muscles

◀ Muscling of the hams.
A. Split up: the hams don't touch
each other all the way down; daylight shows between them at the
bottom. **B.** Cat-hammed: long,
thin thighs; the whole thigh has
inadequate muscling.

Ⓐ

Ⓑ

said to be "split up," or undeveloped. If the whole thigh has inadequate muscling (as in a horse with long, thin thighs and gaskins), the
horse is said to be "cat-hammed." That is, he lacks proper muscle
development and strength for speed and power, reducing his usefulness and abilities. Muscle thickness is due in part to genetics (a Quarter Horse has bulkier muscles than an Arab, for example) but is also
influenced by nutrition and conditioning. A very thin horse lacks
adequate muscling. Fitness conditioning can help a horse develop
more muscle but cannot significantly change his type if he is light
muscled or has inherited poor muscle structure.

STIFLE

The stifle is the largest joint in the horse's body and is the highest joint
visible on the hind leg. Its structure is similar to that of the human
knee. Like the human knee, the stifle consists of the lower end of the
femur and the upper end of the tibia. With the patella, its "kneecap,"
which glides in a large groove on the lower end of the femur at the
front of the stifle, the three bones of the stifle create two joints.

Position and Angle

The stifle should be at about the same height as the elbow on the
front leg. This makes for a low, well-placed stifle joint and creates
better leverage for the muscles of the hindquarters. If the stifle is low,
the hamstring muscles along the back of the hindquarters can be
longer and stronger, continuing down toward the gaskin area. A low
stifle also goes hand in hand with medium-short gaskins and relatively low hocks, which give more power to the hind leg than do a
high stifle and high hocks.

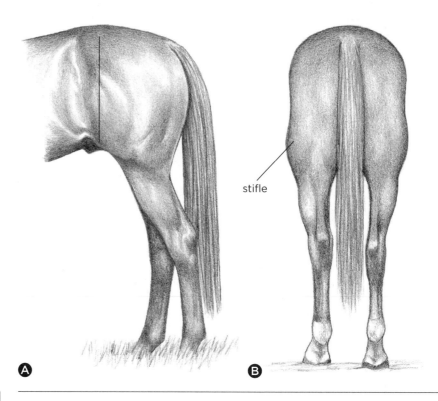

stifle

The stifle should be positioned well forward, nearly in direct line with the hip bone above it. If the stifle is too far back, the thigh will be too short and more V-shaped than square when viewed from the side. If the stifle has good muscling, this will be the widest part of the hindquarters when viewed from the rear; the horse will be slightly wider at the stifles than at the hips. The muscles over the stifles should be adequate, making this area appear fairly rectangular when viewed from the side or rear.

A horse should be wide through the stifles, not narrow, because the stifles need to clear the belly when the hind leg moves forward. Narrow stifles mean the horse will have less freedom of movement. If a horse is too narrow at the stifles, his pelvis may also be narrow and his thigh bones may not angle out as much as they should as they extend to meet the stifles.

The stifle joint is where movement begins in the hind leg, to push and roll the body forward, so the muscles on the inner and outer leg should be well developed. The angle of the joint is also crucial for efficient movement.

The stifle joint and hock joint are synchronized and should have the same degree of angulation; they are the two most important joints in propulsion. A horse with hind legs and stifle joints that are too straight may be more likely to suffer dislocation and locking of the stifle joint. The stifle is also crucial for keeping the leg rigid when

In some horses, the stifle joint is too straight and the hock too crooked; at first glance, you might think the horse has excessively long leg bones because he is sickle hocked and assume that he could never suffer from locked stifles. A closer look at his stifle will reveal that it has the same improper angle as a post-legged horse, making the total length of the leg bones too short. This kind of mismatched hind leg construction is fairly common in Quarter Horses but often goes undetected because the hock joint is much easier to see and evaluate than the stifle, which is generally covered by thick muscle.

The key is recognizing that the stifle joint is not as far forward as it should be. In a properly angled hind leg, the cannon bone is vertical and set directly underneath the point of the buttocks (rather than too far forward or back, or slanting), and the horse's stifle is directly under the point of the hip. If the stifle is too far to the rear rather than under the hip, this makes the horse post-legged at the stifle, even if the hocks are bent and sickled.

A horse with this type of stifle will be just as prone to suffer patella problems and locked stifles as an obviously post-legged horse with too-straight hocks and stifles. Don't be fooled by the sickle-hocked horse. Look closely at the angulation of the stifle as well as the hock to determine whether the horse might develop stifle problems.

weight is placed on it. Due to the arrangement of muscles and tendons, the hock cannot bend while the stifle is straight, and the stifle cannot bend while the hock and fetlock are straight. Whenever the stifle joint closes (the bones above and below it "folding" closer together), the hock joint also folds, as when the hind foot is brought up closer to the body. Whenever the stifle joint opens, the hock joint opens, as when the leg is extended out behind the horse. The whole leg must be either rigid or bent. This locking mechanism, coupled with the locking of the elbow (along with the support for the horse's head by means of the strong nuchal ligament at the top of the neck), allows the horse to sleep standing up.

THE GASKIN

The gaskin, sometimes called the second thigh, is the main group of muscles between the stifle and hock, and it flexes and extends the hock joint. The gaskin should be well muscled, with the stifle well forward to allow for length of muscling between stifle and hock. The muscles on the inner thigh should extend down into the inner part of the gaskin so that the tibial area above the hock on the inside of the leg does not look too thin. The gaskin attaches to the tibia. The gaskin muscles flex and extend the hock joint.

Length

The gaskin portion of the hind leg should be a little shorter than the thigh, but still fairly long, to give the hind leg good leverage and a long stride. This part of the leg supplies much of the power for galloping. Strong, well-developed gaskin muscles are crucial for speed, jumping ability, and pulling power. If the gaskin is too long, however, the leg will lack proper angles for efficient movement. A horse with a long gaskin may have legs that are "out in the country," or he may be *cow hocked* (hocks point toward one another and are too close together) or bowlegged.

The size of the gaskin, when viewed from the side, is partially determined by the length of the tuber calcis bone that forms the point of the hock, protruding upward from the main group of small tarsal bones that make up the hock joint. The longer the tuber calcis bone, the farther back the large tendon is kept from the main part of the gaskin. This allows more room for the muscles, because the tendon forms the back line of the lower gaskin, and more leverage for movement of the leg.

Muscling

Muscling of the gaskin helps control the direction and force of the leg's forward movement if the bone structure is in proper alignment. The large gastrocnemius muscle, one of the main muscles that propels the hindquarters, runs down the back of the gaskin and attaches to the hock joint by means of a tendon. Muscles and tendons that activate the hock attach to the top of the tibia; muscles that activate the lower leg joints attach to tendons just above the hock (the tendons travel down the cannon).

Muscles should be long and broad, with an obvious rise of muscle on the outer leg. If the gaskin is well developed and symmetrical, the hind legs should travel straight, giving the horse balance; this musculature also reduces the risks of limb interference. These muscles are responsible for the final movement in straightening the hind leg during its stride, contributing to the springiness of the gait while trotting or galloping.

◢○ *Conformation Close-up*

Strength for running, jumping, rearing, and other athletic maneuvers depends primarily on the muscles of the quarters, thigh, and gaskin. The length and width of these muscles are important. A long quarter has more range for muscle contraction — and greater effect on the bony levers it works on — for greater range of motion and speed. For power and strength, a horse needs adequate width. A horse with narrow hindquarters isn't as strong, and hindquarters that are too wide create an exaggerated rolling motion and a less efficient gait.

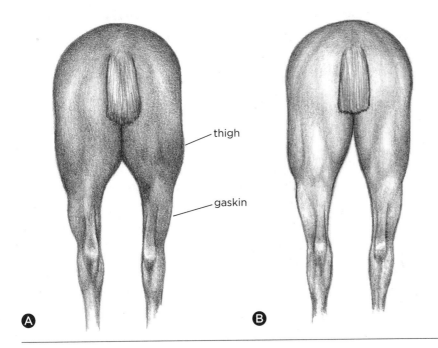

thigh

gaskin

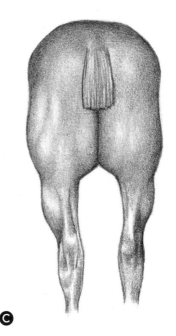

Gaskin muscling. **A.** Normal gaskin muscling. **B.** Inadequate muscling on the inside of gaskin and thighs. **C.** Gaskin too heavily muscled on the outside of the leg (the horse will travel wide).

If the gaskin is too heavily muscled on the inner leg (that is, if there is more muscle on the inner leg than on the outer leg), the leg will be pulled inward as the horse moves it forward, possibly causing limb interference: the horse hits the opposite hind leg above the fetlock joint. If the opposite condition exists (heavy muscling on the outer gaskin and not enough on the inner gaskin), the horse tends to travel wide because the overdeveloped gaskin pulls the leg outward as it goes forward.

THE HOCK

The hock corresponds with the ankle in the human leg, and the point of the hock is comparable to the human heel. The hock has the same function as the knee joint on the foreleg but is located higher on the hind leg.

The hock joint is probably the most complex and hardest worked joint in the body; it must be strong and sturdy. Located between the tibia above and the cannon bone below, the hock is composed of seven bones arranged in rows. When the hock flexes, it brings the horse's hind foot forward. The strain of propelling the body falls primarily to the hocks, and because the hocks flex when weight is put on them, they also dissipate the concussion.

Good hocks give a horse agility, speed, and jumping ability without breakdown. The maneuverability of the body and the horse's ability to lift his feet off the ground with agility and power depend on the strength, position, and soundness of the hocks.

When the hock is well formed, hard use causes few problems in most horses. Poorly formed hocks give rise to a number of problems such as *spavin*, or hock disease, which can lead to lameness and unsoundness. The hocks must be strong enough to withstand a great deal of stress from galloping, jumping, and rearing on his hind legs.

Size and Construction

Because the hock is such an important joint and carries so much weight, it must be large and properly angled. Large, well-formed hocks are always preferable to small, pinched-up hocks. The larger a joint, the greater the surface area for absorbing concussion and for motion and buffering action between the bones. A wider joint surface undergoes less friction and strain than a narrow one. Small joints are limited in mechanical advantage for propelling the horse and are more likely to develop problems from concussion.

A horse with properly angled hocks, at proper height, has a well-balanced hind leg. The lower leg and upper leg are the same length. The way to measure this is to look at the distance from the point of the hock to the ground and compare it with the distance from the point of the hock to the front of the stifle (at the top of the tibia). If this is difficult to eyeball, use a piece of string to measure from the upper edge of the patella to the point of the hock, and from the point of the hock to the ground. These two measurements should be the same and are usually about the same as the length of the horse's head. This gives the hind leg the best leverage and strength.

Viewed from behind, the point of the hock should be directly under the point of the buttocks but with a slightly inward orientation; see page 157. Viewed from the side, the hock joint should be set in a straight line that continues down the back of the leg to the fetlock joint. The cannon bone should be set directly in the center of the hock. The hock should be in perfect alignment with the rest of the leg, so all the joints of the hind leg can move forward in straight lines.

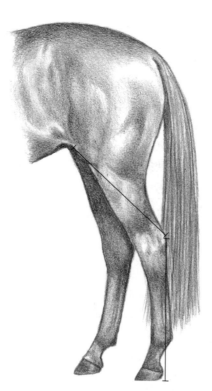

▶ Length of tibia and height of hock. The distance from the front of the stifle to the point of the hock should be the same as from the point of the hock to the ground.

When viewed from the side, the hock should be wide from front to back, and set onto a sturdy cannon (with no "tying in" or narrowing below the joint). The hock should be as large as the gaskin. The hock must be firm and well defined, but not fleshy. The bones should stand out clearly. The hock should be flat on the inner side and only slightly rounded on the outer side. The point of the hock should be fairly square and well defined. The bone forming its point should be long to give adequate leverage power and plenty of room for the gaskin muscles above it.

The front of the hock should be somewhat flat. The bend of the hock should be full and clean-cut, with plenty of width from side to side. A well-chiseled, square, and rugged hock provides better housing for its associated tendons, without inhibiting their movement or creating too much friction between the bones of the leg and moving parts. The hock should not look round; the bones should stand out prominently.

When looking at a horse's hocks, make sure they are identical in size and shape. Occasionally, you will find a horse with odd hocks — one being a different size and shape than the other, possibly due to an old injury. Any obvious abnormality should be avoided when selecting a horse.

Avoid a horse with small, narrow hocks or overly large, clumsy, or rounded hocks. A horse with hocks so large that they look out of proportion to the rest of his body is apt to be clumsy. Too-large hocks are rare, but sometimes you see this, usually in a hunter or jumper or some other horse of mixed breeding that harks back to a heavier ancestor in some of his bone structure. A hock too large can throw the hind leg out of balance, limit the flexion of the hind leg joints (for all joints in the leg are synchronized), and produce a slower, clumsier gait.

Conformation Close-up

A horse is said to be "cut out under the hocks" when the front of the cannon bone just below the hock seems small compared to the size of the hock when viewed from the side. This is similar to "tied in behind the knee" in the front legs. Strength and stability of the hock is reduced with this structure, with less support for twisting motions and more potential for injury to the small hock bones.

Height

The point of the hock should be level with the top of the chestnut on the front leg, which is located a few inches above the knee. This makes the hind cannon a little longer than the front cannon, giving

Did You Know?

A horse with a too-low hock cannot move his hind foot forward as efficiently and has a shorter stride. This reduces his ability to travel with maximum leverage and power. He has less thrust from the hind leg and therefore less speed.

good leverage for greater range of motion and thus more speed. The proper height of hock will depend, therefore, on the overall height and balance of the horse, and whether his front legs have long cannons (high knees) or short cannons.

Because best strength and leverage power of the leg come from a longer forearm (in front) and shorter cannons, the most athletic horses are usually those with fairly low knees and higher hocks that are level with the top of the chestnut. If the hock is in a position other than this, the hind leg is at an improper angle and will have less strength and agility.

If the hock is set lower than the level of the front chestnut, the hind cannon bone will be too short and the tibia will be too long. This puts the hock too far behind the horse's body and gives the impression that he is squatting slightly on his hind legs.

Horses with long tibias and short hind cannons are usually sickle hocked, with the hind feet positioned either too far forward under the body or "out in the country," with the whole leg too far back, both of which strain the hock. The hind legs may also be cow hocked. If the hock is angled too much, this strains the fetlock joint and pastern.

The other extreme is when the hock is higher than the level of the front chestnut, due to a very long hind cannon bone and a short tibia. In this case, the hock is too close under the body instead of directly under the point of the buttocks. Thus, the leg is too far forward, more in line with the stifle than the buttocks. This often makes the hocks and hind legs too straight (post-legged). If the leg is extremely straight, with little bend at the hock joint, there may be a "chicken knuckle" protrusion at the front of the hock joint. In some of these horses, the pastern may be weak. In older horses, the fetlock joints often become arthritic and enlarged.

Due to the longer cannon bone, a horse with a too-straight hind leg may hit his front feet and legs with the toes of his hind feet; his hind feet come too far forward when he is traveling fast. The too-straight hock also undergoes more strain, stress, and concussion than a properly angled hock.

A horse with high hocks may have a croup that is higher than the withers, giving a rider the constant feeling of going downhill. The horse may have trouble getting his hocks underneath himself for good agility and collection. Because the legs are unequal, the hind legs may not move in perfect synchronization with the fronts. Excessive hock action may cause the horse to take high steps behind, or he may strike the back of the front feet or legs with the hind feet.

The Hock Bones

The hock has one free-moving hinge joint between it and the tibia above. Like the human ankle, the hock is made up of seven small bones. Most of these small bones are somewhat flat or square and packed into a rather solid block between the cannon below and the hock's hinge with the tibia. There is only slight movement in the lower block of small bones, but there is just enough to provide shock absorption when the hind foot lands or when force is suddenly transmitted through the bones of the hind leg when the horse pushes off for a jump.

CANNON AND FETLOCK JOINT

The conformation of the lower hind leg is similar to that of the lower front leg. The hind cannon is usually longer and wider than that of the front, however; the hind fetlock is also a little sturdier.

Like the front leg, the hind cannon has two smaller splint bones at the back, on either side; these are slightly longer than the splint bones of the front leg. These three bones in the hind leg are called the *metatarsals*. To adequately support the hindquarters and the longer

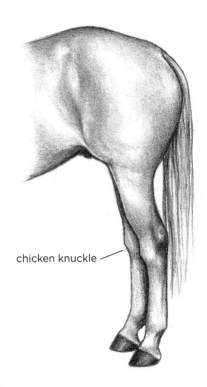

chicken knuckle

▲ A post-legged horse with hock too straight often has a protrusion ("chicken knuckle") at the front of the hock joint.

The Role of the Hock

The hock is the key to the structure of the hind leg. A strong and well-formed hock, placed properly with correct angulation, will make the whole leg stronger, more efficient in movement, and less apt to suffer soundness problems.

and wider cannon, the hind fetlock joint must be strong. As in the foreleg, the back tendons should be parallel to the cannon bone, set back from the bone, and perfectly straight.

HIND PASTERN

For greater strength, the hind pastern should be a little shorter and more upright than the front pastern. The hind pastern plays only a minor role in shock absorption. It must be more upright and solid, with a slightly steeper angle than the front pastern or it may break down, yielding before the strain is taken up by the hock joint.

Length and Angle

The angle of the hind pastern is usually about 49 to 56 degrees and sometimes even steeper. Some horses, however, have similar angles in the front and back pasterns. Excessive length and slope of the hind pastern may not adversely affect a horse unless he is used in a strenuous career. If hind pasterns are too long and sloped, they usually do not hold up over time, breaking down and allowing the fetlock joint to descend to the ground. Most horses with this conformation eventually break down in old age (see chapter 11.)

Evaluating Hind Leg Conformation

The hind legs provide the power and drive for pushing the horse forward and must be straight and balanced to distribute the stress and concussion equally. Proper hind leg angle is critical for speed, agility, and leg soundness. The hind legs should be carefully evaluated from the rear and from the side.

REAR VIEW

Viewed from the rear as the horse stands squarely, each hind leg should be balanced and straight from buttock to hoof. When evaluating a horse, make sure the horse is square on all four legs, bearing an equal amount of weight on each leg, and not stretched or standing with one hind foot ahead of the other. All the joints should be set in a straight line. Hocks and fetlock joints are easiest to see, but remember that the hind leg starts at the pelvis and croup, where the leg attaches to the backbone. The angle and set of the hocks and lower legs is determined by the structure of the pelvis, hips, and stifle joints above them.

Looking first at the top part of the hindquarters, make sure the points of the croup, hips, and stifles are symmetrical on both sides, with no unevenness or protrusions. Take note of whether the horse's tail is set straight and centered, hanging down freely between the buttocks. If the tail is crooked or the quarters seem off to one side, stand above the horse to see if his backbone is truly straight. The horse's hindquarters must be in perfect alignment with his backbone for his hind legs to be symmetrical and work properly.

A line dropped from the point of the buttock (or drawn with a straight-edge on a photo) should bisect the leg, passing through the center of the hock, cannon, fetlock joint, and pastern. A straight leg allows weight and stress to be distributed equally throughout the leg, with no one area suffering extra strain.

An Acceptable Exception

In an athletic horse, the cannon bones should be vertical and parallel. It is also acceptable to have vertical cannons with the hocks turned in and the feet toed out slightly. A line dropped from the buttocks should still bisect the leg perfectly when viewed from the rear.

An athletic horse needs good width of hindquarter between his stifles, which means the stifles point outward slightly. You usually cannot see the horse's belly from a rear view because it is blocked by wide stifles and good muscling above and behind the stifles. When hind feet point outward to the same degree as the stifles, the leg is strong and balanced.

When the hind feet face perfectly forward, there is extra stress on the outer edge of the foot and leg, which leads to lameness problems if the horse is worked hard. A perfectly straight hind leg, with hocks parallel rather than slightly turned in, tends to wobble toward the outside when taking weight. This situation is made worse if the hocks are wide or if the feet toe inward. A strong hock turned slightly inward offers the best support for the hind leg. The hind leg should thus be angled slightly outward at stifles and toes.

Stand directly behind one of the hind legs and envision a line going forward through the stifle joint but angled slightly to miss the horse's belly and shoulders. Then envision this line as a two-dimensional plane that bisects the entire leg, from buttock to fetlock joint and hoof. All the joints of the hind leg should be in that same plane (stifles out, hocks in, toes out).

The wider the horse's rib cage and the shorter his loin (being well ribbed up), the more angled the planes of the legs will be. The stifle must have an adequate angle to move past the wide barrel when the hind leg moves forward. The more narrow and slab-sided the horse, the less angled the stifles need to be and the more nearly parallel the two planes will be.

Did You Know?

In nature, most hoofed animals are cow hocked, that is, the hocks are closer together than are the stifle or feet, which is a much stronger construction than bow-legged hocks. All wild members of the horse family are a little closer at the hocks than they are at the feet.

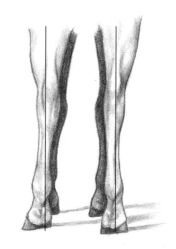

⬤ This is an acceptable exception: the hocks are turned in slightly, the toes are turned out slightly, yet a straight line still bisects the leg.

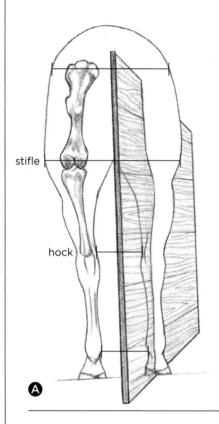
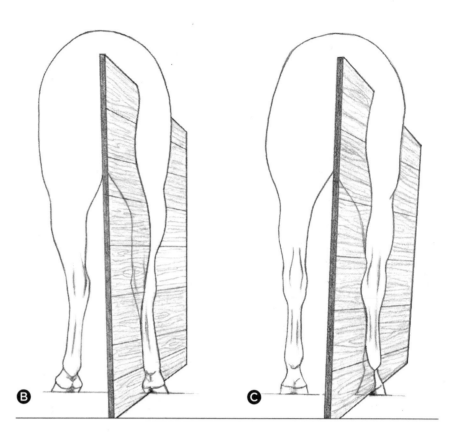

stifle

hock

Ⓐ

Ⓑ

Ⓒ

⬙ **A.** Normal hind leg. The stifle joint is angled slightly outward and the hock is angled slightly inward. A two-dimensional plane angled slightly inward toward the rear of the horse should bisect the thigh, gaskin, hock, cannon, and toe of the foot (and between the two bulbs of the heel). Two such planes will converge behind the horse; they are not parallel. **B.** Cow hocked: the hock is inside the plane instead of being bisected by it. The fetlock joint and hoof are outside it. **C.** Bowlegged: the hock is outside the plane; most or all of the hoof is inside it.

A line dropped from the point of the buttocks of any well-constructed horse will bisect the hock, cannon, fetlock joint, pastern and hoof, but if you look closely at the hind legs you'll notice that the leg does not face directly front. The femur angles outward slightly from the hip socket to the stifle to create wide-apart stifles, then the gaskins angle inward slightly from stifle to hock, and the hocks are angled inward slightly to the same degree that the stifles are angled outward.

From the hocks, the cannon bones go straight down to the fetlock joints and pasterns, and the feet are angled slightly outward to the same degree as the stifles. The pasterns and hooves are still "straight" when viewed from behind and not slanting off to one side or the other, but in front they face slightly outward rather than straight ahead and the feet break over slightly to the inside.

SIDE VIEW

When viewed from the side, the cannon bone should be vertical and directly under the buttocks. The back of the hock and the back of the cannon should be straight and perpendicular to the ground when the horse is standing squarely.

If a line is dropped from the point of the buttock, it should touch the point of the hock and follow the back of the cannon down to the back of the fetlock joint, hitting the ground a very short distance behind the heel of the foot. This is the ideal degree of angulation in the hock joint. If the hock joint is too straight (set too far underneath the buttocks toward the body of the horse) or too angled (hock and cannon not perpendicular to the ground, with hind feet too far under the horse's body and the cannon bone angled), there can be serious problems.

An occasional exception to this conformation rule — straight line from buttock to hock and down the back of the cannon — is seen in horses with exceptionally long quarters and a more protruding

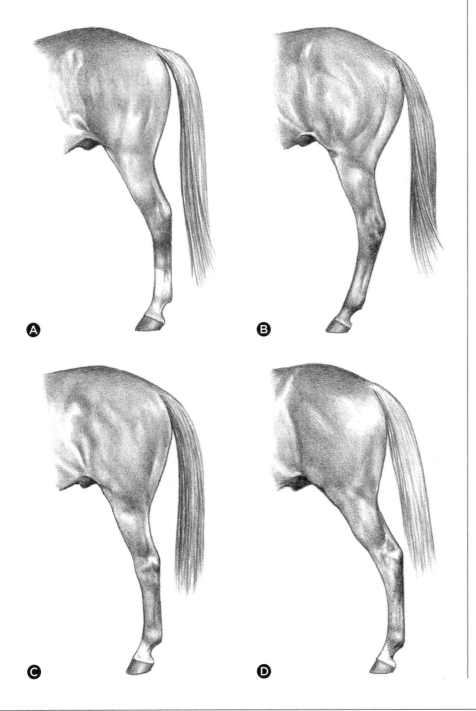

A

B

C

D

◀ The angle of the hock joint is the key to structural strength and durability (soundness) of the hind leg. Strongest construction is when the point of the hock is directly under the point of the buttocks. A line dropped from buttock to ground follows the back of the cannon. If the hock joint is not directly under the buttocks when the horse is standing squarely, the construction is weak. **A.** Proper hock angle. **B.** Sickle hocks (bent hocks). **C.** Post-legged (not enough bend at the hocks). **D.** Out in the country.

buttock than average. The hock angulation may be normal, but the line dropped from the buttock could miss the leg slightly because of the long buttock. The opposite sometimes occurs, if a horse has a too-short rump; a line dropped from the buttock goes in front of the back line of hock and cannon, even though the hock angulation is correct. A very sloped rump might also give this result.

Faults

Abnormal hock angulation and position are a detriment to athletic ability. Faulty hock conformation almost always leads to injury if the horse is used hard.

SICKLE HOCKS

A sickle-hocked horse has too much bend at the hock joints with a sloped rather than vertical cannon bone (any angle of less than 150 degrees between the upper leg bone and the cannon bone); there is greater stress and strain on the joint. This hind leg structure makes a horse more likely to develop *curb* (enlargement of the tendon at the back of the hock), *bone spavin* at the lower hock joints (enlargement on one or more of the hock bones), and *bog spavin* (permanent swelling in the soft tissues of the hock). A horse that is extremely sickle hocked may also damage the bottom or back of his hind fetlock joints when running hard.

If a horse is sickle hocked, a line extended up the cannon bone is at such an angle that it completely misses the buttocks. The horse's feet are too far underneath his body. They are not directly under his hocks and buttocks as they should be. This conformation is sometimes called "camped under" or "standing under" because the feet are too far forward under the body.

Sickle-hocked conformation is detrimental to speed and also makes the horse more susceptible to leg problems and lameness. In order to have strong thrusting power and speed, the hind leg must act as a perfect pendulum; the hocks must be able to straighten quickly as the hindquarters propel the horse forward. Maximum straightening and backward extension of the leg is hindered by sickle hock, making the push-off weaker. Straighter hocks and stifles are better than excessively bent ones for producing speed.

A straight hock (rather than curved and "sickled") has much more closing and opening leverage in its hinge joint, enabling the leg to reach farther forward and give more backward thrust, for greater stride and power. The sickle hock has more binding between the tibia (above the hock) and the top of the cannon, which puts stress on the small moveable bones of the joint. Activities that put a lot of strain on the hocks with quick starts, stops, and turns or bursts of speed can lead to spavin, *thoroughpin* (soft, puffy swelling on the upper part of the hock), and curb in a horse with sickle hocks.

When there is too much bend in the stifle joint and hock joint, motion is less efficient. There is considerable loss of time and energy spent straightening the joints at each stride. There is more circular motion before the hock can get into position to drive the horse's body forward. A leg with proper hock and stifle angulation swings farther and faster, beginning its forward motion from the point of the toe and driving the body forward from a straight line with no loss of motion between the ground and the top of the hock.

OUT IN THE COUNTRY

Some horses have hind legs that are "out in the country," to use old-timer's terminology. This is also called "camped out behind." The phrase describes a vertical cannon that is too far back behind the horse. The gaskin area (tibia) is too long, putting the hock too far back. This conformation is not as weak as sickle hocks, but it is still undesirable in an athlete.

A hind leg of this type cannot produce as much speed or agility as a properly built leg. The leg may have too much swing before the foot hits the ground, creating a lot of wasted motion. This can lead to early fatigue on a long ride or create extra movement when the foot lands, adding stress to the joints and hoof wall. If this type of construction is pronounced, the horse may have difficulty collecting himself; he can't get his hind legs underneath himself very well. A horse with this construction may also have rear pasterns that are too upright.

POST-LEGGED

Hocks that are too straight with too little bend put the entire hind leg too far forward rather than directly under the buttocks. A horse is considered *post-legged* (hocks too straight) if the joint angle between the upper leg bone and the cannon bone is more than 170 degrees. The leg appears as straight as a fence post. When viewed from the side, a line dropped from the buttock falls in back of the cannon on a hind leg that is too straight; the hock is set forward almost under the stifle. The tibia (above the hock) is almost vertical, rather than having a normal 60-degree slope.

Upward Fixation of the Patella

The normal horse rests one hind leg by locking the stifle — the patella is hooked over the bulge at the end of the femur. This enables him to rest a leg without any muscular effort to keep it steady. He can lock and unlock the stifle to stand with a hind leg cocked.

In a horse with too-straight stifles, the patella may inadvertently catch and hook any time the joint is extended — when he is walking, trotting, or galloping. In a horse with proper hind leg conformation, the stifle angle is about 135 degrees. When the joint is extended to about 145 degrees, the patella hooks on the femur. If the post-legged horse has a stifle angle of about 140 degrees to begin with, it doesn't take much of a misstep to move it a few more degrees and hook the patella, which is a serious problem if it happens while he is traveling (see page 314).

Post-legged structure can cause locked stifles. Because the stifle joint is also too straight, the patella sometimes slips out of position and locks the leg in backward extension, creating a condition called *upward fixation of the patella*, or *locked stifles*, in which the patella slips and locks the joint so it cannot flex. When this happens, the stifle and hock cannot bend, and the leg remains extended behind the horse. The joint may just catch temporarily or it may remain locked.

Young horses with straight stifles may suffer from this problem at certain phases of their development; the slackness of the patella allows the bone to slide in and out of its proper position. In some of these horses, the problem disappears as the bones grow and the horse matures. In other cases, the patella slips out suddenly and remains dislocated. A veterinarian can carefully manipulate the leg and move it into proper position to release the patella.

If the problem recurs or becomes chronic, it may cause inflammation and degenerative arthritis in the stifle joint. Surgery to sever the medial patellar ligament offers a permanent solution, but the joint will never be as strong. A horse with hind leg joints that are too straight often has short, too-straight pasterns, as well.

Spavin

The post-legged horse with too-straight hocks may develop bone spavin, a bony enlargement of the hock due to arthritis, and bog spavin, because of extra strain on the front of the hock joint capsule. There is constant tension on the small joints within the hock, which irritates the joint capsule and joint cartilage. Excessive hard work and concussion contribute to these hock problems. Spavin can occur not only in horses that are continually trotted on hard surfaces, but also in cutting horses, polo horses, roping horses, reining horses, hunters, and jumpers — any horse that uses the hindquarters strongly or does a lot of stopping and turning. The excessive concussion and strain from overuse of this joint — particularly if the hock is not large, strong, or well formed — disrupts the bone lining, causes erosion of joint surfaces, and sets up inflammation that leads to new bone growth and bony enlargement of the hock. Not all cases of spavin produce visible swelling or lumps, but when there is active inflammation in the hock, all cause lameness in the early stages.

The bone fusion is essentially a healing process; once the bones are solidly fused, with no movement possible between them, the inflammation subsides and there is no more pain or lameness. Many such horses, after being lame for a year or more with spavin, eventually become sound enough to work again, even if hock flexion is considerably less. The small bones may fuse to one another, to the head of the cannon bone below them, or to the inner splint bone next to the cannon.

If seriously overworked, virtually any hock may develop spavin, but poor conformation greatly increases the likelihood of problems. Spavin was common in heavy horses that traveled on hard roads, but today it is also common in horses with poor hind leg conformation. Spavin is often seen in horses with narrow, upright hind feet and short, straight hind pasterns; they usually have straight hocks and stifles, as well. This conformation creates more concussion. Spavin is also common in horses that do not travel straight; the hind legs swing in or out instead of moving forward in straight lines. Any twisting action at the hock joint adds more concussion and stress to the hock bones.

A hock with too much angle (sickle hocks) undergoes too much strain on bones and joints. The front of the hock is in a cramped, unnatural position; hard use can injure the small bones. The excessive angle also puts more strain on the Achilles tendon at the back of the hock and may produce a *curb*. A hock with not enough angle (post-legged) suffers excessive concussion, which damages the bones and joint capsules and can also lead to spavin. Inflammation within the hock joint from too much strain and stress can interfere with movement of the joint and tendons.

The chronic swelling of bog spavin is caused by too much lubricating fluid in the capsule, a result of pulling and irritating the capsule, which causes the lining to produce excess fluid. The restriction of the tendon sheath (due to improper angle) when the hind leg is moving can also lead to development of thoroughpin. The too-straight leg is easily injured by hard use because of this extra strain on the flexor tendon and its sheath and on the upper part of the suspensory ligament.

⚲ *Conformation Close-up*

A post-legged horse may suffer more concussion on the hind feet because of the way the straight leg causes the feet to stab directly into the ground at each stride, with little flexion. This can lead to cracked hooves, sole bruising, and other concussion-related problems within the foot.

Length of Leg

The post-legged horse actually has a shorter hind leg (in total bone length) than the horse with sickle hocks, even if the two horses are the same height at the croup. This is because a straight line is the shortest distance between two points. If the lines between all the hind leg joints (from croup to buttock to stifle to hock to fetlock) are relatively straight up and down, the horse has shorter hind leg bones than the sickle-hocked horse that has more slope to all of these lines, making his leg a zigzag. The horse with long hind legs is more apt to be sickle hocked and over angulated or "out in the country" (see page 161); the leg bones are too long to be in the proper position.

This is why the horse with a straighter leg has more speed; it takes less time to swing the leg back and forth without having to straighten out all those zigzag angles. The shorter and straighter the hind leg, the more effectively it can deliver power and thrust. This type of hind leg is best for straight-ahead speed and direct thrust. The best jumpers and sprinters often have relatively straight hind legs, but if carried to the extreme (post-legged) they tend to have problems with locked stifles and injured hocks due to the additional stresses on the hock joints.

Horses with more curve to the hind leg have more angled joints with the feet more underneath the horse and hence, longer leg bones and more length of leg relative to the height of the croup. These horses tend to do better at activities that require a lot of flexing. Many of the horses that are easy to "collect," bringing their hind legs farther underneath themselves for more upward impulsion or for precision work and agility, have angled legs.

Horses that excel in dressage or smooth riding gaits, or reining, cow cutting, polo, or any other sport in which they must work off their hocks, are not post-legged; some tend to be slightly sickle hocked.

Taken to extreme, however, sickle-hocked construction makes a weak leg, with more stress on joints, and much more risk for hock injury and spavin. If the legs are too "bent" at the hocks it actually becomes more difficult for the horse to collect and work off the hocks.

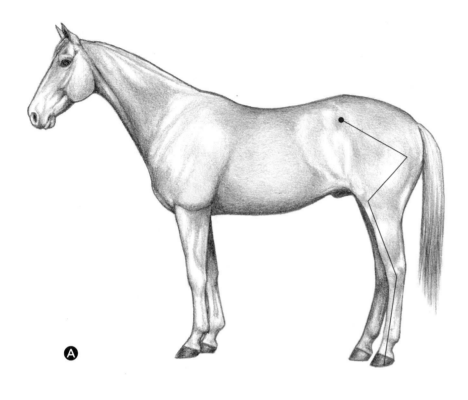

◀ Length of the hind leg bones. **A.** Even though he is croup high, this post-legged horse has shorter hind legs because of his shorter leg bones. **B.** The sickle-hocked horse has longer legs because of the longer leg bones.

A

B

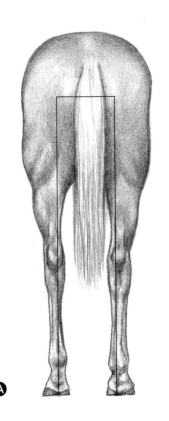
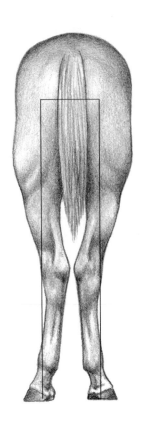

▶ Rear view of hind legs. **A.** Good hind legs (slightly turned in hocks and turned out feet, with cannons vertical). **B.** Cow hocked (nonvertical cannons) with toes turned out (splay footed). **C.** Bow legs (hocks turned out and feet turned in). **D.** Wide behind (feet wider apart than the stifles). **E.** Close behind (hocks, fetlock joints, and feet too close together).

Ⓐ   Ⓑ

⦶ *Conformation Close-up*

A horse with too much zigzag bend in hind legs (which adds up to longer length of leg bones) may not travel level, even if he is the same height at withers and croup when standing still. When moving, he may be croup-high at each stride, because the extra length of hind leg (as it straightens out) pushes the croup higher. This can produce a rough and uncomfortable ride. Ideally, the croup should be no higher than the withers as the horse travels; the hind leg joints will bend and flex smoothly in a horse with proper leg angles, with no abnormal upward thrust of the croup.

BASE WIDE

Base-wide conformation occurs when the hind feet are too far apart (farther apart than the legs at the thighs). The most common type of base-wide conformation in the hind legs is cow hocks. The hocks are too close together and the feet too wide apart. The hocks may point toward one another and the cannon bones are closer together at the top than at the fetlock joints. The feet may be fairly straight or they might be widely separated and pointing outward. Extreme cow-hocked conformation puts strain on the side of the hock joints and can cause bone spavin.

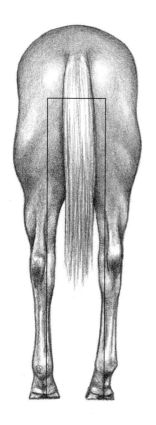

C

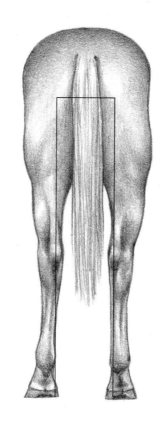

D

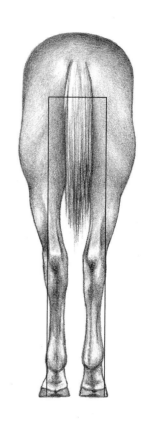

E

The normal horse has stifles pointing slightly outward and hocks pointing slightly inward; toes also point slightly outward. In a cow-hocked horse, there is usually not much width of hindquarters between the stifles (they may seem sunken in or clamped to the body, and may be facing straight forward instead of angled slightly out), and the hocks are obviously too close and pointing toward one another. The cannon bones slant outward as they go down from the hocks to the fetlock joints, with feet widely separated. The toes point outward more than the stifles do; the hindquarters are generally narrow. The slant of the stifles and toes does not match.

Viewed from the side, you might discover that the cow-hocked horse is also sickle hocked. Spavin is usually common in horses that do not travel straight behind, due to a twisting action of the hock joint. This deviation also affects the lower leg, putting more strain and twist on the cannon and pastern, and putting the fetlock joint at greater risk for stress injury. The inner foot must carry more weight, which can lead to uneven wear, cracks, and bruising.

The cow-hocked, splay-footed horse may throw his legs outward (at some gaits more than others), but many horses with this type of leg structure tend to interfere when traveling, striking each foot against the opposite leg, generally hitting the fetlock joint. This is because when the toed-out foot is picked up, the fetlock joint folds crookedly instead of straight, bending the foot to the inside. The inward swing of the foot is usually accentuated when the horse is wearing shoes, due to the added weight on the foot. If the horse is ridden very often, the fetlock joints may be seriously injured by constant hits with the opposite shoe.

In some cow-hocked horses, the hocks wobble inward so much that they actually brush one another as the horse moves. The extremely cow-hocked horse usually has a weak, wobbly movement in the hind legs. Even if the cow-hocked condition is not too extreme, the horse may have problems when running very fast. The hind legs must go forward as the horse picks up the front legs and the hind feet move up alongside them. A horse with hocks too close together may whack his hocks with his front feet. A horse that is cow-hocked may get by without injury while doing slow work, but this kind of conformation can be very detrimental to a racehorse.

In some horses the hocks are too close together but the cannon bones and feet are vertical from there down, rather than splayed out. This type of construction is not as bad, and the horse may not have interference problems. Some horses that stand close behind, however, will interfere, especially at the end of a long ride or race when they become tired.

A normal hock points very slightly inward rather than straight ahead, just because the stifles must point slightly outward in order to swing forward past the abdomen. If fetlock joints are in proper alignment under the hocks, this construction is not viewed as being cow hocked. In a cow-hocked horse the fetlock joints are farther apart than the hocks, making the cannon bones angled outward rather than straight. Because of the angled leg, the horse usually carries more of his weight on the inside portions of his hind feet rather than bearing weight squarely on the whole hoof.

BASE NARROW

When viewed from behind, the base-narrow horse has hind feet too close together. The distance between the center of the feet is less than the distance between the center lines of the legs at the hocks and thighs. Bowlegged horses (with hocks too wide apart) are often base narrow at the fetlock joints or feet.

A base-narrow, bowlegged structure is most common in heavily muscled horses; the hindquarters are wide and bulky (stifles too far apart). The leg bones are quite far apart at the top and at the hocks, but come closer together toward the ground. There is excessive strain on the outside portions of the leg (more stress on the bones, ligaments, and joints). The hocks are often wide apart (and pointing straight back or slightly out rather than slightly inward, as they should) and the cannon bones slant inward to the feet. The toes generally point straight forward or may even point inward. Weight is carried more on the outside edges of the hooves.

Bowlegged hock construction puts great strain on the hock and fetlock joints. The hocks may develop bone spavin, bog spavin, or thoroughpin. The horse with this type of hock structure tends to swivel the hocks outward at each stride, and this puts a twist on the hoof each time it takes weight. When watching the horse walk or trot (from behind), you can see the foot is placed on the ground and twisted as the hock pushes outward to take the weight of the body and is finally straightened again as it pushes off. The twisting motion of the hocks prevents the foot from coming to the ground squarely and the turning action puts more stress on the outside of the hoof wall. This can lead to cracks and bruises, or even ringbone, due to stress on the pastern or coffin joints.

The feet may be facing forward or pigeon-toed. Bowlegged horses are often toed in. In some horses, the legs may be fairly straight down to the hocks, but become base narrow from there on down. Bowlegged and base-narrow structure is weak conformation, and this type of horse may experience limb interference at fast gaits. The hocks roll outward and the feet come too close together as the horse travels. The hind leg does not have much forward reach and has a lot of wasted motion caused by the twisting of the hock as the foot is lifted from the ground. This reduces the hind leg's efficiency for speed. The horse won't be a good athlete because he cannot make efficient use of his muscle power for traveling forward or stopping quickly.

Foot Conformation

FEET ARE CRUCIAL to athletic ability and soundness and require close scrutiny in a horse's evaluation. A horse may have a pleasing overall appearance, beautiful head, good muscling, and willingness to work, but if a foot or leg breaks down he won't be able to achieve his full potential.

Feet must be well built and of adequate size to support the weight of horse and rider; they also must be able to hold up under the stresses of athletic activity and concussion. When the foot is flat on the ground, we see

A horse's feet are amazingly strong for their size, supporting the weight of the horse at fast gaits and when landing from jumps. The parts of a well-conformed hoof work together to minimize and dissipate concussion.

the outer hoof wall, but when lifted we can see the frog, sole, and bars. The frog is a V-shaped cushion of soft, horny material located in the center of the sole, the softest part of the hoof; the bars are the horny wedges that turn in from the heel. These external structures can give insight into the shape and health of the internal parts of the foot. Health of the hoof can also be a clue to the overall health and soundness of the horse. Genetics, nutrition, and environment all play a role in hoof structure and soundness.

Anatomy of the Foot

It is amazing that a structure as small as the foot can support a horse and withstand the impact of his weight when he is traveling swiftly. The normal, healthy hoof is constructed in such a way that its various parts work together to minimize concussion. The material of the hoof wall is similar to the human fingernail, but it is much stronger, with elaborate mechanisms to counteract impact and force.

BONES OF THE FOOT

The short pastern bone in the leg joins the coffin bone within the foot just below the level of the coronary band; half the short pastern bone is within the hoof. The navicular bone lies behind the coffin bone and below the short pastern bone.

▼ Bones of the foot: side view.

cannon bone
extensor tendon
long pastern bone
short pastern bone
coffin bone
deep flexor tendon
superficial flexor tendon
sesamoid bone
sesamoid ligament
navicular bone
plantar cushion

The coffin bone is shaped like a small hoof with "wings" to the sides. Attached to those small wings are the thick cartilage cushions that can be seen and felt protruding above the coronary band. This cartilage can become calcified if injured, creating a sidebone (see page 332). The coffin joint inside the foot has more movement and elasticity than the pastern joint, because of the way the navicular bone is placed behind it, combined with the navicular bone's pulley action with the flexor tendon. The extensor tendons attach to the front of the coffin bone, the flexor tendons attach to the back of the coffin bone, and strong ligaments bind the coffin bone at its joint with the short pastern bone. The fibrous cartilages on each side are closely united with the coffin bone and help keep it in place; when weight is placed on the foot, all of these structures keep the coffin bone from descending too low or tipping too much.

The wedge-shaped navicular bone is supported by the deep flexor tendon behind it and below it, and serves as a pulley-like leverage point for the deep digital flexor tendon that is attached to the back of the coffin bone. A fluid-filled bursa protects the navicular bone from the strain and friction of the moving tendon. If the bursa is injured, disrupting this protection, the horse goes lame with signs of navicular syndrome (see page 330).

HOOF WALL AND OUTER COVERINGS

The hoof wall is a specialized horny shell that protects the bones, nerves, blood vessels, and tendons inside the hoof. This wall grows down from the corium of the coronary band at the hairline. The constant growth of the hoof wall compensates for normal wear and broken edges, replacing them with new horny tissue.

Conformation Close-up

The hoof wall should be fairly thick, pliable, and resistant to dryness, not dry and brittle. The wall is thickest at the toe and thinner at the heels to allow for flexibility and expansion at heel and quarters when the foot bears weight. The toe should be nicely rounded and the heels should be broad, not narrow.

Just below the coronet at the hairline is the *periople*, a narrow strip that functions like the cuticle on a human fingernail. It protects the juncture between the skin and the hoof horn and produces a tectorial layer, a waxy, varnish-like substance that seals the outer surface of the hoof wall to prevent excess drying. When the ground is soft and wet, the hoof becomes softer. As the ground dries and becomes hard, the hoof toughens and dries, to prevent rapid wearing.

The hoof wall is made up of tiny, hollow tubules bundled tightly together, which run from coronet to the ground. These tubules are the outer layer of the hoof wall. They carry and hold moisture within the hoof wall, which is about 25 percent water, but have no nerve endings or blood supply. Because the structure of the foot determines the direction and spacing of these tubules, conformation of the foot is vital for proper hoof health and moisture retention. If the tubules become too spread apart by an imbalanced foot, the hoof wall may lose moisture and dry out. On the inside of the hoof, the innermost

No Foot, No Horse

"No foot, no horse" is a horseman's adage and a fact that has been acknowledged for a very long time. Xenophon, a Greek general who wrote detailed cavalry manuals about horse care, training, and conformation in 400 BC, mentioned the importance of feet. He wrote: "For just as a house would be useless, even if the upper parts were in excellent condition, if the foundations were not properly laid, so too would a war horse, even if his other parts were good" (quoted in Gladys Brown Edwards, *Anatomy and Conformation of the Horse* [Croton-on-Hudson, NY: Dreenan, 1980], 175). This truth was also recognized by the earlier Hittite civilization. Kikkul, the Master of Horse, wrote an essay on clay tablets instructing the horsemen of his day about hoof conformation, about 1400 BC.

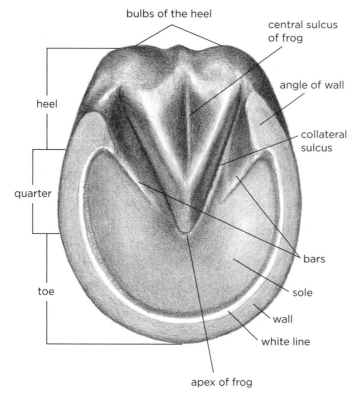

bulbs of the heel

central sulcus
of frog

angle of wall

heel

collateral
sulcus

quarter

bars

toe

sole

wall

white line

apex of frog

🔺 **Bottom of the foot**

tubules (the intertubular horn that merges with the fingers of the insensitive laminae) interface with the sensitive laminae that carry blood and have nerve endings. The sensitive laminae are produced by the laminar corium that covers the front of the coffin bone. The sole and frog corium line the underside of the coffin bone and frog and produce the horn of the sole and frog.

🔍 *Conformation Close-up*

The tough outer covering of the foot consists of the hoof wall, sole, frog, and bars. The outer wall should be hard and thick. When you look at the bottom of the foot, the hoof should be worn evenly, the sole should be somewhat concave, and the bars should be a visible inward continuation of the hoof wall. The bars enable the hoof to expand at quarters and heels when weight is placed on it and serve as a brace to keep the heels from contracting. The V-shaped frog helps absorb concussion in the middle of the sole and regulates hoof moisture.

INNER STRUCTURES

The surface of the coffin bone is covered by the sensitive laminae, tiny "leaves" of soft, velvety, blood-filled tissue. These interlock with tiny plates of insensitive laminae inside the horny outer shell of the hoof wall. The thin, horny plates run parallel to each other and slant forward, as do the outer horny tubules that make up the wall, allowing for firm attachment between the two surfaces.

The *quick*, the sensitive inner sole, is above the horny outer sole. There also is a large cushion in the back of the foot, just above the frog. This fibrous wedge of cartilage, the plantar or digital cushion, helps the foot absorb and dissipate the shock of impact at the rear of the foot — at fast gaits the heel comes to the ground first. On either side of this cushion are cartilage structures, which can be felt easily above the coronary band toward the heel.

In a normal, healthy foot, all structures work together to help minimize concussion. When weight is placed on the foot, the coronet narrows and drops backward, the concave sole flattens, the hoof expands at the heels, and the overall height of the hoof decreases. The sideways expansion of heel and cartilage when weight is placed on the foot creates a sucking action. This pulls blood from beneath the coffin bone into tiny vessels in the side cartilage and distributes concussion impact like the gel-filled sole of an athletic shoe. The plumpness below moves to the side and up to the cartilage. This is the only truly elastic region within the hoof wall where expansion can take place.

WHITE LINE

The junction where sole and hoof wall meet is the white line. This is where the insensitive laminae from the bloodless, nerveless hoof wall meet and interlock with the sensitive laminae at the edge of the living tissues within the foot. The white line has some elasticity, creating a flexible link between the solid hoof wall and the softer sole. The white line is like a hinge that helps with the expansion and contraction of the quarters and heels of the foot, which spread when weight is placed on them.

The white line is actually yellowed at the sole edge and whiter toward the hoof wall; it is typically of uniform width and is very pronounced on a freshly trimmed foot. A relatively thick white line indicates hoof density and strength, whereas a thin line, especially if it has points of separation or tends to flake apart, may indicate structural weakness. A white line that is too wide, however, may be a sign of separation that allows dirt and pathogens to enter between hoof wall and sensitive inner tissues.

CORONARY BAND

The coronary band, also called the coronet, just under the hairline at the top of the hoof, is the outer covering for the specialized area of horn-producing cells, from which the hoof wall grows.

At the top of the hoof wall, the coronary band should be perfectly symmetrical. The hairline around the hoof should be smooth and straight, not wavy or distorted. If, due to poor leg and hoof conformation, there is more impact on one side of the foot than the other, it will drive up the coronet in that area, resulting in an uneven hairline.

The coronary band should be well defined but still blend into the pastern with a nice smooth taper. If the pastern meets the hoof at an abrupt right angle due to a large hoof and a small pastern (the coronary band and hoof sticking out squarely with an almost flat surface in the area just above the coronary band), the horse is at greater risk for sidebones. Such a plateau of coronary band is more common in a draft horse than a riding horse. The foot is more prone to injury and bruising because the expanse of flat coronary band surface is more

The Hoof and Circulation

The horse's foot is his second heart. Hoof expansion and contraction with each stride not only dissipates concussion but helps push the blood back up the leg. In the rest of the body, muscle activity helps the circulatory system return blood to the heart, but the horse has no muscles in his lower legs. Each time the horse puts weight on the foot, the pressure helps force blood out of the foot and up the leg veins. When the foot is lifted, the release of pressure allows new blood to flow into the foot. In nature, the horse is almost always moving and this keeps his feet healthy. Lack of activity creates poor circulation and the horse may "stock up," developing swelling in the lower legs. Inactivity such as stall confinement is therefore very hard on feet and legs.

Did You Know?

When shoeing a horse, a farrier uses the white line to help him place the nails properly. Nails should always go into the outer, insensitive horny wall, not the sensitive inner tissues. If a nail is driven inside the white line, it punctures the inner tissues, causing pain, lameness, and possibly an infection.

Trim Hooves Regularly

For a shod horse, shoes should be reset or replaced every 3 to 10 weeks (6–8 weeks on average), depending on the rate of hoof growth. Some horses' hooves grow very fast, and the toes become too long just 3 or 4 weeks after shoeing, causing the horse to trip and stumble more readily. Others can go a couple months before they need to be reshod, unless the shoes wear out sooner. If shoes are left on too long without proper hoof trimming, the angle of the foot and pastern will change, placing added stress on the leg.

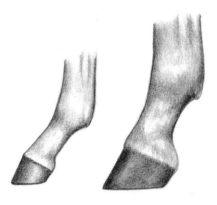

⬙ Foot of a foal compared with foot of a mature horse. A foal's foot is smaller at the ground surface than at the coronary band and his pastern is relatively long. A mature horse's foot is smaller around the coronary band than at the ground surface.

apt to be stepped on and injured. Avoid this type of foot conformation.

How the Hoof Grows

The hoof grows down evenly from the coronary band. Any injury to the coronary band can affect the growth of the hoof in that area. The hoof wall grows about ¼ to ⅜ inch per month, depending on the horse and on nutritional and environmental conditions. Generally, the entire hoof wall is replaced every 9 to 10 months, but some horses have a slower or faster rate of growth. Hooves tend to grow faster in summer and slower in winter. Because the heel is the part of the hoof wall with the least depth, it is the "youngest" part of the hoof horn. The horn at the toe is the oldest and thickest.

The hoof horn is thin at the quarters and thinner at the heels. The heel must absorb the shock of landing and be able to expand, and the thinner hoof wall in this area aids flexibility. It is also thin just below the coronary band all the way around the hoof, giving elasticity to the lateral and medial cartilage beneath it. The cartilage lies partially above the hoof and partially inside the hoof wall. The toe of the foot should be thick and strong to prevent excessive wear as the foot breaks over and pushes off with each stride, digging into the ground at fast gaits. The inner hoof wall — the side closest to the other foot — is usually slightly less sloped than the outer wall.

The hoof is smaller in circumference around the coronary band than at the ground, except in a young foal, whose pastern is also relatively long. In a mature horse, the hoof should angle out slightly as it nears the ground, but not too much or it will be weak and prone to break and crack. In such a case, the horse may also have a flat sole. If the wall angle is too steep, the foot will be small and contracted at the ground.

⊸◎ *Conformation Close-up*

A dished, concave appearance (rather than a straight surface) at the front of the foot may be due to lack of circulation in the toe area or to forces created when the toe is too long. Long toes increase the leverage force in the foot and may cause tearing of the laminae. A dished toe can also be the result of chronic laminitis.

Hoof Rings

The normal hoof wall is smooth, with no rings or ridges. An inflamed coronary band produces a thicker horn that results in a ridge. A nutritional deficiency or lack of circulation to the coronary band may produce thinner horn, which grows out as a groove or shallow area. A single ring at the same location on each hoof may be the aftereffect of an illness. Multiple ripples may be evidence of a mild case of laminitis, or inflammation of the laminae. Multiple rings that are farther apart at the heel than at the toe indicate uneven growth from chronic laminitis. *Founder* is the horseman's term for the aftereffect of chronic laminitis, in which the coffin bone has either rotated or dropped inside the hoof. A foundered horse has a steady progression of large rings and ridges down the hoof wall. Faint rings are normal due to changes in season or nutritional level. Rings may be caused by seasonal variations of hoof growth (warm weather and green grass make a hoof grow faster), dietary changes (as from dry feed to green pasture), or a fever that temporarily altered hoof growth.

A single lump on the hoof is usually the result of local trauma. It may weaken the wall and lead to cracking, or the defect may just move down the wall as the hoof grows until it wears away or can be trimmed away.

BARS AND SOLE

The hoof wall curves in at the heels, creating bars that run along each side of the frog for a short distance. The hoof wall bears most of the weight when the foot is on the ground, especially when the horse is shod, and the bars serve as braces to prevent overexpansion and contraction of the foot. They help take additional weight on the heels, and act as wedges to keep the heels from caving in and contracting. Each time the foot takes weight, the frog forces the bars apart and lifts the plantar cushion, creating pressure that causes the blood vessels within the foot to contract. The bars should be strong and well developed; a foot with good bars is a strong foot.

The sole is a hard plate of horny material that surrounds the frog; it should be firmly and smoothly attached to the wall. The sole should be almost round in the front foot and more oval in the hind foot, with a healthy frog, good strong bars, and well-defined *sulci*, or grooves, on each side of the frog.

Soles should be slightly concave in the front feet and even more concave in the hind feet. The only place the sole should come close to the ground is just behind the toe. A concave foot has more grip and traction at fast speeds and on variable footing. The concavity of the sole in the hind foot helps diminish the effects of concussion because there is some give to the sole. This is especially important in the hind leg, for it is attached to the backbone at the lumbosacral joint and is capable of only minimal shock absorption. Flat feet without proper

Did You Know?

The navicular bone in the flat-footed horse is more at risk for bruising and concussion trauma. Navicular syndrome occurs more readily in flat feet.

In unshod horses, the bottom of the hoof wall, the frog, and bars of the foot are all level and flat to the ground; each helps bear the weight of the horse. On soft surfaces, the sole also comes into contact with the ground and helps bear weight. Bars and frog seldom reach the ground in a shod horse, unless the ground is soft or the footing is uneven; shoeing puts the hoof about ¼ inch or more above the ground, hindering the ability of the frog and bars to accept some of the weight.

concavity are undesirable because the soles are more easily bruised by rocks, which may prompt an abscess to develop beneath the horn.

The sole should always be thick. It is thickest on the outer edges and thinner toward the frog, about ¼-inch. Thin walls and soles are two problems that often go together; the hoof either wears away too quickly or does not grow fast enough to counteract sole pressure.

Pieces of the old dead sole should flake off and shed periodically rather than build up and remain in the foot. The horny sole continually grows downward from the sensitive inner sole above it. Cracks develop in the old sole and help the outer layer of dead tissue flake away in a self-trimming process called *exfoliation*. A horse's sole usually needs no trimming when the foot is trimmed. Trimming the sole may take off too much protective covering, getting close to sensitive tissue.

Occasionally, dead material on the sole builds up, however, especially if the horse lives in wet conditions and the sole never has an opportunity to dry out. Excess sole material must be carefully peeled away to the proper level with a hoof knife. Otherwise, the hoof cannot be trimmed adequately, and the layer of dead sole may continue to build up, providing a place for bacteria to grow.

Conformation Close-up

If the sole is thin, the tissues it protects are more easily bruised. When the sole is checked with a hoof tester (a pincer-like instrument that puts pressure in a small area), a horse with a thin, easily compressed sole may flinch. Foot conformation may look normal, but the horse is prone to have tender feet, especially after being newly trimmed or shod. Because a horse with a thin sole frequently has a thin wall, the foot tends to wear more rapidly than normal. This is often most noticeable at the heels; the foot angle may be different from the angle of the pastern because the heel has worn away too much.

FROG

The frog is a V-shaped cushion of soft, horny material located in the center of the sole, the softest part of the hoof. It is made up of the same fibrous material as the rest of the external hoof, except that the frog contains oil glands that make it somewhat rubbery. By weight, the frog is about 50 percent water. It generally becomes smaller and shriveled during dry seasons. It sheds twice per year; the old dead tissue separates from the new frog underneath.

The frog should be large and healthy, bordered on either side by the bars, and extend a little more than halfway to the toe and point toward the center of the toe.

The frog, being somewhat soft and flexible, functions as a shock absorber, directing concussion outward instead of up the leg when the foot hits the ground. The flexible frog complements the rigidity of the rest of the foot, allowing the hoof wall to have more give and counteracting the shock of landing on hard surfaces.

When the foot bears weight, the frog and digital cushion at the heel area are squeezed between the coffin bone and the ground, causing them to flatten and spread the heels apart. The space between the bars and the frog allow for side expansion of the heels and frog. The overall height of the hoof at the heels decreases and the heels expand about 1/16 inch on each side when the foot takes weight. A horseshoe should be slightly wider than the hoof at the heels to allow for this expansion.

Big, Soft Frog vs. Small, Hard Frog

Horses that live in soft, wet pastures tend to have bigger, softer frogs than horses living and traveling in dry, rocky, or desert terrain. Continually wet footing tends to make a hoof expand and flatten out, and because the hoof sinks into the footing, the frog contacts the ground. The flat, "pancake" feet of draft horses, which were developed in the wet climates of Europe and the British Isles, helped keep them from sinking into soft ground.

In contrast, a horse living in dry country develops harder and more upright hoof walls and concave soles that lift the frog off the ground and out of the way of sharp rocks. Desert animals such as the donkey or burro have narrow, upright feet, and a frog so small and high that it never touches the ground. Most riding horses are in between these two extremes, with feet and frogs that can adapt to different conditions.

◯ Conformation Close-up

The frog is a good landmark for judging the conformation of a horse's foot. If the frog does not divide the sole into equal halves, this is an indication of crooked foot and leg structure; the foot is misshapen or out of balance. The horse may be base wide or base narrow, with feet growing unevenly because they are crooked instead of straight.

Heel Bulbs

The heel bulbs are part of the back area of the digital cushion, a fatty, fibrous, wedge-shaped pad inside the back part of the foot. It is situated above the frog and below the short pastern bone. This cushion, with its heel-bulb extensions, absorbs the impact of landing; the hoof is designed for landing heel first, and this is the area that best handles the concussion.

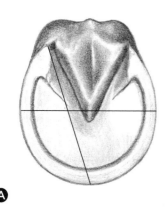

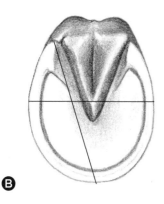

 Measuring a front foot. **A.** A normal foot is the same distance from angle of bars to center of toe as it is at its widest point from side to side. **B.** A contracted foot is longer than it is wide.

Size and Shape of Feet

An athletic horse can maintain speeds of 10 to 15 miles per hour for long distances (endurance horses often travel 100 miles in 7 to 10 hours), and racehorses can run in bursts of speed of up to about 45 miles per hour. These statistics are quite remarkable for such heavy-bodied, small-footed creatures. The horse needs feet with proper shape and conformation to withstand concussion.

MEASURING A FOOT

Feet should be properly shaped and of proportionate size for the horse. The hoof should be of adequate size to support the horse's weight but not so large that he'll be clumsy.

The width of the foot is measured across the widest part of its base, and the length from the center of the toe to the point where the hoof wall turns in to form the bar at the heel. A front foot should have the same measurement from side to side as from toe to heel. A hind foot, being more oval, should be slightly longer than it is wide. The two sides of each foot should also be equal; the measurement from toe to heel on each side should be exactly the same.

Feet Too Small

If feet are too small for a horse's body structure, he will not hold up under strenuous work and hard training. The increased shock of concussion in the small hoof area may cause lameness from various problems, such as navicular syndrome or road founder, or joint problems in the leg. A small foot is less able to dissipate the stress of impact than a large, elastic hoof and may also tend to bruise more readily or develop sore heels. A small foot may easily become contracted and the hoof horn more brittle and dry.

Feet Too Large

If feet are too large, a horse will stumble and be clumsy. If feet are too wide with splayed-out walls, the walls might not provide enough support, and the sole of the foot may be flat. A large foot is sometimes pancaked, and the sole is easily bruised. If feet are too large, the horse may step on himself and bruise his heels or coronary bands or step on a shoe with another foot and pull it off. He may also hit himself while traveling.

Draft horse breeds have the largest feet. Clydesdales have very large feet with round soles and wide heels. The Suffolk has a smaller, more compact foot than other draft breeds, and the Percheron tends to have the strongest, most solid feet.

Selective breeding in some breeds has resulted in individuals with feet too small for their body weight, leading to increased incidence of various types of unsoundness. An example is the "halter type" Quarter Horse that has a massive, muscular body and small, dainty feet. If you must choose between a horse with feet too small or too large, it is usually wise to select the horse with larger feet if they are well conformed, for the horse is more apt to stay sound.

FEET SHOULD MATCH

The two front feet should closely match in size and shape, as should the two hind feet. Pairs of feet are rarely exactly alike, but any obvious difference is cause for concern. Front feet should be slightly rounder and larger than hind feet, because they must support two-thirds of the horse's body weight. The hind feet are slightly narrower and more upright and have a more pointed toe; the front feet should have a round toe. If a front foot is longer from toe to heel than it is from side to side at the quarters, the toe of the foot is probably too long or the foot is contracted.

The shape of each foot is directly related to the conformation, position, and action of the leg it supports. An oddly shaped foot should arouse suspicion about the soundness of the horse, as should any foot that is different in size or angle from its mate. One foot may be more upright and boxy than the other or more shelly (thin, brittle, and easily broken) and thin-walled. Mismatched feet hinder the horse's performance and make it harder to keep him sound.

A horse that has been chronically lame may develop mismatched feet over time because he places less weight on the lame foot. Recall that a foot expands each time it takes weight, springing back to its original shape when lifted. A lame foot, not having as much weight placed on it, tends to have poor circulation and contract over time.

In a horse with good leg conformation, the foot will break over the center of the toe and will wear evenly.

🔍 *Conformation Close-up*

Shape and wear of the feet can tell you a lot about a horse's leg structure. If wear on the feet is uneven, consider it an important reminder to look closely at conformation of the leg it supports. When a horse is standing squarely, each foot should be in proper alignment with the leg it supports. Viewed from front or rear, a line dropped straight down from the point of the shoulder (or buttock) should bisect the foot. Viewed from the side, a line going down

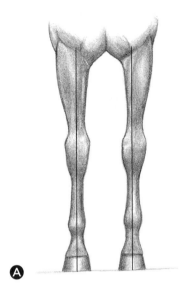

Ⓐ

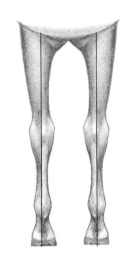

Ⓑ

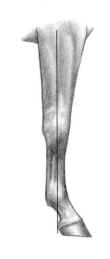

Ⓒ

🔺 Feet should be straight from any view and in proper alignment with the leg above. **A.** Front view. **B.** Rear view. **C.** Side view.

the center of the cannon should come to the ground just behind the heel bulbs. If the foot is not in proper alignment with the leg, this poor conformation can contribute to many types of lameness and unsoundness. Poor leg conformation can have an adverse effect on the structures of the foot, creating abnormalities.

APPEARANCE

The foot should be balanced and symmetrical. When you look at the foot from front or back, both sides should match. Height and slope of the hoof wall should be the same on both sides. Both sides of the coronary band should be the same height from the ground when viewed from the front. The ends of the coronary band at the heels should be the same height when viewed from the back.

Hoof growth and shape respond to the weight placed on the foot; if the leg is crooked and the foot is not bearing weight evenly across its surface, the half that bears the most weight will tend to be steeper and sometimes shorter than the half that has less stress. Most horses tend to have slightly steeper hoof walls on the inner front and hind feet, but if the inner foot is steep and the outer foot is flared, this is an indication of uneven weight bearing. Uneven weight bearing can cause uneven foot shape and sheared heels.

When you look at the bottom of the hoof, it should be the same shape on both sides, with even wear on both sides of the toe, sole, and heel. There should be no outward bulges or flares on the bottom of the foot. The heel bulbs should be even in size and height. If the foot is not balanced, this may be due to poor conformation or to improper trimming or shoeing.

▼ Uneven weight bearing creates a nonsymmetrical foot shape and "flares"; the frog points off-center.

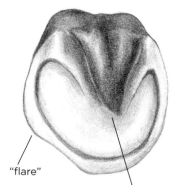

"flare"

frog pointing off center

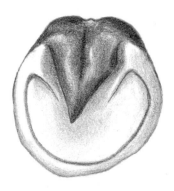

Width of Heel

Hooves should be round and wide at the heels, not narrow or contracted. The shape of the heels should be similar to the size of the widest part of the toe, with strong, well-developed bars. Wide heels give and spring apart when the foot takes weight, absorbing some of the concussion. If this weren't the case, all the shock and jar of hitting the ground would be transmitted directly to the bones of the foot and up the leg to the joints. Wide, springy heels can help absorb some of this shock. Horses with narrow feet tend to be more prone to contraction.

WIDE AND DEEP IS BEST

Heels should be wide and deep. When the foot is shod, there should be at least an inch of horn between the shoe and the back of the coronet at the heel bulb. A thin, narrow heel is not as strong and is more easily bruised. There is not as much wall and buffer between the ground and the inner sensitive tissues. A strong, deep heel usually has strong bars. Navicular disease is more likely to develop if the heels are low and weak, putting extra stress and strain on flexor tendons and increased pressure on the deep flexor tendon that glides over the navicular bone.

Some horses' feet are forced into abnormal shape because of improper shoeing or shoeing that seeks to change the horse's action, as is done in some American Saddle Horses and Tennessee Walking Horses. The hoof wall is allowed to grow excessively long to give the horse a longer stride or higher action, and the feet may contract as a result; tendons may also suffer more stress. The artificial hoof shape may aggravate other conformational weaknesses such as base-wide, splay-footed conformation, making the horse more prone to ringbone, sidebone, and other lameness problems.

Mechanics

When the horse travels at a fast gait, the heel of the foot hits the ground first. The resilient structures at the heel are better equipped to handle impact than is the toe. The heel and relatively thin quarters expand, the flexible digital cushion expands as the short pastern bone rotates down and back against it, and the lateral and medial cartilages are pushed outward. The frog is pressed down and contacts the ground to help absorb the shock of impact. The frog is thickest toward the rear of the foot.

The toe makes contact after the heel. The toe cuts into the ground as it lands and breaks over for the next stride, which helps dissipate impact and gives more traction. As the toe lands and the entire hoof is on the ground, the impact is directed up through the hoof wall, which is made up of tiny parallel horn tubules that absorb some of the compressive force.

The hoof wall is attached to the coffin bone inside the hoof by means of interlocking laminae. The sensitive laminae next to the coffin bone are interlaced with the insensitive laminae of the hoof wall. This creates a somewhat flexible "sling" that supports the coffin bone inside the hoof. Because of these amazing connections, the foot can accommodate impact and wear and tear, while at the same time protecting the inner, delicate living tissues.

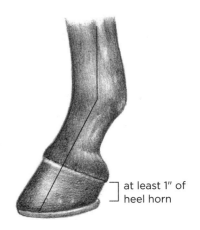

at least 1" of heel horn

⬭ Heels should be deep; there should be at least an inch of horn above the shoe when shod.

Why Not White?

White feet were traditionally avoided. Lack of pigment in the hoof horn tends to make the hoof softer when wet, prone to rapid wear, and more brittle and easily chipped and split when dry. The softer horn does not hold nails as well, so shoes are more easily lost. If the hoof is dry and brittle, it may split when nails are driven. Some horses' white feet are relatively tough, but as a general rule pigmented hoofs are more durable, more resilient, and more resistant to trauma. Despite this, today many horsemen like the flashy look of white socks and a light-colored, nonpigmented hoof.

Did You Know?

The impact of a horse's weight, multiplied by his speed, creates a tremendous amount of concussion on a few square inches of hoof. The size and shape of his feet determine how well they hold up to and withstand this kind of trauma.

Evaluating the Foot

A horse should always be evaluated while standing and while moving. This gives a better indication of how he handles his feet and legs. He should have a good way of traveling, moving "straight and clean," with no wasted motion or deviations that might cause limb interference. A horse with good conformation has straight feet and legs that move forward in relatively straight lines.

Foot flight is the path the hoof makes as it is picked up and travels through the air. The structure of the foot and leg influences *breakover* (the way a foot leaves the ground), foot flight, and how the foot lands. The *breakover point* is the last instant the toe touches the ground, as it is being picked up, and this area of the toe shows the most wear. Foot and leg conformation determine the shape of the feet, how the feet wear, and the flight of the feet. It also establishes whether the feet are picked up squarely and land squarely or start and end their flight crookedly.

⊸○ Conformation Close-up

When evaluating a horse's feet, look at their size, shape, and wear, and pay close attention to the structure of the heels, soles, and frogs, and the all-important hoof and pastern angle. Watch the horse travel at the walk and the trot, from the front and the rear. Observe how he handles his feet, how he picks them up, swings them, and puts them back down. His feet are the foundation on which his athletic ability and future soundness depend.

Some points of poor conformation will show up more obviously when the horse is moving than when he is standing still. For example, when a horse is moving you will clearly see whether his feet paddle outward or wing inward, or if his feet come too close to one another; each of these is a clue to an imperfect structure. If you notice a deviation in gait, take a closer look at the horse's feet and legs. A pigeon-toed horse tends to paddle, and a splay-footed horse tends to wing his feet inward.

WEAR AND BREAKOVER

The hardest and most durable part of the hoof horn is at the toe. When a horse is barefoot, this area suffers more wear than the rest of the hoof wall, due to breakover and thrust at the toe. A shod horse will also tend to have more wear at the toe; the breakover point will be worn the most.

If a horse has good foot and leg conformation, his feet wear evenly because the foot breaks over at the center of the toe. A horse with crooked legs has unbalanced feet that wear unevenly. Forces are not evenly distributed and one side of the foot receives more impact. The side that gets more impact will be steeper (and often taller) because the rate of hoof growth on that side speeds up (due to increased circulation) and the side receiving less impact flares outward. There will probably be a flare in the hoof wall on one side, instead of a symmetrical shape to both sides. The frog will be pointed off-center.

If a leg is not straight, the hoof may grow out of balance due to uneven weight borne by the foot. The coronary band is not symmetrical because the hoof wall pushes up on the steep side of the foot. If one side of the foot continually hits the ground harder than the other, the heel bulb on that side may eventually be driven upward, creating a condition called sheared heels, which may result in lameness (see page 327).

TOE LENGTH

A horse's toe length can be affected by whether the feet are worn down properly if barefoot or whether the feet have been trimmed recently. It is also affected by conformation and foot structure, particularly in front feet, which generally are more sloped than the hind feet. If the foot and pastern slope too much, the horse will usually have a long toe. A long toe with a too-short heel and a long heel with a too-short toe both put the foot angle out of balance.

If the toe is too long — especially if length is accentuated by extra hoof growth — it puts excessive weight on the heels of the foot and extra stress on both the deep flexor tendon and the navicular bone. Navicular problems are often caused by toes that are too long. Conversely, a very short toe is usually indicative of a steep foot. If the toe is short and steep, the horse has a choppy, jarring gait, which increases stress to the foot.

A horse with a short toe often has a relatively high heel and tends to break over quickly. The foot reaches its highest point toward the end of its arc and then comes to the ground abruptly, increasing concussion. A horse with a long toe usually has a shorter heel and breaks over less quickly, which results in a longer stride, with the highest point near the first part of the arc. The foot then comes to the ground more gradually, landing with less concussion but with more strain on the leg tendons due to the delayed breakover (see chapters 7 and 11).

What Is "Normal"?

The angle of the foot and pastern is about 50 degrees in the front feet and about 55 degrees in the hind feet. The traditional "ideal" angle was 45 degrees, but no ideal applies to every horse. More important is the proper angle for the individual: it should be unbroken (toes and heels proper length), pairs should match (both fronts the same, both hinds the same), and feet should be balanced and fit the horse's conformation. Foot angle should match pastern angle and leg structure.

▼ Hoof and pastern angle should be the same. **A.** A broken foot and pastern angle puts extra stress on the foot and leg. Angle broken due to long toe and short heel *(left)*; angle broken due to short toe and long heel *(right)*. **B.** Foot axis: imaginary lines through the center of the toe and across the ground surface of the foot will meet at right angles if the foot is level and the leg is straight. **C.** The ground surface of the foot should meet an imaginary line through the center of the foot and pastern at right angles.

HOOF ANGLE

Hoof angle is measured from the side from the coronary band to the point where the toe meets the ground surface. The angle of the hoof should be the same as that of the pastern (which is measured with a line from the center of the fetlock joint through the center of the pastern to the ground), or there will be extra strain on bones and tendons. A line from the fetlock joint to the ground should be straight and unbroken between the foot and the pastern. If toes are too long, the angle will break backward, putting strain on the back tendons and other parts of the leg. If the heel is too long, the line will break forward, putting strain on the front parts of the foot and leg. If foot angle and pastern angle are not the same, proper trimming is needed to correct it.

FOOT AND PASTERN AXIS

The foot axis, viewed from the front, is an imaginary line going through the center of the toe from the coronary band to the ground. From the back, the line should bisect the foot between the heel bulbs. This straight line should join the pastern axis, passing through the center of the pastern and up to the center of the fetlock joint; the leg should not deviate from fetlock joint down, and the foot should share the same axis.

If the foot is level and properly balanced, the foot and pastern axis will meet the ground surface squarely. Viewed from front or back, the foot and pastern will be straight and perpendicular to the ground. If you pick up the foot and look at the bottom, you should be able to extend an imaginary line down the pastern and foot, crossing the base of the foot (a line from one side of the hoof wall to the other, at the quarters), the two lines perpendicular to one another. If the foot is off-level, the lines will not be perpendicular.

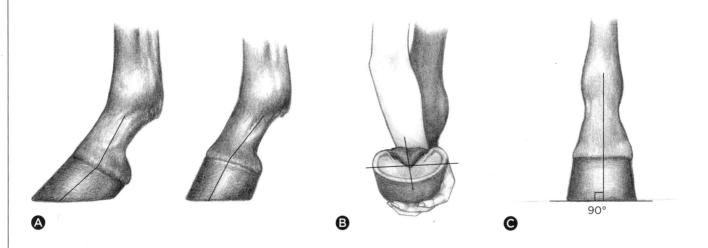

Ⓐ   Ⓑ   Ⓒ   90°

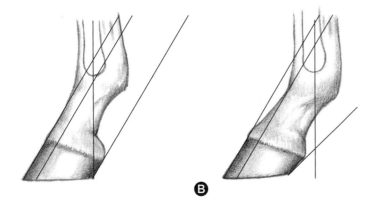

A. Angle of toe and heel should always be the same, and a line dropped from the cannon bone should touch the back of the heel; this gives the best support for the leg. **B.** Underslung heel; the angle of the heel is not the same as that of the toe, and there is not enough hoof under the back of the foot to adequately support the horse's weight. A line dropped from the cannon bone entirely misses the heel. This puts more stress on the heel and on the leg tendons.

Conformation Close-up

The angle of the horse's heel should be identical to that of his toe. The height of the heel should be about half the height of the hoof at the toe. This makes a well-balanced, healthy foot.

Unshod vs. Shod

Horses that go barefoot all their lives in natural conditions (with room to roam, where they can travel and wear their feet properly) usually have tougher, thicker walls and soles, and a shorter toe and higher heel, which makes a steeper hoof angle. Horses in confinement or on soft ground that are unable to wear down their hooves naturally often do not have natural hoof angles, even if they go barefoot, because their hooves grow too long.

Wild and feral horses have few of the hoof problems common to domestic horses, partly because their feet are doing what they do best: carrying the horse over dry ground, with almost constant, moderate activity. Most domestic horses are kept in unnatural conditions, and feet typically must be trimmed because they don't get enough natural wear. They usually must be shod for riding to protect them from too much wear. The art and science of shoeing began many centuries ago as a way to keep the hoof from wearing away too fast with extra work and hard use.

Trimming and shoeing became the norm for the domestic horse, but these measures don't always give the foot optimum conditions for retaining its proper shape, angle, and balance. Often the shod foot is quite different from the way nature would shape it under ideal conditions. In nature, the hoof wall wears away at the same rate it grows, keeping the wall and toe very short, but not so short that the horse is tender-footed.

Expansion Is Key

The open heel and wedge-shaped frog allow the hoof to expand as weight is placed on it and to contract when the foot is lifted. This hoof design also provides better traction for the foot. The foot is well adapted for counteracting effects of concussion, but it is most effective when the foot is of proper size and shape, with strong, deep heels that can expand. An improperly shod foot, with nails too far back at the quarters, can limit and hinder this expansion.

THE NATURAL HOOF

Beginning in the 1980s, some farriers took a closer look at the feet of wild and feral horses in an effort to improve trimming and shoeing techniques. In a wild horse, the hoof at the toe (from coronary band to ground surface) is rarely more than 3 inches long, whereas in a domestic horse of similar body weight and hoof size the toe length is often 3.5 inches or more, creating a different foot angle and forcing the hoof breakover point farther forward. The hoof wall of the free-roaming horse makes only four points of contact with the ground when standing on a flat surface — at each heel and at either side of the toe. The toe is usually worn off, making a square front to the foot, and the wall at the quarters is often worn down or broken away to sole level.

With the toe worn off, the hoof has a breakover point that is usually only about 1 to 1.5 inches in front of the tip of the frog. The shod horse (or one trimmed in traditional fashion, leaving all the hoof wall at the toe instead of shortening it at the front) has a longer toe, with the breakover point 2 inches or more from the tip of the frog. This creates a different hoof angle and often forces the foot to land flat or toe first instead of heel first. Landing flat-footed stresses the navicular bone, tendons, and coffin joints, which are not designed for shock absorption and are more easily damaged by excessive concussion.

THE FOUR-POINT TRIM

Some farriers use a four-point trim to simulate the wild hoof, shortening the toe so the hoof is more naturally shaped; the hoof is blockier, without such a long toe. This creates a steeper hoof angle and helps many horses to "get back under themselves," with more support to the leg and less strain on tendons from an overly long toe. This type of trimming and shoeing can help correct dished hoof walls and allows toe cracks and quarter cracks to grow out by removing ground-bearing surfaces between the four supporting pillars.

This trimming method shifts the breakover point of the foot farther back (not so far out in front) and eventually increases the depth of the heel. This makes the hoof angle steeper — a more normal 50 degrees or more instead of the farrier's traditional 45 degrees. This decreases strain on the deep digital flexor tendon, increases the strength of the suspensory system in the lower leg, and increases efficiency of movement.

Some farriers have found that the quickest and most effective way to correct many problem feet is to let a horse go barefoot in the four-point trim for several months. Until a foot can produce dense, tough

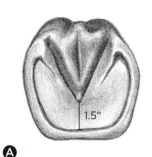 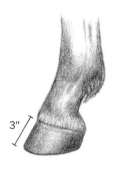 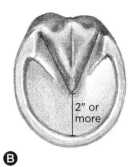 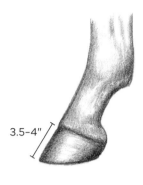

A **B**

horn, it is hard to balance it or have shoes stay on properly (nails are often pulled loose when a hoof wall is weak and crumbly). Repeated shoeing of a foot with a weak hoof wall that lacks strength and mass will often make it even weaker. Putting the foot at a more natural angle allows the hoof to remodel itself if it has become unbalanced from improper trimming or shoeing. The foot can often become healthier in the process, with its structures working more as nature intended. When a problem foot is trimmed this way, it looks quite different, at first, from the symmetrical circular foot that most farriers look upon as ideal. But over time it attains a structural integrity that enables it to maintain itself at or near ideal shape, without having to continue the four-point trim.

Bad feet can often be corrected by Mother Nature if the horse is turned out on dry ground for a year with total "neglect," where the terrain wears the feet adequately. The hoof will remodel itself accordingly. Turnout on soft wet ground, or in small enclosures where the horse doesn't get enough exercise, may not accomplish this goal and may only make bad feet worse. The hooves can't wear adequately and will grow too long, putting strain on legs and joints. They may also suffer hoof breakage or cracks and splitting, due to the long feet.

For a shod horse, the best foot is usually attained by keeping the toe short (for proper breakover and foot angle) and allowing the horse to have adequate heel. The wild horse does fine without shoes because hoof growth balances travel wear. A horse carrying a rider on hard or rocky ground day after day, or competing in strenuous athletic endeavors with the added weight of a rider, may wear his feet faster than they can grow. Proper shoeing will always be needed for certain horses. Farriers and horse owners can learn, however, from the natural foot and hoof angle of the wild horse. This knowledge can help improve shoeing in a way that more closely simulates the normal hoof.

A. Wild horse foot (or four-point trim) has a shorter toe at both the ground surface and a side view. The hoof has four points of contact with the ground (worn away at toe and quarters). The short toe puts the breakover point just 1 to 1.5 inches from the point of the frog, and the toe is only about 3 inches long from coronary band to ground surface. **B.** Typical domesticated foot (trimmed and/or shod regularly); the toe is 3.5 to 4 inches long. Toe and breakover point are usually 2 inches or more from the point of the frog.

PART II

Evaluating a Horse

Always remember that there are no "ideal," perfectly conformed horses; even the best horses have some faults. A good horseman realizes that the guidelines for evaluating conformation are simply guidelines, not concrete rules. Guidelines should be flexible. They simply give us ways to evaluate a horse and to compare him with other horses; they should not dictate selection.

A horse may have a fault in one area, such as a short neck or a slight cow hock, but he may have enough good points to still be an effective athlete and useful for many purposes. If the good points outweigh the less desirable traits and if the faults are not serious, the horse may be fine for what you want him to do. When choosing a horse, be sure he is able to do what you want him to do.

Remember that a horse must be judged while moving as well as while standing still. His action, and the way his conformation translates into movement, is critical. Some points of poor structure and lack of body balance will be more obvious when he is moving. The key to evaluating a horse is to know what you are looking for, what constitutes good conformation, and how to weigh the strengths and weaknesses of an individual horse.

Body Proportions

THE BEST HORSES in every breed display an overall balance and symmetry, with each part of the body being proportionate. Body balance is crucial to athletic ability. The length and proportions of a horse's body and back play an important role in the form and function of his legs. So even though a horseman may be tempted to focus on the feet and legs when evaluating conformation and soundness, the entire body must be carefully considered.

A good horse is well balanced, symmetrical, and proportional and can be visualized in thirds. Such conformation allows for optimal balance, speed, and agility.

Ideal conformation varies somewhat among breeds, but the differences are minor. For example, a champion cutting horse from the Quarter Horse breed, a winning Thoroughbred racehorse, a great Standardbred trotter, and a versatile Morgan or Arabian share the same basic structural traits, despite differences in body dimensions. Without good proportion and balance, the horse may be limited in what he can do well and may not remain sound if worked hard.

Visualize the Horse in Thirds

The ideal horse can be visualized in thirds. His body should be one-third shoulder area (the front part of the horse that is measured from the point of the shoulders to a line dropped from where the withers meet the back), one-third body (the section of his body measured from the withers to the point of the hip), and one-third hip area (from the point of the hip to the point of the buttock). A common fault in many horses is being too long in the back; the horse is not evenly proportioned. This fault makes it harder for a horse to carry a rider at fast gaits and also creates more leg problems (see chapter 6 for more on back conformation).

▼ A horse with ideal conformation for athletic ability and durability is one-third shoulder area (front end), one-third back area, and one-third hip area (hindquarters).

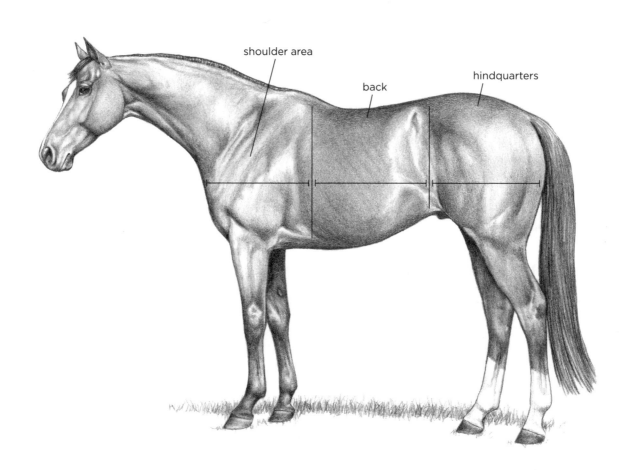

shoulder area

back

hindquarters

Conformation Close-up

Some people admire a horse with a long shoulder but fail to notice whether the shoulder is laid back or too upright, especially if they are looking for tall horses. A long, upright shoulder may add several inches to the horse's height, but this is not a trait that contributes to athletic ability or soundness. An upright shoulder puts more stress on the leg. The rule of thirds can help you judge the shoulder. If it's too upright, even if it's long, it makes the front of the body less than one-third of the horse.

A Good Horse Is Square

For best athletic ability, a horse should be the same height at the withers as he is at the croup, the highest point of the rump, and his height should be proportionate to his length. A good horse is a "square" horse, with the withers being approximately the same height (measured from the ground to the top of the withers) as the distance from the point of the shoulder to the point of the buttocks. The length of the body is thus the same as his height at the withers. Excluding his head and neck, the horse's body fits neatly into a perfect square.

A good horse is square. The distance from the point of his shoulder to his buttocks is equal to his height (from the ground to the top of his withers). The depth of his body (from the top of his withers to the underline) is the same as from underline to fetlock joint. He is the same height at the withers as he is at the croup. In addition, a horse's topline should be shorter than his underline.

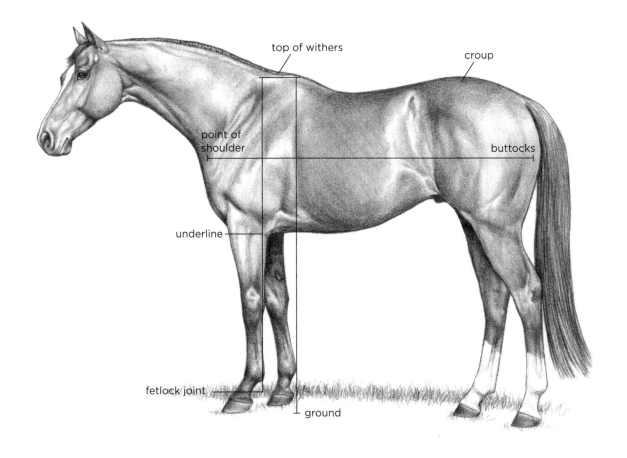

Croup and Wither Height

Generally, the withers do not obtain their full height until a horse is mature. In young horses up to 3 years old, the croup may be higher than the withers. Yearlings and 2-year-olds sometimes look like they don't have much withers at all; the upright spines of those vertebrae are still short. By the time they are 3 or 4 years old, though, this changes. The withers catch up with the croup, the horse looks more balanced, and his back holds a saddle better. As the horse matures, the withers reach their full height and he has a properly conformed back.

Until the spinal processes of the thoracic vertebrae (at the withers) and the bones of the forelegs have completed their growth, most young horses are taller at the croup than at the withers. By the time the horse has reached full mature height, however, the withers will be level with or slightly higher than the croup.

In some horses, a high croup is a hereditary trait. The horse finishes his growth and remains an inch or more taller at the croup. When riding this type of horse, the rider feels like the saddle is sliding forward and she is going downhill. The saddle tends to go too far onto the shoulders, which hinders shoulder movement and may cause pressure and chafing sores on the withers, girth, and behind the shoulders.

In order to keep the saddle from going onto the neck when traveling down a steep hill (or if the horse bucks, which the discomfort from a too-far forward saddle may cause him to do), the rider must have the cinch uncomfortably tight. Some riders on a horse with this kind of "downhill" balance use a crupper (a strap that goes back to the tail and is anchored under the dock of the tail). Neither remedy is very comfortable for the horse.

The range of hind leg movement depends more on the length of the tibia and the degree of flexion and extension between the lower

Did You Know?

Some people believe that a high croup is a sign of speed if the muscles of the loin and quarters are strong, suggesting more power in the hind legs, and, in fact, many sprinters have "downhill" balance. However, a high croup does not necessarily mean that a horse has longer hind legs or a greater stride; this depends on the angles of the legs (see chapter 8).

end of the femur and the upper end of the tibia within the stifle joint than on the length of the hind leg in a croup-high horse. Whether the croup is high or low, the angle that the upper part of the pelvis makes with the sacrum will vary according to the length of the ilium and the tilt of the pelvis.

A high croup and low withers can be a great disadvantage to athletic ability in a riding horse. When the croup is higher than the withers, the horse's weight is shifted forward onto the front legs, which reduces his front-end agility, especially when the horse is asked to collect himself, jump, or make quick changes of direction. He must work much harder to lift his forehand, and many of his muscles — especially in his back, loins, and front legs — become easily fatigued. The downhill balance also puts more concussive impact on the front legs. This can lead to injury and breakdown, in addition to the jarring effect on the rider.

Some horses have withers higher than the croup. Withers that are too high make the saddle slide back toward the loins, placing the rider too far back on the horse. This makes it difficult for the rider to maintain proper position and balance and interferes with the horse's balance when doing active maneuvers. If the girth or cinch slides back a few inches, it may inhibit expansion of the lungs and rib cage if the horse must exert. A breast collar will be needed to keep the saddle in place.

Is the Horse Built "Uphill" or "Downhill"?

Body balance is partly determined by the relative height of croup and withers but also by the position of the backbone from front to back: how low or high the base of the neck is, and where the neck vertebrae join the thoracic vertebrae. This helps determine whether the horse will be heavy in front and how he moves. A front-heavy horse with downhill balance is often best at straight-line activities such as racing and performs poorly when actions require collection and lightness or stops and turns.

Body balance is often assessed by comparing the height of the withers with the height of the croup, but this is not always a true indication of the actual balance of the horse. Sometimes a horse with withers and croup of the same height is still built "uphill" or "downhill." The most accurate way to determine the balance is to look at the vertebral column and whether it is level. Compare the level of the widest part of the horse's neck at its base with the level of the lumbosacral joint just below and often slightly in front of the point of the croup.

Did You Know?

If the saddle slips back, it puts the rider's weight over the loins, where the back is least able to support it, and more weight on the hindquarters. This may increase strain on joints and ligaments of the hind legs, especially if the rider is heavy.

To locate the widest point of the neck, stand in front of the horse and place your hands on either side of his neck. Slide your hands down toward the base of the neck until you feel the point where the vertebrae and muscling are thicker. This is approximately where the fifth and sixth vertebrae are connected and is the neck's widest point. Mark this spot with a piece of masking tape or something that will temporarily stick to the horse's hair.

Next, on the same side of the horse, mark the level of the lumbosacral joint, where the lumbar vertebrae end and the sacrum begins. It is usually just a little forward of the croup, slightly ahead of the highest part of the rump. How close it is to the croup depends in part on whether the horse has a long loin or a short loin. The joint may be very near a line drawn from one point of hip to the other or it may be behind this line.

You can usually feel and see the place on the horse's backbone where the lumbar region ends and the sacrum begins. The actual joint, however, is deeper in the back; the top spines of the vertebrae create several inches of space between the surface of the horse's back and the spinal column itself. The lumbosacral joint is located about 4 inches below the surface.

To mark the area of the joint, drop down about 4 inches from the topline of the back, and put masking tape on the side of the horse, just below where you determined the joint to be; this is a short ways down the horse's side from the loin area. The loin is the muscle-

▶ A horse with relatively level balance makes a good riding horse.

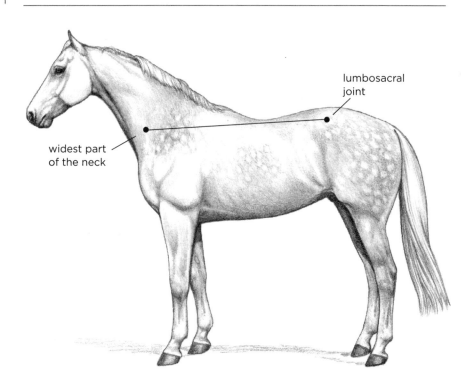

widest part
of the neck

lumbosacral
joint

covered hollow spot between the last ribs and the hip bone. After marking the lumbosacral joint at the back and the area between the fifth and sixth vertebrae on the neck, visualize an imaginary line running between these two marks; it will roughly be the line of the horse's backbone.

The horse must be standing squarely on level ground. The slant or levelness of the line between these two points (on neck and

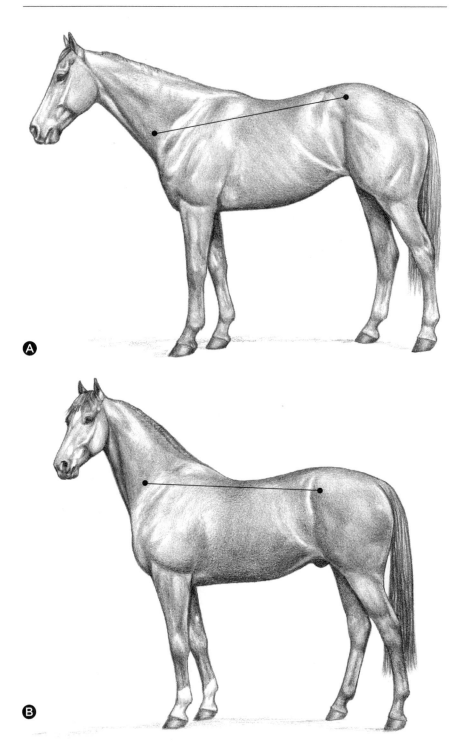

◀ **A.** Downhill balance typical of a sprinter. **B.** Uphill balance.

A

B

hindquarter) will be an indication of the horse's body balance. If the line is nearly level, no more than 4 inches higher on one end than the other, the horse has relatively normal balance and should be able to handle himself with all-around agility.

If the line slants too sharply downhill toward the front, with the neck mark more than 4 inches below the mark near the croup, the horse is front-heavy with a downhill balance. It will be difficult for him to collect himself and transfer weight to his hindquarters for pivots and turns and to be light on his front end. A horse with this build is best suited for traveling straight ahead. If he has strong hindquarters and legs, he may excel at racing.

If the line between the base of the neck and lumbosacral joint slopes up toward the neck, the horse has an uphill balance and is light on his front end and heavy on his hind end. The joints of the hind legs may undergo more stress and strain because of the overbalance in that direction.

Leg and Body Length

Do not choose a horse that is long bodied and short legged or short bodied and long legged. Disproportionate conformation can result in leg problems and a lack of agility. A long-bodied horse should be long legged, and a short-bodied, short-backed horse should have short legs for the horse to be properly proportioned and square.

If the short-backed horse has legs that are too long for his body, he will be more likely to overreach when moving, striking his front feet with his hind feet. A horse with a too-short back will also be somewhat stiff and inflexible, with a more jarring ride.

A horse that is too long in the back may have a swing to his gait, changing the forward movement of his legs so they do not travel perfectly straight. They come forward in arcs, making limb interference more likely. A long back may also be weak and the horse will be unable to round it for proper weight carrying.

Deep Heart Girth

When judging the body of a horse, look for a deep heart girth (the depth between the top of the withers and the bottom of the chest cavity) and well-sprung ribs (rounded, rather than flat). A horse needs plenty of room for his lungs to expand when he is exerting. If he has a shallow body, he will look like his legs are disproportionately long for his body and will have less lung capacity and endurance.

Horses with a good "barrel" (wide through the ribs and deep through the heart girth and flank) usually have more staying power for a long, hard job. They also do not draw up so much in the flank after a long workout. By contrast, the "bacon-sided" or "slab-sided" horse with very little curvature of rib, and the "wasp-waisted" horse with tucked up, shallow flank and ribs that don't extend far enough back at the abdomen generally don't have much staying power and endurance (see chapter 5 for more on the chest).

In a well-balanced horse that is agile, athletic, and fast, the distance from the fetlock joint (in the front leg) to his underline at the girth is usually the same as the distance from his underline to the top of his withers. In other words, the depth of his body, or heart girth, is about the same as the length of his legs down to the fetlock joint.

If the horse's legs are longer than the depth of his body or he's so short legged and deep bodied that his legs are shorter than the depth of his body, he not only looks out of proportion but he usually moves awkwardly. For gracefulness, agility, and stamina, he needs balance between legs and body. Remember, the ideal horse is a "square" horse; his proportions are equal. The distance from ground to withers is the same as the length from front to back, and the length of his legs and the depth of his body are the same.

Other Helpful Measurements

The length of a horse's head usually matches some of his other body proportions and can be used as a guide. If a horse is well proportioned and balanced, the length of his head is nearly the same as the length of his neck and about as long as the distance from girth to withers. His head also is about the same length as his hind leg from the point of the hock to the ground (which is also the same as the height of the chestnut from the ground on the front leg).

This length is nearly the same as the distance from the point of the shoulder to the highest point of the withers, as well as being the distance from the withers to the hip bone, and the same distance as from the point of the stifle to the point of the croup. There should be at least 2.5 head lengths between the point of the buttock and the point of the shoulder, and the same from withers to ground. These guidelines can give you a good idea about whether or not the horse has proper body proportions.

Symmetry

The horse should be balanced in his body proportions, and his left and right side should match. It can be difficult to tell whether the sides match unless you look at the horse from above as well as from the front and back. One way to get a good look is to stand behind him

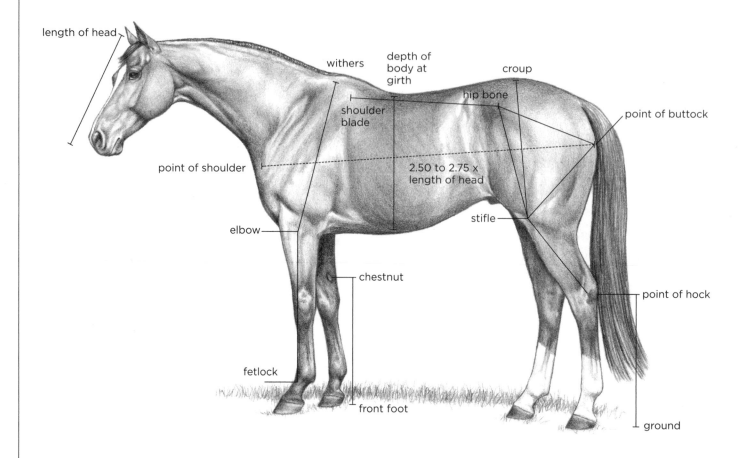

length of head

withers

depth of body at girth

croup

hip bone

point of buttock

shoulder blade

point of shoulder

2.50 to 2.75 x length of head

stifle

elbow

point of hock

chestnut

fetlock

front foot

ground

⚫ The length of the head should be similar to these lengths: point of hock to ground, point of hock to front of stifle, front foot to chestnut, depth of body at girth, fold of stifle to croup, and rear edge of shoulder blade to hip bone. The length from point of shoulder to point of buttock should be 2.50 to 2.75 times the length of the head. Distance from fetlock to elbow is the same as the height from elbow to withers. The lines from buttock to hip, buttock to stifle, and stifle to hip should be similar.

in such a way that you are tall enough to look down on his back (as when standing on a bale of hay or a fence). If there is a twist to his spine or any lopsidedness, it will be obvious from this higher vantage point.

Even if a horse doesn't have perfect conformation, his imperfections should be symmetrical. A horse with matching front legs (whether slightly toed in or out, or over at the knees) is more likely to stay sound than a horse with just one abnormal leg. A horse with one crooked front leg or hind leg, or one hock or hip or point of shoulder higher than the other, will more likely go lame from the abnormal way of traveling. Body parts that don't match put even more strain on the various stress points because of the defect in gait. Asymmetry also decreases the efficiency of the horse's action and hinders his athletic ability and agility.

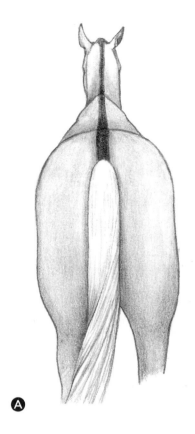

A

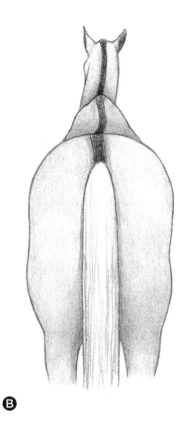

B

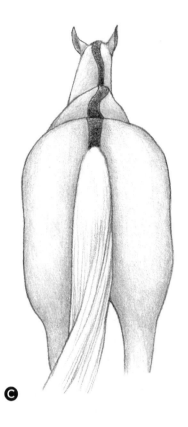

C

Balance Is Key

Feet and legs are often our main focus when evaluating a horse's potential athletic ability and durability, but body proportions are also crucial and play a role in proper leg structure. A good horse has a well-balanced body shape. The best equine athletes in any breed have an overall balance and symmetry. Each part of the body is in proper proportion to the other parts. If there is a mismatch or imbalance in some aspect of a horse's conformation, no level of perfection in certain other parts can make up for this lack. Overall body balance and proper angles are critical to optimum athletic ability and soundness.

◬ Check for symmetry. Always compare one side of the horse with the other. **A.** Normal. **B.** Twisted. **C.** One shoulder blade is higher than the other (one front leg is longer).

Body Angles

WHEN ASSESSING A HORSE'S athletic potential and the likelihood of future soundness, carefully evaluate the angles of the body. Some of the most important angles to consider include the slope of the shoulder, the slope of the pastern, and the angle formed by the line running from the point of the hip to the buttock and then to the stifle joint. For an efficient gait, athletic ability, speed, smoothness, and durability, always choose a horse with good angles.

Shoulder, hindquarter, stifle, hock, and pastern angles determine the length of a horse's stride, how fast he can run, how much impact his bones and rider must endure, and how sound he will be. Horses with proper angles are better able to withstand and distribute concussion.

Angles and Soundness

The angles in the shoulders, hindquarters, and pasterns govern whether the horse will be smooth and fluid in his movement and whether he will stay sound. These angles help determine how much concussion the bones of the feet and legs must absorb. Concussion stress is a contributing factor in the breakdown of many vital structures, causing lameness and sometimes permanent unsoundness.

SIMILAR ANGLES

Most horses tend to have the same degree of angle at important locations. A horse with a steep shoulder usually has a steep pelvis, and a horse with a relatively horizontal shoulder usually has a more level pelvis, for instance. The slope of the pelvis (downward and back) mirrors the slope of the shoulder (downward and forward). The slope of the thigh is similar to the slope of the humerus. The slope of the shoulder is often the same as the slope of the pastern.

A traditional rule of thumb is that a good riding horse has about a 45-degree angle in the slope of the shoulder in relation to a horizontal line drawn from the point of shoulder to the point of buttock, and a similar 45-degree angle in the front pasterns. (A draft horse has a steeper shoulder and wider angles at shoulder and hindquarters.) Many good horses, however, have a slightly steeper angle in the pasterns than in the shoulder. Very few horses have the "ideal" 45-degree pastern angle; front pasterns are actually more "normal" within the 47- to 55-degree range, depending on the individual horse. The angles in shoulders and pasterns may not be identical, but this does not seem to be a detriment to performance ability and soundness.

A horse with upright shoulders that are short and steep, with a wide angle between the shoulder blade and the humerus, will generally have short, upright pasterns and a short hip with a wide hip angle. By contrast, a horse with long sloping shoulders and a narrower angle between shoulder and humerus tends to have more sloping pasterns and a longer hip, with a more acute angle in the hindquarters.

In order to accommodate speed and a long stride, the angles of shoulder and pelvis must be fairly acute rather than obtuse. A long, laid-back shoulder (that is, one more horizontal than upright) and a long, horizontal rump are essential for speed, because they enable the legs to swing forward and back with a greater range of motion. In a draft horse, by contrast, speed is not required; the stride can be shorter. The shoulder of the draft horse is more upright and the rump is equally slanted, rather than level.

shoulder angle

pastern angle

Shoulder Angle

Since humans have been breeding horses, a great deal has been said and written about the length and position of the shoulder and its role in athletic ability. In early writings about horses by the Mongolians and the Arabs (two cultures that depended on their horses), much was made of the "line" of the shoulder. In English texts of the late 1700s, a desirable shoulder was defined as being oblique, or slanted. In more modern times, a good shoulder is referred to as "well laid back," and horsemen talk about the "slope" of the shoulder.

Assessing the horse's shoulder angles provides one of the best clues about the smoothness of his gait, which is a significant factor in the degree of concussion to which leg bones and joints are subjected. It also gives insight into his potential for speed and length of stride.

SHOCK ABSORBER

The well-sloped shoulder acts as a shock absorber, decreasing the amount of concussion transmitted to the body. Concussion affects the front end of the horse more than the hind end because of its anatomy and because the front legs carry more weight. The bending

⏾ Slope of shoulder and pastern are usually similar, though not always. Sometimes a horse has a slightly steeper slope to the pastern than in the shoulder.

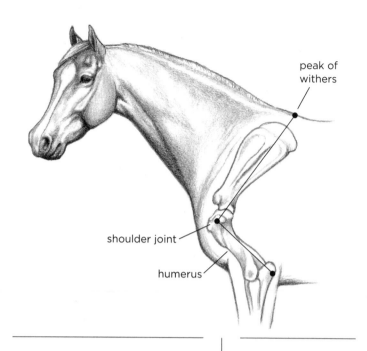

peak of withers

shoulder joint

humerus

🔺 Measuring the shoulder angle from the peak of the withers to the shoulder joint between the shoulder blade and humerus.

of the hock joint, accompanied by stifle flexion, absorbs nearly all of the concussion in the hind leg. Because of the way the knee and elbow joints are formed, the front leg (except for the pastern) becomes an unyielding column each time weight is placed on it. The knee absorbs some concussion through two rows of overlapping bones (see page 115), but it cannot make use of flexion as the hock does. Instead, the front legs depend on movement of the shoulders and pasterns for cushioning; therefore, the shoulders and pasterns must slope adequately to allow for this. Otherwise, the horse is more likely to suffer concussion-related problems such as navicular disease, ringbone, sidebone, splints, road founder, bucked shins, and joint deterioration (see chapter 16).

Definitions of a sloping shoulder vary. Some horsemen measure from the point of the shoulder to the start of the mane on the withers to create the angle, while others use the highest point of the withers as their reference. Some measure the angle of the shoulder joint between shoulder blade and humerus; others measure the slope of the scapular spine — the raised ridge in the center of the flat part of the shoulder blade — in relation to the ground. These different methods of measurement can yield different results. The easiest angle to measure is the line of the shoulder in relationship to the ground.

⭕ *Conformation Close-up*

If you measure the angle of the shoulder blade in relation to the ground, this gives an idea of the leverage and shock-absorbing potential of the shoulder. In some sports, length of the shoulder is often more important than the slope. A good jumper, for instance, usually has a long shoulder, but it may be a little more upright than that of a good racehorse or dressage horse.

The angle made by the shoulder blade and the humerus varies from the angle made between the shoulder blade and the ground, depending in part on whether the humerus is nearly level or tilted; this varies greatly. Most jumpers have a shoulder blade/humerus angle of 100 to 105 degrees because the humerus is relatively level, but horses in other disciplines may have a slightly different angle.

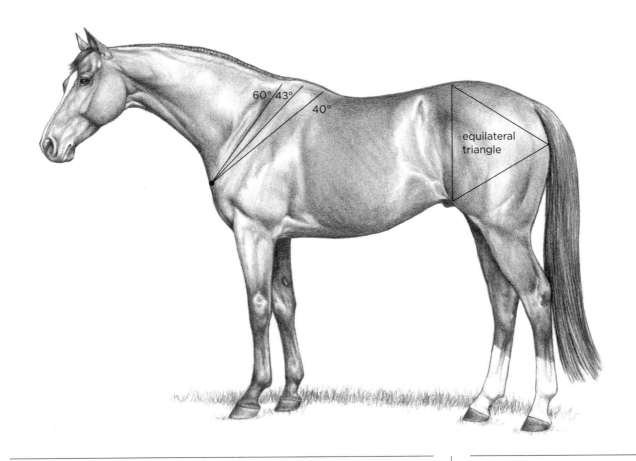

equilateral triangle

TAKING MEASUREMENTS

Most authorities recommend that you measure the angle of the shoulder by first envisioning a reference line, parallel to the ground, from the point of the shoulder to the rear of the horse or by drawing one on a photo. Then draw a line from the point of the shoulder to the highest point, or peak, of the withers. (This line typically follows the spine of the shoulder blade; see illustration on page 207.) The angle made by these two lines is the shoulder angle, and it should be about 45 to 50 degrees; an angle greater than 50 degrees indicates an excessively upright shoulder.

Some horses have an upright shoulder that is set so far forward at the top that the angle is hard to see; if the point of the shoulder is used as a reference, the shoulder appears more sloping than it actually is. Checking the angle of the scapular spine will give you the true slope.

WITHERS AND SHOULDER ANGLE

A well-built, athletic horse usually has relatively acute body angles and good withers (see page 83). A horse without adequate withers doesn't hold a saddle well and does not have proper bone structure for a good shoulder or athletic action. Withers that are too thick and

▲ A good shoulder, well laid back, will have about a 60-degree angle using the line from point of shoulder to junction of neck and withers, and about a 40-degree angle using the line from point of shoulder to junction of withers and back. The line from point of hip to point of buttocks should be long. The angle made by this line and the line from buttock to stifle should be sharp. As in the shoulder, the sharper the angle, the greater the range of motion in the legs.

low hinder the freedom of shoulder movement, causing poor action in the front legs. The low-withered horse usually has a short, upright shoulder and choppy leg action, with a shortened stride and limited forward reach. With up-and-down leg action, instead of low and extended action, the front legs undergo more concussion.

🔍 Conformation Close-up

The withers are the upright spines of the third through ninth thoracic vertebrae. The height of these vertebral spines has an influence on how the front of the horse's body is conformed. They provide the anchor for muscles that attach the shoulder blade to the body. Without well-formed withers, it is almost impossible to have a well-laid-back shoulder. The set of the shoulder blade depends largely on whether the withers are set forward or extend well back, which in turn depends on the height of the vertebral spine.

The withers begin shortly after the neck ends. A horse with withers of adequate height usually has a long, laid-back shoulder. The combination of long shoulder blade and good withers, set back from the neck, gives proper angle for good front leg propulsion, whether a horse is used for jumping or racing. Unlike a racehorse, however, a jumper can often get by with a shoulder that is slightly more upright, as long as it is not too short.

Withers with adequate height also provide better suspension of the chest than do short, flat withers. The rib cage is suspended entirely by muscle attachments (see chapter 5). The shoulder blade is loosely attached to the ribs and can glide up and back over the outer surface of the ribs when weight is placed on that front leg. This gliding action helps dissipate concussion.

The more upright the shoulder blade, the shorter it generally is, with less potential for backward gliding movement over the ribs. There isn't much room for shoulder flexion when the top of a short

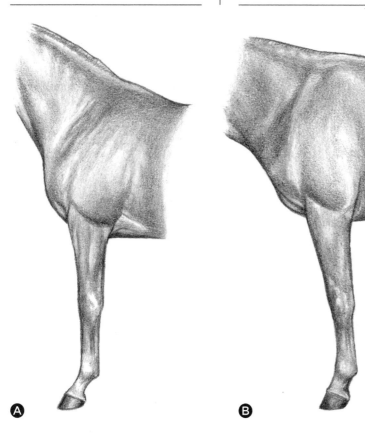

▼ **A.** A horse with a long, sloping shoulder and good pastern angles has a longer stride and a smoother gait, and is less likely to suffer breakdown and lameness due to excessive concussion. **B.** A horse with short, upright shoulders and pasterns has choppier action and a more jarring gait, and is more likely to develop concussion-related problems such as splints, navicular syndrome, and road founder.

Ⓐ   Ⓑ

shoulder blade is directly over the joint instead of behind it; there is more concussion at all gaits. A horse with short, upright shoulders usually has a short neck and short, upright pasterns, as well. This type of conformation puts a horse at increased risk for lameness from concussion and jars the rider at each step.

🔍 *Conformation Close-up*

Good withers and laid-back shoulders go together. A horse with good withers tends to have properly sloped pasterns and good angle in the hindquarters, making for better speed and less concussion, both of which are easier on horse and rider. When selecting a horse, choose one with acute rather than wide angles, a long, sloping shoulder, and properly sloped pasterns, rather than one with shorter lines and steeper angles.

SLOPING SHOULDER

A sloping, laid-back shoulder is essential for speed because there is more room for complete extension and flexion, and it allows for maximum range of motion. The leg can advance farther forward, improving the action of the horse at all gaits and increasing his potential for speed.

When you look at the shoulder and foreleg while the horse is standing, notice that the point of the shoulder is the extended bone structure of the upper arm bone. There is a gap between the lower part of the front edge of the shoulder blade and the extension of the humerus. When the shoulder and foreleg are extended to make a stride, this extended part of the arm bone fits into the lower part of

◀ **A. Laid-back shoulder. Shoulder blade should slope back so the humerus and foreleg can swing freely. B. Upright shoulder.**

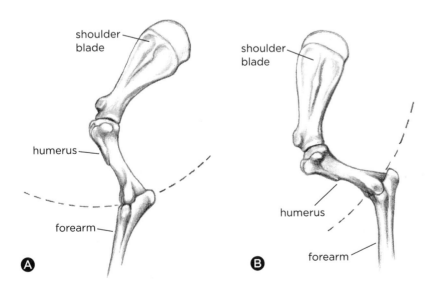

shoulder blade

humerus

forearm

Ⓐ

shoulder blade

humerus

forearm

Ⓑ

the shoulder blade, creating a locked position, which determines the extent of the forward reach of the leg. If the shoulder blade is upright, the gap between it and the forearm is greatly reduced, shortening the degree to which the leg can extend.

STEEP SHOULDER

If the shoulder is too upright, the front legs will be set too far under the horse, making him unable to extend forward as he should. He has a short, choppy gait, with increased concussion and less speed. His feet lift higher (with higher knee action) rather than forward, and they hit the ground with greater impact and frequency than feet in a longer-striding horse.

When traveling fast, the horse should be able to reach out well past his nose with his front feet, and he can only do this if his shoulder is long and sloping rather than short and steep.

LENGTH OF SHOULDER

A horse with a long, sloping shoulder also has room for optimal length of muscle. Because the inner side of the shoulder blade is attached to the body by muscles, a long shoulder offers more room for these muscle attachments, providing greater support and smoother movement. It also distributes this attachment and its burden of weight over a greater area, with a larger bearing surface against the body. This minimizes the jar and strain on any one part of the shoulder and allows for extended stride and freer movement of the leg.

The greater the length of the muscles on the outer side of the shoulder blade, the more they can contract, providing the horse greater range of motion at each stride. A shorter, more upright shoulder carrying the same muscle mass will be heavier and bulkier, inclining the horse to be awkward and clumsy. Any extra bulk will also make the horse heavier in front, reducing agility, speed, and endurance.

A sloping, well-laid-back shoulder gives a jumping horse more room to lift and tuck his front legs when going over an obstacle. As the horse prepares to take off, the shoulder muscles pull the shoulder blades into a nearly horizontal position, enabling him to lift the front legs. The more horizontal the shoulder can become, the easier it is for the horse to tuck up his front legs more tightly. The greater the length of the shoulder blade and humerus, the greater the horse's ability to lift and tuck his front legs. The mobility of this long shoulder also gives more shock-absorbing capacity when the horse lands from the jump.

In a short shoulder, the muscles must be tighter and tend to become overdeveloped in order to withstand the increased jar and concussion. The cartilage and ligaments suffer more wear and tear and become less flexible, which can result in stiffer shoulder action. With less bearing surface against the body, the muscles must become stronger, thus more fibrous and rigid, in order to bear all the weight, reducing shoulder action and causing premature stiffness. The stress of impact also tightens the shoulder muscles, making the stride even shorter and the horse less supple and flexible in his movements.

Conformation Close-up

Ideally, the length of the shoulder should be about the same length as the neck, from the top of the neck at the poll to the bottom of the neck at the front of the withers. When the neck and shoulder length are similar, the horse is well balanced.

CORRELATION OF HUMERUS AND SHOULDER

The humerus connects the point of the shoulder with the elbow, creating an angle with the shoulder blade that should match the angle between the pelvis and the femur. The exact angle is not important, as long as it's similar to the angle in the hindquarters of that particular horse. If you use the centers of the bones as reference points, the angle between the humerus and the shoulder blade should be between 105 and 120 degrees; if you use the point of the shoulder as the junction of the angle lines, the angle should be about 85 degrees.

If the angle between the humerus and the shoulder is too acute, the horse will be pigeon-breasted. This is common in horses with a

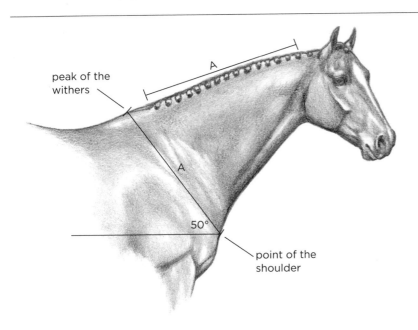

The shoulder, from the peak of the withers to the point of the shoulder (A), should be about as long as the neck, from poll to front of the withers (A).

⚠ A pigeon-breasted horse has a long, upright shoulder with a low point of shoulder, and a horizontal humerus sets the front legs too far under the body.

long, upright shoulder blade, which sets the point of the shoulder too low and the humerus too horizontal. The end of the humerus that meets the elbow is therefore set too far back, placing the front legs too far back under the body. The horse appears to stick out in front, like a pigeon. His front legs cannot extend as far as they should and he swings them more to the side instead, creating a rolling, uncoordinated gait. The problem is accentuated if the front of the chest is also too wide.

The horse with an optimal shoulder angle is more agile and better able to cope with uneven terrain or sudden changes in direction. Likewise, the rider endures less jarring and bounce because concussion is better dissipated. A sloping shoulder places the withers farther back. Ideally, the withers should be set well behind the elbow, rather than directly over the foreleg. This gives a smooth ride, decreasing the jarring felt by the rider. With a sloping shoulder, the rider is farther back and also sits on the most flexible part of the horse's back, thereby reducing concussion on the leg joints. If the horse has an upright shoulder, the rider's weight is more directly over the front legs and increases stress and impact on the front legs (see chapter 6).

Hindquarter Angles

While the shoulders and forelegs are attached to the spine by muscles, the hindquarters are firmly attached to the spine and pelvis by bone joints. Thus, the hind legs can give direct driving power to propel the horse forward. Because the hind legs do not receive as much concussion as the front legs, the bony attachments of the hind legs (at the sacroiliac joints, between the sacrum and the ilium of the pelvis) usually do not suffer undue shock.

Ideally, the angles in both the shoulder and hindquarters should be very close to an equilateral triangle (see illustration on page 207). In the hindquarter, this triangle is created by an imaginary line drawn between the point of the hip and the point of the buttock, from buttock to stifle, and back up to the point of the hip.

LENGTH OF STRIDE

The angles in the hindquarters help determine the length of the horse's stride. The sharper the angles, the longer the reach he has with his hind legs. Just as in the shoulder, if the angle is too wide, there is less forward reach of the leg. Range of motion in the legs depends on the hip joint in the hind leg and on the rotation point of the shoulder blade in the front leg.

The hip joint is deep under the muscles, not at the outer wing of the point of the hip. You can locate the position of the hip joint by looking at the point of the buttock and drawing an imaginary horizontal line from the buttock to the concavity below and slightly behind the point of the hip. The hip joint beneath all that muscle is a few inches forward of the buttock, at the level of the imaginary line. The hip joint should be level with the rotation point of the shoulder blade: the point that rotates as the leg moves forward or back without changing its forward or backward position.

SPEED AND AGILITY

The closer the rotation point of the shoulder is to the withers, the longer are the swing of the lower part of the shoulder and the horse's stride. For athletic speed or stride length, the rotation point of the shoulder should be somewhere in the top third of the shoulder blade. For a sprinter that may need a shorter, quicker stride, however, the rotation point can be closer to the middle of the shoulder blade; hindquarter angle will match.

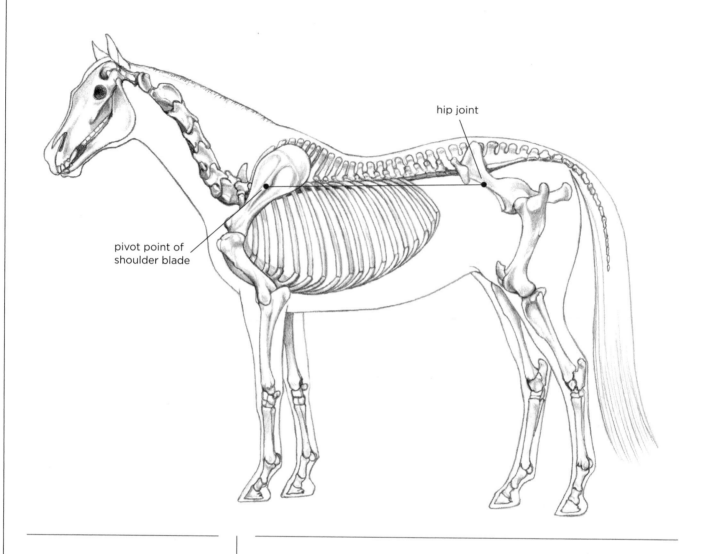

pivot point of
shoulder blade

hip joint

⚠ **The hip joint should be level with the rotation point of the shoulder blade.**

Hindquarter angles play a significant role in a horse's speed and agility. When a horse runs, much of the driving power and thrust comes from the hindquarters. A horse with acute angles and a longer swing of the leg has more freedom of movement and usually more agility. He can typically outrun a horse with wide angles and a shorter stride and won't have to work as hard while doing it.

Pastern Angle

The angle of the pasterns should match the angle of the foot. The pastern axis and foot axis create one continuous line running through the core of the pastern and down through the hoof. If this line breaks forward or backward with a different angle in the foot, the bones, joints, ligaments, and tendons will experience increased stress.

The angle of the pasterns is important in the equine athlete and crucial to length of stride, ease of gait, and durability. The actual "ideal" angle varies depending on a horse's leg and body conformation. A 45- to 55-degree angle in front pasterns is usually appropriate,

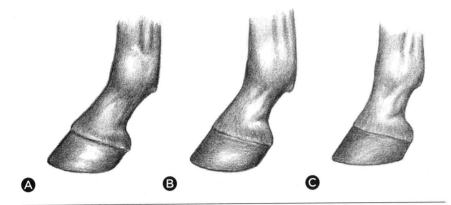

◀ Long pasterns are often more sloped than short pasterns; the latter tend to be more upright. **A.** Long pastern. **B.** Normal pastern. **C.** Short pastern.

with a corresponding 49- to 59-degree angle in the hind pasterns. If pasterns have steeper angles and are too upright, the front legs will suffer excessive concussion and the horse will ride rough. Pasterns that slope too much, with an angle less than 45 degrees, tend to be weak and more prone to breakdown.

PASTERN LENGTH

Pasterns may be long, short, or "ideal." Sloping pasterns often tend to be a little longer than upright pasterns. If well formed, front pasterns can be long and springy without being weak. The hind pastern should be a little shorter (with a wider, more upright angle) and heavier boned than the front, though it should never be straight and rigid. If the hind pastern is too long and flexible, the weight of the body may cause it to yield before the hock can take up the strain, which puts a lot of stress on the pastern and fetlock joint.

HOW MUCH SLOPE?

The stacked angle of the pastern bones allows the lower leg joints to absorb more of the shock of impact concussion. This gives more spring and smoothness of gait than bones stacked end on end can give. In light horse breeds (especially racehorses), properly sloped front pasterns decrease the risk of tendon strain and breakdown, as well as sore shins, splints, and knee injuries due to concussion. Navicular disease is more common in horses with upright pastern conformation than in those with more sloping, springy pasterns and a lighter step. Navicular disease can also occur in horses with excessive pastern slope and too long a toe. This conformation puts more strain on the heel area and on the tendons that glide over the navicular bone.

Occasionally, a horse has pasterns that are too long and "springy" (too sloped) to provide adequate support for the leg. Front pasterns that slope too much may be weak, with the fetlock joint coming clear

Pasterns as Shock Absorbers

The horse's pasterns are his best shock absorbers, especially in the front legs. Pastern angles help dictate whether a horse has a smooth or jarring gait and whether he will be prone to concussion-related injuries to feet and legs. In the hind leg, the hock joint flexes whenever the leg takes weight, and this counters most of the shock and concussion. But in the front leg, the knee joint is fully extended and the elbow is locked when weight is placed on the leg. The job of absorbing concussion falls largely to the pastern joint. Thus, the front pasterns should be properly angled and flexible.

down to the ground when the horse is running. If a front pastern does not slope enough, having an angle greater than 50 to 55 degrees, it is too steep. If the pastern is both steep and short, the foot will not have much give when it hits the ground. The horse will have a choppy, jarring gait, which is damaging to feet and legs and uncomfortable for the rider. The front pasterns are typically more sloped than the hind pasterns.

The heavy draft horse, with less pastern slope than most light horses, is susceptible to excessive concussion and related problems, such as ringbone. Concussion problems are common if draft horses are worked on hard surfaces. Pastern angle is usually similar to shoulder angle (though it is not uncommon to have pasterns a little steeper than the shoulder), and in a draft horse the shoulder is more upright than in a riding horse. For pulling, the draft horse's pasterns must be very strong and relatively upright. Short, straight, upright pasterns give more leverage when a horse digs in to pull a heavy load, but they also increase the risk of concussion injury and arthritis. The Clydesdale and Percheron generally have better-sloped pasterns than the Shire, and fewer problems when trotting on hard surfaces. Percheron horses have Arabian blood in their ancestry, giving them more sloped angles and freer action.

If the pastern slopes adequately, it transfers some of the stress and weight bearing to the tendons as the horse travels. Because the tendons are more elastic and resilient than bones, there is less damage from concussion. If the pastern is too upright, however, a far greater amount of concussion is transmitted directly to the bones of the leg. Over time, this can lead to many types of injury, as well as unsoundnesses (see chapter 16).

STRIDE AND BREAKOVER

Ideally, the foot should break over smoothly and reach the height of its arc as it passes the opposite leg. A properly sloped foot will have a strong, well-built heel that is not too low or shallow. It will have less heel than a foot having a short, steep pastern and hoof angle, however. A horse with a sloped pastern will break over a little slower at each stride and have a longer stride than a horse with an upright, stumpy foot (a boxy foot that is shorter from front to back). The more angled pastern has a corresponding, slightly longer toe, as well as a longer stride and a different foot flight. A horse with a pastern angle of less than 45 degrees and a long toe usually has a delayed breakover, lifting the foot higher and reaching the highest point of its arc before it passes the opposite leg. Then the foot flight settles into a long stride, touching down gently. Horses such as this may have a sloped shoulder and a graceful long stride (and a very comfortable ride), but care must be taken to be sure the toe of the foot is not too long or the angle too sloped, or there will be more strain on parts of the leg.

By contrast, the horse with an upright shoulder and short, steep pasterns will often have a high heel and a short toe. He has a quick breakover because of the short toe, but also has a shorter stride and more jarring gait. The decreased effort needed to raise the already high heel, and the quick breakover of the short toe, are reflected in his foot flight. The arc is lower at first (because it takes less effort for the foot to leave the ground), and more forward, not reaching its full height until it is well past the opposite leg, at which point the foot may be raised quite high. Then it comes abruptly and forcefully back to the ground. This type of conformation makes for a very choppy, pounding gait with short strides.

The longer-striding horse with more sloping pasterns doesn't lift his feet quite as high but makes a longer sweep over the ground. The horse with upright pasterns usually has higher leg action, bringing his feet to the ground much more quickly and sharply, and expending more energy in up-and-down motion than forward motion.

Height

THE IDEAL HEIGHT for a horse, as it pertains to athletic ability, is debatable. Even in breeds where the majority of individuals are shorter or taller than the average horse population, some enthusiasts prefer that horses be taller or shorter than the breed standard.

Horse height is measured in hands from the ground to the top of the withers. A hand is 4 inches. The average riding horse is about 15 hands tall (that is, 60 inches, or 5 feet tall), depending on breed. Ponies are usually less than 14.2 hands (14 hands 2 inches, or 58 inches tall) — the height that differentiates a horse from a pony — though some horses are shorter and some ponies are

The height of a horse must be evaluated in relation to his overall body balance. Whether a horse is tall or short, for best speed and agility his body needs proper proportions. Height alone does not guarantee athletic ability.

taller than this. There are short and tall individuals in every breed, but some breeds are taller than others, on average.

Is He Balanced?

Height in a horse should always be evaluated in relation to his overall conformation and balance. Height alone won't tell you whether a horse will make a good athlete. Body balance from front to back, whether the horse has uphill or downhill balance and is front heavy or rear heavy, and body proportions — shoulder, middle, and hindquarter — are more important than size (see chapter 10).

LEG AND BODY MUST BE PROPORTIONATE

Length of leg should match body build. Body length from the point of shoulder to the buttocks should be the same as the horse's height from the ground to the top of the withers; that is, his body should be square. For most horses, and particularly for the smaller Thoroughbreds, a square body is a good guide for the ideal height and length relationship, but a few good hunters may be a little longer than this in body.

The type of conformation to avoid when selecting or breeding horses for athletic ability is the tall, leggy horse that lacks depth of body, and the short-backed horse that has long legs. If a horse is shorter in body length than he is tall, he will usually have a stiff gait, because of his too-short back. He will also tend to forge, striking his hind feet against his front feet, because his legs are too long for his body length.

If a horse's legs are too long in proportion to the length or depth of his body, he will not be agile. He may also have problems with balance or efficient locomotion and a tendency toward incoordination. The leggy horse without depth of body and chest (being high off the ground, without sufficient depth of chest to compensate and balance it out) may be fast on a straightaway and for short distances, but he lacks balance for speed work of an intricate nature. He also lacks staying power due to limited room for lung expansion. Depth of chest, allowing good lung room, should always be a consideration; when looking at a horse's height, also look for depth of chest equal to leg length.

SHORT LEGS VS. LONG LEGS

It is probably a more serious fault for a horse to have long legs and no depth of chest and body than to have short legs and a deep chest and body. A shorter-legged horse has a lower center of gravity and better base of support, with securer balance than an overly leggy horse. During the gallop, for instance, a shorter-legged horse has better equilibrium. Horses with short legs rarely overreach and forge, yet this is a common problem in a disproportionately long-legged horse.

The best speed comes most consistently from a properly balanced horse whose legs are equal to his body proportions. A short-legged horse can be swift if he can move his legs fast enough to compensate for his shorter stride. Stride length is not affected as much by the size of the horse as by the angle of his hip and shoulder.

Short-legged horses may be either lazy or fast, depending on their individual nature. When a short-legged horse gallops well, he can often compete with the best of the taller, leggier horses, due to better balance and body control on turns and uneven terrain, especially on

Did You Know?

A tall horse is usually heavier than a small horse and is more apt to have insufficient bone support for his body. Many large, tall horses lack adequate bone circumference and thus are too "fine boned" for their size and weight, which can lead to leg injuries and soundness problems that might not occur in the smaller horse (see chapter 7). Adequate bone size and strength ensure durability and future soundness. It is often difficult to find these traits in a large horse.

Legs and body proportions should match. **A.** Long legs and shallow body. **B.** Long legs and too-short back (the horse will usually forge, or strike his front feet with his hinds).

the downhill slopes. On a long uphill grade, however, the longer-legged horse, if he is not too heavy in the body, has the advantage.

For good athletic ability, you don't want a horse with legs too short; this puts him at a great disadvantage and also means his back is too long in relation to his height. The slightly short-legged horse or the perfectly square horse usually excels in most athletic activities and careers, so always consider this when evaluating height in relation to a horse's conformation.

Height and Rider Size

If you are selecting a horse for yourself for a certain career or selecting a horse for a child or young rider, it's important to chose a horse of appropriate height and size for the person who will ride him. A very tall horse may be awkward for a short rider. A small, short horse may have a more difficult time performing while carrying a large or heavy rider.

HORSE TOO TALL

A short rider on a tall horse may have trouble communicating with the horse by use of seat and leg aids, because the rider's legs are too short to reach far enough down the sides of the horse. A horse's sensitivity to leg aids is not as fine higher up on his sides. He may not be as responsive as he would be to a rider with longer legs. A short rider on a tall horse is also at a great disadvantage when mounting and dismounting, because the stirrups are too short.

HORSE TOO SHORT

A tall, long-legged, or heavy rider may feel uncomfortable on a small horse. It may be hard for a long-legged rider to find her balance and use leg aids properly. If the rider's legs hang too far down the horse's sides, the calves of the rider's legs may not be able to contact the horse effectively.

A tall or heavy rider may hinder a small horse's balance and athletic ability. If a rider is tall, this may make the horse-rider balance top-heavy, throwing the horse off balance during certain maneuvers. If the rider gets off balance or loses proper position in the saddle, the horse may be more apt to trip and get out of position.

WEIGHT CARRYING

Generally, it is wise to match the size of the horse to the size of the rider. If the rider is too heavy for the horse, this may lead to back soreness, particularly if the rider does not always ride in a balanced position. Carrying extra weight may tire the horse more quickly; he may not be able to perform as well or as willingly as he would with a lighter rider. In addition, increased concussive force may lead to front leg injury or lameness.

Typically, a horse should not be asked to carry more than 20 percent of his body weight. Thus, an 800-pound horse should not be asked to carry more than 160 pounds of weight (combined weight of rider and tack). This is a relative figure, however, because tack is deadweight and a rider is live weight. It is usually easier for a horse to carry additional live weight than additional deadweight: the rider can move to keep in proper balance with the horse, as when going uphill or downhill, for instance. Avoid using a big, heavy saddle on a small horse.

Another factor to consider is that many small horses, especially those of Arabian breeding — due to their strong, short backs and stamina — have more weight-carrying ability for their size than do larger horses. The 20 percent rule may not always apply. A 900-pound Arabian may easily be able to carry 25 percent of his weight on an endurance ride, whereas some larger horses would have a hard time carrying 20 percent of their weight on a long ride.

What Height Is Ideal?

Big is not always better. An adage states, "A good little horse will beat a good big horse any day." A smaller horse is often better proportioned than a tall horse and, therefore, more agile and able to collect himself, making him more maneuverable for fast work. A tall horse may have a lot of speed, but unless he has excellent body proportions, it may take him a long time to stop and turn. A long leg without the body proportions to match can be a detriment to speed and balance. Overall body balance is more important than size: the horse must "fit" together, regardless of size and height (see page 258).

◯ Conformation Close-up

An upright shoulder can add height but is undesirable. A horseman should never select for height alone, especially if extra inches are gained in the shoulder. An upright shoulder creates an abnormal wither and a lot more concussion on legs and body. A horse with an upright shoulder and pushed-up withers is often taller at the withers than at the croup, an imbalance that may hinder athletic ability and agility.

ALL-AROUND ATHLETES

When agility and staying power are considered, a well-built small horse will often do better than a well-built tall horse. The best cutting horses, for instance, are generally small: 15 hands or less. Several breeds, including Quarter Horses, Arabians, and Morgans, have done well in this sport, and many of the best have been short, well-proportioned individuals.

The Quarter Horse, for instance, is known for its bulky muscles and quick burst of speed; many individuals weigh as much as 1400 to 1600 pounds at 15 to 16 hands in height. But the cutting horse is the petite ballet dancer of that breed. A good cutting horse rarely weighs more than 1200 pounds and is usually less than 15 hands high.

Racing and jumping enthusiasts often prefer a taller horse with more leg, because a well-proportioned tall horse has longer legs and can take longer strides. Likewise, a tall or heavy rider usually prefers a tall horse.

In general, smaller horses tend to be more agile than the larger, taller horses. Even for speed, the short, compact horse (like the Quarter Horse) usually outruns the taller, leggier horse (such as the Thoroughbred) over short distances, but may then tire if he is heavily muscled. Over long distances, a lean horse will ultimately outrun a bulky horse, and the small, light-muscled horse (such as the Arabian) generally has the most endurance for the longest races.

Many good "little" horses have been successful in grueling sports because of their compact strength and perfect balance. In sports that require great maneuverability, a well-balanced small horse is generally more "handy" than a larger one. Even in straightaway racing, legginess in a tall horse may be a detriment to stamina. As soon as the horse begins to tire, he begins to sway. He may start changing leads more frequently to rest his leading legs and aid his balance. If he does this too frequently he will lose ground. He can probably keep running in a straight line while switching, but if he changes leads too much on a turn, this may cause him to wobble off his course.

Cross-country races and steeplechase tracks often have a variety of uphill and downhill slopes where the smaller, compact horse has an advantage over the tall horse because he is closer to the ground and has better balance, especially when a number of running horses are crowded together. The taller horse is often not quite as sure-footed and is more easily thrown off balance. Occasionally, a taller horse may have an advantage over a smaller one because hunt courses are sometimes designed for horses with long strides.

DRAWBACKS OF HEIGHT

From foalhood, large, leggy horses tend to have higher risks for injury and problems. A horse genetically programmed for a lot of growth is often large as a foal and may have a difficult birth and complications related to prolonged birth.

The large, fast-growing youngster may also be more prone to skeletal problems. He may be too heavy for his soft, immature bone structure and be at risk for skeletal deformities. He may have weak spots in the fast-growing bones due to nutritional imbalances; his fast growth creates special needs and problems that do not affect a

Did You Know?

A small horse almost always has better endurance than a large, bulky horse. A small horse has lighter muscles and therefore less body weight to pack around. A small Arabian (under 15 hands and less than 1000 pounds) has tremendous weight-carrying capacity for his size and weight. Because he has an extra pair of ribs and, in most cases, one less lumbar vertebrae, he has a very strong back. The small Arabian has superior endurance over a long course and has proved the abilities of the "little" horse.

smaller, slower-growing foal. Developmental orthopedic disease (DOD) includes a wide range of ailments — from *physitis* (inflammation of the growth plates at the ends of long bones) to *osteochondritis* (inflammation of both the bone and the cartilage at the bone ends) and contracted tendons in the legs. DOD is more common in large youngsters than in small ones.

The large horse tends to have more foot and leg problems, especially if his feet are small for his body weight. If his feet are not structurally adequate for his size, he is more apt to develop concussion-related problems, such as navicular syndrome, ringbone, and sidebone. His hooves may not be strong enough to withstand the pounding and may develop cracks in the hoof wall. Excess concussion may also lead to splints and bucked shins.

The larger the body, the harder the fall. If a large horse is uncoordinated, he is more apt to fall down than a smaller, more balanced horse. A small horse taking a tumble may not injure himself as severely as a big horse whose heavier body crashes to the ground with tremendous force.

In any sport where agility is needed, excess size and height can be a serious handicap. Very few barrel racers, polo horses, cutting horses, and reining horses are large. If a horse needs quickness and balance, being large or tall is usually a detriment. Size is occasionally an advantage but is rarely a necessity; in fact, in more instances than not, it can be a liability.

JUMPING ABILITY

Even among show jumpers, the tallest horse is not necessarily the best at clearing the highest jumps. In earlier days at country shows, for example, it was not unusual for a heavy half-bred horse (part draft, part light horse) to perform just as well or better than the taller, more gangly Thoroughbred. In fact, the shorter, compact half-bred might have done some plowing on his owner's farm in the morning, only to be ridden into the show ring in the afternoon to clear a high obstacle with ease.

The height of a horse does not seem to make a significant difference in jumping ability; some short horses are natural jumpers and do as well or better than tall ones. But if the horse is heavy bodied, he may not have the endurance of a lighter-muscled, taller horse. The main drawback to the staying power of a jumper is his body build, not his height. A heavy-bodied horse, whether short or tall, has more deadweight to carry over a jump, which requires him to expend more energy and effort. There is a point at which the extra power derived from the heavier muscles is no longer sufficient to compensate for the additional weight that must be carried over the jump. For stamina, the jumping horse should not be too heavy in body.

The well-balanced, moderately muscled small horse, however, often does very well on the jump or hunt course. It's quite common for a strong pony or a very small horse to carry a lightweight rider over fairly high jumps. There is no reason a well-built 15-hand horse cannot tackle any type of obstacle he may encounter in the jumping ring. The smaller horse has some advantages in competition jumping because it takes less room for him to turn and adjust his strides; he can go through a difficult course in less time than the leggier, more awkward or less balanced horse. If both individuals are of equal jumping ability, the extra agility and balance can enable the smaller horse to make his way through an intricate course faster than the taller, longer-legged horse.

PROBLEMS WITH LONG CANNON BONES

Proper cannon length has suffered greatly in many modern breeding programs, particularly in breeds that people have tried to make taller. Many of these taller horses have longer cannons, but the forearm has not changed proportionately; it is still about the same length as that of a shorter horse. The "normal," well-proportioned, athletic horse has a forearm that is longer than the cannon bone. A one-to-one ratio of cannon to forearm length diminishes the likelihood of durability and long-term soundness.

Thus, the taller horse that has long cannons and relatively short forearms for his size has a leg bone structure that is not balanced. A horse with a long cannon and short forearm is never as agile and doesn't hold up as well under hard use as a horse with a better muscle-to-tendon ratio. For speed and agility, horses need long muscles and short tendons.

Estimating Mature Height

If you are evaluating a foal, yearling, or even a 2-year-old, it may be difficult to estimate what height he will be at maturity just by looking at him. Horses grow and mature at different rates. One individual may be smaller than his peers as a yearling but catch up by the time he is 2 or 3 years old. Some horses may not reach full height and maturity until they are 6 years old. Some breeds grow more slowly than others. For instance, a young Quarter Horse may reach full height by the time he is 2 or 3 years old, whereas an Arabian may not reach his mature height until he is age 6 or 7.

WAYS TO ESTIMATE MATURE HEIGHT

The foal's legs are quite long in proportion to his body size and depth; cannon bones and pasterns are nearly as long as they will be when he grows up. His forearms and hooves, however, do more growing in comparison. By the time he is a yearling, his legs have grown about as long as they are going to be at maturity, but his body depth is still incomplete.

A mature light horse from a riding horse breed measures about the same from the center of the fetlock joint to his elbow as he does from his elbow to his withers. One way to guess a foal's eventual height is to use a string or flexible tape measure to determine the distance from fetlock to elbow, and then use that measurement to see how far up it will go from his elbow. The usual rule of thumb is to take that height and add 2 inches, which yields his approximate mature height at the withers. This method is fairly accurate unless at maturity a particular horse will have very low withers ("mutton withers") or exceptionally high withers. In these instances, an estimate made at foalhood could be off by an inch or two.

Estimating the mature height of a yearling is probably a little more accurate than estimating the mature height of a foal, especially in horses that mature to approximately 15 to 16.3 hands. The animal

▶ Estimating the mature height. Determine the distance from fetlock to elbow in the foal, then project that distance up from his elbow and add 2 inches.

add 2 inches to this height

is measured from ergot (the small waxy lump on the skin surface at the bottom and back of the fetlock joint) to elbow, then this measurement is projected from elbow to where the withers will eventually be.

The yearling's leg measurement is about the same as it will be as an adult; he will do the rest of his growing by becoming fuller and deeper in body and gaining more withers. By measuring his leg length from ergot to elbow, then holding that same length of string from the elbow straight up to where his withers will be and adding 1 inch, you can get a fairly good estimate of his final height.

Measuring Tip

On the outer surface of the elbow joint, just below the rounded triceps muscle, there is a small pit or dimple. At the lower edge of this pit, on the bony part of the elbow, you will feel a small bony protrusion about the size of a pea. This little prominence is the point from which to measure, when holding your string or measuring tape, to estimate the horse's mature height.

How a Horse Moves

KNOWING HOW A HORSE travels and handles himself at various gaits can help a horseman become a better rider, trainer, and judge of horses. A working knowledge of the anatomy, gaits, and abilities of the horse can show us the "why" of good horsemanship and the reasons a horse may or may not be able to perform a certain task or do well in a certain career. Different gaits and activities put different stresses on the horse's legs. His movements at various gaits can give a better idea of his athletic ability.

Conformation influences the gaits that come most naturally to a horse. Understanding leg action and various gaits will help you evaluate a horse's athletic potential and ability. Knowing what normal looks like can also help you detect lameness.

Center of Gravity

The center of gravity, or point of balance, is the point at which a horse's body would hang in perfect balance if suspended. Like the center of a wheel, this spot stays relatively still when a horse is moving.

Because the front end of a horse is heavier than the hind, when standing still his center of gravity is located toward the front of his body. For most horses, the center of gravity is near the front of the rib cage, about two-thirds of the way down an imaginary vertical line from just behind the withers to a few inches behind the elbow. More specifically, if a vertical line is dropped from the seventh thoracic vertebrae, where the withers join the back, and another line is run horizontally from the point of the shoulder toward the buttocks (parallel to the ground), the point at which these two lines intersect is the center of gravity when the horse is standing.

With the added weight of a rider, the point of balance is where the rider can most easily "stay with" the horse during movement.

▼ Center of gravity

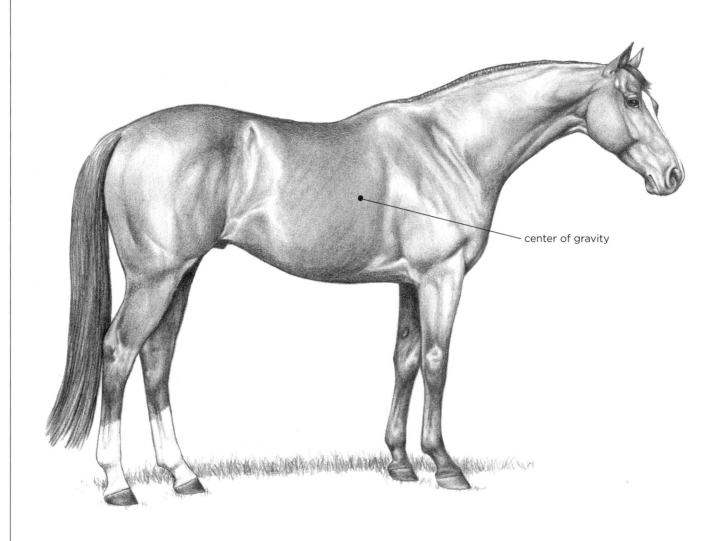

center of gravity

Because the horse is front heavy, the best place for the rider is near the front of his back, which is also the strongest part of the back and the most logical place for the rider to sit.

When a horse moves, notice how he must compensate for the fact that most of the weight is carried by his front feet. He can lift a hind foot at any time, but because of the extra weight on his front end, he can't lift a front foot when standing squarely unless he first shifts his weight toward the rear. If you start to lead a horse forward when he is standing squarely, he must raise his head before he takes a step. He then crouches a little at the rear or moves one hind foot forward to shift his body weight back so he can lift a front foot.

During various gaits, the horse constantly uses his head and neck for balance, lowering and raising his head to shift his center of gravity forward or back.

Gaits

The horse is capable of four or five different gaits, but most horses do only three naturally: the walk, the trot, and the gallop. The canter is a slow, collected gallop and so is not considered a separate gait. Through selective breeding and training, some horses can do other gaits, as well, such as the running walk, the rack (also called the singlefoot), the stepping pace (a highly collected rack), the amble, and the fox-trot. In addition, various Paso breeds have a distinctive gait and leg action, and the Icelandic horse does a tolt, a natural fast rack.

THE WALK

The walk is a four-beat gait in which the legs move independently of each other in a definite sequence; it is a horse's slowest gait. Unless he is standing off balance, a horse will generally start his stride with a hind leg. The horse's conformation and the speed of the walk determine how the feet are picked up and set down. Some horses take long strides, whereas others take short, choppy strides. Some horses' hind feet overstep the tracks made by the front feet by a few inches to a foot or more.

During the slow walk, a horse usually has three feet on the ground at one time. As a hind leg comes forward, the front foot on that same side prepares to push off. It leaves the ground a split second before the hind foot lands. Each foot moves in order, creating a distinct four-beat gait.

At the slow walk, the hind foot lands in back of the front foot that is leaving the ground. At a faster walk, the hind foot usually lands in the same track or a little in advance of where the front foot was. As the

Leg Sequence at the Walk

When the right front moves forward, the next leg to leave the ground is the left hind, then the left front, then the right hind. This sequence continually repeats itself: right front, left hind, left front, right hind, right front, and so on. As a hind comes forward, the front foot on that side is lifted, getting out of the way of the approaching hind foot. If the horse starts moving with his left hind, the next foot to move will be the left front. He moves both legs on one side first, then both legs of the other side. Thus, the walk is classified as a four-beat lateral gait — *lateral* because both legs on the same side move one after the other, then the legs on the opposite side move one after the other.

speed of the walk increases, each foot is raised a little earlier. The fronts are picked up more swiftly to get out of the way of the approaching hinds. At the fast walk, each foot is raised before the diagonally opposite foot comes to rest. In other words, the right hind is lifted before the left front foot strikes the ground.

The front foot of one side is lifted before the hind foot on that side has reached the ground, causing the horse to roll a little toward the unsupported side. Thus, at the fast walk, the horse has only two feet on the ground at once, and he shifts his weight alternately onto a lateral pair and then to a diagonal pair.

At a fast walk, the hind foot will usually land well forward of the track made by the front foot that has just been picked up. At the fast walk and at the faster gaits, the horse's heel comes to the ground first, unless he has a serious foot or leg problem that makes him land on his sole or toe. At the slow walk, however, the foot is often put down squarely.

Conformation Close-up

When a front foot comes forward and lands, the weight is rolled from the heel to the toe, then the toe grips the ground and helps pull the horse forward as that foot breaks over and is lifted again. Until the sole of the front foot reaches a vertical position (just before the foot breaks over and is picked up again), the front foot pulls the horse forward. Some authorities believe that any unnatural interference with the front feet, such as shortening the toe too much, can affect how fast a horse can travel. In a mile race, it can account for several feet or yards.

What to Look For

The ideal walk is a long-striding, free-flowing gait. If the horse walks well, there will be some swing to his back and tail and a nice fluid motion: his whole body moves, not just his legs. He moves from hips and shoulders, and the hips rise and fall evenly with each stride. The head and neck swing evenly up and down and slightly side to side. If you see any unevenness or stiffness, the horse may have a problem that could interfere with his athletic ability.

THE TROT

The trot is a two-beat diagonal gait. The left front and right hind move in unison, as do the right front and left hind. During the fast trot, there is a moment of suspension in which there are no feet on the ground. During the slow trot, this suspension is not obvious; one

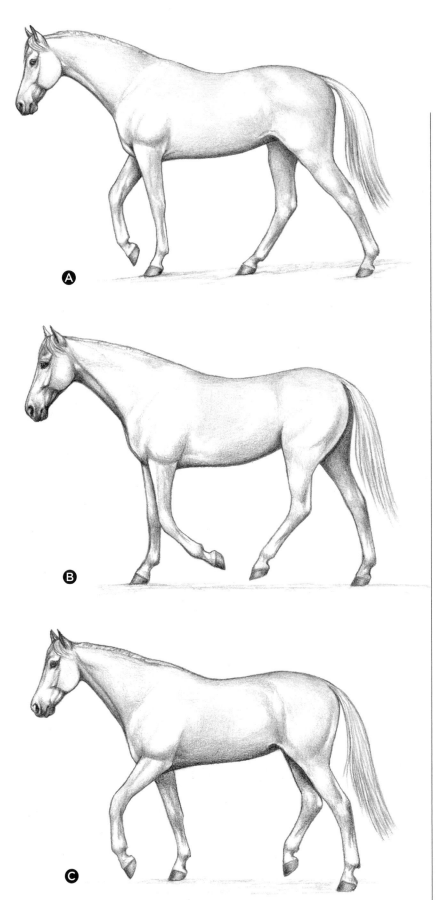

◀ **A.** Slow walk: three feet on the ground at once. **B, C.** Fast walk: only two feet on the ground at once, alternating from a pair of lateral legs (B) to a pair of diagonal legs (C).

Ⓐ

Ⓑ

Ⓒ

diagonal is coming to the ground at nearly the same time the other is pushing off. The trot has constant, equal rhythm. The horse's head stays level instead of bobbing up and down as it does in the walk and gallop.

A trot can be slow, medium, fast, collected, or extended. At the slow trot, the horse takes short strides. He takes longer strides at a medium trot and very long strides at the extended trot. Horses that do an extended trot cover the ground faster by lengthening their stride, not by accelerating their leg movements.

What to Look For

When evaluating a horse's trot, look for even strides. This is the most symmetrical gait, and any abnormality or slight gait defect will be obvious. The trot is a useful gait for detecting soreness and lameness (see chapter 16), because it is faster than a walk and the horse only has two feet on the ground at once. In the walk, two other legs are usually on the ground to help share and lessen the weight on a lame leg. In the trot, the horse's head and neck stay still (no bobbing motion for balance as in the walk or gallop), so any little bobble indicates a problem. At a normal trot, the horse should swing along freely, with hind feet overstepping the tracks made by the fronts. He should have good hock flexion and thrust from the hind legs.

● The trot: diagonal legs work in unison.

Conformation Close-up

How a horse's body is structured plays a major role in what gaits come naturally and also determines at what point he changes gait. Some horses are natural trotters (or pacers, or do a single-foot instead of a trot), whereas others prefer to gallop. You may not be able to tell this by looking at him at rest, however, which is another good reason to evaluate him when he is moving and when he is standing still.

THE GALLOP

The gallop is the fastest natural gait of most horses. This is a fully extended gait: the horse stretches his head and neck as far forward as possible and takes long strides. The gallop is a four-beat gait with a brief moment of suspension in which all four feet are off the ground.

At the fast gallop, the hind feet break the shock as the horse lands from each stride, and the forelegs take a large share in propelling and pulling the horse along. The long muscle in his neck helps pull the front legs forward, causing the head to bob at each stride. At the fast gallop, the horse extends his head and neck to make his head a fixed point from which this neck muscle can help pull the front legs farther forward at each stride. A well-laid-back (long, sloping) shoulder is essential for speed. The humerus can be flexed more rapidly and completely, and the front leg has a freer, more forward swing and thus a longer stride, unlike that of a horse with an upright shoulder whose leg action is cramped because his forearm cannot swing forward as far.

The horse's back remains fairly rigid during fast gaits. Most of the movement occurs in the neck and at the lumbosacral joint to enable the hindquarters to move forward under the body so the hind legs can reach well forward in a long stride. The longer the stride and the more time the horse can spend in the air between strides, the faster he will be, for his forward propulsion is hampered somewhat each time a foot hits the ground.

At a fast gallop, a horse never has more than two feet on the ground at once. The horse can begin the gallop by pushing off with either hind leg, reaching farther forward with the leading hind leg. The next foot to land is the nonleading front foot, then the leading front foot. A period of suspension follows before the hind feet land again (nonleading hind, followed by leading hind), but each foot strikes the ground separately to produce a distinct four-beat gait. There is more distance between strides at the gallop than at the canter.

Did You Know?

The cruising speed of each horse is different. There is a speed at which a horse feels most comfortable at the walk, trot, and gallop. He will automatically change to the faster or slower gait when he feels less comfortable speeding or slowing the gait he is currently doing. Some horses prefer to break into a trot rather than speeding up the walk, or prefer to trot faster rather than breaking into a canter. Some are natural trotters, while others are natural gallopers and prefer to gallop rather than to trot faster.

▶ At the gallop, the horse never has more than two feet on the ground at once, and these are always in pairs (both hinds and both fronts), except for the phase where he is on diagonal legs (leading hind foot and nonleading front — see C).

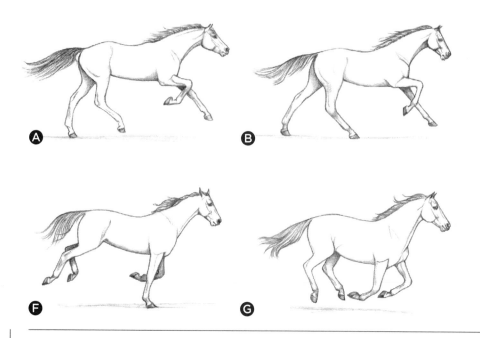

A   B

F   G

What to Look For

At the gallop, the horse should be balanced and able to extend with long strides. There should be obvious flexing in the hindquarters (rotating the hind legs forward from the lumbosacral joint), so he can reach well underneath himself with his hind legs, for a strong thrust. Shoulders should rotate freely so forelegs can extend well forward. The galloping horse should change leads effortlessly, whether to make a turn or just to give his leading legs a rest now and then when running in a straight line.

THE CANTER

The canter is a slow, collected gallop. The horse is not as extended as at the gallop, and this gait is steadier. His head is up, his neck more arched, and he carries his weight farther back on his hindquarters rather than so heavy in front. He is more ready for a quick change of direction at the collected canter than he is at an extended gallop.

When he canters, he has one or three feet on the ground at once, except for the phase of his stride in which all four feet are off the ground. The canter is usually a three-beat gait, unlike the gallop. If a horse is cantering on the right lead, his left hind lands first, then the right hind comes to the ground farther forward and leads, landing simultaneously with the left front for the second beat. Then the right front leg reaches farther forward (leading), coming to the ground for the third beat.

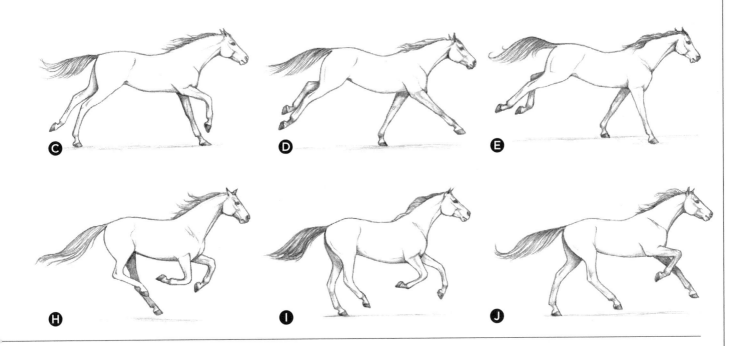

What to Look For

At a canter, the horse should demonstrate good natural balance with good stifle and hock flexion. Lameness is hard to detect at a canter, unless the horse is very lame, because he has several feet on the ground at once for support. When cantering at liberty (no rider), the

▼ At the canter, the horse has one or three feet on the ground at once, except for the phase of his stride in which all four feet are very briefly off the ground.

horse should change leads easily when changing direction, and his gait should be light and effortless.

THE PACE

Some horses, due to heredity and conformation, pace instead of trot. A few horses can do both, but most horses do one or the other. Standardbreds (a breed used for harness racing) are either trotters or pacers, and this is their fastest gait. They can trot or pace as swiftly as other horses gallop. The fastest racing pacers can usually pace a little faster than racing trotters, because the period of suspension in the pace (when all feet are in the air) is slightly longer than in the trot.

Unlike the diagonal trot, the pace is a lateral gait. The legs on the same side come forward together. In the pace, the horse is supported first by legs on one side of the body and then by legs on the other side. This produces a rolling motion from side to side in order to maintain balance.

The pacer does not have the balance and support that a trotter has. Therefore, the pace is not as surefooted as the trot in mud, snow, or on any other type of slippery terrain. More weight is thrown onto

▼ The pace: lateral legs work together in unison.

the legs at a pace, as each lateral pair hits the ground, than at the trot. The fast pace is actually more stressful, with more concussion, than a fast trot.

THE AMBLE

In this gait, the horse is moving each leg separately, as in the walk, but his legs are moving faster. Just as in the walk, the amble is a four-beat, lateral gait (right hind, right front, left hind, left front), but it is swift and smooth. Horses with this gait were popular years ago, before the advent of improved roads and wheeled vehicles.

In the amble, the horse's back remains level, with a gentle side-to-side rocking. There is a slight pause between the two lateral pairs of feet hitting the ground, creating a rapid one-two, one-two beat. This gait was the forerunner of the racing pace and is often described as a pace performed at walking speed, though the hind foot lands a split second before the front on the same side.

THE RACK (SINGLE-FOOT)

The rack, or single-foot, is similar to the amble in that it is also a swift, smooth, four-beat gait, but the beats are completely even; there is no pause between them. The hind foot strikes the ground an instant before the front foot on the same side. The horse makes very little balancing movement with his head, and there is little or no overstep with the hind feet. The rack is much faster than a walk; its speed is similar to a trot or pace.

A slow rack is often called a *single-foot* or a *broken amble*. It is a comfortable, ground-covering gait, faster than a walk. In a fast rack, the horse lowers his body slightly and keeps his head still, moving his legs in a flashy high gait. The fast rack is usually accentuated by training (encouraging the horse to move his legs even higher) for the purposes of show.

The *tolt* is a natural fast rack done by the Icelandic horse but without the high leg action required of a five-gaited show horse. The horses that do this fast four-beat gait naturally can keep it up for hours; they do this instead of trotting.

THE FOX-TROT

A fox-trot is like a slow, shuffling trot, with the horse taking short strides. He seems to walk with his front legs and trot with his hinds, and the hinds land in the tracks of the front feet. It is a smooth gait for the rider. The horse bobs his head at each stride, similar to a walk, but this gait is faster than a walk.

This gait is classified as a four-beat diagonal gait; the hoofbeats have a break in the sequence (left hind, right front, then a short pause, then the right hind and left front). Some horses naturally do a fox trot when hurrying (wanting to trot but being held to a walk). They shift into this very fast version of a walk, moving their front legs in fast, short, walking strides while doing what looks like a medium-slow trot behind.

In the Missouri Fox Trotter breed, the gait is exceptionally smooth and fast because the action of the hind legs creates a sliding motion rather than the jarring impact of a trot. This creates less concussion for the horse and makes for a pleasant ride; the rider can easily sit this gait.

THE RUNNING WALK AND STEPPING PACE

These are similar gaits. Both are four-beat, lateral gaits, much like the amble, but have more leg action. A five-gaited show horse must be able to perform one of these gaits as well as the walk, trot, canter, and fast rack. The running walk is a loose-action movement with each of the four feet hitting the ground separately and at regular intervals (left front, right rear, right front, left rear). The horse's head nods in rhythm to the beat rather than remaining steady and level as it does in the single-foot or rack.

PASO GAITS

The various Paso breeds of Central and South America descended from Spanish horses that were bred for their swift and smooth walking and ambling gaits. In Paso horses, these gaits are fast and flashy and the front legs have a distinctive sideways action. Paso horses have been selectively bred for these ground-covering gaits for more than

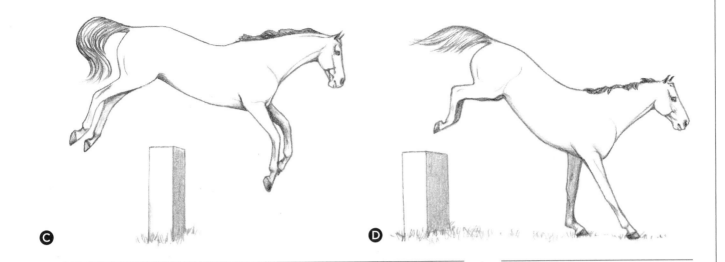

C   D

300 years and have some conformation differences that enhance the gaits. They have flexible joints (for the exaggerated action), long pasterns, and long hind legs.

Jumping

To be a jumper, a horse needs good balance, using head and neck to reach out and help move his body over the obstacle in an arc. The best way to evaluate a horse's jumping potential is to watch him jump without a rider. Observe a young, untrained horse by creating a jumping lane: put a low jump across an alleyway or make a lane with panels around an arena. Unhindered by a rider or a longe line, the horse will show his true jumping form and ability, or lack thereof.

APPROACH AND TAKEOFF

A horse can jump from a standstill or from any gait, though most ridden horses are asked to jump from a canter or a gallop. As the horse approaches the jump, he pauses briefly to gather himself so he can push off effectively with his hind legs.

If the horse is cantering as he approaches a jump, he lowers his body, especially his head and neck, during the last strides. Just before takeoff, he brakes with his front legs to slow himself. The normal stride sequence of the hind legs is interrupted as he plants them underneath his body in a flexed position and shifts his full weight onto them. He crouches as his hind legs prepare to push off.

He brings his front legs off the ground in a flexed position as his body rises, with head and neck swinging up and back to balance this action. He rapidly straightens his hind legs with a push-off thrust to propel himself over the fence. When the hind feet leave the ground,

▲ **Jumping. A.** The horse flexes his front legs to clear the jump and rapidly straightens his hind legs to push off. **B.** His head and neck go forward to balance his action over the jump. **C.** He straightens his front legs as he starts to come down. **D.** His head and neck swing up and back to shift his weight and minimize the force of the landing. All weight is taken by the leading leg and transferred immediately to the other leg; knees remain rigid and straight to support his weight as he lands.

the hind legs begin to flex again as the horse clears the fence, and the head and neck stretch forward and down to balance the body.

LANDING FROM A JUMP

As the horse goes over the fence and prepares to land, he keeps his hind legs flexed to clear the obstacle and begins to unfold and extend the front legs to receive his weight. He swings his head and neck up and back to help shift his weight and minimize the force and impact on the landing leg. As he lands, the leading leg takes the weight, but it is immediately transferred to the other leg as he continues on.

The fetlock joints are stretched to their fullest as the pasterns "give" and the fetlock joint descends to absorb the impact. The knees remain straight and rigid to support the horse's weight as he lands. The hind feet land in sequence, usually well forward of their normal position to help take the weight and minimize the impact and sudden stopping effect, enabling the horse to continue striding forward smoothly after the jump.

Stopping

When a horse is asked to stop, the momentum of his body is still moving forward. He uses his front heels as brakes while he straightens out his front legs and shifts back his weight farther. To shift his weight, he raises his head and plants one or both hind feet on the ground more forward than in his normal standing position. He flexes his hocks and stifles and crouches a little on his hindquarters to get more weight back onto his hind legs.

⚲ Conformation Close-up

When forced to stop unexpectedly or when asked to stop from a fast gallop, the horse must shift his weight to his hind feet to regain the freedom and control of his front feet. If he doesn't put his hind legs well underneath himself to shift the weight back, he bounces to a stiff-legged stop on locked front legs, and is over-balanced in front. Stopping requires as much agility as the gaits. How he handles himself when stopping can give insight into a horse's athletic ability.

Conformation and Equine Locomotion

When watching a horse travel at any gait, evaluate the manner in which he moves, looking for symmetry, balance, ease of movement, and fluid action. Each gait should have an even rhythm and strides of even length.

The way a horse is conformed influences gait significantly. If the horse is overly front heavy, having a wide front end or thick-muscled shoulders and neck, or a long neck and heavy head, the tempo and manner of his gait will be somewhat different than that of a horse with a more streamlined build or a lighter head and neck or heavier hindquarters. The way a horse moves is closely related to his balance and stability and the length of his back and legs. All aspects of his conformation combine to give him his own unique balance and method of moving and determine which gaits he does best.

THE BASICS

A horse's center of gravity is behind his withers. His front end (including head and neck) is heavier than his hindquarters, so in order to pick up a front foot and move, a horse has to overcome the fact that he is front heavy. If a horse is standing squarely on all four feet, he cannot lift a front foot until he shifts some of the weight back from his front end; he does this by raising his head slightly (see page 234).

Propulsion

The front legs help pull the horse along, but most propelling power comes from the hind legs. If for some reason (soreness in his back or a hind leg, ill-fitting tack or harness, or improper riding), a horse finds it painful to push with his hind legs, he may learn to compensate by pulling himself more than usual with his fronts. This may lead to abnormal muscle development along the underside of his neck and behind his shoulder blades. He also may travel with a twist in his gait, rather than straight. Normally, most of the thrust comes from the hindquarters.

The power of his movements comes from the horse's hindquarters but is accentuated by his ability to round or lift up his back and make it stronger. The horse uses his back and belly muscles to help transfer power from the hindquarters to the rest of his body. He can effortlessly raise his front end, making it lighter for a variety of actions, and even lift the front end off the ground completely when rearing or jumping. He does this by using his hindquarters (bending the lumbosacral joint at the loins), rounding his back, and flexing (lifting and shortening) his neck to help shift his balance.

The Back and Hind-Leg Action

Because of the back's rigidity and lack of spinal flexion, the horse's hind feet can extend forward only about as far as the middle of his abdomen. The hind leg moves in pendulum fashion from the rigid

⬤ Rounding the back: shortening and collecting.

pelvis at the hip joint, but most of its swing comes from the stifle joint. Due to the mass of muscle surrounding the thigh, the femur has limited movement.

The stifle works in unison with the hock. When one flexes, the other flexes. The hock supports and distributes the weight and is the strongest, most resilient joint in the horse's body. It is hock action, rather than back flexibility, that makes most of the horse's athletic activities possible. The rigid back serves as a relatively fixed point from which the hind legs can swing.

Balancing Movements

Whenever a horse moves, he shifts his weight from one leg to another, raising or lowering his head to lengthen or shorten his neck and keep himself in proper balance. Whenever he moves a leg, he must also overcome the fact that he is front heavy. When he walks, he brings each leg forward at the exact moment, and in the proper order, to keep himself balanced.

The head is like a small weight at the end of a lever, the neck. The head and neck work together, moving up and down from a fixed point, or *fulcrum* (the horse's center of gravity, which is below the withers in the front part of his body), to balance the hindquarters, a much heavier weight. The horse uses his neck to help maintain proper balance and equilibrium in all of his body movements.

A long neck is usually more desirable than a short one; the horse with a longer neck is generally better able to balance himself. He can more easily raise and lower his head to whatever position is required for balance. A long neck is also an advantage in a race, especially when a horse may win by a head or a nose.

The Head and Neck at Various Gaits

The horse uses his head and neck for balance in the same way humans use their arms for balance when walking or running. At the walk, canter, and gallop, the horse's head bobs at each step. His head drops each time a front foot comes to the ground, and his hip drops whenever the hind foot on that side comes to the ground. If he is lame, there will be an exaggerated movement of his head or hip (see chapter 16).

At the trot, the horse does not make balancing movements with his head and neck as he does at the walk and canter. Diagonal legs strike the ground and push off simultaneously. Thus, at each stride of the trot, the horse is supported by a leg at each side and on each corner of his body, rather than just one leg (or two or three) as at certain phases of the walk and canter, when his weight and balance must continually shift. When trotting, the horse's head should be steady, with no up-and-down movement, though some horses will have a very symmetrical tiny head bob. It is very easy to tell when a horse is lame at the trot, because any nod of his head or drop of his hip suggests soreness.

The horse's long neck and relatively large head are important to his balance and his ability to maneuver quickly and run swiftly. A galloping horse makes good use of the following balancing principle: when the hind feet hit the ground and push the horse forward, the horse raises his head and neck (see illustrations I and J on page 241). Then as the front legs hit the ground, the horse drops his neck and head to help raise and counterbalance the rising hindquarters, so the hind legs can come forward again for another stride (see illustrations C and D on page 241). As the hind legs hit the ground, the horse again shifts his weight back so he can lift his front legs off the ground to come forward, and the cycle repeats itself: the head and neck rise, reaching forward and down, then rise again. The head acts as a counterweight for the rest of the body: the downswing of the head and neck pulls on the back and neck muscles, which helps propel the horse forward when traveling.

LENGTH OF STRIDE

The position of the neck bones, along with their muscle attachments, determines the way the horse will carry his head and neck. To a large extent this will also determine the swing of the shoulder and amount of forward reach in the front legs. Thus, the carriage and gait of the whole body is influenced by the conformation of the head-neck-shoulder relationship.

The ability of a horse to propel himself over the ground swiftly is greatly affected by the movement of his shoulders and front legs. Their movement is enhanced (or hindered) and partially controlled by the muscles of the neck. In the last part of a long race, for instance, the horse with the best neck muscles will be able to keep running strongly because they will help pull his front legs forward with longer, stronger strides.

For speed and agility, there must be proportionate length of neck and a well-carried head. The longer-necked horse is able to take longer strides and is usually able to carry himself more gracefully and with greater ease, hence with more stamina and endurance, and is generally the better athlete, if the rest of his body is in balance. A long, low stride takes the horse farther, with less effort (and less concussion to himself and the rider) than a short, choppy stride where leg action is shorter and higher.

The short-necked horse must move his legs more rapidly and, by comparison, more often to keep up with the long-necked, longer striding horse. Over short distances, the short-striding horse may be able to keep up and even have a short blaze of speed due to the sheer energy of moving his legs faster, but over a long course he will tend to tire more quickly because he has to take many more steps than his longer-striding competitor. The short-striding horse usually lifts his feet higher and brings them back to the ground more forcefully than the longer-striding animal, and hence expends more effort and suffers more concussion.

HORSE SIZE AND STRIDE LENGTH

The size and height of the horse has less influence on stride length than does his conformation. A well-balanced and properly proportioned small horse (with good neck length and shoulder angle) can usually keep up with the longer-legged taller horse and is often more agile. Any horse, large or small, must have proper proportions and angles to have good balance, agility, and endurance.

It doesn't take as much energy for the horse, large or small, if he takes long strides. Usually, the short-necked, short-striding horse doesn't compete well at longer distances unless he is an exceptionally strong individual with great heart and endurance. He will usually wear out before the longer-striding animal gets tired. The longer-necked, longer-striding horse has more economy of motion and can cover a course with more speed and less effort.

⊶○ *Conformation Close-up*

A horse that strides well at the walk will also have a good stride at the trot and gallop. The horse with a short, choppy stride at the walk will not be able to extend the trot or gallop very well. A good natural stride at the walk will take the horse forward the full length of his body (as measured from withers to buttocks), and his hind feet should overstep the track of his front foot by a few inches at a fast walk.

14

Athletic Ability

THE MAIN REASON for evaluating a horse's conformation and structure is to relate it to his function and
use. Certain aspects of conformation are essential for
all breeds and types. Conformation is a key factor in
how a horse travels and whether he'll stay sound or go
lame. As we've already learned, no horse has perfect
conformation. Opinions and preferences vary among
horsemen as to what constitutes ideal conformation in
the equine athlete.

There are general guidelines to follow when selecting
or evaluating a horse for an athletic career, or a stallion
or broodmare that will be used to produce athletic

We evaluate a horse's conformation to determine whether he can do the job we want him
to do. Ideal conformation enables a horse to perform smoothly and safely, moving with
optimal balance, agility, and speed. It also helps him stay sound while doing it.

horses. This chapter examines the factors applicable to any light horse (saddle horse) used for dressage, barrel racing, jumping, racing, cattle work, endurance riding, and other athletic activities. (For draft and driving horses, see chapter 15.)

The usefulness of a saddle horse depends on his ability to carry a rider while performing various tasks. The riding horse must be built for functional movement. He must have long, slender muscles, a streamlined frame without unnecessary weight, and body and leg angles that optimize speed and maneuverability. He usually needs both speed and agility: surefootedness at fast gaits and the ability to change speed and direction for quick maneuvers while carrying a rider.

Evaluate a Horse in Motion

The study of conformation is more than assessing a horse's various parts. The main goal when evaluating a horse is to see how the parts fit together and whether they form a harmonious whole. You want a horse that moves well. Good movement is not only beautiful to watch, it also ensures that a horse can do the job and stay sound while doing it.

A horse that travels with pleasing and fluid action is usually a good candidate for an athletic career. A horse should be evaluated while he is moving as well as while standing still, because many aspects of poor conformation are more obvious when the horse is traveling. Similarly, if you were to study a horse only while he is standing still, you may not see the inherent athletic qualities that may be present despite minor imperfections in structure. You can often make do or even do well with a less-than-perfect horse if he has strong leg construction and strong joints, a good "engine" (heart and lungs, for endurance), and the willpower and drive to be a good athlete in spite of minor imperfections.

HOW HE MOVES IS MOST IMPORTANT

Whenever you evaluate a horse, keep in mind that all horses have faults, or conformational flaws. It is important to determine the impact of a fault on a horse's ability to perform. Does he have strengths that compensate for the flaw? Can he move well in spite of the flaw? Your goal is to determine which faults hinder him and which ones can be overlooked.

Only when he is moving at various gaits can you observe some of the traits you must evaluate, including how well (or poorly) he might be suited to a certain career and how easy (or difficult) he might be able to train for a certain type of activity. What counts is the way various aspects of conformation translate into movement.

⟲○ *Conformation Close-up*

As riders, we want to know if a horse can move with agility, grace-fulness, and in a manner that suits what we want him to do. If we have a chosen sport in mind for a horse, we must make sure he has the ability to perform well. When considering a horse for an athletic career, watch him move. If he is not in your immediate area, ask the owner to send you a video of the horse in action, as well as photographs. Then you can decide whether you want to invest the time to see him in person.

MANY THINGS ARE MORE OBVIOUS WHEN HE'S MOVING

You may not notice that he's slightly splay footed (toed out) until you see his feet winging inward as he walks. You might not see that his elbow joints are turned out until he moves his front legs in swinging action rather than straight. His hind legs might look fine while he's standing still, but if you stand behind him when he walks and the hock joints seem to have a twisting motion, look more closely at his hind legs.

A judge of horses usually begins an evaluation by looking at the horse standing squarely on a level surface to study various body angles and proportions, as described in part I. Yet the most important aspect of conformation is how that horse moves: whether he will be smooth to ride, able to respond to a rider adequately to collect and extend, turn swiftly around a barrel or after a cow, and have the speed to compete in a chosen career. You need to know whether he moves in a manner that will minimize or increase his risks for future injury and unsoundness. His preference for certain gaits (whether he is a trotter or pacer or has another gait, such as a rack or a fox-trot) will not become apparent until he moves.

⟲○ *Conformation Close-up*

Look at a lot of horses while they are moving to get an idea of what is normal. For the best view, have someone lead the horse straight away from you, straight back toward you, and parallel to you, at both the walk and the trot — several times, if necessary — so you can get a good view of his leg action.

OBSERVE HIM AT LIBERTY

The best way to evaluate a horse's action is to watch him travel at liberty in a large paddock, pasture, or arena, without the interference or balance-altering influence of a rider or handler. Carrying weight or

▲ Watch the horse moving at liberty, if possible.

Did You Know?

A slightly pigeon-toed horse may sometimes be a better risk as an athlete than a splay-footed horse. In either deviation, the joints are not lined up correctly, but a pigeon-toed horse often seems to withstand the stresses better than a splay-footed animal. The horse with toes turned in won't strike himself because he paddles outward when in motion.

tack may change the horse's way of going, and an ill-fitting saddle or girth can make him shorten his stride and affect the way he travels. Thus, the best possible scenario is to watch him at his various gaits with no tack on at all. A hilly pasture is an ideal location to see how he handles himself going uphill and downhill as well as on level ground. You want to be able to see him move naturally at slow gaits and fast ones. If it is not feasible to watch him travel under totally natural conditions, watch him run free in a paddock or large arena.

If there is no place to observe him running free, the next best option is to have someone lead him for you at the walk and trot. If he is being led, however, make sure the person leading gives him complete freedom of head, walking and trotting him on a loose lead with no tension on the rope that might affect his action or balance. Tension on his head may make him travel crooked or in some other way affect his balance or way of traveling.

⊸○ Conformation Close-up

Run your hands over the horse when he is standing still (especially up and down his legs) to check for lumps or swellings, and then watch the horse travel at the walk and trot. If he has a leg with a blemish or enlargement, make sure it does not affect the way he moves. If you are evaluating a horse to purchase, have a veterinarian examine the animal also, especially if the horse has any abnormality you are unsure of, to determine whether it is an unsoundness or just a blemish (see chapter 16).

WAY OF GOING SHOULD BE STRAIGHT AND CLEAN

Leg action should be free flowing and fairly straight, moving forward in straight lines. The horse with crooked legs and a crooked flight path puts more strain on leg structures. When working at speed, he may also strike himself and injure his legs. Any horse with legs that are out of alignment and deviate from straight foot flight may have problems when he is working fast.

If feet aren't hitting the ground perfectly square (both heels of the foot striking the ground at the same time), this is hard on the entire leg. If a foot lands first on one side, due to a crooked foot or leg, this puts extra stress on parts of the foot and leg and causes strain or injury, leading to breakdown and unsoundness if the horse is used often and hard. The horse with correctly conformed feet and legs tends to handle the stresses of athletic exertion with less injury. He'll be less inclined to develop arthritic joints.

DEVIATIONS FROM STRAIGHT ACTION

Most horses are not perfectly straight in the legs, but some types of deviation are less problematic than others.

Paddling

A horse with toes turned inward even slightly will tend to pick up his feet near their outside edge rather than squarely at the center of the toe. This starts the foot flight crooked, with the leg swinging outward. This outward swing (called *paddling* or *dishing*) may be just a small deviation from a straight line or an obvious arc to the outside. A horse that paddles will almost never hit himself, but his gait is inefficient; the extra effort of moving the leg in an outward arc rather than a straight line will cut his speed and may also cause fatigue on a long ride.

Winging

The splay-footed horse picks up his feet to the inside, winging them inward, and tends to hit his other leg if the foot flight comes in close to the opposite leg. Winging is less desirable than paddling because the horse is likely to injure himself.

Limb Interference

A horse that interferes is one that accidentally strikes a leg (anywhere from the coronary band to the knee or hock) with the opposite foot. At high speed, he may crack or break a sesamoid bone in the fetlock joint or suffer other leg injury because of the way he hits himself. A horse with crooked legs generally hits the opposite fetlock joint when walking but may strike himself higher up the leg at faster speeds. At a fast trot, for example, he may hit the opposite cannon bone.

A horse that only strikes himself once in a while and not too harshly (brushing the leg rather than striking it forcefully) may merely break the skin and create a sore on the fetlock joint, or a series of sore areas along the cannon bone. But a horse that hits himself frequently and forcefully may damage the bones, causing inflammation that creates a bony lump or a series of bony nodules up and down the cannon bone, or a large splint. A forceful blow from a hoof striking the opposite leg may break a sesamoid bone in the fetlock joint or fracture the splint bone on the inside of the opposite cannon bone.

Forging

The horse that forges strikes his front foot or leg as it is being picked up with the approaching hind foot on the same side. In most cases, the toe of the hind foot hits the heel of the front foot. This problem may

Other Types of Leg Contact

In addition to paddling, winging, limb interference, and forging, there are several other types of leg contact.

- *Cross-firing:* Hitting the inside part of the front foot (usually at the quarters) with the diagonal hind foot; a problem most frequently seen in pacers.
- *Scalping:* At the instant it breaks over and leaves the ground, the toe of the front foot hits the coronary band or pastern of the approaching hind foot. Sometimes the contact and injury to the hind leg is even higher, at the front of the fetlock or even the cannon bone.
- *Elbow hitting:* The horse strikes his elbow with the shoe of the front foot; occasionally seen in horses that have long feet and weighted shoes to accentuate their gait.
- *Speedy cutting:* Any type of limb interference at fast gaits. Most of these contact problems are directly due to poor conformation but can sometimes occur with improper shoeing that throws the hoof off balance and alters its flight.

be due to improper shoeing but is most common in horses that have long legs and short backs. The horse may not strike himself when running free and barefoot, but the added weight of a rider changes his balance, and if he is shod the increased swing of the foot (from the added weight of a shoe) may be enough to cause this problem.

Balance and Body Proportions

Most outstanding horses, in whatever field of performance they are used, have well-balanced conformation. In the well-balanced and athletic horse, the legs fit the body, the depth of the body and length of the legs are similar, and the back is neither too long nor too short compared with the length of leg, as discussed in earlier chapters.

The ideal equine athlete in any breed or size tends to have the same body proportions: one-third shoulder area, one-third body, one-third hip. Whenever we deviate from these proportions when breeding horses, we create problems for the horse and hinder his athletic ability and durability — he's less apt to stay sound.

IMPORTANCE OF BODY PROPORTIONS

A horse must have good legs, but a horse can have a good body and minor leg faults and stay sound. Good legs cannot compensate for stresses put on them by bad body angles. We have bred horses with different muscling and head styles, and in some breeds the whole body is more elongated or more compact, but the ideal proportions do not change much.

Stand back and evaluate the horse's body proportion and angles, for these make a big difference in whether or not the legs will suffer strain and concussion. To judge body proportions, learn to find and define the horse's front end (shoulder area) and hips. Locate the

One Breeder's Opinion

Heidi Smith, a retired veterinarian who bred and rode endurance horses for more than 30 years, says that the most ideal example of conformation she has ever seen was a Thoroughbred stallion in Kentucky. He had the perfect conformation for dressage, polo, roping, and endurance rides. He was a huge horse but had a short back and perfect body proportions (one-third shoulder, one-third back, one-third hindquarter). Unlike so many of today's Thoroughbreds, he also had good feet and legs.

Smith says that old-time horsemen always looked first at legs when judging a horse, but she feels body proportion and back conformation are just as important. She's seen too many poor bodies contribute to the breakdown of good legs, whether on the racetrack, endurance circuit, or other types of competition. She says she would never select a horse for riding or breeding purposes unless it has a good body. Improper body proportions and angles always put too much stress on the legs.

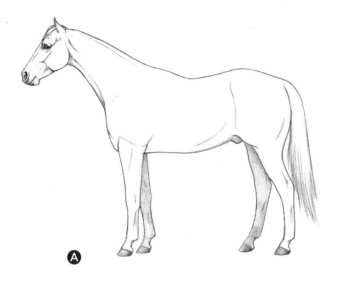

◀ Various breeds have some basic and similar body proportions, in spite of breed differences. **A.** Basic conformation for a riding horse of any breed. **B.** Quarter Horse. **C.** Thoroughbred. **D.** Standardbred. **E.** Morgan. (*Note:* The dotted lines in illustrations B through E are the body outline of A.)

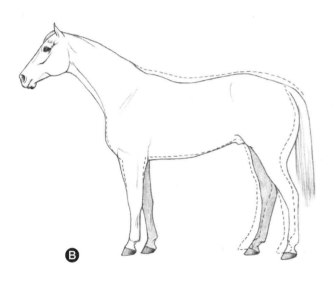

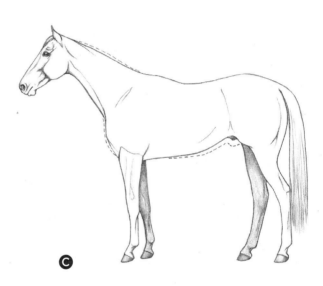

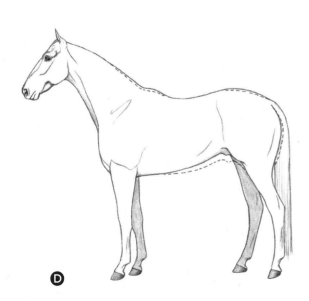

A good horse is usually about 2.5 to 2.75 times as long as his head, measuring from the point of the shoulder to the point of the buttock.

front and back of the pelvis, so you can pinpoint the hip bones and relate their angle to the lay-back of the shoulder. Then evaluate the horse's proportions and body angles (see chapters 10 and 11 for additional information).

The horse's back should never be longer than the front end or the quarters. Old-timers used to measure the horse from point of shoulder to seat bone (point of buttocks) and state that this length should be equal to two and a half times the length of the head, in a horse with good proportions. With a good shoulder and a long quarter, a horse would not be unreasonably "long" if his actual length is two and two-thirds the length of his head. But all the additional length should be in the shoulder and quarters, never in the back and loins. The length should still be broken into thirds: one-third shoulder, one-third back, and one-third quarters.

STRIDE IS DETERMINED BY ANGLES IN SHOULDER AND HIP

The angle of hip and shoulder, rather than a horse's size, length of leg, or height, is what governs his stride. No matter what size he is, the horse should have good balance; all his parts should fit together pleasingly. Angles in the body (shoulders and hips, especially) should match and be of good length and slope for maximum shock absorption and a good stride that is not too short and choppy. If he is well proportioned and his shoulder matches his hip, with good overall conformation, he will probably be a good athlete whether he is large or small.

A horse with a long, well-sloped shoulder and hip will usually be fast and agile and move with minimum effort, compared with a horse that has a short, steep shoulder and hip, with choppy action. A well-laid-back shoulder (see chapter 11) permits a greater swing of the leg. The horse can reach out farther with his front feet, with a longer stride. In the hindquarters, too, the sharper the angle, the greater the length of hip and the more freedom of leg movement.

_◯ Conformation Close-up

No matter how long a horse's stride or how good his shoulder action, at the walk few horses bring the front of the knee farther forward than a line dropped vertically from the point of the shoulder. At the trot, the knee may advance as far forward as a line dropped from the poll. At the gallop, the front foot may reach as far forward as the nose, when head and neck are moderately extended. At the fast gallop when the head is fully extended, the front foot may not actually reach forward as far as the nose.

When evaluating a horse's shoulder, some people look for a long shoulder, but angle is just as important as length. A long shoulder is not the same as a laid-back, well-sloped shoulder. Some people praise a long shoulder but fail to judge whether it is laid back or too upright, especially if they are selecting for tall horses. A long, upright shoulder may add a hand (4 inches) to the horse's height, elevating the whole body, but it puts more stress and concussion on the legs.

Many horsemen are familiar with what a shoulder angle should be like (sloping rather than upright), but fail to look at angles in the hindquarter (stifle and hip). A triangle is made when you draw a line from the point of the hip to the point of the buttock, and then down to the stifle, and from the stifle back up to the point of the hip (see page 209). This triangle should be roughly equilateral, with all sides nearly equal in length and all angles similar.

The side from the stifle to the point of the hip may be a little shorter in horses best suited for endurance work rather than sprinting. This side of the triangle may be a little longer in the sprinter. But if the angle is too wide and open in the sprinter, it creates the problem of post-leggedness, with not enough angle in the stifle and hock. This can be the cause of serious breakdown problems.

▶ Angles in hindquarters are a little different in the endurance horse and the sprinter; the triangle formed by points of the hindquarter may not be equilateral. **A.** In a horse geared for endurance, the line from hip to stifle may be a little short. **B.** In the sprinter, the line from hip to stifle may be a little longer.

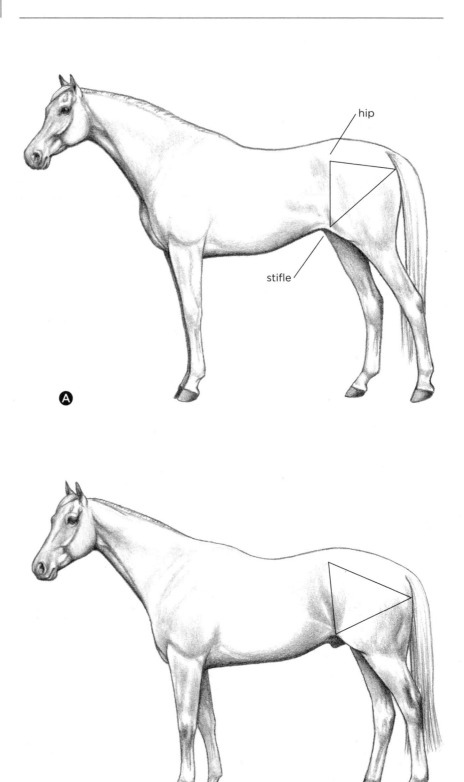

hip

stifle

Ⓐ

Ⓑ

SYMMETRY

The horse should be perfectly balanced. Whatever his body and leg conformation, it should be the same on both sides. A mismatch may be due to injury or to inherited poor conformation, but regardless of cause, asymmetry should be avoided when selecting an equine athlete.

One shoulder may be smaller than the other (a condition called *sweeny*) due to atrophy of the muscles from nerve damage created by an injury (see chapter 16). One hip may be higher than the other due to an injury caused by running into something solid. One front foot may be smaller due to injury in which the horse was lame for a long period of time and did not put as much weight on that foot, causing it to contract. Any time one foot or leg does not perfectly match its mate (as a left or right mirror image), suspect a conformational flaw or an earlier injury that created stresses, altering the way leg, foot, and joints developed and grew.

Contraction of one foot may be due to poor conformation that creates an uneven stride. A horse may inherit uneven structure in which one leg is slightly shorter than the other, making his gait irregular. Or he may inherit clubfoot conformation on one or both sides. A *clubfoot* is one in which the hoof angle is steeper than pastern angle: a foot with a very short toe and a high heel.

Carefully check the horse from front and rear to see if both front (and both hind) legs and feet match in size, shape, and angle. Also look at him from above (standing on something if you have to) to see if his back is straight and symmetrical from side to side. If a horse has one front leg shorter than the other, this may show up more obviously from a top view. You can see a twist in the topline (at shoulder and neck) or mismatched shoulders. A horse with uneven legs will have an uneven stride, creating a hitch in his gait that is not only uncomfortable to the rider, but also a hindrance to his best athletic performance.

No Horse Is Perfect

Sometimes an imperfect horse can perform well in a career that does not require perfection. A horse can be useful, in spite of his limitations, especially if you recognize his faults at the beginning and use him carefully and wisely within his abilities to perform. This can prevent serious conformation-related injuries and breakdowns that could lead to lameness or unsoundness.

As judges, breeders, and riders, we tend to have a mythical ideal in our minds about what a horse should look like and what aspects of conformation constitute the perfect horse. This picture will vary, however, for the roper, eventer, dressage competitor, racehorse owner, and cow cutter. In some sports, a horseman may be most concerned about whether a horse has perfect front legs (because they take so much extra stress), while in other sports the concern may be focused more on the hind legs because the horse will be working primarily off his hocks. Even within a certain discipline, however, the picture of ideal conformation may vary with the individuals judging the horses.

CAN HE STILL DO THE JOB?
We all have a somewhat different set of guidelines within our minds but need to realize that it is highly unlikely that any horse will fit that perfect picture. Therefore, we must weigh each horse's various points of conformation to determine which characteristics are acceptable and which are not.

A lot of people can see a horse's flaws, but very few people are able to evaluate the degree to which faults will or will not hinder a horse's abilities in the sport chosen for him. If you followed all the rules of conformation, you would reject many good horses because they didn't fit the perfect picture. On the other hand, if you ignore the basic principles of conformation, you may be disappointed in the horse's lack of ability or his inability to stay sound while doing his job.

Is his body build and type suitable for jumping? Or cutting cattle? Or racing? Before you evaluate and judge his conformation, you must understand what kind of structure would be a help or hindrance to the horse's job. Compare him with other horses in similar occupations. Horses at top levels of their particular sport or activity tend to have similar conformation — a body build and leg angles that enable them to excel in their job and stay sound while doing it. Even if their structure is not "perfect" in terms of the traditional ideals, it may be the most correct for their specific activity.

A reining horse or cutting horse may have a little more angle in his hocks than a racehorse, for instance. The stock horse may be a little more sickle hocked than the ideal and a racehorse may be more post-legged, but they both do well in their jobs because these types of leg angles suit their specific activities. As long as their leg angles are not extreme to the point of putting extra stress on bones and joints that would lead to breakdown, these are the angles that help make them superior performers.

If a horse has physical limitations and is thrust into training or a career he is ill equipped to handle, he may have trouble performing well. He may also become sour and ill tempered because of pain or discomfort due to the abnormal stresses these activities put on his body. It is much easier for the horse and for the rider and trainer to accomplish a job if the horse's structure enables him to do the work easily. If he cannot, he may become resistant to the trainer or rider's efforts and develop adverse reactions or bad behavior. Sometimes a perceived "bad temperament" is merely the result of problems we are causing a horse by trying to make him perform in ways that he is not well constructed to accomplish.

HEART AND WILLINGNESS

There is more to performance success than having perfect conformation. Some horses with great legs and angles are mediocre in their performance, while others with not-so-perfect structure become champions. There are many good horses that become tremendous athletes in spite of structural shortcomings. A horse may have slightly crooked legs but make up for it with strong joints and a lot of heart. He may stay sound during a long life of hard use in a career that would take a hard toll on most other horses.

No two horses are built alike, and it's not always easy to determine just by looking at conformation which one will hold up under hard use and which one will break down. *Structural integrity,* the strength and soundness of the stay apparatus (the system of muscles, tendons, and ligaments that helps support the horse while standing and acts to prevent overextension of the joints and reduce concussion during movement) also plays a role. Some horses with serious conformation faults still manage to go the distance, holding up well through many years of strenuous work. Old-timers used to say that such a horse had "good leather," and this made up for the structural imperfections. They are able to stay sound and perform well in spite of conformational handicaps.

Some good ranch horses have conformational faults but are able to work many hard miles chasing cattle without going lame; some endurance horses with crooked legs can go thousands of miles with never a sore step; and some jumpers, steeplechasers, and racehorses have imperfect structure but never break down. These individuals defy the usual principles of good conformation. When judging a horse, we can evaluate conformation but only guess at durability.

Some horses can fool you, because they have the good leather to hold together in spite of great odds against them. They are the exception rather than the rule, but these horses demonstrate that there is more to success than perfect conformation, and that good leather and willingness are part of the equation for becoming a winner. There is an elusive quality to athletic ability and superior performance that is not measurable in terms of what we like to think of as definable traits. This goes beyond measurable angles, length and straightness of leg, or body proportions.

Some horses love their jobs so much that they always give their best; their "heart" may carry them through. Sometimes the only way to find out if a horse is really a good one is to try him. Look at his athletic ability and how he performs, try to evaluate the defects that might cause him problems, weigh the risks against the benefits, and then decide if he's worth a gamble.

WEAK LINKS IN THE CHAIN

It's usually better to have a few minor faults in several areas than perfection in one area and some very major faults in other areas. After all, if all the links in a chain are at 95 percent strength, you'll still have a strong chain. But if you have some links at 100 percent strength and some at only 30 percent, the chain may break.

When searching for a great athlete or trying to breed horses with ideal conformation, aim for the overall package; look at every aspect of the horse's body and legs. Some breeders and judges of horses focus on only one or two things that they feel are most important and lose sight of other aspects. This can lead to selection of horses that might have a pretty head and a nice topline and tail carriage, but poor hind leg conformation, or selection of horses that have bulky, muscular hindquarters but no withers or slope to the shoulder, or small feet.

Don't base horse selection or breeding decisions on pedigree, economics, or popular bloodlines without considering conformation, or somewhere down the road you or your horse-buying clients will be severely disappointed. If a horse has a major fault, don't buy him or use him for breeding, no matter how much you like him.

LOOK AT THE WHOLE PICTURE

If you select a poorly constructed horse to be part of a breeding program, you may produce horses that develop the same lameness problems that affected their parents, grandparents, and great-grandparents. Crooked legs, bad feet, improper shoulder angle, among other things, can be passed from one generation to the next, perpetuating a tendency toward certain unsoundnesses.

Some undesirable traits can be a ticking time bomb, especially if you use the affected horse only for breeding and never stress him enough in an athletic career to have him suffer breakdowns from a predisposing weakness. He may never go lame, but if his foals are used athletically, they may become a huge disappointment to their owners. Broodmares and stallions that are only shown at halter and do nothing more strenuous may stay sound but may produce offspring that won't.

Type

THERE ARE MANY BREEDS of horses that excel in a range of activities and in similar performance events. Within a certain breed, there can be several variations of type. When determining whether a horse is well suited for a particular kind of performance, the criterion is often type rather than breed.

Many people have breed preferences, but all good horses of a certain type share some similar abilities, regardless of breed. For example, a horse of sturdy draft-horse type will be good at pulling, no matter his breed, whereas a lighter-muscled horse will be better at carrying a rider in speed events. Horses of stock-horse

If you have a specific career in mind for a horse, make sure he has the proper body for that type of work. Certain aspects of conformation make horses better choices for some jobs than for others.

type are more heavily muscled than those used for endurance. Many Quarter Horses, Paints, and Appaloosas, as well as some Morgans and Arabians, are of stock-horse type.

A Horse's Build Determines What He Does Best

Through selective breeding, breeds and types of horses have been developed to excel in certain kinds of work or sport — racing, pulling a heavy wagon, sorting and chasing cattle, to name a few. Some aspects of conformation that aid these activities have become standardized in certain types of horses. Each type has a characteristic body build that makes it easier for that horse to do the intended work. If you have a specific job in mind, choose a horse whose conformational attributes will help him excel in that particular activity.

NOT ALL HORSES ARE CREATED EQUAL

It is easy to see why draft horses are better suited for pulling heavy loads, and light horses are better for riding, but there are some differences in type, especially among the light horses, that determine whether they can do well in the career we want for them. Conformation features and temperament make some horses better suited for certain jobs than for others. Body and muscle type, for instance, partially determine whether a horse is better suited for sprinting a few hundred yards at top speed, running swiftly for a mile, or finishing a 100-mile endurance race in winning time.

Short, thick muscles contract quickly and provide the power for sprinting; they function well with little or no oxygen. Because the horse can't generate oxygen fast enough to meet the muscles' requirements, the muscles rely on stored fuel in the form of glycogen. Longer, leaner muscles are more efficient for endurance activities, with the body supplying oxygen as needed.

CONFORMATION FOR ALL-AROUND ATHLETICISM

A well-built horse can do virtually any job reasonably well. If a horse is well balanced with good body proportions, proper angles, and straight, sound legs, he can be a good all-around horse.

Outstanding all-around athletes are seen in almost every light-horse breed. Look for a horse with an average length of neck, relatively short back, long and well-sloped shoulder, good withers, fairly level rump with long quarters, deep heart girth and flank, good straight legs with proper hind leg angles, and reasonable body proportions and balance. Certain breed traits may hinder individuals within a breed when performing tasks that fall outside their particular specialty. For instance, gaited horses may not make good racehorses or cutting horses, and some of the more heavily muscled stock horses won't make good endurance horses.

Some breeds tend to have faults or conformational traits that limit their usefulness in certain disciplines. If you hope to use a horse in a discipline unusual for its breed, you may need to search longer to find a horse that won't be hindered by an undesirable trait or fault. For example, if you want to find an American Saddle Horse to do cattle work or a Quarter Horse to do dressage or gaited classes, you may have to look a little harder than if you select from a breed that has been specifically bred for those kinds of activities.

Some breeds have conformational traits that are not ideal but have been accepted or tolerated in the breed. There are Quarter Horses and Arabians with low withers, for instance, which makes it more difficult to keep a saddle in place. Some Arabians have quarters and shoulders that are too short for speed, and some are cow hocked. Some Thoroughbreds are shallow in the flank, and many have low heels, insufficient bone, and weaker hoofs (for their size) than an Arabian.

A number of Quarter Horses are too heavily muscled for any activities except those that require short bursts of speed, and many are sickle hocked or post-legged. Some have feet too small for the weight of their bulky bodies. There are Saddlebreds with pasterns that are too upright, and some are calf-kneed. Some Tennessee Walkers have too much slope to the quarters, and some are sickle hocked. The Standardbred may be short in the quarters and long in the back. The Morgan comes in two types: the stocky, compact, traditional type, and the taller, leaner Saddlebred type. The compact Morgan is often heavy crested, an easy keeper, and prone to grass founder.

Other breeds also diverge from good basic conformation and usefulness because they have been bred for specific purposes, and conformational features of one breed may not be desirable in another. Still, the general balance and conformation of a good riding horse that can do many things remain and should be considered before initiating a breeding program.

Though each breed has advantages and disadvantages for specific kinds of activity, you can usually find individuals within a breed that have good general conformation for all-around athleticism. You will also find some with very poor conformation that cannot perform or hold up in their own discipline — for example, racehorses that break down in training or can't run fast; Quarter Horses that are not agile

Did You Know?

Animals that do well in desert regions are usually smaller, not only because of sparser feed but because of a different kind of metabolism and better heat dissipation. They have more body surface per pound of body weight than their larger counterparts.

enough or fast enough for cutting, reining, barrel racing, and other speed events; Arabians lacking endurance; gaited horses that can't do their gaits; and warmbloods that fail at jumping or dressage. If you have a favorite breed and are choosing a horse from within its ranks, be selective and always pay close attention to conformation.

The Bloods

There are basically two types of horses: hot-blooded and cold-blooded. A third type is a blend of the two and is appropriately called *warmblood*. The hot bloods and cold bloods evolved in different environments, and their body type and metabolism reflect their adaptation to that environment. The large-bodied draft horse evolved in the colder climates of northern Europe, while the hot-blooded Arabian evolved in the warmer deserts of North Africa and the Middle East.

CHARACTERISTICS OF "HOT" BLOOD

The term *hot-blooded* does not refer to the temperature of the blood or body. All breeds have a normal body temperature of about 99°F to 101°F (37–38°C). A hot-blooded horse has more red blood cells per similar volume of blood than a cold-blooded horse, to facilitate greater oxygen supply to the working muscles used for running fast over long distances. The hot-blooded horse also has a lively mind and flighty temperament; his personality is programmed for quickness and speed. Some people would call this attitude "hot" or "hyper." By contrast, the cold-blooded horse has a more lethargic metabolism and attitude.

The hot-blooded horse has some major body differences when compared to a cold blood. Because he evolved in a warm climate, he has a smaller, finer, and more oval body structure to allow efficient heat dissipation. He has less distance from his body core to the external surface, thin skin for easy heat loss, and many efficient sweat glands for better cooling. His blood vessels stand out prominently under the thin skin, especially when he is hot or exerting, to bring overheated blood to the body surface for cooling and to provide fluid for sweating. His neck is long and slim for greater heat-loss ability. The hair coat is shorter, even in winter, than that of a draft horse, so as not to hinder heat loss.

The hot-blooded horse has longer legs in proportion to body size than a cold blood; the longer length provides speed and allows more airflow around and under the body. He also has larger, thin-skinned ears to promote heat loss, and a smaller head than a draft horse, with a less bushy tail and mane. The finer mane and tail hair retain less heat, and the tail is usually carried well away from the body (often carried quite high when traveling at fast gaits) to allow for more airflow and less heat retention.

CHARACTERISTICS OF "COLD" BLOOD

The cold-blooded, or draft, horse has fewer red blood cells per similar volume of blood and thus lacks endurance for long-distance speed. Proportionally, his air passages and lungs are not as large as in a light horse, so the draft horse has less "wind" for speed and endurance. Large, well-rounded bodies for retaining heat were important for survival in cold northern climates. A short, thick neck has less body surface for its mass and retains heat better than a long, thin one. Short legs minimize the space underneath the body for airflow and heat removal. Feet are relatively large and flat (an aid in traveling over soft or boggy ground), in contrast to the smaller, more concave feet of the desert horse that traveled in the rocks.

The thick skin of a cold-blooded horse holds in the heat. Long, thick hair also provides good insulation, along with a layer of fat under the skin. Due to thick skin and its adaptation for insulation, the draft horse does not sweat as easily or as profusely as a hot-blooded horse when exerting. Sweating was not needed as much in a cold climate, and the body is programmed for retaining heat rather than dissipating it through sweat and evaporation. The thick mane and tail also add protection against wind and cold temperatures. The tail is carried low to protect the thin-skinned area between the buttocks from wind and cold.

Short, small ears help minimize heat loss. A large head (with relatively long air passages) and small nostrils (often partially closed) help keep the horse from damaging his lungs in cold weather; the small nostrils let in only a small amount of cold air and the long airways help warm it before it gets to the lungs.

CHARACTERISTICS OF "WARM" BLOOD

Warmbloods are a blend of hot and cold blood. There are many European breeds (including Belgian Warmblood, Dutch Warmblood, Hanoverian, Holsteiner, Oldenburg, Trakehner, and Swedish Warmblood) that were specifically created by crossing these different types. Many other horses also fall into this category because of their mix of genetics. A warmblood can be created by crossing a draft horse and a Thoroughbred, for instance, or even by mixing Thoroughbred blood with some of the old Quarter Horse bloodlines that were predominantly "colder" than most light horses.

Strengths of Hot-Blooded Horses

The hot-blooded horse has several attributes, developed for survival as a prey animal, that make him an ideal athlete for many of the sports in which he now excels. He can leap into action from a standstill (which makes him good at racing, speed events or working cattle), reaching a speed of up to 45 miles per hour within about 4 seconds. He can maintain good speed for long distances (as for endurance sports), and also has great efficiency of energy. Conformational factors that aid his energy efficiency, speed, and agility (compared to draft horse conformation) are legs that are long and light compared to body size and relatively small, light feet. Less energy is needed for moving his legs swiftly.

Some people prefer warmbloods for certain sports because they like the substance and mellow attitude of cold blood mixed with the more athletic features of the hot blood. Any cross between hot and cold blood is technically a warmblood. Some of the older breeds that fall into this category because of early mixing include the ancient Iberian type (which includes the Spanish Andalusians and Lusitanos), Friesians, Lipizzans, and many pony breeds.

The Specialists

There are many types of horses today because horses have been bred for so many different purposes. If you have a specialized job in mind for a horse, you'll want to select one from the ranks of specialists.

Although all equine athletes have many conformational traits in common, certain types of horses have aspects of structure that help them perform specific activities more successfully than others. The traits that give the draft horse his power would be a hindrance to a racehorse, for example. The conformation that enables a gaited horse to give his rider a smooth, free-flowing extended traveling gait may hinder his ability to collect himself and change directions with swift agility when chasing cattle on a mountainside or performing reining patterns. Various types of horses have been selectively bred for different jobs, and they have some conformational differences that make them better at some jobs and less proficient at others.

Conformation Close-up

Even if a horse was bred to race, cut cattle, or be a sport horse, he may not be up to the task if he has certain structural weaknesses. The horse you hoped would be a good jumper may not hold up very long in that career if he has calf knees or offset cannons. A horse with weak hocks won't make it as a cutting horse or reiner. If you are choosing a horse for a certain discipline or sport, pay special attention to the points of conformation that are crucial for soundness and durability in that type of activity.

THE RIDING HORSE

Most of the breeds in use today are riding horses, and most riding horses are either hot-blooded or have a large influence of "hot" blood in their ancestry. Arabians are the original "hot-bloods." Thoroughbreds also fall into that category because of the large infusion of Arabian blood in the formation of their breed. Almost all breeds of light horses today have some Arabian or Thoroughbred blood in their

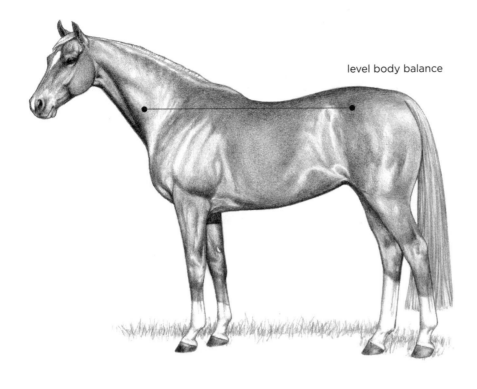

level body balance

◀ Riding type: good "riding" conformation with good angles and relatively level body balance (not too downhill) from the lumbosacral joint to the widest part of the base of the neck.

background. Most riding breeds have more "hot" blood than "cold" blood in their background, but many are various mixes of both.

Suitability for Carrying Saddle and Rider

A relatively short back is usually stronger for carrying weight than a long back, due to a shorter, stronger coupling. A riding horse must be able to carry weight, and this depends in part on his ability to raise his back rather than having it "hollow." The horse with good withers, strong loins, and ability to flex at the neck and at the croup, bringing his hindquarters more underneath himself, has the best weight-carrying ability. The ribs should be well sprung, coming outward from the spine almost perpendicular to it (rather than downward) before they taper downward, to give a good, strong foundation for the weight of a rider.

A slab-sided horse with little spring of rib and a "peak roof" shape to the back cannot carry weight as well as the horse with round ribs and is also harder to fit with a saddle (see illustration on page 97). The upper edge of the bars of the saddle tree will rub on the horse's ribs, and the lower edge will not make good contact with the horse because the lower edge of the saddle will typically be wider than the horse's back. The center of the saddle may rest on the top of the spine, creating too much pressure and a sore back.

Ideal Horse Conformation, According to Xenophon

Much has been written over the years about horse conformation, and some of the early descriptions are still valid. When the Greek general Xenophon described preferred conformation for a cavalry mount in 400 BC, he could just as well have been describing ideal conformation for the average riding horse today — a horse that could do well in nearly any career. He evaluated certain points of conformation by comparing them with those of well-known equine athletes of his time (rather than using an arbitrary angle or measurement), and used some generalities that allowed for the balance and symmetry of the individual animal. For instance, he wrote, "the pasterns should neither be too upright, like a goat's, nor yet too sloping." He also said that "from the breast, the horse's neck in its natural position should not point outward like a boar's, but like a cock's should rise straight to the poll, and be flexible at the bend" (quoted in Gladys Brown Edwards, *Anatomy and Conformation of the Horse* [Croton-on-Hudson, NY: Dreenan, 1980], 8).

A horse with a round back and low withers has the opposite problem. Sores are likely because the saddle is perched on the back without much to hold it in place, except a very tight cinch and a breast collar. It will tend to roll sideways or forward and cause rubbing and chafing.

A horse with low withers usually must have a breast collar, and this handicaps him when traveling uphill. A horse must work with his head fairly low while climbing to be balanced and have maximum push with his hindquarters. The breast collar puts excessive pressure on his windpipe, restricting his breathing. The best back for carrying weight and for holding a saddle with the fewest problems is one with well-shaped withers and topline, with properly shaped ribs.

Riding Position

The natural position of a rider on a horse with a well-sloped shoulder and withers set well back on the topline is over the center of gravity, which is behind the withers and forward of the loin muscles. This position places the rider over the "spring of the back," where the back is most flexible. The rider's weight is close to the driving power derived from the thrust of the hindquarters and loins, yet not so far back as to inhibit the loins. The rider is back far enough to be away from the direct concussion of the front legs and shoulders, and thus receives a smoother ride in this position than in any other place on the back.

This position is easier on the rider and the horse; extra weight is not pounding down directly over shoulders, knees, and fetlock joints. In a horse with upright shoulders and more forward withers, the rider is usually sitting a little more forward on the back, with her weight more over the front legs. This makes for a more jarring ride and is hard on the horse's front legs. They suffer more concussion from the extra weight bouncing directly over them.

If a horse carries the rider forward of the center of gravity, the ability to spin and pivot on his hind legs is somewhat hindered because the horse is made even more front heavy by the forward weight of the rider. For best athletic ability, balance, and durability (staying sound through years of hard use), choose a horse with sloping shoulders, good withers set well back, and a strong, short back.

The Withers and Saddle Fit

The conformation of the withers is a key factor in determining whether you will have saddle problems. A saddle that does not fit your horse's back will create sores. Withers too sharp and high can be easily bruised if a saddle rubs them at the top. If the saddle is too narrow, it may put too much pressure on the muscles just below and behind the withers. Pressure hinders blood circulation, producing sores, and killing pigment-producing cells so new hair grows in white. It can also cause the horse to restrict his movement to avoid pain, causing muscles to atrophy. Make sure the saddle fits the horse and does not put pressure on top of the withers.

Sometimes a horse with high withers will have a dip in the back just behind the withers, making it hard to fit a saddle, for there is less muscle for the saddle to rest on. Just as with a swaybacked horse, the saddle tends to form a "bridge" between the withers and the loin area. When this happens, it may rest too heavily on the withers, creating a pressure sore at the top of the withers, or pinch them, causing back pain or a sore spot from excessive pressure and rubbing.

Take special care when selecting a saddle for a horse with this type of conformation; it should fit him properly and may need a breast collar to stay in place. If the saddle slips back too far, it will shift the rider's weight too far back (hindering the horse's action and balance) and won't fit properly in that position. On a high-withered horse, the saddle may also need extra padding to keep from pinching or rubbing the withers.

THE JUMPER

The basics of good conformation apply to the jumper. The jumper, however, must withstand some extra stresses. Take care in selecting a horse for this type of career, especially when evaluating his strengths and weaknesses.

Horses Need Training

Many athletic horses are graceful when running free but do not handle themselves as well with a rider on their backs until they have been trained. The added weight of a rider affects the horse's balance. Most horses need a lot of work and training at all gaits in order to develop needed dexterity, good balance, and the ability to adjust their stride to meet any new situation.

The jumper must have strong, correct leg conformation to withstand the trauma and concussion of landing from a jump without suffering breakdown. He needs strong, well-built hindquarters and hocks to give him the power and mobility to jump, and a strong back. The loin area, especially, must be well developed.

Length of Back

There have been good jumpers with short backs and long backs. Length of back is not as important as strength of back, especially in the loin. Keep in mind, however, that constant jumping puts great strain on the spinal column; the shorter the back, the more concentrated the concussion it must absorb. The shock is greatest on the lumbar bones, which are toward the rear. The back should be long enough to carry a saddle without putting much pressure on the loins. The loins need freedom of movement to function without hindrance over a jump. A back that is too long, however, will usually have a weaker loin and tire more easily.

Light in Front

The jumper needs good overall balance because he uses his head and neck for jumping balance. He needs well-developed hindquarters and a relatively light front end with center of gravity a little farther back than the racehorse, for instance. He needs well-made shoulders and front legs because they bear all his weight when landing from a jump, but his front end should not be too massive. Very few horses with heavy forequarters make good jumpers. A wide breast is a disadvantage in any equine athlete and especially in the jumper. It cuts down speed and agility, reduces his stamina, and hinders his ability to jump well.

He should be wider in the hindquarters than in front. He will be more agile and better balanced and have freer use of his front legs for clearing a jump if he is not front heavy. His body should be wedge-shaped: narrow in front and wider behind. He should not be too narrow (front legs too close together), however, or he may be narrow chested, with less stamina and less ability to handle himself well when landing from a jump.

If the breastbone is too wide and pectoral muscles too bulky, front legs will be too wide apart, creating a poor way of traveling and loss of agility. The horse will be too heavy in front. If his breast is too wide, he will have a rolling gait and may paddle outward with his front feet, resulting in less speed and coordination. He will tire more easily. A heavy front end makes it harder for him to rise up over a jump and makes for a heavier landing with more concussion on the front legs.

Conformation Close-up

Heaviness of muscle on thighs, arms, and forearms is a hindrance to free action and jumping ability. The heavier-muscled horse has more bulk and weight to get over the jump and will tire more quickly than a lighter-muscled animal. The thicker, heavier horse carries more body weight and won't hold up as well over a long course. The heavy horse is also less efficient at cooling himself when exerting.

Front Legs

The jumper's front legs must have proper angles to hold the complete weight of horse and rider when landing from a jump, without putting excessive strain on any of the joints (see chapter 7). All the weight is on one front leg when first landing. Poorly built front legs add to the risk of breakdown and unsoundness for the horse and unsafe landings for the rider. Proper angles enable the horse to fold his front legs up tightly and raise his knees to get cleanly over a jump. If he can raise his front legs enough, he won't have to lift his body so high to get over a large jump. A long forearm and short cannon are desirable for jumping ability.

Conformation Close-up

A well-laid-back shoulder and a mobile neck of adequate length are necessary for agility and safety in jumping. Adequate length of neck is more important to a jumper than is the length of his back; the horse needs a relatively long neck for balancing himself over a jump. The horse can change his center of gravity quickly by raising or lowering his head and neck. When landing from a jump, his head lifts up when a front foot hits the ground, transferring some of the weight farther back.

When the horse lands from a jump, his foot hits heel first, throwing the strain onto flexor tendons in back of the cannon. The tendons use the sesamoid bones at the back of the fetlock as a pulley block and the navicular bone as another pulley block. At the instant of landing, the front foot hits the ground on its heel, with toe up and the fetlock joint sinking almost to the ground.

The second foreleg hits the ground a split second after the first. Weight is transferred instantly from the first leg to the second. The

⬤ When the horse lands from a jump, his foot hits the ground heel first, throwing all the strain on the flexor tendons, and the fetlock joint sinks almost to the ground. The second foot hits the ground immediately after the first.

heel of the first foot skids along the ground a little with the toe raised, putting tremendous strain on the tendons and their pulley blocks. Yet these structures, if properly conformed, are able to withstand the stress because they have some give. If the horse landed flat-footed without the give, the resulting impact could break the cannon bone, pastern bone, navicular bone, or even the coffin bone. This damage sometimes occurs if a horse lands wrong.

Jumping accident-free is possible through a combination of conformation and strength of the leg structures and good timing. The long pastern bone and navicular bone are probably the weakest links in the leg structure, but the unique arrangements of tendons and pulley-like surfaces created by the sesamoid and navicular bone make for very little direct strain on the long pastern bone if the horse has a strong sloping pastern that is not too upright. Short, steep pasterns and feet too small for the weight of the horse put more strain on these bones.

For strength of leg, the horse should have well-made cannons; the sides should be flat and broad and the tendons behind them firm and smooth. Knees should be wide, and flat in front. Large, strong knees are important to a jumper, not only for athletic ability, but also to minimize risks for breakdown of these joints. Feet should be of proper size for the weight of the horse, well built, and sound. Sooner or later, any fault in the front feet or legs of a jumper will lead to trouble.

The jumper must have good bone with tendons set well back from the cannon bones (giving a larger total circumference of the leg), for less friction between the moving parts (see chapter 7). For strength and soundness in a jumper, it's better to have above-average bone circumference than below average. You don't want the horse too large for his bone structure. He must be of adequate size to carry a rider effortlessly over a jump, yet he also needs enough bone to support that size and weight.

Size and height are not as crucial as build to jumping ability. But if a small horse has short, choppy strides he will have more trouble placing his strides for perfect spacing between jumps in a show ring. Most jump courses are designed for the strides of tall, long-striding horses.

Strong Hindquarters

A strong but not overweight forehand must be coupled with powerful loins, big quarters, strong gaskins, and very sound hocks to carry a horse over a jump. Hocks should be evaluated carefully when selecting a hunter, jumper, or steeplechaser. The hocks should show no signs of spavin (bone spavin or bog spavin), thoroughpin, or curb (see chapter 16).

Hocks should be large, flat in front and at the sides, and wide from front to back. A line dropped from the horse's buttocks should fall straight down the back of the hock and cannon (see chapter 8). If hind legs are too straight (post-legged), the stifles will also be too straight. This can lead to the patella slipping out of place, with the stifle joint catching or locking. A slipping patella during jumping can be disastrous for both horse and rider. The tibia (between stifle and hock) in a good jumper is usually large and long; the best jumpers have a very strong gaskin.

⭕ Conformation Close-up

Hindquarters should be strong, with fairly level quarters. A too-sloping quarter (goose rump) has shorter muscles and less strength for jumping.

Evaluating a Jumper

A good jumper will lengthen his stride as he approaches the obstacle, slow his speed briefly in the final stride before the jump, and lower his front end slightly as he brings his hind legs more underneath himself for the takeoff. He should stretch his head and neck forward and tuck up his front legs and fully flex his hind legs to clear the jump, making a nice arc with his body. While going over a jump, the highest point of the horse should be his withers, not the top of his head.

If a horse seems uncoordinated or hesitates too much before getting himself organized to jump, he may not make a good jumper. If he twists his body while jumping, kicks out with his hind legs, bucks when landing, or charges off afterward, he may be experiencing discomfort or pain in his back or legs. If he consistently shows these tendencies, he may be a poor gamble as a jumper.

Good conformation is crucial for a jumper's success, but so is willingness and heart. A show jumper also needs good temperament, intelligence, and an ability to stay calm and listen to his rider. Always assess the conformation and the character of a horse — one without the other rarely produces a superior performer.

THE RACEHORSE

A racehorse must have good conformation to have speed and to stay sound under the stresses involved in running at top speed. Size is generally not as important as good feet and legs, but a horse that is quite tall or heavily muscled will generally not do as well as a more balanced animal. A relatively long neck is usually an advantage to the runner for balance and speed; a horse with a short, thick neck cannot extend himself as fully and will have shorter strides.

A sprinter that runs at top speed for a short distance is often built a little differently than a long-distance runner. Sprinters have more muscling on quarters, thighs, and gaskins, and sometimes more length in the hindquarters. Pasterns may be shorter and straighter and hindquarters more massive in the sprinter. The distance horse generally has longer, leaner muscles, longer legs and longer stride, and thus may be taller than the sprinter. The exception would be the Arabian racehorse, which is generally not as tall as a Thoroughbred but can outrun any other horse over long distances. The distance runner is generally leaner, like a greyhound. He has a good front end (long withers, deep girth and well-sprung ribs) and a leaner hindquarter.

For any runner, the body should be wedge-shaped, with a light front end. A wide breast cuts down on speed because it is less streamlined and has more wind resistance; it also makes it harder for the horse to have rapid front leg movement. The shoulders should never be so wide that you can't see the hindquarters behind them when standing in front of the horse.

▶ Racing type: sprinter conformation (Quarter Horse) with downhill body balance, croup higher than withers, and relatively straight hind leg angles.

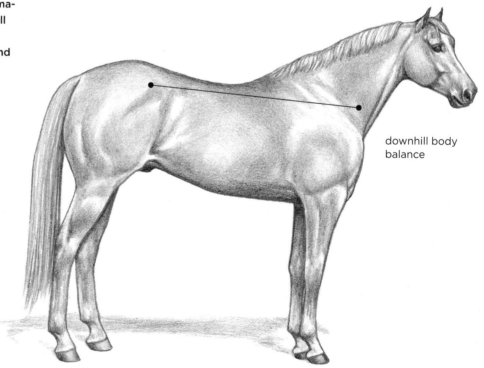

downhill body balance

Because the horse is naturally front-heavy due to his head and neck, anything that decreases the weight of the front half of the body (without decreasing its strength) and increases the power and weight of the hindquarters can be an aid to speed, especially in the sprinter, who is usually built with "downhill" balance (see chapter 10). The runner not only needs strong loins and quarters, but the additional weight of powerful hindquarters shifts the center of gravity back farther, enabling him to have freer and greater use of his front legs. A good racehorse usually has a long quarter (more than one-third of his total body length) and may have a longer back and loin than the average riding horse.

In a racehorse, feet must be strong, well formed, and of adequate size for the body. Front legs should be close to ideal conformation to minimize concussion. Racehorses start training very young. Stress on immature bones and joints can cause breakdown and unsoundness if there are faults in the front legs or feet that cause uneven weight bearing or deviation from straightforward motion.

A horse with crooked legs may develop splints or any number of joint problems. A splay-footed horse may interfere and strike himself. He may fracture the inner sesamoid bones on the fetlock joints due to additional stress on these bones. A pigeon-toed horse may injure the outer sesamoid bones or suspensory ligament. A calf-kneed horse has extra stress on knee joints and may get bone chips in his knees. A calf-kneed horse may be slow breaking out of the starting gate because his weight is more toward the rear of his feet. A horse with shallow heels and long toes may suffer chip fractures in the knees and bowed tendons because of extra strain on the knee bones and tendons during exertion.

Racehorse vs. Riding Horse

The ideal racehorse (built for maximum speed) and the ideal riding horse (built for smoothness of gaits and good weight-carrying ability) are somewhat different in structure. A horse destined for a sport other than racing needs a shorter, stronger back, and a level or slightly uphill body balance. The latter is a disadvantage to a racehorse. For maximum straight-ahead speed, the racehorse must not "lift up" in front. He carries his neck straight out to give the most leverage power for pulling his front legs forward. This trait goes hand in hand with downhill balance and lower set of his neck. A horse in any other sport must be able to raise his head and neck for shifting his weight farther back to become light on his front end. There is an obvious difference in the build and balance of a racehorse versus a riding horse and in the way they carry themselves. This does not mean a racehorse can't be successful in other disciplines, but it may be more difficult to train him to be light and collected if he has a sprinter build; his body type is designed for speed rather than agile maneuverability.

For strongest conformation and least risk of injury when stressed, front legs should be straight or very slightly in at the knee (carpal valgus). Studies by Dr. Wayne McIlwraith and colleagues at Colorado State University showed that racing Thoroughbreds with a slight inward angle at the knees (knees slightly closer together than fetlock joints) suffered fewer knee injuries than horses with perfectly straight front legs (T. M. Anderson, C. W. McIlwraith, P. Douay, "The role of conformation in musculoskeletal problems in racing Thoroughbreds," *Equine Veterinary Journal* 36 [2004]: 571–75). The researchers believe this is due to decreased weight bearing on the inner knee joint, where most chip fractures and arthritis occur. If the cannon bone is angled slightly, some of the load is taken off the inner knee. Conversely, if a horse is out at the knee (bowlegged, or carpal varus), he will rarely stay sound. If the fetlock joints and feet are closer together than the knees, there is enormous stress on the inner knee.

To have exceptional speed, the racehorse needs proper leg and body angles for freedom of movement and long stride (sloping shoulders, good angles in shoulders and hips). For extended speed, the leverage action of the front legs should be great, with long forearms and short front cannons. A well-laid-back shoulder that is not overburdened with heavy muscle enables the front leg to swing far forward and back very quickly.

In the hind leg, the longest stride (greatest amount of "ground gain" per stride) is attained only if the hind legs can straighten fully. A good racehorse has a relatively level rump and proper hock and stifle angles to allow the hind leg the greatest swing, like a pendulum. If the hocks and stifles are too bent (sickle hocks), there is loss of time in straightening out the joints at each stride.

Some racehorse breeders select for straight hocks and stifles, because the straight leg can swing faster. Many good racehorses have relatively straight hind legs, but if joints are too straight this can lead to problems with slipped patellas and locked stifles (see chapter 8). For good speed, the thigh bone between stifle and hock should be relatively short, with a longer cannon for more pushing leverage.

Some sprinters have long hind legs and a croup higher than the withers. This can lead to overreaching and injury to front legs unless the horse has a relatively long back or travels wide behind. In most cases, well-balanced conformation is preferred, but there are some high-crouped horses that race well. Most good racehorses have downhill balance (the base of the neck is more than 4 inches lower than the lumbosacral joint in the hind legs; see chapter 10), but this does not always mean the croup is higher than the withers.

Sprinter vs. Stayer

Sprinters, horses that have blazing speed for short distances, usually are built a bit differently than *stayers*, horses that excel over longer courses. Sprinters are often longer in the back, which helps keep them from being so front heavy, because they generally have a more obvious "downhill" build than the distance racer. The sprinter usually has a shorter thigh and shorter forearm, while the distance horse has longer legs and his body is not so close to the ground. The humerus in the sprinter is more horizontal and shorter than that of the distance runner. Rump and pelvis of the sprinter is often steeper; a distance horse has a more level rump.

A. The sprinter has more muscling and sometimes a longer back and more length in the hindquarters — and more downhill body balance — than the stayer. ***B.*** *The stayer has long, lean muscles and may be taller than the sprinter.*

THE RACING TROTTER OR PACER

Horses that race in harness are trotters or pacers, and almost all of them are Standardbreds. Because they are bred to pull a racing cart rather than carry a rider, they have some conformational differences. Most harness-racing horses have a longer neck and back, more sloping rump, and higher head and neck joint than a riding horse. They are bred for maximum speed at the trot or pace, rather than the gallop, and for ease of pulling a light cart. Many of them can, however, make good riding horses, especially for pleasure riding. But if they are very long in the back with somewhat upright shoulders, they are not as capable in activities that require a high degree of collection or quick maneuverability.

The harness racer needs a long, powerful, and well-sloped shoulder for length of stride, and good straight legs to minimize any interference problems. If a pacer's front toes point outward (splay footed), he may hit the opposite knee when pacing at racing speed. A trotter may strike the opposite cannons or fetlock joints with the swinging-inward foot.

▶ The Standardbred has a long, powerful, and well-shaped shoulder, with a high neck joint, a long neck, and a long back. Long legs (with long forearms and short cannons), long barrel, and deep heart girth are an advantage for speed at the trot or pace.

Good knee action is very important, as are strong, well-conformed knees. Just as in the galloping racehorse, calf knees cannot withstand as much stress as a straight leg; the calf-kneed harness racer may also develop bone chips.

Legs should be long (for length of stride) and well muscled, with long forearms and short cannons. If a trotter has long cannons and a short back, he will tend to overreach and strike his front feet with the diagonal hinds. Some trotters travel wide behind, bringing the hind feet up alongside the fronts, which enables them to avoid injury from overreaching. Pasterns should slope adequately to help dissipate concussion.

🔍 Conformation Close-up

The feet of a harness racer should be very strong and well formed to withstand the concussion of trotting or pacing at racing speeds. There is more concussion at these gaits than there is at the walk and the gallop.

A good harness racer has a relatively wide rib cage, deep heart girth, and a long barrel. The hindquarters should be well balanced and fairly muscular, with proper hind leg angulation when viewed

▼ The harness racer needs good, straight legs to minimize interference problems, good knee action, and a long stride.

from the side. Some trotters and pacers can be slightly sickle hocked without problems, but extreme angulation will impair the horse's action and stride. It can also lead to hock injury and strain of the back tendon (creating curb) at the lower part of the hock.

THE STOCK HORSE

Some activities require both speed and agility. The stock horse (cow horse, cutting horse, barrel racer) must combine both. Originally developed to work on Western ranches handling cattle, this type of horse has a quick burst of speed and the agility to maneuver after a dodging cow. Some must be sturdy enough for roping.

Today, the stock horse has become a specialist, however. Few are as versatile as the old-time ranch horses that had to be able to outrun a calf for roping (and powerful enough to hold him afterward), able to outmaneuver the wildest cow to cut her from the herd or head her back to the herd if she ran away, and travel all day when gathering cattle in rough country.

Today's *roping horse*, for instance, is generally used only in the show arena for short bursts of activity. He must have size, power, and speed to catch and hold a steer, but is usually too heavily muscled to have the endurance needed to work cattle all day in steep country. He needs strong hindquarters for quick bursts of speed, but his leg structure must also be correct for a quick stop with good balance. A roping horse must be able to burst into full speed from a standstill. A good roping horse breaks from the "box" faster than a racehorse breaks from a starting gate.

A calf-roping horse must be able to catch a fast calf, putting his rider into position to rope it, and then make a quick stop. A good calf-roping horse can be any size. A steer-roping horse, by contrast, is usually larger and stronger, with more weight to hold against the pull of a larger animal.

In team roping, the heading horse that runs up behind and alongside a straight-running steer while the rider ropes the horns of the steer must be quite sturdy, whereas the heeler, whose rider ropes the hind legs of the steer, must be more maneuverable to get his rider close to the steer that is bouncing around at the end of the header's rope. A heading horse is generally tall and heavy (1200 to 1350 pounds) while a good heeling horse may be smaller.

The *cutting horse* is probably the most agile and maneuverable equine athlete, but today's top performer works mostly in an arena under controlled conditions and does not have the durability and endurance of the earlier ranch horse. When selecting a horse for

cutting, the most important things are agility and strength, along with "cow sense," the ability and willingness to work cattle.

The horse must have the drive and speed to outmaneuver a cow, and correct leg structure to withstand the stresses involved in darting, twisting, turning, stop-start actions. The best cutting horses are relatively small (rarely more than 15 hands); a smaller horse has more quickness and agility than a taller, heavier horse and can stop and turn more readily.

A *barrel-racing horse* must be very fast and agile enough to make a smooth, quick turn around a barrel and head off in another direction. Most good barrel-racing horses are well balanced in their body conformation, with strong, well-sloped shoulders and strong hindquarters. Racehorse-like sprinting ability, combined with the skill to quickly shorten the stride to make a turn around the barrel without losing valuable seconds, are what count in this sport.

▲ The heading horse, whose rider ropes the horns of the steer, must be quite sturdy, whereas the heeler, whose rider ropes the hind legs, must be more agile and is often smaller and not as heavily muscled.

The horse with a short, strong back can turn with more speed and agility than a horse with a long back; the short-backed horse can get his hind legs under himself better for making the turns. The powerful takeoff and quick turning action put a lot of stress on feet and legs, so they must be well constructed and straight. Crooked legs not only create more stress on certain parts, but also take longer to extend and straighten, losing the crisp efficiency needed in a sprinter that is trying to beat the clock.

The *reining horse* also must have the conformation necessary for speed and agility. In this sport, the horse must be able to make a smooth stop from a gallop and then pivot either way (rollback) to where he is facing the opposite direction, to gallop off again. The horse must also be able to do a sliding stop from a gallop, back up swiftly, do a flying lead change in circles at the gallop, and spin in a small circle, pivoting on one hind leg.

For reining competition, some horsemen prefer a slightly sickle-hocked horse, thinking that having the hind feet farther underneath the body (rather than directly under the buttocks) helps the horse make the pivots and turns more easily. If a horse is very sickle hocked, however, this type of activity puts too much strain on the hind legs; the horse is more likely to develop hock problems.

THE POLO PONY

Horses used for the very active game of polo are not ponies in the true sense (see page 303); this term came into use because the average polo horse is smaller than a typical racehorse or jumper. A 14.3- to 15.3-hand horse is generally preferred because he can stop and turn quickly. The smaller horse has an agility advantage over a larger, taller horse in making fast stops and turns at high speeds. In this regard, the polo horse is similar to the stock horse, but with lighter muscling due to the need for greater endurance.

All the principles of good conformation apply to polo horses: strong, straight legs; a well-laid-back shoulder; a very short, strong back; relatively long and flexible neck for good balance; and short front cannons and strong hindquarters. Straight legs and strong, well-shaped feet are essential or the horse will not hold up under this hard use. Most polo horses are small Thoroughbreds or Thoroughbred crosses. Small, light-muscled Quarter Horses also do well, as do some Quarter Horse-Thoroughbred crosses.

The ideal polo horse has enough muscling for the job and a certain sturdiness for withstanding rough knocks — the game demands a lot of action, and there are many collisions between horses. All aspects of conformation should be ideal for durability to withstand the stress and strain of this activity, with a well-proportioned and balanced body. Good head and neck conformation and carriage are essential for natural balance and for the control and communication (via the bit) necessary for perfect maneuverability at the rider's command.

Long, sloping shoulders and good withers are needed for speed and agility and to hold the saddle in place, because the rider often leans away from the horse to hit the ball. Feet and legs must be well built and durable to stay sound and minimize tendon strain.

THE DRESSAGE HORSE

Dressage requires great athletic ability; a horse must have good conformation and proper muscle conditioning to do well. Well-constructed legs and body, with proper angles, allow freedom of movement and agility, and enable the horse to collect and extend himself more fully. A long, well-sloped shoulder is essential for great extension of the front legs, and a relatively flat rump with good straight hind legs and proper angulation in stifles and hocks enable the horse to work with his hindquarters underneath himself for collection and impulsion. The horse must have free-flowing straight action.

A short, strong back is important; the horse must be able to round his back to carry the rider and collect himself. A long back or sway-back makes it much harder for the horse to fully collect. The back should not be *too* short for a dressage horse, however, because this will create stiffness and less flexibility. The back should be very strong and straight from withers to loin, without a downhill balance toward the front end (see chapter 10).

⊸○ *Conformation Close-up*

In a dressage horse, the withers should be fairly long from front to back, making the back look fairly short if the horse has a strong loin. Withers should blend nicely into the back, well behind the top of the shoulder blade.

Body shape must be balanced and symmetrical, although many dressage riders prefer a horse that is slightly "uphill" (higher at the withers than croup) rather than perfectly square. The quarters should never be higher than the withers or too level, or the horse will have a harder time lowering his hindquarters to get his hind legs well underneath himself for proper collection and propulsion needed for advanced dressage movements. With good withers conformation and a slightly lower croup, the horse's topline will have the proper

▶ Dressage requires good conformation, proper muscling, and conditioning.

appearance during dressage work, especially when the hindquarters are lowered (with hind legs flexed), with the horse's neck lifted up from its base and his poll flexed.

The head and neck connection is very important in a dressage horse, for ease of collection and proper carriage (see chapter 3). The throatlatch should be open enough that the horse can truly flex at the poll rather than having the flexion point farther down the neck. Avoid horses with short, thick necks or long swan necks with an extra kink in the lower half (in front of the withers) in spite of its arch behind the ears. The swan neck cannot attain proper flexion. Without correct flexion at the poll, the horse cannot carry his back properly for sustained collection.

The humerus must have proper angle with the shoulder blade to have good action in front legs. If the humerus is too horizontal (at a right angle or less to the midline of the shoulder blade), the front legs may be too far underneath the horse for good extension (see chapter 7). He'll have more stress on his front legs and travel heavy in front.

Proper hind leg angles (rather than too much or too little angle) are important for good action, collection, and flexion in dressage.

Long legs can be an advantage to a dressage horse, whereas too much length of leg decreases agility and balance in other types of athletes that work in varied terrain. The dressage horse, however, works in a very controlled environment and needs springy, light gaits with extensive reach, which can be aided by longer legs. The front and hindquarters still should be in balance, however, with the hip joint no higher than the pivot point of the shoulder blade.

For a competitive dressage horse, the somewhat elusive and indefinable quality called *presence* is also important, along with size. Even though a small horse can do well, judges seem to prefer horses 17 hands high or taller, which is why many dressage riders choose warmbloods.

THE EVENTING HORSE

Eventing (combined training) is a sport that originated with early cavalry competitions to test the army horses' speed, fitness, and agility and to ready them for the long marches and difficult conditions encountered in battle. The event horse used to be called a jack-of-all-trades: he had to be good at dressage, steeplechasing, and show jumping. Today, this sport still combines several tests — dressage, cross-country work (assessing endurance and speed), and jumping ability. A good event horse can also excel as a steeplechaser or point-to-point racehorse.

Eventing is probably one of the ultimate tests of a horse's athletic ability and versatility, so proper angles and body build are very important. A successful event horse needs the conformational traits of a good jumper, with the balance and back strength of a dressage horse, along with the attributes required for endurance, including adequate wind for speed and distance work.

He must be a good all-around athlete with the physical and mental ability to do the precision work as well as the speed work. He needs ideal conformation to combine jumping ability with speed. Horses in the height range of about 16 hands seem to be ideal for this sport, since small horses may not have quite enough speed or stride and taller ones may not have as much stamina or agility for the obstacles of the cross-country courses.

Feet and legs must be strong and sound, with straight action, for efficiency of motion. The horse must have speed and agility. He needs long strides but also the ability to pick up his feet well to get himself out of bad spots, deep footing, and water obstacles and to avoid falling. He must be nimble enough to keep his footing and to jump efficiently at high speeds.

THE ENDURANCE HORSE

Arabians and Arabian crosses often are best suited for long-distance work because they have the heart and lungs for it, are light muscled, and can carry more weight for their size. Thoroughbreds, a breed with a lot of Arab blood, also do well. The hot-blooded horse (Arabian or with Arabian ancestry) has more oxygen-carrying capacity in the blood, which enables him to work longer and harder without fatigue. This type of horse also has a more efficient cooling system than the heavier-bodied cold-blooded horse.

Size is a key factor in whether a horse will have exceptional endurance. The small horse has a significant advantage in that he has more body area for sweat evaporation (and cooling) in comparison with his overall weight and bulk than the larger horse. A lightly muscled horse usually has more stamina than a heavily muscled horse. Long, lean muscles can keep working longer. Thick muscles have difficulty getting rid of the waste products from exertion and tend to become sore or to "tie up" on a long ride. Heavy muscles also overheat more readily and cannot easily dissipate the heat produced during exercise. The muscular horse tires more quickly because he has more of his own weight to carry. The small horse (15 hands and under, and with little body bulk) is often more efficient in his feed requirements and can go more miles before "running out of gas."

In order to hold up under many miles of riding, however, the endurance horse must also have excellent conformation in body, feet, and legs. He must have good balance and symmetry of body, so all body parts work well and smoothly. A deep, wide rib cage and heart girth are essential for lung room. Head and neck should be well constructed for proper airflow, with large nostrils and plenty of room for the windpipe in the head-neck connection.

Legs should be well constructed and straight, with straight action. A minor deviation might not make much difference to a pleasure horse that only travels a few miles each day, but can make a very big difference to an endurance horse. The added strain over a 100-mile course or the continual brushing of a foot against the opposite leg when interfering may create lameness and unsoundness problems. A minor interference can become a major problem toward the end of a long ride when the horse becomes tired and his gait becomes sloppier.

Front pasterns should slope adequately to minimize concussion. Leg length and angles should be ideal for long, easy strides. Feet should be large enough to support body weight without extra stress, but not so large that the horse is clumsy. A strong, thick hoof wall is essential for withstanding many miles and to tolerate the constant reshoeing needed through a season's work. All factors discussed in earlier chapters pertaining to ideal foot and leg conformation apply to the endurance horse, as he puts more miles on these structures than any other equine athlete.

Back construction is of great importance, not only for good traveling ability (good legs require a good spine) but also for holding a saddle properly and carrying the weight of a rider that far. Most good endurance horses have short backs. If a horse is too long in the back or has a weak loin, he cannot round his back to carry the weight and his back will become tired and sagging. This leads to poor leg coordination and a tendency to interfere. Many leg problems in endurance horses originate as back problems, so make sure the horse has a strong, well-constructed back. He also needs good withers to hold the saddle in place. If the saddle doesn't fit properly or moves around too much, a horse's back will become sore; he will not be able to go the many miles required.

The endurance horse needs good conformation and very strong construction to withstand the training and fitness conditioning necessary for this sport. The horses that do best have natural stamina and are usually hot-blooded. A rider gives them the proper kind of work and training to develop fitness and traveling efficiency by strengthening the back and hindquarters for carrying weight over distance without fatigue or strain.

THE GAITED HORSE

A gaited horse (e.g., Saddlebred, Tennessee Walker, Fox Trotter, Peruvian Paso) is constructed a little differently than other light horse breeds. He is often longer in the back (loin area), with a short hindquarter and long gaskin. The lumbosacral joint is always a little farther back in the gaited horse than in the non-gaited horse. Femur placement is also a little farther back, more toward the rear of the pelvis, which helps produce his distinctive movement.

Because it has more give, the long back tends to give a smooth ride. The back tends to go hollow, which helps incline the horse to gait, with more side-to-side swing and lateral action. The longer tibia helps create a long overstep in the hind legs, which is prized in a gaited horse. Some of the common hind leg problems in these breeds, such as spavin and locking patella, can be minimized, by avoiding extremes. A gaited horse should never be too long in the back, sickle hocked, cow hocked, or too "camped out behind" — these faults put more strain on the joints.

Horses bred for a long stride in the hind legs, with too much distance from stifle to hock, are often too short in the femur and may have straight stifles that are prone to patella problems. Unless the cannon bone is short to compensate for the longer tibia, the horse will be camped out behind, with the hocks too far back behind the buttocks. Long hind cannons and a long tibia make the whole leg too long, putting more stress on hips, stifle joints, and hocks. Less length in the hind limb is better, because the horse is more likely to stay sound.

Some gaited horses have an extra motion in the hind legs, the leg swinging to the inside as it takes weight. When the hind foot comes to the ground, the hock wobbles to the outside, and then the foot breaks over toward the outer hoof when it leaves the ground. This puts a swiveling torque on all the joints. Weak construction such as this has been perpetuated in some gaited horses by breeders who select for the look of the gait rather than for sound performance. Likewise, some breeders select for sickle hocks because the excessive hock angle makes it look like the horse is taking a longer stride. A correctly conformed hind leg also takes a long stride and is by far the better choice.

⌕ Conformation Close-up

A gaited horse is not built like other riding horses. A typical gaited horse will have a slightly longer back and shorter quarter and a longer tibia. A line dropped from the point of the buttocks may pass through the center of the hock rather than the back of it, and this is quite acceptable. If the hind legs are set so far back that the entire hock and cannon is behind that line, however, there is more potential for leg injury.

In a well-built riding horse, the hip socket is about halfway between the point of the hip and the rear of the pelvis, but in many gaited horses the hip socket is farther back, which changes the pivot point for the whole leg. Most gaited horses do not have long quarters; some are very short, which makes the hind leg placement even less ideal, especially if the pelvis is also short and excessively angled, as in goose rump. This construction can lead to hind leg problems, so it's best to avoid extremes and select for more balanced structure.

THE PLEASURE HORSE

A wide variety of horses make good pleasure animals. Often a horse that does not have ideal conformation for more demanding sports like racing or eventing (or has a slight impairment that would create

The gaited horse has uphill body balance; his angles and proportions are suited more for a smooth ride and traveling ability rather than for extreme speed.

a handicap or make him more likely to be injured with harder use) can still make a good pleasure horse. But the rules of conformation should still be considered; you don't want the horse to go lame with ordinary use.

You also want to make sure the horse has adequate athletic ability to travel comfortably and safely, with no discomfort to his rider. A smooth, easy gait is preferable to a jarring one. A well-built body, head, and neck (enabling the horse to collect and extend and be responsive to the bit and to proper communication from the rider) are very important in a pleasure horse.

Avoid selecting a horse that stumbles because he can't collect himself or pick up his feet properly, or a horse that is always fighting the bit because his neck is not well constructed for flexing at the poll and giving to the bit. A horse with good conformation is always more pleasurable (and safer!) to ride than a horse with poor conformation.

THE DRIVING HORSE

A good carriage horse is usually strong and compact (with adequate bone for durability), with good legs and feet and a good neck. The ability of the horse to pick up his front feet and extend them well

Carriage type (Cleveland Bay); strong and compact, broad and muscular, with uphill body balance and neck set high on the chest.

forward depends a lot on the set of the neck and development of the neck muscles.

Ideal size is considered to be about 15 to 16 hands to combine speed and agility. The shoulder can be a little more upright than in a riding horse and covered with more muscle, as this makes it easier for the horse to lean into a collar for pulling his load by pushing his body against the collar. A broad chest can be an advantage to a driving horse, whereas it is usually a disadvantage to a riding horse.

A carriage horse should have a broad, strong back, and can have a longer back than a riding horse (and a longer loin) because he does not have to carry weight on his back. He should be deep in the flank (from loin to groin), not shallow. His body balance should be level or "uphill" from back to front (he should never be higher at the croup than at the withers).

A driven horse needs strong hindquarters to pull his vehicle by pushing into his collar or breastplate. Well-constructed hind legs are vital to withstand the extra stresses of pushing while traveling, especially at speed. If the horse does not have proper hind leg angles and good hocks, he may develop curb from the constant stress of pushing his own weight and that of the vehicle he is pulling.

The hindquarters should be well muscled, with quarters of good length, and slightly sloped for ease of getting his hind legs underneath himself for pushing. Thighs and gaskins should be strong. When viewed from behind, the hindquarters should appear square, with plenty of width and muscling.

The driving horse needs a fairly long shoulder and a well-set head and neck of adequate length to flex at the poll and travel well. His neck should be set high on his chest for good head carriage. He needs a free-swinging, ground-covering walk, with ability to lengthen and shorten his stride as needed in order to traverse all kinds of terrain. A little knee action (lifting the feet a bit higher than a riding horse) is often desired to negotiate bad footing or deep mud. Showy action is sought in some breeds (such as Hackneys), but excessive high action can be a detriment to efficiency and endurance in a driving horse.

Good feet and legs are essential, with correct structure and angles for straight action and for dissipating concussion. Good hock angles are important in the harness horse, because the hock is often overworked either in pulling or in flexing to keep back the weight of the vehicle on the downslopes. Proper feet and leg angles are always important. If the horse will be trotting for miles, you don't want him

A good carriage horse has adequate bone for durability, strong hindquarters, and proper hock angles, and a well-set head and neck (of adequate length) to be able to flex at the poll and travel well.

interfering. If he must travel on hard ground or roads, especially at a trot, he needs good feet and legs to withstand the concussion.

THE DRAFT HORSE

Draft horses were once the horsepower on our farms and roads, pulling farm equipment and wagons. Today, some are still used for farm work and for show in parades and pulling contests. They are also used in crossbreeding with light horses to create warmbloods and heavy sport horses; the crossbreds are often used in dressage, jumping, and other events.

There are only a few draft horse breeds, compared to dozens of light horse and riding breeds. Draft breeds include Clydesdale, Belgian, Shire, Suffolk Punch, and Percheron. The basic body build for a draft horse is broad and muscular. Most draft horses weigh more than 1600 pounds and many of the larger breeds are closer to 2000 pounds. The typical draft horse is more than 16 hands tall and can be as tall as 19 hands.

A good draft horse has a deep, wide chest and a massive, crested neck, making him heavy in front. This gives him greater pulling power as he leans into a collar, and allows him to easily pull more than his own weight. His back is usually very broad. He is much wider than a riding horse and is proportionally wider than his size might suggest.

Several conformation traits are acceptable in the draft horse that would be unacceptable in a riding horse. The draft horse generally has a straighter, more upright shoulder, which is better for leaning his weight into a collar, and less withers. (He does not need to hold a saddle, and his neck and shoulder angle make for low withers.) His hindquarters may slope more, and his legs are often shorter in proportion to his body height, partly because he has low withers. Because the draft horse has short legs, his body length is usually longer than his height. His body is deeper from withers to underline than the length of his legs from belly to ground. The short legs in comparison to body height give more leverage and power when pulling.

Draft horses of all breeds tend to have large heads, which is not detrimental to their type of work. The neck should be short, thick, and very muscular compared to the neck of a riding horse. Length and flexibility of neck are not needed (for balance at fast gaits) because the draft horse is not required to have the speed and agility of a riding horse.

A good draft horse has a thick, powerful shoulder and is wide in front. His neck is set onto his chest fairly high, and his body balance

◀ Draft-horse type (Belgian).

should be relatively level or only slightly downhill from back to front. The sternum is wide in a draft horse; the space between the forearms is much wider than that of a riding horse to allow room for the massive pectoral muscles. The draft horse should not be too wide (with front legs very wide apart), or concussive forces on the front feet may be too much, making the horse more likely to develop sidebone and ring-bone. A good draft horse travels with his feet relatively close together and straight; he is not shaped like a barrel with a leg at each corner.

The draft horse does not need as much slope to his pasterns as a riding horse, for there is less concussion to dissipate because he is not working at speed. Upright pasterns are more efficient for pulling. But if pasterns are too short and upright, the horse may develop sidebones, especially if trotted on hard roads.

Legs should be short and solid for pulling power and stability (balance when pulling), with muscular forearms, thighs, and gaskins and short, sturdy cannon bones. Because of his large size, the draft horse rarely has as much bone per 1000 pounds as does a smaller horse (see chapter 7), but needs as much as possible to support his weight. Joints should be large and strong. Feet should be large, for good support of

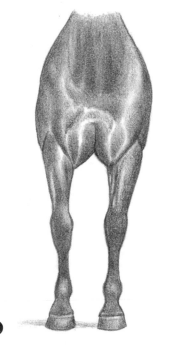

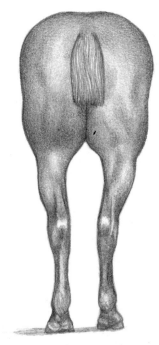

△ Good front leg (A) and hind leg (B) conformation for a draft horse: a good draft horse is wide in front, with a thick, powerful shoulder. Space between the forelegs is wider than that of a riding horse. The draft horse has well-muscled hindquarters, sturdy legs and bones, thick stifles, and strong hocks (set low, for pulling leverage). He is wide through the hips and narrower at the hocks, fetlocks, and feet.

a large body, dissipation of concussion, and good traction. The ideal draft-horse foot is very round and should be wide and deep at the heels. A draft horse often has flatter feet than light horse breeds, but if they are too flat they will bruise easily. Flat feet or contracted feet should be avoided; the horse will probably not stay sound.

The draft horse needs a strong back and very strong loin (which aids in pulling power), with deep flanks and belly. He must have well-muscled hindquarters and a long, wide pelvis, strong sturdy leg bones, thick stifles and strong hocks — set fairly low — for maximum leverage while pushing and digging in with his hind legs. Strong shoulders and forearms give him power to pull against the collar and dig in with his front feet.

Hind leg angles should be proper, though a little angulation in hocks and stifles can be tolerated in a draft horse, as long as it is not excessive (sickle hocks). Some angle is always preferable to a leg that is too straight (post-legged), as a draft horse with straight stifles is liable to dislocate the joints. When pushing hard with the hind legs to move or pull a heavy load (straightening out the angle between the femur and tibia), the patella may easily slip upward if the stifle joint is already too straight. If the patella becomes lodged on the front of the femur, the stifle joint becomes locked.

Several draft breeds are more cow hocked than would be desirable in a riding horse. The draft horse is wide through the hips but close at the hocks. The leg bones from hock to fetlock joint are closer together than you see in most light horses. Some breeders contend that the draft horse's hind legs should be "close" so as not to be bumped or troubled by the traces of the load being pulled, but taken to extreme this structure makes a weaker leg.

Breeders who use draft horses to cross with Thoroughbreds to produce warmbloods and sport horses try to select draft horse individuals with conformation and disposition that will complement the light horse and make a sturdy, levelheaded, athletic cross. A draft horse that crosses well with light horses is one that has good balance and action, with less-than-average width and coarseness in the front end. The warmblood breeder hopes to combine the desirable aspects of both types while minimizing the aspects of cold blood that would be detrimental to speed and agility.

THE PONY

Most ponies evolved in cold, northern climates; they are more closely related to draft horses than to hot bloods. They have body builds similar to draft horses (in smaller size), unless they've had an infusion of light horse blood in their ancestry. Early on, many of the pony breeds were used for pulling and draft work as much or more than they were used for riding.

Ponies have a different body type than riding horses, and it is this, not height or size, that makes them ponies rather than horses. Technically speaking, any animal taller than 14.2 hands is a horse and anything shorter than 14.2 hands is a pony, but this is not a very accurate defining trait. Some horses are shorter than 14.2 hands and some ponies are taller.

When choosing a pony for riding (rather than driving), pay close attention to body and leg structure, since many ponies tend to have chunkier, stockier bodies than horses, and poor angles for good riding qualities. The body and leg angles of a chunky pony can make for a rough ride and more concussion on feet and legs. Evaluate a riding pony as you would a riding horse, taking into consideration that he may still show some of his "cold-blood" characteristics. The more these can be minimized, however, the better, for a good athletic riding pony. For driving, it will not matter if the pony shows more *cobbiness* (short-legged, close coupled, and stout) or cold-blood traits.

◀ Ponies are closely related to draft horses (but of much smaller size) and tend to have chunky, stocky bodies with relatively steep angles.

Select Only the Best Breeding Stock

The purpose of breeding horses is to try to improve the breed (or type, if you are crossbreeding and trying to create a specific type of athlete) by selecting only the most outstanding individuals as breeding stock. They should have outstanding parents as well as an outstanding pedigree, because conformation is inherited and some characteristics can skip a generation or two. If criteria other than excellent conformation and soundness are selected as the desired traits, the resulting offspring will probably be a detriment, not an asset, to the breed or type.

Eye appeal and fashionable pedigree are not enough. Horses must be selected for structure and soundness, not just popular bloodlines. The individual must have the basic structure to hold up to hard use and the ability to function properly. Without good feet and legs, a well-balanced body, and a strong, well-constructed back, sooner or later the horse will become useless as an athlete and unable to compete in the rider's chosen sport.

UNACCEPTABLE FAULTS IN BREEDING ANIMALS

By knowing the basics of good conformation and which injuries are likely to occur with which faults, it is easier to select broodmares and stallions that can produce athletic offspring that will excel in their careers.

If you don't pay attention to conformation when selecting breeding stock (and ancestors' conformation, even if you only have photos to evaluate), you may perpetuate problems in offspring and subsequent generations. Inherited defects include ewe neck, long back, parrot mouth and sow mouth, poor body and leg angles, flat feet, shallow heels, and weak hooves that won't hold a shoe.

Conformation Close-up

If a horse has a defect, determine whether it is inherited or acquired. Is it merely a blemish (caused by an injury that could have happened to any horse) or an unsoundness due to stress from poor conformation? Any lameness or unsoundness should be carefully scrutinized. If it stems from poor structure that was inherited, do not use that animal for breeding, or you may perpetuate the problem in future foals.

When selecting breeding stock, the basic principles of good conformation should be evaluated. Any deviations from good conformation should be carefully weighed. Minor faults may be tolerated in a mare you already own, if you can select a stallion that is structurally correct in the area where she is weak. But the last thing you should do is compound a weakness by choosing a stallion that shares the same fault as the mare; this almost guarantees the same weakness will show up in the foal, perhaps to an even greater extent.

UNACCEPTABLE CONFORMATION FADS

Faults that are often tolerated or even selected for in some breeds only bring heartbreak when the animal cannot perform up to expectations. For instance, some breeders feel that sickle hocks (hind feet too far underneath the body rather than directly under the buttocks) are desirable for quick starts and stops, but this conformation taken to extreme puts great strain on joints and can lead to hock problems and a lame horse.

Other breeders desire heavy muscling in the hindquarters and forelegs and select for a bulging rear quarter with stifle and hock too straight. But this type of conformation (often called "halter conformation" in the Quarter Horse breed) will not hold up with strenuous activity. If a horse is too post-legged, this structure leads to spavin and to locked stifle joints (upward fixation of the patella; see page 162).

In some breeds, certain weaknesses are often tolerated, such as cow hocks in Arabians, shallow heels in Thoroughbreds, sickle hocks (and the opposite extreme of post-leggedness) in Quarter Horses, and long backs in Saddlebreds. Breeders who tolerate serious faults or follow fads of poor conformation hurt their breed immensely; it becomes more difficult to find sound individuals who can perform as athletes in a variety of careers.

There are still riders who want horses that can hold up under general use or compete in a strenuous sport. Sound, hardy horses are becoming the exception, rather than the norm. Young, good-looking animals become a disappointment later when they develop unsoundnesses that halt their promising athletic careers.

CONFORMATION IN REPRODUCTION
AND FOALING

Mares with physical traits that make it hard for them to breed, carry a foal to term, and deliver it should not be bred. Some of these traits include narrow hips and pelvis (which make it hard for a foal to be born), tipped-up pelvis, tipped vulva, and malformed udder or teats. A mare with a serious lameness should not be bred; as she gets heavy with foal it may become more difficult for her to travel around or get up and down.

A mare with a level rump (which sometimes goes with post-legged conformation) and a too-level or tipped-up pelvis may have problems delivering a foal. A horizontal rump may be accompanied by a pelvis that is level or slanted upward toward the rear, making it harder for the foal to come up over the brim of the pelvis and into the birth canal, especially in older mares that may be swaybacked. The pelvis may tip up more than it did when she was young. If a mare has a level rump and high tail set, check the slant of the pelvis (by looking at the line from croup to point of buttocks) to see if it has a proper angle or is tipped up; this is sometimes accentuated by swayback. Tail set alone is not enough; look at the angle of the bones.

Another problem for broodmares is a tipped vulva; the top part of the vulva is pulled forward and is horizontal, not vertical. A tipped vulva can lead to inflammation and infection of the reproductive tract, resulting in infertility. Anus and vulva are not in a vertical line; the anus has sunk forward into the body instead of being directly over the vulva. Feces may fall into the vulva and vagina to cause inflammation and infection.

A thin mare may have a tipped vulva just because she doesn't have the flesh and muscle covering to fill out her hindquarters over her bones. Older mares often develop this problem because the anus tends to sink forward as body structures sag with age and from having several foals, but sometimes this condition is also found in young mares that have never had a foal.

Selecting for long hindquarters, which increases a horse's rear leg thrust and speed, produces a conformational trait that leads to tipped vulva. If the rear part of the pelvis (that forms the point of the buttocks) is quite long, the lower part of the vulva is quite far back and the top part of it is pulled forward, creating the tipped-vulva condition. Many athletic mares have fertility problems because breeders have selected for the conformational traits that lead to power and speed. With these mares, a Caslick's repair must be done to prevent infertility.

In a Caslick's repair, the lips of the vulva are scraped (to create a raw edge), then sewn together so that they grow together, creating a seal to keep out contamination. This seal must be opened, however, whenever the mare is to be bred — or whenever she foals — so the act of breeding or foaling will not tear the vulva. When selecting a mare for breeding, this aspect of reproductive conformation should be taken into consideration; good vulva conformation can prevent a lot of problems.

In the breeding stallion, conformation is also important in order for him to do his job. Any hind leg problems or weaknesses will make it more difficult for him to mount and breed a mare. For best fertility, he also needs normal testicles of adequate size, to produce adequate numbers of sperm.

Any horse, mare or stallion, under consideration for breeding purposes should be examined by a veterinarian to evaluate breeding soundness.

◀ Tipped-up pelvis sometimes accompanies a level rump and high tail set; this can be a problem for foaling. It is often accentuated in an older mare that has become swaybacked.

cutaway view

◀ Tipped vulva on mare with long hindquarters; anus is forward rather than directly over the vulva (feces can fall into the vulva). The cutaway view shows the position of the anus and the vulva.

Soundness

CONFORMATION AND TENDENCIES to certain unsoundnesses are inherited. A sound horse is a healthy horse that has no injuries or impairments. An unsound has a problem that interferes with his usefulness, making him lame, unsafe to ride, and unable to perform normally and hold up to steady use.

Not all conformation flaws are the result of genetics, however. Some are the result of injury and may happen to any horse. Others are due to excessive strain and overwork, and these tend to occur more readily in a horse with poor conformation. For example, faults such as crooked legs and poor body angles can predispose a horse to ringbone, splints, curb, navicular syndrome, and fractures.

An unsoundness may be mild or severe, its level of impact determined by the horse's career. Unsoundnesses that might hinder a horse used for endurance

Conformation determines if a horse will be a good athlete or a poor one and if he will stay sound or not. The feet and legs of a well-conformed horse undergo less stress and strain because all forces are distributed equally, with no extra pull or concussion on any one part.

riding, racing, and jumping, for example, may not hinder a horse used for pleasure riding.

Although some unsoundnesses may be detrimental to a horse's athletic ability, they may not impair his ability to produce well-conformed foals. Be aware, however, that if a horse has hereditary conformational flaws, those traits may be passed on to future generations if the horse is bred.

Thoroughly evaluate a horse for soundness before making a purchase or initiating a breeding program. It's always wise to arrange for a veterinary pre-purchase examination for soundness. If you plan to breed an animal, the examination should include an evaluation of breeding soundness, as well.

The Physical Examination

The feet and legs are often a horseman's first priority when checking for soundness, but to get the full picture, take time to make a thorough physical examination, and don't forget the head and neck. With the horse at the halt, check his sight, hearing, mouth, and teeth (see chapters 3 and 4). Excessively worn incisors can be a sign of cribbing, and an abnormal depression just ahead of the withers may indicate torn neck ligaments, for instance. Common conformation problems are discussed under the appropriate body part.

BODY

When examining the horse's body, check for possible injury to the point of the shoulder and to the nerves that stimulate the shoulder muscles. If the nerves have been damaged, the shoulder muscles will be atrophied, or shrunken (a condition called *sweeny*), and will lack symmetry. Atrophied muscles are weak and can hinder a horse's performance if he is used in athletic activity.

A kick or sharp blow to the shoulder can cause shoulder injury. Sweeny also can be caused when the shoulder is in a forward position during a stride and suddenly slips back, tearing the nerve fibers. This kind of slippage is most common when a horse is trying to climb a steep hill or is pulling a heavy load on wet ground. A draft horse working in wet, muddy ground or on wet, slick streets may experience this problem, but any horse can slip if his feet cannot cut into the ground to provide adequate traction.

Check the withers, back, and girth area for any evidence of saddle sores or cinch sores. Most saddle marks are merely blemishes, such as spots where the hair grew in white or areas of thickened skin. If there is significant scar tissue, however, it might cause the horse

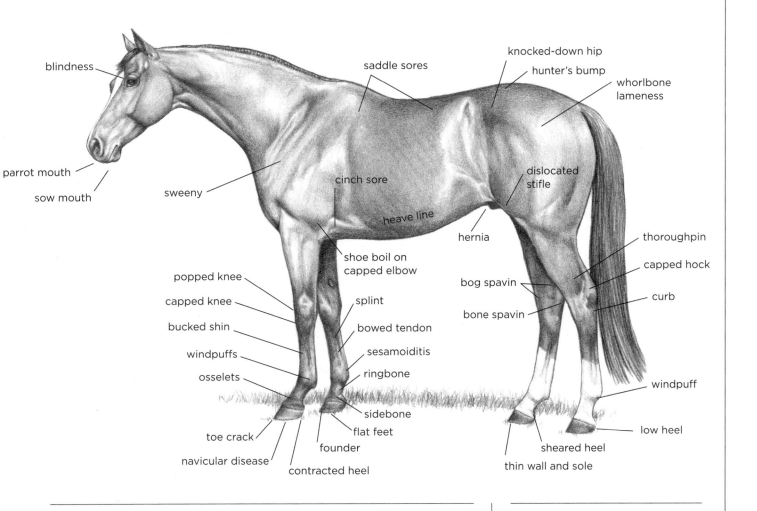

blindness

parrot mouth

sow mouth

sweeny

saddle sores

knocked-down hip

hunter's bump

whorlbone lameness

cinch sore

heave line

dislocated stifle

hernia

shoe boil on capped elbow

popped knee

capped knee

bucked shin

windpuffs

osselets

splint

bowed tendon

sesamoiditis

ringbone

sidebone

flat feet

toe crack

founder

navicular disease

contracted heel

bog spavin

bone spavin

thoroughpin

capped hock

curb

windpuff

low heel

sheared heel

thin wall and sole

discomfort and soreness each time a saddle is used. An abrupt sag in the back just behind the withers may indicate torn ligaments.

Look under the belly to check for any abnormal enlargements or swellings. Some horses have a hernia at the navel, a few inches ahead of the udder on a mare or the sheath on a male horse. There should be only a tiny bump at the navel. If the area is larger than a small marble, there may be a weak spot. If the protrusion is as large as a golf ball or orange, the horse has a hernia. Some male horses have scrotal hernias in the area just behind the sheath. Hernias are rare but can cause problems, so it pays to check.

Check for abdominal muscle lines that indicate *heaves*, a respiratory problem caused by sensitivity to dust and molds. Heaves is a condition similar to asthma in humans. Air passages react to irritants such as dusty hay by swelling and becoming obstructed. Because simple relaxation of the diaphragm is not enough to force the air out of his lungs, a horse with constricted airways must follow up with an additional push with his abdominal muscles. These muscles become

⬥ When evaluating a horse, check these hot spots for unsoundnesses.

larger than normal, creating a heave line, an obvious groove along each side of the belly.

Heaves is most easily detected by listening to a horse's lungs after you have walked and trotted him. If he has a bad case of heaves, he might cough or wheeze as he walks or trots. In a mild case, the problem may only be detectable with a stethoscope after he exerts. If you suspect that a horse might have a respiratory problem, have him checked by a veterinarian. A horse with heaves is seriously impaired during strenuous athletic activity and is not a good choice for a competitive career.

HIPS AND PELVIS

Injury to the hindquarters, as from a blow or fall, may create enlargement or disfigurement. To detect such an injury, look at both hips at once to determine whether they are symmetrical or not. If not, the horse has probably been injured.

Hunter's Bump

With the horse standing squarely on his feet, look at him from behind. Enlargement at the top of one side of the croup or a misalignment of the croup with the pelvis or lumbar vertebrae results in an obvious bump and one hip being more forward than the other. This is usually due to a tearing of the ligaments at and a dislocation of the sacroiliac joint. One side of the croup is higher than the other, and the rump slants to one side. From the side, a sharp rather than a rounded protrusion is visible at the croup. Occasionally, if the joints on both sides have been affected, bumps appear on both sides of the croup.

This injury causes displacement of the pelvis on one side of the backbone and is called *hunter's bump* or *jump bump* because it occurs most frequently in jumpers. It is most common in horses with a long back and weak loin. This type of conformation makes it harder for the horse to gather himself properly to go over a jump. It can also occur in a horse with good conformation if he has been jumped a lot or experiences bad footing, as when one hind leg contacts the ground too far forward or slides forward on landing. In such a case, all of the horse's weight is supported for an instant by the hind leg that is too far forward, thereby twisting the sacroiliac joint and tearing the ligaments.

The injury may be caused by excessive strain on the hindquarters when jumping or even when trotting up a

▼ Hunter's bump is usually due to a tearing of the ligaments at and a dislocation of the sacroiliac joint.

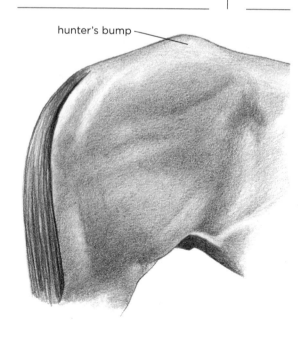
hunter's bump

steep hill. It may also occur if a horse falls down and the hindquarters slip out from under him, straining the ligaments to the point of tearing. When the injury heals, the horse usually can be used again, but the bump remains and the area is prone to reinjury.

Misalignment of the hindquarters can also occur if a horse suffers a twisting of his pelvis, which disrupts the joint. In this case, one hip is higher than the other, making the hind legs asymmetrical. The leg with the higher hip appears longer and the angles of the stifles and hocks more "open," while the leg with the lower hip looks shorter, with the angles more closed.

Knocked-down Hip

When viewing the horse from behind, hips should be level, but sometimes one side is lower than the other because of injury to the point of the hip or due to a dislocation or fracture of the pelvis on that side. This type of injury can be caused by a hard blow to the hip bone, such as running into a gate post or doorway, being hit by a vehicle, or a kick from another horse. If the point of the hip is crushed or fractured, it will be small or sunken, not prominent. If the hip has been bruised rather than crushed, it may be enlarged.

Even if the injury has healed, a horse with knocked-down hip may not be able to perform in strenuous activities because his gait is affected. Uneven muscle development may interfere with his strength for speed or jumping. He is also more apt to suffer muscle soreness and be at risk for strain and reinjury if worked strenuously. He may be able to do slow work without adverse affects, however.

ELBOWS

Check the horse for capped elbow and shoe boil. A *capped elbow* is an enlargement on the point of the elbow due to bursitis. It can be caused by a blow (such as being kicked on the elbow joint) or by the horse's shod foot pressing against his elbow when he is lying down. A horse may strike himself in the elbow when stamping off flies with his foot. Occasionally, a horse with high leg action (such as a Hackney pony, for instance) might hit himself on the point of the elbow with the heel of his shoe when trotting.

The swelling is caused by trauma or irritation of the bursa, the capsule that produces lubricating fluid for the joint. When irritated, the bursa produces excess fluid, distending the capsule.

If infection develops in the swollen bursa, the fluid turns to pus, creating a *shoe boil*. A shoe boil usually bursts and drains but may not heal. In such a case, it becomes a permanently draining fistula. An injured bursa may also fill with fibrous tissue. This is a problem you want to avoid when selecting a horse, because it can be difficult to resolve, so check the elbows for any enlargement.

STIFLES

Check the stifle to be sure it isn't swollen or dislocated. A stifle injury aggravated by arthritis in the joint can render a horse unsound. The severity of the injury and the damage done to the joint determine the degree of lameness. Fractures or bony changes cause a horse to be permanently lame and unsound.

If the injury occurred in the soft tissues only (a sprain or pulling of the connective tissues, or trauma to the joint capsule or to ligament attachments without rupturing those tissues), a lengthy 6 months to a year of rest may allow for complete recovery.

A horse with any degree of stifle lameness should be evaluated by a veterinarian. Horses with stifles that are too straight are more prone to joint injury than are horses with normal stifle angles. A horse whose stifles are too straight often has hocks that are too straight, as well. If a horse with a too-straight stifle seems sound, be alert for an occasional, telltale clicking of the joint or an intermittent "catching" of the patella; both are warning signs that the horse may develop stifle problems.

A horse with too-straight stifles is at risk for upward fixation of the patella, in which the hind leg locks in an extended position behind the body (see page 162). Generally, avoid choosing a horse with hind legs that are too straight. If you are tempted to select this type of horse because he has some strong qualities, carefully check his stifles and have him thoroughly examined by a veterinarian to make sure he has no history of stifle injury.

KNEES

Well-constructed knees rarely cause problems, but they can become injured with hard use. Check the knees for signs of swelling or enlargement.

Popped Knee

Popped knee, or *carpitis*, is inflammation of the knee joint and often involves the joint capsule as well as bones and ligaments. It is caused by trauma or excessive concussion. Horses with poor front leg conformation or horses that are worked too strenuously when soft and out of condition are the most likely candidates for this problem. Front leg conformation that may predispose a horse to carpitis includes calf knees (back at the knee) and bench knees (cannon bones too far to the outside of the knee joint).

Occasionally, a blow to the knee, such as a kick, or direct injury when the horse paws with a front leg and hits the knee against something solid, will cause this condition. Whatever the original cause of injury, the inflammation stimulates new bone growth in the knee area. A bony enlargement is visible at the front of the knee, and lameness is obvious at fast gaits.

Capped Knee

Like capped elbow, capped knee is a soft enlargement caused by an injury, such as falling on the knees, getting up and down on hard ground, or blunt trauma. If the swelling becomes cystic and calcifies, the bony enlargement impairs knee action. Otherwise, the swelling remains soft but the condition is chronic; the extra lubricating fluid permanently stretches and distends the knee joint.

No matter their location, most types of bursitis cause permanent swelling. Often the swelling is unsightly but does not interfere with a horse's usefulness. If capped knees make a horse lame, however, it is considered an unsoundness.

HOCKS

The hock joint can suffer injuries that are obvious when examining the horse. These will usually appear as soft-tissue swellings or bony enlargements.

Capped Hock

Capped hock is a firm swelling or enlargement at the point of the hock, usually caused by injury such as a blow to the hock or the horse kicking his hind legs against a wall or trailer tailgate and banging his hocks. It is sometimes accompanied by curb, a thickening a few inches lower. Capped hock by itself rarely causes lameness, but the blemish is permanent. The scar tissue within the bursa keeps it enlarged.

Curb

Curb is an enlargement at the back of the hock, a few inches below the point of the hock. It is caused by tearing or inflammation and thickening of the plantar ligament and usually results from poor conformation of the hind leg, such as sickle hocks or cow hocks, putting strain on the plantar ligament. After the ligament heals, scar tissue causes permanent thickening. In some cases, inflammation of the bone lining causes new bone growth and enlargement. Curb is

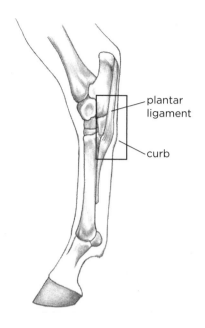

▲ Cross section showing enlargement in plantar ligament that creates
a curb.

Garde

Garde is a problem similar
to but different from curb.
The upper end of one of
the splint bones protrudes
beyond the profile of the
hock and presses on the tendons, creating irritation and
a small swelling that is often
mistaken for curb. In garde,
however, the bump is shorter
and more abrupt than in curb
and is off to the side of the
tendons rather than directly
underneath them. The small
swelling is usually permanent
and may or may not cause
lameness, depending on how
hard the horse is worked.

considered an unsoundness if it interferes with proper action of the
hock joint.

Occasionally, a horse with good hind leg conformation will
develop a curb from violent exertion (disrupting that ligament) or
from kicking his hocks against something solid. A permanent blemish results, but he will usually be sound after the injury heals. The
enlargement generally does not interfere with the function of a well-
conformed leg.

In horses with poor hind leg conformation, however, curb is
considered an unsoundness, because the problem will likely recur
whenever the horse exerts. With poor conformation, the hock is continually under greater stress than it should be. Exertion only magni-
fies the stress. The plantar ligament is easily reinjured, making the
horse sore and lame again.

Spavin

Spavin means disease of the hock joint; there are several types of
spavin, most of which cause swelling or lumps in the area of the hock.

Bone Spavin

The hock joint is made up of a number of small bones with slightly
moveable joints that allow for a wide range of flexion and extension.
Bone spavin generally causes fusion and eventual immobility of
some of these moving bones.

As the hind leg takes weight and the large muscles of the hindquarter begin to drive the leg back to propel the horse forward, the
small bones shift into a close-packed position to make the hock joint
solid and strong. Too much strain on these little bones as the leg
takes weight (when the hock is already overbent — as in a horse with
sickle hocks or in a draft horse pulling with his hocks flexed) causes
damage to the joints between them, creating spavin.

The characteristic bony enlargements of spavin generally appear
on the lower and inside portion of the hock, though occasionally they
occur higher on the joint or even on the outside of the hock; some are
never visible. Bone spavin usually results from poor conformation
such as sickle hocks or cow hocks, which increase the concussion and
stress within the joint, especially on the front or inside of the hock.
Bone spavin can also be caused by excessive stress and strain, as in
roping and reining competitions, when a horse must do a lot of quick
stops or turns on his hind legs.

Horses with narrow, thin hocks are more likely to develop bone
spavin than are horses with strong, sturdy, well-developed hocks.

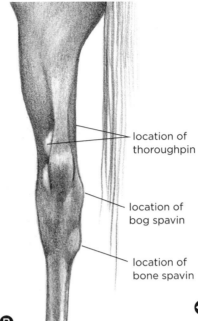

A

B

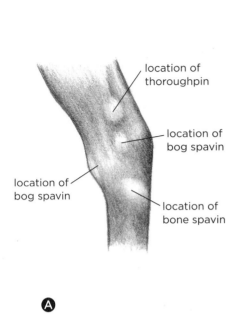

○ Locations of bog spavin, bone spavin, and thoroughpin. **A.** Side view of hock. **B.** Rear view of hock.

Rope horses, cutting horses, and reining horses are less apt to get bone spavin if they have good strong hock joints and good conformation (no sickle hocks or cow hocks) and are not started into heavy competition until their bones are fully mature (4 years old).

The most common location for bone spavin is at the junction of the lower part of the hock and the cannon bone or splint bones. Bone spavin causes lameness and pain when the horse flexes the hock joint, making him take a shorter stride. The inflammation creates an enlargement on the inner surface of the hock, which may only be detectable by X-ray. Even after the inflammatory phase has passed and the bones have healed and fused, the horse may travel stiffly due to lack of flexibility in the joint.

─○ *Conformation Close-up*

A horse with bone spavin usually has a shortened stride in the affected leg. His foot makes a lower arc and he tends to drag the toe in an attempt to limit the action of the sore hock joint. He tries to land on the toe of the foot rather than the heel, and the toe is usually worn excessively. When standing, he often tries to favor the hock joint by resting the toe of that foot on the ground, with the heel slightly raised. Often a horse will damage both hocks and then may try to shift his weight forward onto the front legs to relieve his pain.

Bog Spavin

Bog spavin is a chronic swelling of the joint capsule of the hock. The capsule creates too much synovial fluid, which permanently distends the lubricating sac. Bog spavin usually results from stresses caused by poor conformation, especially if the hocks are too straight. It also can be caused by injury to the hock joint as a result of quick stops and turns or other athletic stresses. Less frequently, it is caused by nutritional deficiency when the horse is young and growing.

Bog spavin creates a large, soft swelling that bulges on the inner part of the lower front of the hock joint. Sometimes two smaller swellings occur on either side of the hock, toward the rear. These should not be confused with thoroughpin, in which the swellings are higher. Pressing one of the points of swelling in bog spavin displaces the synovial fluid, causing the other two bumps to bulge.

Lameness is usually present only if the bog spavin is caused by trauma. In such a case, there will be heat, pain, and swelling over the hock joint. If the bog spavin is caused by poor conformation, treatment is of little value because the condition will likely recur.

Thoroughpin

Thoroughpin is similar to bog spavin but is a puffy swelling in the web of the hock; it is located in the usually empty space between the large back tendon and the gaskin above the hock. The swelling is a few inches higher than that of a bog spavin. It is caused by distention of the sheath that surrounds the deep flexor tendon, due to strain of the tendon. Once it is stretched and swollen, the tendon sheath often remains that way, becoming a permanent weakness, though the horse may not be lame.

CANNON BONES AND LOWER LEGS

Many of the unsoundnesses that hinder a horse's athletic ability originate in the lower legs, below the knees and hocks. These problems are generally caused by strain or concussion, and may be due to cumulative stresses or sudden injury.

Splints

Splints can be an unsoundness or merely a blemish, depending on their location or stage of development. Splints are most common on the front legs because they bear more weight than the hinds. The bony enlargements on the cannon bone may appear at any point along the juncture of splint bone and cannon. The splint bones are located on either side of the cannon, starting at the knee joint and ending about two-thirds of the way down the cannon bone (see chapter 7).

When the horse is young, the splint bones are only loosely attached to the cannon bone by the thick, strong interosseous ligament located between the splint bone and the cannon bone, and there is some movement between these bones. Eventually, the splint bones fuse to the cannon, usually by the time a horse is 4 years old, but sometimes as late as 5 or 6 years old.

If there's excessive movement between splint bone and cannon bone, the ligament attachment creates a pull and disruption of the bone lining. The resultant irritation stimulates new bone growth, eventually creating the splint. In early stages it is called a *green splint*. There is heat, swelling, and pain in that area.

After the acute inflammation subsides, new bone forms where the ligament was torn from its attachment. The new bone then acts as a bridge, fusing and holding the splint bone in place on the cannon so it cannot move, preventing any further tearing. A large splint is easily seen; a smaller one may not be as obvious but can be readily felt when you run your fingers down the leg.

Because of the way splint bones are formed and attached to the cannon in the front leg (directly under the knee), the inner splint bone is pushed downward and back each time the leg bears weight. By contrast, the outer splint bone is merely pushed down. There is

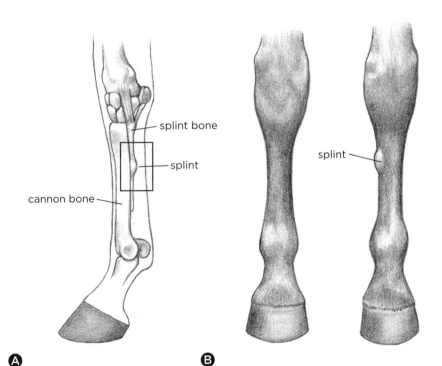

◀ Splint. A. Cross section showing enlargement on a splint bone. B. Location of splint on inner aspect of cannon bone.

splint bone

splint

cannon bone

splint

Ⓐ Ⓑ

more movement for the inner splint bone. If a young horse is overworked before his legs mature, the inner splint bone is too often pushed in two directions at once, and may be pushed so far that the ligament tears. In the hind leg, the outer splint bone carries more weight (supporting the hock) and is the one that moves in two directions at once. If a splint forms, it is usually on the outer leg. But because hind legs carry less weight and suffer less concussion, splints are rare on the hind legs.

Trotting on hard ground is a common cause of front leg splints in young horses. Often a young horse will develop splints from concussion and overwork, though the same kind of work will not hurt a mature horse whose splint bones are already firmly attached to the cannon. Until the bones are fused, there is always risk of a splint developing whenever there is too much movement between the bones from overwork or concussion.

Poor conformation puts additional stress and concussion on splint bones. Two types of front leg conformation increase the likelihood of splints: upright shoulders and pasterns (which give the horse a more jarring gait and a lot more concussion on the leg bones) and offset cannons (also called bench knees). When cannon bones are set too far apart, at the outside of the knee joint rather than squarely under the center of the knee, this puts more strain on the inner splint bones. A horse with offset cannons almost always develops splints on the inner side of the upper cannon bone, especially if worked on hard surfaces before age 5 or 6.

Splints accompanied by poor conformation or those that interfere with moving parts (toward the back of the cannon where it is rubbed by a tendon, or a high splint next to the knee joint) are considered unsoundnesses. A splint that interferes with a moving part will hinder working soundness of the horse and can lead to impaired leg action, soreness, and lameness. A splint accompanied by poor conformation — even if the horse is no longer lame after the inflammation is past — is a problem if you ever breed that horse; the offspring may inherit the same poor conformation.

⟋◯ *Conformation Close-up*

Splints can develop on any part of the splint bone, on either side of the cannon, but most are on the inside of the front legs because the inner splint bones are more subject to stress. Most splints occur about 3 inches below the knee. A splint on a hind leg (or on the outside of a front leg) may be due to injury such as a blow or a kick.

Splints can be caused by injury (such as one foot striking the other leg and disrupting the bone lining, a common problem in a splay-footed horse who wings his feet inward when trotting), poor conformation that puts more stress on one of the splint bones, or strain to the leg or overwork, which creates concussion and stress on attachments between splint bone and cannon bone.

Splints usually cause lameness only in the early stages, but some never cause lameness. Lameness is most noticeable at the trot and is most severe after exercise on hard ground. After a few weeks, the heat and swelling subside (if the area was swollen), the splint calcifies, and the hard, permanent lump appears. Lameness then usually disappears, at which time the splint is considered a blemish, unless it interferes with movement. If struck by the opposite foot or reinjured, an old splint may flare up and again become a problem for the horse.

Bucked Shins

Bucked shins, or metacarpal periostitis, is the term for inflammation of the periosteum on the front of the cannon bone. This usually occurs only in the front legs and is most common in young racehorses during their first weeks of training. Strain and concussion injure their young legs. Mature horses are rarely affected this way, because their periosteum is mature and fully attached, and the bones are stronger.

A horse with bucked shins is lame (or takes short strides if both front legs are equally affected), and there is heat, swelling, and tenderness on the front of the cannon bones. As the shins heal, there may be enlargements on the front of the cannon bone. Sometimes trauma and concussion can lead to stress fractures on the front of the cannon bone, which are more serious than bucked shins.

Bowed Tendon

Bowed tendon is an unsoundness resulting from severe strain to the flexor tendons and the sheath that surrounds and protects them. The deep flexor tendon and the superficial flexor tendon lie one behind the other behind the cannon bone. They extend down the length of the cannon bone and attach to the hoof, flexing the hoof when the muscles at the back of the forearm are contracted.

The tendons are encased in a sheath that produces lubricating fluid. When the tendons and their sheath and attachments are injured or torn, bleeding and inflammation cause swelling that

Did You Know?

The periosteum, or bone lining, protects and nourishes the bone and serves as an anchor for ligaments and tendons. It also contains a layer of bone-forming cells that contribute to bone growth when the horse is young or when healing a fractured bone. Injury to the periosteum causes inflammation, heat, and swelling. As the blood supply to the area increases, the bone-forming cells are stimulated to form new bone, creating a lump.

bulges outward. The affected area is hot and tender. Adhesions form, binding the tendons to each other and to the sheath. Fibrous scar tissue forms between the tendon sheath and the surrounding tissue; the bowed appearance is due to this fibrous scar tissue. A bow can occur high or low on the tendon; a severe case may involve the whole length of the tendon.

Bowed tendon is most common in the front legs. If it occurs in a hind leg, it is usually low. A horse with chronic bowed tendon may appear sound at the walk and trot but quickly goes lame when worked hard or fast.

Bowed tendon is usually caused by strain and overwork of the flexor tendon. Horses most likely to bow a tendon have long, weak pasterns or are too soft and not in proper condition for the work being asked of them. Horses that undergo rigorous training or strenuous exercise, horses with long toes, and horses whose tendons cannot support their weight are at greater risk for bowed tendon. Such a horse can bow a tendon when running hard, galloping uphill, turning quickly, bucking, suddenly accelerating to full speed, or floundering in boggy ground. A severe blow to the back of the leg can cause damage that may result in a bowed tendon. Once a bowed tendon becomes chronic — that is, once scar tissue is present — it becomes a permanent unsoundness, limiting the horse's ability to perform at fast speeds.

FETLOCK JOINTS

Several problems can affect a horse's fetlock joints, making him lame and unsound. Most are due to the stresses created by poor conformation and include injuries to bones, tendons, and ligaments.

Sesamoiditis

Sesamoiditis is inflammation of the sesamoid bones within the joint. These two small bones are located on either side of the fetlock joint, toward the rear. Sesamoiditis is usually accompanied by periostitis and new bone formation; the suspensory ligament may also be affected. This problem is generally caused by excessive strain to the fetlock joint, creating pain, swelling, lameness, and later new bone growth. The fetlock joint will never be as sound or strong again. Horses with long, weak pasterns are more likely to suffer this type of injury.

Osselet

Osselet is a term for traumatic arthritis of the fetlock joint, characterized by calcification within the joint. There is periostitis at the front of the fetlock joint, between the cannon bone and the long pastern bone (first phalanx), just beneath the fetlock joint. It may also occur on the front of the lower end of the cannon bone or long pastern bone.

Osselets result from extreme stress and strain that stretches and tears the joint capsule. *Green osselets* refers to the early stages of this condition, when there is soft, hot swelling on the front of the fetlock joint before the new bone growth begins. Inflammation of the joint capsule due to damage in the cartilage on the front edges of the juncture between the cannon and the long pastern bone may lead to chronic, permanent swelling. There may be a thickening of the joint capsule as well as an increase in the lubricating fluid that distends the capsule.

Osselets occur most frequently in the front legs, because they undergo more strain and concussion at the fetlock joint than do the hind legs. Horses with steep front pasterns are most vulnerable to osselets, due to the excessive concussion created by this type of conformation. Osselets may progress to the point that the underlying bone is involved: the fetlock joint becomes arthritic, with resulting calcification, stiffness, and chronic pain and accompanying fibrous enlargement of the joint capsule. Osselets may lead to small chip fractures at the front edge of the long pastern bone, which leave bone fragments in the enlarged joint capsule.

Windpuff/Windgall

Windpuff, or windgall, is a distention of a joint capsule, tendon sheath, or bursa anywhere on the leg, but the area of the fetlock joint is most commonly affected. Windpuff is usually caused by strain, especially when a horse is immature. It is considered a blemish unless there is accompanying lameness, in which case it is considered an unsoundness. Lameness is rare, except when windpuff is accompanied by arthritis, bursitis, or tendonitis. Windpuff is a chronic condition characterized by firm swelling in the fetlock joint, most commonly just above and in front of the sesamoid bones. The swelling is usually soft but may be hard in some cases.

Windpuffs in the fetlock area can occur in two locations: the lubricating sac where tendons pass around the sesamoid bones at the back of the joint, and along the tendon right behind the joint and the cannon bone. When these areas are irritated by friction, jarring, and pounding, extra lubrication fluid is produced, which distends the bursa or tendon sheath, creating the swelling. A horse with short, upright pasterns is prone to develop windpuffs because of the excessive concussion caused by his leg conformation.

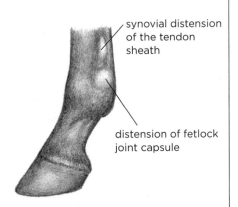

synovial distension of the tendon sheath

distension of fetlock joint capsule

▲ Locations of windpuffs. Windpuffs may result from excessive synovial fluid in the joint capsule or in the sheath covering the superficial and deep digital flexor tendons.

FEET

The old saying, "no foot, no horse" is true, especially as it pertains to soundness. Many of the common unsoundnesses that have plagued domestic horses for centuries originate in the feet. Avoid poor foot conformation such as flat feet and weak hoof walls, as these will often result in breakdown and lameness (see chapter 9).

Flat Feet

Flat feet are more easily bruised than normal concave soles and are more prone to corns and hoof abscesses. *Corns* are bruises near the bars and are caused by excess pressure. A flat-footed horse is likely to go lame if ridden without shoes and may need hoof pads to protect his soles in some cases. Flat feet are a serious fault for a horse that will be ridden a lot.

A *dry corn* or bruise leaves a red stain in the horny tissue, due to injury of the sensitive tissues underneath, and a little bleeding under the sole. A *moist corn* or bruise is the result of more severe injury to the tissues; serum oozes from the injured sole. An *abscess* (suppurating corn or bruise) may develop if the area becomes infected; the horse will be noticeably lame. Treatment is often needed to open and drain an abscess.

Corns and sole bruises can also be caused by pressure from improper shoeing, and sometimes by overreaching. When a horse overreaches, the toe of the hind foot (especially when shod) strikes the sole of the front foot.

A corn at the bars of the foot is most often due to a shoe left on too long and may also occur in a horse with contracted feet. A too-small shoe that puts pressure on the foot at the angle of the bars, rather than on the hoof wall, may cause bruising. In a properly fitted shoe, the heel of the shoe is wider than the heel of the foot, allowing room for hoof expansion each time the horse puts weight on the foot.

If left on too long, however, even a properly fitted shoe can cause problems. The hoof wall grows at a forward angle and pulls the shoe forward toward the toe. Soon the heel of the shoe no longer fits; the hoof horn at the heel starts to grow down around the shoe, and the shoe puts pressure on the angle of the bars rather than on the hoof wall. As the foot comes to the ground and takes weight, the heel of the shoe is driven upward against the angle of the bars because the hoof wall has grown out around the shoe instead of resting on it. Frequency of shoeing depends on individual growth rate: some horses need to be shod every 6 weeks, and others can go 10 weeks between shoeings. Appropriate and regular shoeing is key.

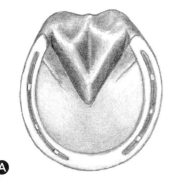

A

corn under shoe pressing into bar

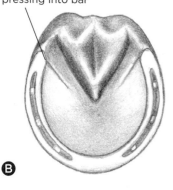

B

▲ **A.** A properly fitted shoe gives support at the heels. **B.** An improperly fitted shoe or one left on too long causes the heel of the shoe to press on the angle of the bar and hoof wall and can cause a corn.

Dropped Sole

A dropped sole is usually thick and made up of heavy flakes of horny material. If this is removed when trimming the foot, the quick is close to the surface and the sole will be pink or start to bleed. The accumulation of dead flaky material can sometimes harbor infection or thrush, which may penetrate the inner tissue and make the horse lame.

A dropped sole is more serious than a flat foot and is due to chronic laminitis, in which the coffin bone inside the hoof rotates down below the level of the bearing surface of the hoof wall; such a horse is said to be foundered. The tip of the bone may actually penetrate the sole in severe cases. The sole is very flat and in some instances may even be convex, protruding downward. The horse with a dropped sole will usually be lame or will readily go lame with use. It is difficult to keep the horse sound enough for hard use.

Contracted Heels

Contracted heels are generally due to injury or improper trimming and shoeing rather than inherited conformation. A horse with a leg injury or lameness may favor that leg or foot by bearing less weight on it, which eventually causes the heels to contract. If only one front foot is affected, the problem may be due to an old injury. The heels are pinched in and narrow, and the frog is generally small and atrophied, with deep grooves (sulci).

Due to loss of shock absorption and restricted elasticity, a foot with contracted heels is more prone to concussion problems. Also, the narrow heels tend to trap and hold dirt or manure, keeping the foot full of debris and at risk for thrush. The sole may stay moist and dirty, creating a perfect environment for pathogens that cause thrush. If contracted heels are not corrected by proper trimming and shoeing, the whole foot may eventually become contracted.

Contracted Feet

Contracted feet are sometimes called *mule feet*, because they are narrow like a mule's foot, not rounded like a normal horse foot. In addition to having an oval shape, a contracted foot has steep walls. This condition generally results from poor foot care, injury, improper shoeing, or consistent shoeing with no opportunity to go barefoot, but some horses inherit their narrow feet. Irregular trimming (allowing the feet to grow too long between trimmings) or keeping a horse shod year-round can cause contraction, especially if shoes are left on too long.

Lameness from any cause can make a horse put less weight on a foot, and over time the lack of frog pressure and heel expansion can result in contraction. When a foot is badly contracted, it may take a year or more of proper care for it to return to normal. A contracted foot is generally narrow at the heel, but its whole width may be narrow; the frog is typically small and atrophied. The foot does not absorb concussion very well and is more vulnerable to sole bruising, corns, road founder, navicular syndrome, sidebones, or ringbone.

Hind feet are normally narrower and the soles more concave than the front feet. If a front foot is narrow and the sole is exceptionally concave ("dished"), the foot is contracted. If the hoof wall contracts too much, especially at the heels, there may be inadequate room for the inner workings of the foot. If the hoof wall presses too firmly against the coffin bone, it causes pain and lameness and a condition called *hoof bound*, due to the pinching of sensitive tissues.

Thin Walls

Thin hoof walls and soles are a severe handicap, often associated with flat feet or with hooves too small for the horse's size and weight. Thin walls tend to break, chip, and split more readily than healthy hoof walls and don't hold a shoe well. Thin walls and soles are considered an unsoundness.

Some horses inherit thin, weak hooves, thin soles that tend to bruise easily, or shallow heels. A thin hoof wall is not as strong and elastic as a normal foot and cannot expand and flex as readily without cracking. The structure of the foot may look normal, but it wears down quickly and tends to crack and split. The narrow hoof wall reduces the weight-bearing base of support and the sole is often flat or thin.

If the horse is barefoot, he soon goes lame because he wears down the hoof and walks on thin soles, which are easily bruised. Even when shod, a horse with thin, weak hoof walls may have trouble holding a shoe: the nails may pull out or the hoof wall may split where the nail is driven; there isn't enough wall thickness to easily hold the nails.

Low Heels

Low heels should be avoided, as the foot has inadequate depth of sole at the heel, and the sensitive inner tissues are close to the outer surface. Because the horse normally lands heel first, a horse with shallow heels is prone to bruising. The heel bulbs may even strike the ground when the foot lands.

A low heel is often accompanied by a long toe, which shifts the weight to be carried toward the back of the foot, creating excessive

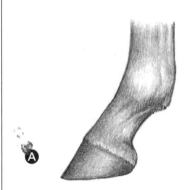

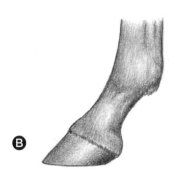

▲ **A.** Low heel. **B.** Low underrun heel.

wearing and concussion at the heels. Such a horse may be more likely to develop navicular problems due to excessive concussion and added pressure on the navicular bone by the tendons that glide over it. A long toe puts more stress on all support structures: flexor tendons, suspensory ligament, and sesamoid bones. A horse with a long toe and low heel is at greater risk for developing osselets, as well as injury to the sesamoid bones, due to strain and overflexing of the fetlock joint.

Underrun Heel

An underrun heel may occur with low heels and a long toe. The base of support is forward rather than directly under the heel. The angle of the heel is vastly different than the angle at the front of the foot, and the heels have no support.

Sheared Heels

Sheared heels result from a severe imbalance in the foot; the hoof wall at the heel is higher on one side of the foot than the other. This condition is sometimes caused by improper trimming and shoeing that leaves the foot unbalanced, or by injury or trauma that causes the horse to favor one side of the foot to avoid pain. If weight is borne more on one side of the foot, the foot tends to grow unevenly at the heel and the heel bulb on one side is pushed up.

High Heels

High heels are often due to improper trimming and shoeing or a clubfoot. If heels are high and long, they cannot expand as they should, which can lead to contracted heels. If the condition is not corrected, the whole foot may become contracted. The pastern of a foot with high heels is often too short and upright.

Clubfoot

Avoid a horse with clubfoot. Clubfoot is characterized by a steep pastern, and a hoof and pastern angle of more than 60 degrees. The heel is high, and the hoof is box-shaped. Often, the hoof angle is steeper than the pastern angle. If just one foot looks this way, an injury may have caused it. Lack of use due to pain and lameness can cause contraction and shortening of the tendons, which raises the heel and shortens the toe; the heel does not wear as much as the toe and grows longer. In some lines of horses, one front foot is steeper than the other because the leg is shorter than the other. Asymmetry in the front legs can cause an uneven stride and clubfoot.

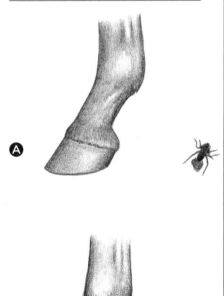

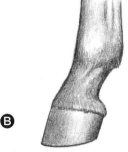

A. Normal foot. B. Clubfoot with short, upright pastern, short, stumpy toe, and long heel.

If both fronts or both hinds are too upright, the problem may have been inherited or caused by a nutritional deficiency when the horse was young and growing or by contracted tendons during foalhood. Clubfoot makes a horse less agile, with a rough, choppy, stumbling gait, which can hinder an athletic career. He may be less surefooted and unsafe to ride at fast gaits. A clubfoot is also more likely to suffer sole bruising in the toe area, for it bears too much weight and the horse tends to land on the toe.

⚲ *Conformation Close-up*

In severe cases of clubfoot, the coronet and fetlock joint are too far forward, due to contraction of the tendons and ligaments. In some instances, the front of the hoof wall is cocked so far forward that it touches the ground at each step.

The coon-footed horse has long, weak pasterns. The angle of the hoof is steeper than the pastern, which puts extra strain on tendons, ligaments, and bones. The fetlock joint cannot adequately support the weight of the horse and may hit the ground and be bruised when the horse travels fast over rough ground. The coon-footed horse is at risk for strain of the suspensory ligaments and injury to the fetlock joint on uneven terrain.

A coon-footed horse may have an easy, soft ride due to the extra give in the pasterns, but he won't hold up under hard or strenuous use. Adequate slope of the pastern is desirable in a riding horse, but too much slope — especially when the pastern has more slope than the hoof — weakens the leg.

Coon foot can occur in front and hind feet. Horses having too-straight hind legs may have severely sloped pasterns. Even if hind pasterns are normal initially in post-legged horses, they are prone to breakdown with age and hard use. The stretched suspensory ligaments may cause the fetlock to drop, causing the pastern to slope almost to the point of being horizontal as the structure weakens.

Hoof Cracks

If severe, cracks in the hoof wall can make a horse unsound. Toe cracks, quarter cracks, and heel cracks start at the ground surface and travel upward. Too-long hooves are the usual cause of cracks; the excessively long hoof wall is often broken, chipped, or split. Cracks originating at the coronary band usually result from injury to the coronet, which damages the horn-producing cells and weakens the hoof horn at that area, making it prone to further cracking.

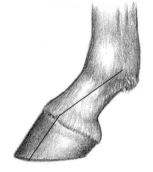

▲ Coon foot.

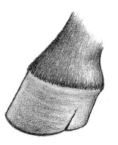

▲ Quarter crack (hoof crack at the quarters).

Quittor

Quittor is traumatic injury to the coronary band that causes chronic inflammation in the underlying structures, especially the cartilage surrounding the coffin bone. At the site of injury, necrosis (cell death) and constant drainage of pus are common. A wire cut or puncture wound, being stepped on, and being struck by another hoof if the horse has limb interference can damage the coronary band.

Founder/Laminitis

Founder and laminitis can make a horse unsound for work. Conformation generally does not play a role, but a horse with poor conformation is more susceptible to *road founder*, which is caused by excessive concussion on hard surfaces.

Digestive tract upsets that precipitate endotoxemia are the most common cause of founder. These include carbohydrate overload from too much grain or lush green grass, and some types of intestinal infection, such as Potomac horse fever and colitis-X. Endotoxemia is a serious condition in which toxin-forming bacteria proliferate in the gut and toxins leak through the intestinal wall and into the bloodstream, causing problems in other areas of the body; one such side effect is founder. Severe infection elsewhere in the body, such as that caused by retained placenta, can also cause founder.

Rings, ridges, and ripples in the hoof wall are signs of founder. Due to chronic irritation and inflammation of the coronary band,

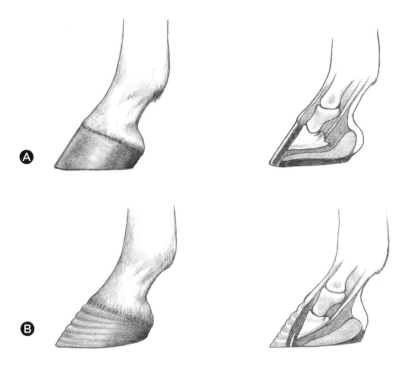

◀ **A.** Normal foot. **B.** Foundered foot with hoof rings and ridges and a dropped sole (coffin bone has rotated and tipped down through the bottom of the foot).

the hoof grows more rapidly than normal. A dropped, flaky sole is also seen. This causes sole bruising and lameness in the horse when ridden, unless he is shod with a shoe or hoof pad that supports and protects the sole. Unless trimmed frequently, toes may grow long and curl upward. *Seedy toe,* separation of the hoof wall at the white line that allows bacteria into the sensitive tissues of the foot, causing infection, is common in foundered horses.

─○ *Conformation Close-up*

When checking a horse for soundness, always look closely at the feet for evidence of founder. The hoof wall will have telltale rings, ripples, or ridges around it, and the sole will usually be dropped: either flat, or bulging rather than concave. Sometimes rings are caused by other factors that change the rate of hoof wall growth, such as diet, fever, and even improper trimming and shoeing, but the rings and ridges of a foundered hoof are more pronounced.

Navicular Syndrome

Navicular syndrome is a serious unsoundness. It often begins as inflammation of the *navicular bursa*, the fluid-filled sac next to the navicular bone in the center of the hoof. (The bursa lies between the deep flexor tendon and the navicular bone in the foot, which is above the middle area of the frog.) To avoid painful pressure on the frog, the horse tries to land on his toe rather than on his heel. A horse with navicular problems therefore has a shuffling gait and shortened stride.

Navicular syndrome usually affects only the front feet because they bear more weight and the small navicular bone is more susceptible to shock and crushing from concussion and strain. A puncture wound that penetrates the navicular bursa in the hind feet can also cause navicular syndrome.

Navicular syndrome is most common in horses with long toes and low heels, which puts greater strain on the tendons and crushing force on the navicular bone. But it is also common in horses with upright conformation (pasterns too short and steep, upright, short shoulders), weak navicular bones, feet too small for a heavy body, and horses continually subjected to excessive concussion. Anything that increases concussion to the foot increases the risk for navicular syndrome. A strong, well-conformed foot and good leg conformation minimize the effects of concussion.

The first indication of navicular syndrome may be recurrent and worsening lameness. It may take several years for all symptoms of the syndrome to appear. These include lameness; standing with the involved foot pointing forward instead of placing weight on it; moving with a choppy, stumbling gait when ridden; and progressive changes in the appearance of the foot. Over time, lameness will cause atrophy and shrinking of the foot and contraction and raising of the heels due to lack of weight-bearing. The foot becomes brittle, with an arched sole and shrunken frog. One or both front feet may become somewhat contracted and smaller than normal.

Ringbone

Ringbone is a bony enlargement on the first, second, or third phalanx (long pastern bone, short pastern bone, or coffin bone). There may be inflammation of the joints between the affected bones or fusion of the pastern or coffin joints. A bony enlargement may appear at the coronary band where the hoof wall grows down from the hairline (due to ringbone at the coffin joint inside the hoof), or higher at the pastern joint.

Bone growth can be caused by injury to the periosteum, such as a blow that bruises the bone, a wire cut, or stress due to poor conformation. Horses that are base narrow or base wide, pigeon-toed or splay footed, are more likely to develop ringbone than are horses with good straight legs. A horse with crooked legs has constant strain on the limb below the fetlock joint, which translates to greater force pulling on the bone lining; the attachments for ligaments and tendons are constantly under stress. Because of increased concussion at the pastern joint, short, steep pasterns also increase the likelihood of a horse developing ringbone.

Ringbone can either be high or low. High ringbone is visible near the pastern joint, causing that part of the pastern to have a bell-shaped appearance. If the joint is not involved, there may be no lameness after the inflammation subsides. Low ringbone is near the coffin joint, usually at the extensor process of the third phalanx — the protrusion at the front of the coffin bone — creating a bulge in the coronary band at the front of the foot.

Ringbone can be articular (involving the joint surface) or periarticular (around the joint, but not involving the joint surface). Low ringbone is often more serious than high ringbone, because it is usually articular and occurs underneath the coronary band, inside the hoof, causing severe pain and lameness.

Chronic low ringbone is called *pyramidal disease* or *buttress foot* because of the bulging of the coronary band. The hair on the coronary band stands up at the front of the foot, there is heat and tenderness in this area, and the shape of the toe of the hoof wall changes.

Did You Know?

Ringbone is most common in the front feet because they carry more weight and are under greater stress than the hind feet. Because of their crooked leg structure, pigeon-toed horses are most likely to develop ringbone on the lateral aspect of the joints, while splay-footed horses are more likely to develop ringbone on the medial aspect of the joints.

▶ Various types of ringbone.
A. Low periarticular (around the joint). **B.** Low articular (involving the joint between coffin bone and short pastern bone): "buttress foot." **C.** High periarticular. **D.** High articular (involving joint between long and short pastern bones).

Sidebone

Sidebone is calcification of the cartilage on the side of a horse's foot. In a normal horse, the large areas of cartilage on each side of the foot, back toward the heel and above the coronary band, are firm but movable structures. If they calcify and turn to bone, they are considered sidebones. Sidebones are brittle and less flexible than normal cartilage.

Concussion is a major cause of sidebones, especially in horses of upright conformation, because it increases trauma to the cartilage. Pigeon-toed horses tend to get lateral sidebones and splay-footed horses tend to get medial sidebones, but it is not uncommon for sidebones to eventually develop on both sides of the foot.

Sidebone may or may not cause lameness. Lameness usually occurs only when there is inflammation — as the cartilage calcifies and becomes bony — or when an old sidebone gets bumped and reinjured. A sidebone may fuse with a ringbone and cause severe lameness or it may fracture and cause sudden, severe lameness. Sidebone that has healed usually doesn't cause problems unless it is large.

Identifying Leg Lameness

When trying to determine whether a leg is lame and where, it's best to start at ground level and work up the leg, as most lameness problems originate in the feet. Watching the horse standing still can often provide important clues and is a good way to start an examination. A horse with a sore foot or leg will generally be reluctant to put weight on it and therefore will not stand squarely. If it is difficult to detect a subtle problem, observe the horse in motion.

OBSERVE THE HORSE STANDING

If a front foot is sore, he may stand with that leg forward, holding more of the weight on the other leg. If the horse stands with both front legs angled forward, this could be a sign that both are sore (perhaps with navicular problems); he is trying to take more weight on his hind legs. If he is obviously shifting his weight onto his hind feet, this may mean his fronts are very sore, perhaps with laminitis.

Cocking a hind foot is not necessarily a sign that it's sore, because horses often rest a hind leg. But if he always rests the same one, it may mean that he doesn't want to put weight on it. If he continually shifts his weight from one hind foot to another, this is usually a sign that both hind feet are sore.

Thoroughly Check the Suspect Leg

Once you determine which leg is sore, the next step is to locate the problem. The first place to look if a horse is reluctant to put full weight on a leg is the foot. The problem may be as simple as a rock caught in the hoof or shoe. If there's nothing obvious when you pick up a foot, a veterinarian may need to use a hoof tester to see if there is a sore area, which may indicate a stone bruise or abscess under the sole.

If the bottom of the foot seems fine, check for heat in the hoof wall. Compare it with the warmth or coolness of the other foot. This is easiest to do in the morning, when a normal hoof will tend to feel cool. In the heat of the afternoon (and after the horse has been active), the normal hoof will be warmer. Also check for pain around the coronary band and heels by squeezing.

If you are still at a loss, check the leg from top to bottom. For a front leg, stand right in front of the horse's neck, with his head over your shoulder. Run both hands down either side of his withers and shoulders, pressing with your thumbs to detect any sensitivity around the points of the shoulders. Run your hands on down the legs to compare the joints for thickness and swelling, heat or sensitivity, then feel the back tendons.

Raise each front leg and check for sensitivity in the knee joint, and in the relaxed tendons (by pressing on them) when the knee is flexed. Press on the sesamoid bones toward the rear of the fetlock joints, and check the pulse there to determine whether there is a difference in

Did You Know?

Sidebones typically occur in the front feet only, but a wire cut or some other injury to the cartilage of any foot can cause sidebone.

the strength of the pulse in one leg or the other. While the leg is off the ground, twist the foot to check for pain in the fetlock joint. The horse will flinch or try to take his foot away from you if moving the foot to the side causes pain.

For a hind leg, feel the hock and stifle joints to check for swelling, and check the back tendons. With the leg held up, feel the relaxed tendons and also check the sesamoids at the rear of the fetlock joint. Flex the fetlock joint to check for soreness. Your hands can feel if there's any heat or swelling in a certain area. The horse's reaction to your touch or pressing can also tell you if it's sore or sensitive. A difference in the strength of the pulse can tell you there's inflammation somewhere in that leg; the blood vessels dilate to permit more blood into a damaged area.

You can usually pinpoint a problem by observing the horse while standing and moving, to tell which leg it is, and narrow it down to the specific area by careful observation and feeling that leg with your hands. Once you've located the area of soreness, the next step is to determine what is causing it. You may need a veterinarian to help you diagnose the problem, determine whether the condition is temporary or a long-term unsoundness, and whether treatment is warranted.

OBSERVE THE HORSE IN MOTION

Always check for soundness in motion. The horse's primary value to most owners is his mobility and athletic agility; a lame horse cannot perform at his best. The lameness may be due to a temporary injury or even a rock stuck in a shoe, but it may be a sign of serious unsoundness that could make the horse useless for work. Some problems are not noticeable until the horse is moving.

Plan to thoroughly check the horse while he travels at a walk and a fast trot. The trot is often the best gait in which to detect a subtle lameness. Every horseman should become familiar with the way a sound horse moves — the perfect regularity of gait and stride — especially at the walk and trot, to be able to detect when a horse is "off" (see chapter 13). Lameness is merely an alteration of gait as the horse tries to reduce the pain of weight bearing on a certain part of his leg structure. If the horse is lame, the reason for the lameness should be determined. Which part of the horse's body is sore, and why?

Unsoundnesses Detectable with Movement

Several problems will show up only when the horse travels. There are no swellings or other visible signs that suggest a problem when the horse is standing still.

Stringhalt is the term for an involuntary jerking (spastic flexion) of the hock joint. The cause of this disorder is unknown. The horse jerks his foot up toward his abdomen as he travels. This jerking is exaggerated if he is making a turn. Usually, only one hind leg is affected. As the horse lifts the leg to take a stride, it jerks up too high and then hits the ground sharply when it comes down. In some affected horses, the extra motion is barely noticeable, while in others there is a very obvious jerking. The horse may do it at every step or only occasionally.

Whorlbone lameness (trochanteric bursitis) is another unusual problem that can only be detected when the horse is moving. It is caused by inflammation of a bursa in the hip region, due to bruising from a fall or straining of the involved tendon during strenuous exercise, with one leg slipping forward on bad footing.

The injury can also occur when a horse is trotting fast. A galloping horse can flex his back and tuck his hindquarters under his body because both hind legs are off the ground at the same time, with less pressure on the hip joints. But the trotter is always moving his hind legs in opposite directions. At high speeds, he has to flex his hip joints more than he does at a gallop, and this puts more pressure on the bursa, sometimes causing injury.

If the bursa has been injured, the horse is lame. The forward phase of the stride of the affected hind leg is shorter than that of the good leg. The horse travels dog fashion, with the hindquarters moving toward the good side, away from the pain. He tends to carry the affected leg toward the midline of his body while the foot is in the air, and then set it wide when it comes to the ground. That leg does not come as far forward as the good leg, as he tries to avoid the pain.

The Walk and the Trot

The horse compensates for pain by getting off the sore leg as quickly as possible and moving his other legs and body in such a way as to take more of the weight. These compensatory movements signal lameness. By watching closely, you can usually determine which leg is lame and get a better sense of the source and location of the problem. An upper leg problem in the hips and shoulders may sometimes be harder to determine, and a back problem may be mistaken for a leg problem because a sore back may cause the horse to shorten his stride and travel more stiffly. Watch from the side as the horse is led past you at the trot, in front of a horizontal point of reference like a fence. The easiest way to tell which leg is affected and at what point of his stride he is compensating is to watch his head at the trot. A horse's

Watch for Signs of Trouble

A sore horse can do only a few things to lessen the pain caused by using the affected area. You will be better able to identify the problem area if you know what the normal rhythm of gait should be, then watch the movement and listen to the hoofbeats on hard ground. The walk may not reveal much unless the horse is quite sore, whereas the trot is an ideal gait for pinpointing lameness. The horse makes more obvious deviation (seeking to compensate for the sore area) at the trot because the trot is the most regular and symmetrical gait, with diagonal legs striking the ground together. It's more difficult to detect the lameness at the canter or gallop, as these are not symmetrical gaits, and it's easier for the horse to minimize his lameness at these gaits, especially if he uses the lead that reduces strain on his sore area.

head normally remains steady at the trot, because he does not use it for balance. If there is even a hint of head bobbing at the trot — other than a symmetrical little bob at each step, which is common in some horses — this is a clue that the horse is trying to shift his weight by making extra balancing movement with his head and neck.

TYPES OF LAMENESS

A veterinarian will classify lameness originating in the legs as to its type and degree. There are basically four types of leg lameness.

• *Supporting-leg lameness:* The horse favors the leg whenever he puts weight on that foot or lands on it; he is compensating for pain in the supporting column itself (foot, leg bones or joints). He tries to reduce the impact of landing on that leg. He also gets off it as quickly as possible. His lameness is most obvious during the time the leg is fully weight bearing until it leaves the ground again.

• *Swinging-leg lameness:* There are two phases to a horse's stride: the forward (anterior) swing of the leg and the rearward (posterior) movement after the foot lands. If either phase is abnormally shortened, this means the leg has a problem, and the limb hurts in motion. The pain may be in a tendon or ligament, muscle, or joint capsule. If the pain is in the muscles of his upper leg, for instance, the forward swing of his leg will be most affected. If a horse has a shortened anterior phase and lengthened posterior phase in a hind leg he may have a hock or stifle problem.

• *Mixed-leg lameness:* A problem in which lameness is evident in both the supporting and swinging phase of a stride. The horse tries to avoid weight bearing, as well as shortening the forward or backward phase of his stride.

• *Complementary lameness:* Lameness in one leg causes the horse to overuse the opposite leg and it becomes sore, too. How the foot lands can give a clue as to where the problem is located. If the horse has pain in the heel area (such as from navicular soreness), he will try to land on his toe. If he has a problem in the toe (such as a sole abscess near the front of the foot), he will land harder on the heel than usual.

FRONT LEG LAMENESS

In almost every front leg lameness (and even in a serious hind leg lameness), the horse's head bobs at the trot as he tries to take weight off the sore leg and put it more quickly on the good leg. If pain is occurring when the hoof hits the ground (soreness in the support column), the horse throws his head up just before nodding it down, taking as much weight as possible off the bad leg and then throwing it more strongly onto the good leg.

If a horse is lame on the left front, his head drops farthest when his right front (the good foot) comes to the ground, trying to keep weight off the lame left foot. He takes a shorter stride with the sore left foot, and as it comes to the ground he keeps his head up. He tries to pull his body along without landing very much weight on that foot. He lets his head bob down with more emphasis (and more weight) when the sound right front foot lands.

If his tendons and ligaments are sore, he dips his head down after the sore leg reaches full support so the other foreleg (that is just getting ready to take on the full load) can take more weight and lighten the effort of push off (posterior phase of the stride) in the sore leg. If the horse has equal pain in both front legs (as in a case of founder or navicular syndrome), he will not bob his head but may hold it higher than normal as he tries to keep his front legs unweighted while pushing his hind legs farther underneath himself to take more of the weight. His strides will be short and shuffling.

HIND LEG LAMENESS

Compensation movements for hind leg lamenesses are more difficult to detect, for the horse will only bob his head for severe hind leg pain. This can be misinterpreted as lameness in a front leg. A more reliable way to pinpoint hind leg lameness is to stand behind the horse as he is led directly away from you, and compare the up-and-down motion of his hip bones. The hip drops farther on the good leg. If he is lame on the left hind, the right hip drops farther than the left. He will also drop his head more when the lame hind foot is coming to the ground.

If the pain occurs early in the stride (support column of bones or joints), the rest of the stride will be quite shortened and the hip will

Other Ways to Diagnose Lameness

Another way to tell which leg and which part of the leg is sore is to lead the horse on hard ground, or in circles, or up or down a hill. A hard surface can accentuate some types of lameness (as from splints), due to increased concussion. A turn or circle puts more stress on certain parts of his feet or legs; he makes more obvious compensation movements if those parts are sore. Going up and down a hill can also be revealing. Leg bones and joints are under greater stress when the horse is going downhill. Ligaments and tendons have to work harder to propel him uphill (or through soft, loose ground). Under these conditions the lameness may become more obvious.

pop upward as the horse gets off that leg quickly. If pain comes later in the stride (due to soreness in the tendons or ligaments), the hip will sink lower and then bounce back up as that leg comes to the next support phase. To evaluate the hip movement better, it helps to imagine a big T on the back end of the horse, with the tail dividing him in half and the horizontal top of the T connecting the points of the hips. As the horse moves, the rise and fall of the hips will then be quite obvious as you visualize the movement in this horizontal line.

A hind leg lameness will make some difference in how the horse carries his head, but it won't be pronounced unless pain is severe enough to make him try to take more weight on the front legs. When he's trotting, you'll see him drop his head during the support phase of the diagonal leg (when the sore hind leg should be taking weight). If the right hind leg is sore, the horse's head will drop as the left front foot takes weight. If you are only looking at his head carriage and not evaluating hip movement, as well, you might mistakenly assume he is lame in the right front leg.

Working Soundness vs. Breeding Soundness

Working soundness is different than breeding soundness. A horse that is sound for work can be unsound for breeding due to a fertility or conformation problem. Likewise, a horse unsound for work can be sound for breeding, as long as his problem is caused by injury and is not genetic or hereditary. When selecting a horse, keep this difference in mind, especially when choosing a horse for athletic purposes (and not intending to breed it) or choosing one to breed, making sure he has no faults that will be passed to offspring. A horse may be unsound for work yet still acceptable for breeding as long as his problem is not heritable and does not result from poor conformation that is heritable. He might have a bowed tendon, a bad hoof crack that penetrates sensitive tissues, an injury that impairs leg action, or other problems that hinder working ability, such as heaves, yet still be sound to breed.

When selecting breeding stock, avoid hereditary conformation problems. A mare or stallion with an unsoundness caused by poor conformation should *not* be considered sound to breed. Cases in point would be a mare or stallion that developed spavin and hind leg lameness from improper hock angle, a horse with navicular syndrome because of poor foot structure, and a horse with chip fractures in a knee due to weak front leg construction. Even in breeds used for strenuous sports, many talented athletic individuals have little durability due to conformational weaknesses that lead to early

Be a Responsible Breeder

All too often when a horse becomes lame and unsound for work or must be retired from a competitive career due to breakdown and injury, he or she is used for breeding and passes on the very conformational weaknesses that contributed to the unsoundness. This is a big problem in many breeds today, often because a "valuable" horse that breaks down seems a natural choice for breeding.

Similarly, popular bloodlines and expensive horses used primarily for showing in careers that do not require top athletic performance, such as halter classes or pleasure classes, are often selected for breeding solely based on eye appeal or "breed type" fads that have little to do with athletic ability and soundness. *Never* breed a horse with conformational faults that could lead to unsoundness.

breakdown. If a promising youngster does well in a certain sport for a few short years or in the early phases of his training and then becomes unsound, he should not be used for breeding. It would be foolish and irresponsible to breed any horse with conformational faults, for this perpetuates the faults and sentences the next generation to early breakdown.

The Senior Horse

AT SOME POINT, you may consider getting an older horse, perhaps as a safe and dependable mount for a child or a beginning rider. An older horse may have some sags and shifts in body and muscles and some "honorable blemishes" from his years of hard work. Learn how to distinguish which aspects of his appearance might cause problems and which are unimportant to his abilities and soundness.

Some people who breed horses and want to perpetuate the qualities of certain bloodlines will occasionally

The first signs of aging in a horse may be sharper withers and a little sway in the back. By age 21, he is gray around the eyes, he is more swaybacked, and his muscles have sagged, but his skeletal structure and body angles are essentially unchanged.

consider adding an older mare or stallion to their herd. An older horse may have the needed pedigree, but if there are no photographs available of the animal at a younger age, an inexperienced horse judge might be dissuaded by the horse's appearance. Normal changes you can expect to see in an aging horse include sagging muscles, drooping lower lip, and swayback.

Signs of Old Age

Some individuals age more quickly than others. By his midteens, one horse might have a few gray hairs in his mane and tail and around his eyes, and a sag to his back and lips. Another horse may show no signs of aging until he is in his mid-20s or older. Just like people, individual horses age at different rates, and some family lines have greater longevity than others. One horse may be "old" and slowing down in his athletic ability by his late teens, while another horse may be still doing team roping or endurance riding in his late 20s.

▼ By age 28, this gelding's muscles have sagged away from his skeletal structure and he is more swaybacked. He is thin, and his skeletal anatomy is more pronounced. He's also grayer around the face and eyes, with a deeper hollow above his eyes.

Some of the signs of old age that are most obvious are sagging back and muscles. The muscles of the neck and hindquarters may not have the full, fit look they once did; the neck may look thinner and the tail head may become more pronounced. The withers become more sharp and prominent, and the back dips down behind them. The lips become droopier and the shape of the muzzle changes. The horse may develop an "elk nose" (see page 346). Deeper hollows appear above the eyes. More gray hairs crop up in the mane and tail, and often on the head and body, as well, especially around the eyes. The face may have a grizzled look, flecked with gray.

The jawbones of an older horse become thinner. The incisors angle forward more and more, rather than meeting in a straight up-and-down position (see chapter 4). The teeth become very long, except in extreme old age when they may be worn down or even fall out. Teeth can often be a good clue to the horse's age.

Skeletal Anatomy and Body Proportions

The best way to determine whether an old horse has good conformation is to study his basic skeletal structure and the various points of anatomy (see chapter 2).

THE RULE OF THIRDS

In an older horse, ideal body proportions are the same as for any horse: one-third front end, one-third body (back), and one-third hip (hindquarter area) (see chapter 10). Sometimes when you look at a fat, sleek horse, these distinct areas all merge together; it is hard to know where one part ends and the other part begins, as there is very little indication for differentiation. The horse might be pleasing to the eye and you might not immediately notice that he actually has a long back and a short hip, which is considered poor conformation for any equine athlete, no matter his age.

In a skinny horse, the proportions are more obvious. In an old horse or a thin one, the muscles are sunken down and you can see the bony outline better. When looking at a fat young horse, you can actually be more easily fooled than when looking at an old one, unless the old horse is very fat. The old horse generally does not have as much cosmetic cover-up with muscles and fat. The main thing when selecting or judging an older horse is to know the basics of anatomy and conformation and not worry about the cosmetics. To the uneducated eye, fat can cover a multitude of sins and can mask a number of faults.

Did You Know?

Genetics plays a significant role in how fast a horse ages, but so do environment and nutrition. A horse that has been fit and active all his life but never overfat or overthin or worked to the point of breakdown will usually stay sound and healthy longer. And, of course, the horse with good conformation will hold up longer with hard work than a horse with poor structure.

Learn how to find and define a horse's front end and the hips so you can judge his conformation more accurately. By pinpointing the front and back of the pelvis, you can locate where the hip bones are and then relate that hind end to the lay-back of the shoulder in the front end. Compare the proportions as well as angles.

CHECK OUT THE BODY ANGLES

No matter a horse's age, the ideal body proportions and angles remain the same. For example, if a horse becomes swaybacked, the basic body angles do not change. Look at the shoulder joint and how it goes back and hooks into the withers. Where are the withers, and how does the shoulder blade slant from the withers? When judging any horse's conformation, visualize his skeletal structure. Then flesh it out in your mind's eye and see what the animal used to be.

Evaluate the horse's shoulder to see whether it is long or short, upright or well sloped back (see chapter 11). Many people consider a long shoulder desirable, regardless of its angle. But a long shoulder is not ideal unless it is well laid back. A long shoulder is not the same as a laid-back shoulder.

The rule of thirds can help you judge a horse's shoulder. If the shoulder is too upright (even if it is long), the front of the body is too short. A more sloping shoulder will create a greater shoulder area, more nearly approaching one-third of the horse.

Likewise, the angle of the hip and pelvis can affect the body proportions. If the hip is too short, the hind end of the horse will not form an equilateral triangle in the lines drawn from the point of the buttocks to the stifle and back up to the point of the hip. You need to visualize the triangle created by these lines. Ideally, the angles will be about the same, with all sides of the triangle nearly equal in length.

If the triangle has one side that is much longer than the others, the rear end of the horse is less than one-third of the total length of the horse; the horse's back will usually be too long. Because angles in the body tend to be similar, a horse with an upright shoulder usually has improper angles in the hindquarters, as well; the shoulder area and hip area generally will be short and the the back will be too long.

Legs

Similarly, the basic angles in a horse's legs do not change with age, especially if he had good conformation early on. The horse with proper leg angles will usually stay sound in old age, whereas the horse with poor leg angles may be lamer.

LOOK BEYOND THICKENINGS, LUMPS, AND BUMPS

In the old horse, there may be some knots and thickening on bones and joints from old injuries, but the bone structure itself is not going to change. Even with serious injuries, you can usually tell what the basic conformation is. A scar or some other indication of an injury is usually obvious.

Most acquired problems that are due to accident rather than breakdown due to poor conformation will not affect both front legs or both hinds unless there has been a breakdown in the good leg due to the extra strain from favoring an injured leg. If a horse has the same problem in both legs, however (such as navicular syndrome in both front feet, splints on the inside of both front cannons, ringbone on both front pastern joints, contracted heels on both fronts, curb on both hocks, or sore stifles on both hind legs), suspect that these problems were caused by poor conformation.

BREAKDOWN OF THE HIND PASTERNS

One leg problem that sometimes shows up in an older horse is a breakdown of both pasterns in the hind legs, which drops the fetlock joints lower. This can happen through many years of wear and tear. It occurs more often in post-legged horses, however, so thoroughly check the hind leg conformation. A lot of people initially overlook a horse's post-leggedness, until the horse starts to break down in the hind pasterns.

As with any other consideration of leg conformation, you must be able to relate the pastern angle to the horse's basic structure and evaluate whether the angles correlate. If the horse has a nice, long hip, and the femur comes down at a reasonable angle (instead of being upright), then there is little risk of breakdown. The horse is not post-legged and should have a strong and proper pastern angle.

But if all of these angles are too straight, there tends to be more breakdown in the fetlock joints and pasterns, and this becomes more obvious in an older horse. A person might look at the pastern problem and think it doesn't matter that the pasterns are broken down. You might think that because the horse is old, this is a natural result of aging and hard work. The coon-footed (too sloped) pastern angle might be considered an age-related breakdown that doesn't really matter. But it does matter if you plan to use the horse for riding or breeding, because this is an indication that poor conformation caused the pasterns to break down. If you ride the horse, his hind legs may suffer lameness problems from this weakness, and if you raise foals, they may inherit the same poor conformation.

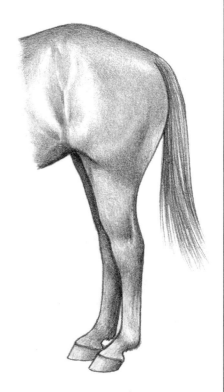

⬤ Broken-down hind pasterns in an older horse occur most frequently in individuals with post-legged conformation.

HEIGHT OF HOCK AND KNEE

Check the cannon-to-forearm ratio in the front legs (height of the knee), and the height of the hock in the hind legs. These will not change with age. Height of knees and hocks can give you a clue as to whether the horse has proper length of cannon. Cannons should be short in the front legs and longer in the hinds. The hock should be the same height as the "chestnut" (horny growth) on the inside of the front leg, above the knee (see chapter 7). If the hock is too low, this may be an indication that the pasterns have broken down, lowering the fetlock joints.

The Aging Head

The basic shape of the head tends to change as the horse gets older. What was once a good-looking head may begin to look more coarse and less beautiful. It may be hard to tell, at first glance, whether the horse's basic head conformation is coarse or whether the changes are due to old age.

WHAT IS *NORMAL* AGING?

In the older horse, the cartilage in the nose softens and changes, creating more of an "elk nose." All of the features tend to coarsen to some degree. When judging an older horse, be aware of what is normal for that breed with aging. It is helpful if you have seen many older individuals, especially if you have seen them at different times over the years and have observed how they have aged. In this way, you get a better idea of what is normal and how a horse looks as he ages.

AGING TEETH AND THE MUZZLE

An older horse is likely to have dental problems and even some missing teeth, so be sure to check his mouth. He may not be able to keep up his weight and energy if he is unable to eat properly. If you are unsure about the condition of his teeth, have them checked by an equine dentist or veterinarian.

Increasing angulation of the front teeth (pointing forward rather than being straight up and down) will create some corresponding changes in the muzzle. The nose and muzzle of the older horse may look quite a bit different than when he was younger. The upper lip will protrude somewhat over the angled top incisors, and the lower lip may droop away from the teeth.

▲ Elk nose typical of an older horse.

CHECK VISION AND HEARING

When evaluating an older horse, remember to check his vision, as described in chapter 3. Hearing loss in horses is rare but can occasionally occur, especially in an older animal. Check to see whether the horse responds to sounds such as clicking and hissing. Make the sounds without moving so he won't respond just because he sees you moving. If he can hear the noise, he will usually look toward it or point an ear in that direction.

Swayback: Age or Bad Conformation?

There will always be some sag in the back as a horse ages, creating more prominent withers. A properly built horse, however, will still have the same good angles despite the dip in the back and the more defined withers.

SWAYBACK DUE TO WEAK CONFORMATION

Swayback, or *lordosis*, can be caused by any number of things. Some horses are born with this condition. In other cases it is nutritional: The young horse was improperly fed (unbalanced diet with inadequate calcium, or an improper calcium-to-phosphorus ratio) while growing. If a young horse is fed too much grain, which is high in phosphorus, this may skew the calcium/phosphorus ratio and he will not be able to utilize enough of the calcium in his other feeds. The bones became demineralized and weak, and by the time the horse is a yearling he begins to look high in the hip and swaybacked. Older mares often become saggy from the strain of carrying many foals. Other horses become swaybacked from old age.

Conformation can play a role in whether a horse will sag with work and age. In order to carry weight, the horse's back should be relatively short, muscular, and fairly flat, not dipping down excessively behind the withers. A long-backed horse has a greater distance between the support points for his back, making him more prone to developing swayback.

Swayback in older horses may be due to the stress of work. The horse's own weight tends to pull the back downward, but this saggy bending is usually counteracted by the pull from muscles, ligaments, and tendons that give the back its strength and support. A horse that travels and works with his head and neck somewhat lowered and his

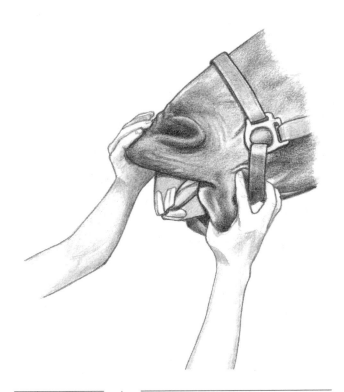

⬥ Checking the teeth of an older mare. The forward slant of her teeth is an indication of her advancing age. Close examination of the incisors (and whether they meet properly) can also give a clue regarding whether the molars meet properly or might have uneven wear that needs dental attention.

Did You Know?

Horses born with swayback show this condition while they are still foals. This congenital problem is due to underdeveloped portions of the thoracic vertebrae. If a young horse starts out with a swayback, the condition persists throughout his life.

▶ Some horses become sway-backed in old age.

body collected can help keep the back from sagging, making the back stronger and less apt to dip downward. The collected horse has his back "rounded" upward, using his back muscles to help support the weight of the rider.

If he travels with his head too high and his nose stuck up in the air, however, his back dips down. It is not as able to resist the downward force of carrying the weight of a rider. Over time, this may accentuate a swaybacked tendency. The high-headed, ewe-necked, or uncollected horse is more prone to develop swayback from work stress and age, especially if he is somewhat long in the back to begin with. Whether or not a horse will become swaybacked depends in part on his basic conformation (long back or short back, strong loins or weak ones) and on how he carries himself, his training, and the work he performs.

RIDING AN OLDER, SWAYBACKED HORSE

Swayback in itself, if not too severe, is usually not a hindrance to a horse's athletic ability. The older horse with a dip in his back can still perform well if he is ridden properly and collected. But more care must be taken to make sure the saddle fits him properly and that the rider's weight is well balanced and does not hinder or injure the horse.

Choose His Job Wisely

With good care, the older horse may be an ideal mount for the pleasure rider or for a young or novice rider who does not use him hard. If the horse is not asked to perform in a demanding sport, he may give many more years of service, especially if his conformation is good and he can continue to work without risks of unsoundness.

Fit of the saddle over the withers is crucial. If the saddle rubs the top of the withers or puts too much pressure on the sides of the withers, it may cause saddle sores or bruising. The saddle tree must be the proper width for his withers. Extra padding is usually needed. The hollow in the back can often be filled with a firm padding such as felt or an extra pad to increase thickness. Don't use a long saddle. If the support points are at the withers and hips (bridging the sag), the pressure will be too concentrated in very small areas, creating a sore back.

PART III

Appendixes

A SERIOUS HORSEMAN always wants to learn more. The horses we know and see every day and the horses we encounter have much to teach us. They help us to train our eyes and fine-tune our "feel" for what a good horse looks like at rest and in motion. The more horses we study, the more readily we are able to recognize their good points and their faults. Learning to correlate form with function is key.

The appendixes that follow should help you in your quest to become a serious horseman.

Applying What You've Learned

WE'VE COVERED A LOT of material in this book, but learning how to evaluate conformation doesn't stop here. It's a lifelong process. The more horses you see and evaluate, the better you will be able to judge conformation. Experience will help you develop a good feel for what is normal and what is not; it will also help you identify what type of conformation holds up and stays sound with hard use and what does not. Evaluating conformation is an art as well as a science — practice is key.

If you want to become a good judge of horses, study many horses. Observe them while they are standing still and while they are moving. This will help you make connections between a particular type of conformation and a horse's action and performance.

It also helps if you can follow certain individuals over the years as they progress in their various careers, to see firsthand what kind of structure makes a top performer. You will see which ones last a long time and which ones wash out early due to breakdown.

Horses in different breeds may vary somewhat from basic conformation ideals — sometimes subtly, sometimes obviously, depending on what is popular and favored in that breed. But generally speaking, all light horse breeds have the same basic conformation. The body proportions of the best individuals are the same. Muscling and head styles may vary, and the body may be longer or more compact, but the proportions of the ideal horse do not change.

When judging any horse, the key is looking at the basic skeletal structure. If you know the basics of equine anatomy — the bones and their angles — then the fat and muscle overlay won't distract you from what is actually underneath.

Evaluation Strategies

What follows is an overview of the steps to follow when buying a horse. It quickly walks you through the evaluation process. For a more in-depth discussion of specific points of conformation, see the relevant chapters.

BEFORE YOU GO

Speak with the owner to get an idea of the horse's history, training, and breeding, and ask for photographs or a video of the horse. It always helps to see a video of the horse moving, at liberty if possible, or at least being led at the walk and trot. This will give you a good sense of the horse before you see him, particularly if he isn't in your immediate area. If you are intrigued by what you hear and see, make arrangements to see the horse in person.

WHEN YOU ARRIVE

When you inspect a horse, arrange in advance to observe him first in his natural environment — stall, paddock, or pasture —before the owner brings him out for you to look at. In this way, you'll not only see how the horse responds to being caught and haltered but can also study how he moves at liberty or on first being led out of the stall.

If the horse is already haltered and waiting for you, this might suggest he has a training problem (perhaps hard to catch) or that the owner wanted to exercise the horse a bit beforehand to warm up so he won't move stiffly when first being led out of the stall. Some problems (mild spavin, early navicular syndrome, some cases of arthritis) are most noticeable when the horse first starts exercising, then he "warms" out of the soreness.

If you are there to observe the horse as he is caught and haltered, you'll get an idea about his disposition and attitude (friendly and at ease with being handled, or not) and training. Also watch how the owner leads the horse out of the stall or pasture to see if the horse moves well. If a horse is prone to travel a little sore when first coming out of the stall, an unscrupulous owner might try to cover this up by keeping a short hold on the halter and making the horse walk with his head high to mask the effects of a slight limp.

CHECK THE HORSE WHILE HE STANDS

After the horse is caught, have the owner let him stand quietly on a slack lead rope so you can observe the horse's natural stance and whether he tends to rest a hind leg or "point" with a front one.

As the horse is being held for you, look closely at head and body. Starting with the head, examine the eyes (for vision) by carefully and gently passing a hand in front of each, without creating air movement, to check for a response. Open the mouth and look at the teeth, to make sure upper and lower teeth match, and that the incisors are not excessively worn, which would suggest the horse is a *cribber*. When a horse cribs, he grabs a wooden surface such as a fence rail or manger (called a crib, in earlier times) with his teeth, sucking in air with a grunting sound. Don't buy a horse that has this bad habit. Angle and wear of the teeth can also give a clue to the horse's age.

Closely inspect the rest of the body, as well, running your hands along the neck and back, checking the back for evidence of saddle sores, old scars, and sore muscles. If the horse flinches when you move your hands along his back (especially over the loin area), you might suspect soreness. Check the girth area for sores and old scars indicating earlier galls. If a horse is hard to fit with a saddle, there will be evidence of old sores, scar tissue, or white hairs; the latter are most commonly seen on the withers and back. Run your hands down each leg to check for lumps, heat, or swellings, especially on the joints.

Have the owner stand the horse squarely on all four feet (on level bare ground, rather than grass, which might obscure your vision of the feet) and make a thorough inspection of body and leg angles. Look at him from a slight distance (and from several perspectives) as well as close at hand, to get a proper impression of body balance and leg angles. A horse may look good from one view, yet show poor conformation from another. He might have one front leg that is well conformed and one that isn't, for instance.

When standing directly in front of the horse check his legs for straightness and distance apart. The hind legs should be just as straight as the fronts, practically hidden behind them. Check the width of the chest, look at the length and muscling of the forelegs, the width and flatness of the knees. Make sure the cannons are perfectly straight and centered beneath the knees, in perfect line with the forearms.

Look at the size of the feet and whether they match in size and shape. From the side, check the angle of hoof and pastern, to make sure they are the same, and note whether the pasterns are long or short, sloping or upright. Pick up all four feet. Check the shape and balance of each foot, and evaluate the sole (concave or flat), the condition of the frog and bars, and determine the soundness of the hoof horn. Make sure the heels are wide and deep, and not contracted. Look for the breakover (wear) point on hoof or shoe to see if the horse travels straight or crooked.

Study His Shape

At some point, stand at a slight distance in front of and then behind the horse to get a perspective of his body shape. Look past the head and shoulders to see if the rib cage is visible and "well sprung" or if the horse is slab sided. The hindquarters should be wider than the shoulders. A good way to check a horse's shape is to stand on a bale of hay (or a fence) directly in front of him and then directly behind, but out of kicking range, so you are high enough to see the actual shape of his body. It should be wedge-shaped, and both sides should perfectly match one another.

Stand high enough to look down on his back to check it for symmetry and length. The horse should be standing squarely, with nose pointing straight forward, not looking to one side or the other. From above the horse, you can see whether his topline is straight and if the muscles on the left match those on the right. If there are obvious differences in shape from one side to the other, or crookedness in the topline, it may be a clue that the horse has a back or leg problem.

If you detect asymmetry, look at the legs more closely and watch the horse move to see whether he has some abnormality in gait due to the asymmetry. Some horses have front legs that are not exactly the same in length or development, for instance. The difference may be very small, or it may be enough to create noticeably uneven stride length and a twist in his topline. Looking at him from above can help give a clue.

Looking from directly behind the horse (far enough back that you can see both sides of his hindquarters at the same time), observe the quarters and loin area. Note the width of the hips and whether the two haunch bones are at exactly the same level. Also note the height of the croup and slope of the quarters — whether level or "goose-rumped" — and whether the horse has a high tail set or low. Note the width and shape of both quarters, and their muscling. Buttocks should be full and rounded, and thighs should meet all the way down to the level of the stifles, with no daylight between them ("split up," or cat-hammed). From behind, you can also see the muscling on the gaskins, above the hocks.

Hocks should match. Check straightness of the hind legs and whether hocks are close together or far apart. If the horse has a full tail that obscures your vision, hold it aside and check the hocks closely to see their shape and inner surfaces. Make sure they match and that there are no swellings or bony enlargements. Check for capped hock or curb. Looking on down to the cannons and fetlock joints, make sure they are straight, and that the feet do not toe in or out too much. The feet should match perfectly.

Study His Angles and Proportions

After thoroughly checking the horse from front and rear, check him from each side. Look closely at his legs to make sure front legs are straight and hocks have proper angle (neither sickle hocked nor post-legged). Evaluate pastern angle, along with angles in shoulders and hindquarters. Note the length of the horse's back and evaluate his topline — shape and height of withers, back, loins, and croup, and level or slanted quarters.

Pay close attention to body proportions. Are his front end, middle, and hindquarters roughly equal (body divided in thirds) or is one part too long or too short? Look at his underline (elbow to sheath or udder) to make sure it is longer than the topline from withers to croup, and that he is well ribbed up and not too shallow in the flank. While you are at it, watch his breathing (flank movements) to make sure it is normal. Look at the lower portion of the abdomen to see if the horse has a *heave line*, a ridge of muscle that makes an obvious groove along the edge of the belly, on each side. This can be a clue that the horse suffers from *heaves*, a respiratory problem caused by sensitivity to dust and molds (see page 311). If so, his lung capacity is diminished and he has trouble forcing the air out of his lungs.

WATCH HIM TRAVEL

After you have thoroughly checked the horse while he stands, ask the handler to lead him straight away from you at a fast walk, for about 30 yards, and straight back again on a loose line so you can see his natural action. Stand directly in front of him and watch his foot flight. Have the owner trot the horse briskly away from you and back, as many times as you need to, to see whether the horse travels straight and has good action (hocks and knees well flexed) or shows any hint of lameness.

After watching the horse move in straight lines, have the handler lead him in a small circle at the walk and at the trot, in both directions. Some lameness problems show up more readily when the horse is turning and putting more weight on one side of the foot than the other. Have the horse walked and trotted past you, so you can view his action from the side to see how he flexes his joints and whether his strides are long or short. Finally, have the owner back the horse up for several strides.

If the horse is old enough to be trained to ride, have the owner saddle and ride while you observe. This will give you clues as to the horse's attitude, manner, and training, as well as his action under saddle. If you like what you see, try him yourself after the owner puts him through his paces. You should get a fairly good picture of whether the horse is sound, and whether he has the athletic ability to perform well. The exercise will also be a clue to his respiratory health (whether or not it makes him cough). If you are satisfied with the horse and wish to purchase, arrange with the owner to have a veterinarian examine the animal to rule out health or soundness problems that were not obvious to you.

Using Photographs to Judge Body Proportion

To judge a horse, look at him from all angles, as well as close up and from a distance. Plan to take some photographs. If you are looking at horses to purchase, you should always allow time to compare and make a decision; few horses are purchased at first sight.

Have someone hold the horse while he stands square and straight on a level surface. His legs should be parallel to each other, and from the side you should see only the legs nearest you. Then take photographs from the side, front, and rear. These will help you visualize the horse and make it easier to study body proportions and their relationships. When taking a photograph from the side, stand 10 to 20 feet away from the horse, opposite the center of his body, so his entire body fills the viewfinder. Keep the camera parallel to his body to avoid distortion. If you are too close to his front, his head and shoulders will look disproportionately large, for example.

When evaluating the photo, create a grid. With pen and ruler, draw a horizontal line on the photo to represent the ground as a level surface. Then draw vertical lines up through the horse's poll, the highest point of his withers, the point of his croup, and the base of his tail. Draw a horizontal line at the breastbone (girth area) and at the top of the withers. You can also draw a horizontal line from the point of the shoulder to the point of the buttocks. These lines can give you reference points for evaluating body proportions and angles. They also can serve as guidelines for measuring various aspects of the body (such as from withers to breastbone and breastbone to fetlock joint, or from withers to ground, and from shoulder to buttock). A racehorse may have a slightly different body shape than a champion roping horse or jumper, but the basic balance and proportions should be similar. The lines you draw on the photo can help you visualize the proportions of his body and can also help you determine whether he has proper angles in body and legs (see chapter 11). Working with a ruler may give you insights you didn't have when looking at the horse in person.

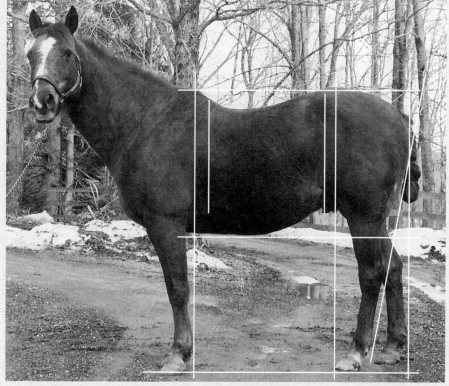

Drawing straight lines on a photo can help you evaluate a horse's body proportions and angles. Here, the lines help show that the horse's croup is slightly higher than his withers, his legs are short in relation to body depth, and his hindquarters are too short and his back too long compared to his front quarters.

When viewed from the front, if the horse is standing squarely, the forelegs should look like two straight columns: legs and feet should be equidistant, and a vertical line from the point of the shoulder down the leg should bisect it. The front feet should be one hoof-width apart.

From the rear, the thighs should have about the same width of muscle as the hips above them. The hindquarters should fill a square, with the croup being the highest point, hips and thighs being the same width, and the bottom of the square being a line drawn between the thighs. In a horse with "ideal" hind leg conformation, a square the same size will also encompass the lower portion of the legs, from the point of the hocks to the ground.

From the front, the forelegs should be two straight columns, with a straight line equally bisecting each leg. Here, the lines show that the forelegs are not straight and the toes turn out (splay-footed).

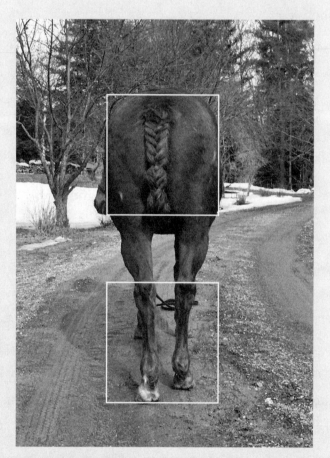

Rear view: Two identical squares can help you evaluate the balance and conformation of the hindquarters. Here, the muscling of hips and thighs is equal, and the distance from point of hock to ground is about the same height as the top square.

POSITION THE HORSE so he is standing squarely on level ground, then view him from the side and evaluate the critical points of his conformation. Take a photograph of him in this position for future reference. Marking up a photo with pen and straight edge helps you to accurately determine lengths and angles of various parts and clarifies how critical points relate to each other. It also reinforces your understanding of the principles of good conformation and helps train your eye to see a horse's strengths and weaknesses. Most important, these evaluations will help you decide whether his structure lends itself to athletic ability and durability, and whether his conformation is desirable for the job you want him to do. (For more on choosing the right type of horse for a particular job, see chapter 15).

Study how the horse's head joins his neck (is it normal, a ewe neck, or heavy crested?) and the length of his neck. Check length and angle of his shoulder, his back conformation (length and shape of topline, shape and height of withers, loins and croup, and slant of the quarters), and conformation of his front and hind legs. Are withers and croup of equal height? Are the front legs straight (or do they deviate in buck knees or calf knees)? Do the hind legs have proper angle (not sickle hocked or post legged)? Evaluate length and angle of the pastern and angles of the hooves. Does he have strong, deep heels, or undesirable shallow or underrun heels?

Use a ruler to check his body proportions. Are the front quarter, back (from base of withers to croup), and hindquarter of equal length? Is the back too long or short? Is the front quarter or hindquarter too long or short? Is his body square — are length and height the same? Is the depth of his body the same as the length of his front leg (from underline to fetlock joint)?

Draw a line from the lumbosacral joint (just ahead of and below the point of the croup) to the widest part of the base of the neck to see if his body balance is level, uphill, or downhill. Measure forearms and cannons (forearms should be longer and cannons shorter). Is the distance from the front of the stifle to the point of the hock equal to the distance from the point of the hock to the ground?

Six photographs follow. I have labeled areas of interest on each with letters, which are cited in the explanatory text below. Test your knowledge of conformation and your evaluative skills by studying the photograph before reading the corresponding text. Can you identify the strengths and weaknesses of the horse? Next, read the text and study the photo again. Then compare the horses with one another.

Training Your Eye: Six Case Studies

Horse No. 1

This horse's neck is a little thick, which may make him more front heavy, but it has adequate length and joins the head fairly well (for flexibility and collection), although it is somewhat straight. The neck meets the shoulder nicely. The long, well-sloped shoulder (A) contributes to good reach (long stride) in the front legs.

The horse's body (front, back, hind) is not quite in equal thirds. He has an adequate front end and hindquarter but is slightly long in the back and is not square. He is longer from point of shoulder to buttock than his height is from withers to ground, even though the withers are slightly higher than the croup. His body depth matches his leg length, however, and he is fairly deep through the flanks (well ribbed up; B). With his long shoulder, slightly long back, and uphill balance (from lumbosacral joint [C] to base of neck [D]), he is probably smooth riding. His uphill balance should make him easy to collect. The horse's overall structure makes him better suited for riding than for racing.

He has well-defined withers, but a hollow (E) directly behind the withers (compare with horse no. 3), which may make him difficult to fit with a saddle; the saddle may tend to slide back. His elbow is directly below the front of the withers, a sign of good shoulder angle and proper length and angle of humerus (neither too upright nor horizontal).

His front legs are reasonably straight, but are slightly back at the knee (F). He has a long forearm and short cannons (which provide better leverage than short forearms and long cannons), pasterns with adequate length and slope, and feet with good depth of heel. He has good flat bone (G) and his knees and fetlock joints are of adequate size and sturdiness. His hind legs have proper angles in hocks and stifles, and the angles of the hindquarter (point of hip to buttock to stifle to point of hip) nearly make an equilateral triangle.

Viewing the horse from the front and rear would help us better evaluate the correctness of his leg structure (and determine whether he will travel straight), but from the side it looks fine.

Horse No. 2

This horse has an obvious swan neck/ewe neck (A). Even though he has a reasonably good throatlatch and head/neck connection, the rest of his neck is an upside-down ewe neck. With a low neck hookup at the shoulder, a low point of shoulder (B), and a relatively upright shoulder, the horse's elbow is directly below the peak of the withers rather than below the front of the withers. The upright shoulder contributes to a long back and less-well-defined withers (compare with withers on horse no. 1 and no. 3). His short front quarter and short hindquarter make his back proportionately longer (compare with the back of horse no. 1). He has a longer and likely weaker loin (C; compare with horse no. 1) and has less depth of flank and is not as well ribbed up (compare with horse no. 3). He is slightly longer than he is tall.

His croup and withers are the same height, but he is a bit slack in the back (and may become more sway-backed as he gets older) and has downhill balance (the base of the neck [D] is lower than the lumbosacral joint [E]). He will probably be best at traveling straight, not activities that require turns and side-to-side action, precision, and collection. He may have trouble collecting himself and may go hollow in the back when traveling.

The angles of his hind legs (stifle and hock) are acceptable, and the angles of the hindquarter (point of hip to buttock to stifle to point of hip) nearly make an equilateral triangle, but he is a little long in the gaskin (F; longer from front of stifle to point of hock than from point of hock to the ground) and thus has a lower hock (shorter hind cannon) (compare with horse no. 1). He also is a little shorter in the quarters (compare with horse no. 1), with a more slanted pelvis (G). Due to his more upright shoulder and similarly angled pelvis, his stride may not be as long as that of horse no. 1.

This horse is also a little fine boned. His long, sloped pasterns may give a fairly smooth ride (to compensate for the upright shoulder), but it's hard to say if they'll hold up under hard use. He also may have underrun heels (H).

Horse No. 3

This horse has a good head/neck/shoulder connection and a slightly better neck arch and neck angle than horse no. 1, but is a little too thick at the throatlatch (A). He has a strong front quarter, with a well-sloped shoulder and good withers (well covered with muscle and not too sharp) and is probably easy to fit with a saddle. His elbow is directly below the front of his withers, putting his forelegs well forward for good movement.

The base of his neck meets the shoulder at a point higher (B) than that of horse no. 1, but because of his hindquarter structure and more level pelvis, his body balance is slightly downhill. He has a short, strong back and is strong over the loin. His hindquarter is a little shorter than his front quarter (body not in thirds), but he has a level quarter (rump) to match his laid back shoulder, and the angles of the hindquarter (point of hip to buttock to stifle to point of hip) nearly form an equilateral triangle. He is not quite as long in the quarters as horse no. 1, which may diminish his stride length and speed. He is deep through the flanks and well ribbed up, for good lung capacity.

He has good hock and stifle angles (not sickle-hocked or post-legged) and relatively straight front legs,

though they are slightly over at the knee (C). He has better bone (D) than horse no. 2 and stronger-looking joints and feet, with more depth of heel (E).

He is a little longer than he is tall and a little deeper from withers to girth than the length of his leg (from elbow to fetlock joint). His neck length is in proper proportion to his body, but is a little longer (from poll to front of withers) than his leg. The shorter legs may be due in part to his being a little too short in the forearm (F). A short forearm and long cannon is not the best combination for leverage and may reduce speed and agility. He has a shorter gaskin (G; tibia) and longer hind cannon (H) than horse no. 2, so his hocks are higher.

Horse No. 4

This horse has good head and neck carriage. The curve of his neck is more normal than that of horse no. 2, and his throatlatch is better than horse no. 3. Someone evaluating this horse in person should inspect his mouth to see if his incisors meet properly; his upper lip appears to protrude slightly beyond his lower lip, suggesting possible parrot mouth (A).

His shoulder is less sloped than that of horses no. 1 and 3 (his slightly upright shoulder matches his slanted pelvis, and he is less level than horses no. 1 and 3), but its slope and length situate the elbow nearly below the front of the withers (closer to the front of the withers than to the peak of the withers). His withers are not quite as well defined as those of horse no. 3. The width of his back (which can't be evaluated from this view) will determine whether a saddle will tend to pull to the side.

His body proportions are fairly close to equal thirds, except for his short quarter and long loin. The loin (B) is well muscled rather than hollow so it may be strong.

Except for his short quarter and apple rump (with low tail head [C] and slanted pelvis), his hind leg angles (stifles and hocks) are good. He is well ribbed up and deep through the flanks (D).

His body is only slightly longer than his height. His depth of body and length of leg are proportionate (depth from withers to underline equals distance from underline to fetlock joint). He has slightly downhill balance (E–F).

His front legs are straight and his long-to-short forearm-to-cannon ratio is better than the short-to-long ratio of horse no. 3. He also has a more balanced gaskin-to-cannon ratio (length from stifle to point of hock equals length from point of hock to ground) than horse no. 2. He has adequate pastern length and slope, but his heels may be shallower than those of horse no. 3 and perhaps slightly underrun (G).

Horse No. 5

The head of this horse joins his neck nicely. He has a relatively clean (not too thick) throatlatch and a desirable neck arch, but the juncture of his shoulder and neck (A) and the angle of his shoulder aren't as good as those of horse no. 3. This horse is a little pigeon-breasted: his elbow is directly below the peak of his withers (B; instead of below the front of his withers), which positions his front legs somewhat farther back than they should be.

His shoulder is a little more upright than desired (not quite as laid back and level as in horses no. 1 and 3), but is relatively long, like his hindquarter. The hindquarter is slanted (pelvis tipped down), but perhaps not as much as the shoulder. The angle of his front end doesn't quite match that of his hind end.

At first glance, his withers and croup appear to be the same height, but it's hard to know from this picture. The horse's position is not perfectly square (his front feet are a little closer to the photographer than are his hind feet), and the ground he's standing on is not level or the photo was taken from an angle, which makes his stance hard to judge. When preparing to take a photograph of a horse for the purpose of evaluating confor-

mation, position the horse so he is standing squarely on level ground. Then, to avoid a distorted view, shoot at the center of his body.

This horse is long in the back and has a too-long loin (C). His topline from withers to tail, therefore, is too long in relation to the length of his underline from elbows to stifle. He is obviously longer in body (D–E) than he is tall (F–E). His body depth (from withers to underline) matches the length of his front legs (from underline to fetlock joint), but his too-long back makes him disproportionate. He appears to have slightly downhill balance. He has a deep flank and ribs well back, for good lung room.

He has a long quarter with down-tipped pelvis, and his stifle (G) is back too far (not directly below his hip [H] as in horses no. 1, 2, 3, and 4), making his thigh more triangular than square and his thigh muscles shorter. The angles in his hindquarters (point of hip to buttock to stifle to point of hip) do not create an equilateral triangle. His pasterns are of adequate length and slope, and his hoofs appear to be strong, with better heels, than horses no. 2 and 4.

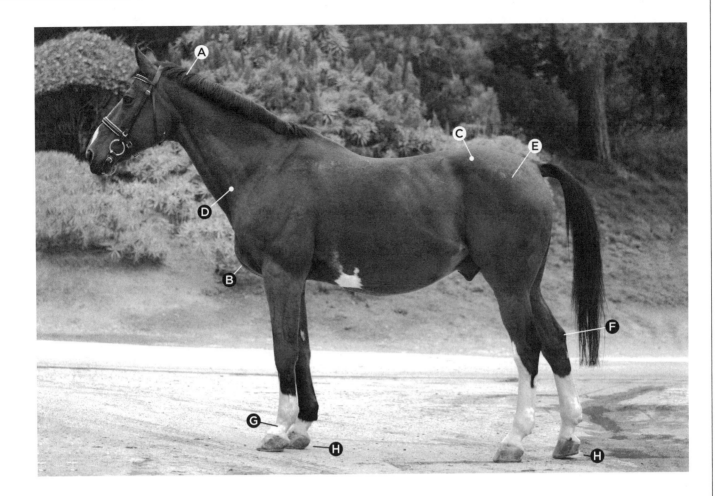

Horse No. 6

This horse's head/neck connection is acceptable, but he has no arch and doesn't have as nice a crest (A) as horses no. 3 and 5. He has a serviceable, functional straight neck, however, and is not as ewe-necked as horse no. 2. He looks like an older horse — a little hollow over his eyes and a bit saggy in his back and belly — but his leg and body angles are satisfactory. His shoulders are reasonably long and laid back, which puts his elbow under a point fairly close to the front of his withers. Even though his pectoral muscles (B) protrude (perhaps from some old swellings, injuries, or injections into these muscles), he is not as pigeon breasted in his front leg conformation as horse no. 5, because his front legs are set forward, as they should be.

His withers are higher than his croup, but this may be partly due to the angle at which the photo was taken. He has relatively level body balance (from lumbosacral joint [C] to the base of the neck [D]) and is only slightly downhill, which means he is probably relatively easy riding and easy to collect. He is about as tall (from withers to ground) as he is long (from point of shoulder to buttock); he is squarer than some of the other horses we have studied.

The horse's body is not quite in equal thirds. His front quarter (shoulder area to the base of the withers) is a little longer than his back (from base of withers to hip). He has a nice short back (a good trait), but his hindquarters are even shorter, which may limit the reach and stride of his hind legs. His pelvis is a bit slanted (slightly goose-rumped [E]) despite the relatively high position of his tail.

His front legs are straight, but a little over at the knees, possibly from many years of hard work. He has good hock and stifle angles, though he may be a little short in the gaskin (shorter from stifle to point of hock than from point of hock to ground). He has a bit of swelling at the point of his hock (capped hock [F]), possibly from an old injury. He has short but well-sloped pasterns (G) that look strong and good strong feet with deep heels (H).

GLOSSARY

abdomen. The belly; the midsection of the body.

accessory carpal bone. The largest knee bone; the small disk-shaped bone that forms a ridge at the back of the knee. Also called the trapezium or pisiform bone.

Achilles tendon. The large tendon at the back of the gaskin on the hind leg, which attaches to the point of the hock.

action. Movement of the horse's legs (straight or crooked, high or low) as he travels.

amble. A slow, four-beat gait that resembles the pace. The hind leg and front leg on the same side move forward together but land separately, so there is no moment of suspension during which all legs are off the ground.

anatomy. The structure of the body and the relationship of its parts; the science that examines the form and function of the body.

angular limb deformity. An abnormal alignment of leg bones caused by differences in growth rate on each side of the bone; this usually results in a toe-in or toe-out stance.

ankle. The fetlock joint.

annular ligament. A ring-shaped ligament around a joint.

anterior. Situated in front of; toward the head end of the body.

apple rump. A short, round rump with a low tail head.

arcade. The surface of the jaw that holds the teeth; the row of cheek teeth.

arthritis. Inflammation of a joint that is sometimes severe enough to cause lameness or abnormal bone growth.

articular. Involving a joint.

articulation. Joint; junction between two bones.

atlas. First vertebra of the cervical region, just behind the head.

atrophy. Wasting away of a muscle; decrease in size from nonuse.

axis. Second cervical vertebra.

back. Topline area between the withers and the point of the croup.

back at the knee. Conformational fault; when viewed from the side, the knees are too far back. Also called calf knees or sheep knees.

bacon sided. Slab sided; narrow rib cage with no "spring" or roundness to the ribs.

balance. In conformation, desirable body proportions; each part of the horse is proportional. Also, keeping the center of gravity over its base — not too far forward or back.

barrel. Portion of the body between the front legs and the loin; the rib cage and abdomen.

bars. On the bottom of the hoof, the portions of the hoof wall that turn in at the heels and run parallel to the sides of the frog. In the mouth, the interdental space between the incisors and the cheek teeth.

base narrow. Conformational fault in which the fetlock joints are closer together than the top of the legs.

base wide. Conformational fault in which the legs are wider apart at the bottom than at the top.

belly. The abdomen; the large cavity that contains the stomach, liver, intestines, kidneys, and bladder. The soft underside of the horse's barrel behind the rib cage.

bench knee. Poor front leg conformation in which the cannon bones are offset to the outside of the knee when viewed from the front. Also called offset knees or offset cannons.

bilateral. Pertaining to both sides.

bit seat. An improvement an equine dentist makes when smoothing the front portions of the cheek teeth (top and bottom) so the horse will not suffer discomfort from the bit.

blemish. Any mark or deformity that diminishes the appearance of the horse but does not affect his usefulness; it may be unsightly but does not make him unsound.

blind spavin. Hock soreness without visible bony growth.

blood spavin. An enlargement of the saphenous vein on the inner hock, above the usual location of bog spavin.

body. Trunk of the horse, excluding head, neck, and legs.

bog spavin. A swelling in the natural depression on the inside and front of the hock; inflammation of the synovial membrane in that part of the joint.

bone. One of the 205 solid structures that compose a horse's skeleton. The amount of support under the horse; *adequate bone* means he has enough thickness of bone to support his size. Measurement of the circumference around the cannon bone, below the knee.

bone spavin. Bony enlargement (bone spur) on the hock, usually located on the inner aspect or front of the lower hock.

bowed tendon. Enlargement of the flexor tendon at the back of the cannon bone due to strain and injury; visible bulge or thickening at the back of the lower leg.

bowlegged. Conformation fault in the hind legs in which the hocks are set too far apart; the feet may be too close together. The front legs are out at the knee (carpal varus).

box foot. A hoof with a too-high heel.

breakover. The point in a horse's stride at which the hoof leaves the ground: the foot rolls forward onto the toe and lifts up.

breast. Front of the chest (muscular area just above and between the front legs); pectoral muscles on either side of the breastbone.

breastbone. See *sternum*.

broken crest. Heavy neck that falls off to one side; also called fallen crest.

brushing. Limb contact. One foot strikes another foot or part of the leg when the horse travels, usually wearing off the hair but not breaking the skin.

bucked knees. Conformation fault in which the knees are bent slightly forward; also called over at the knees, sprung knees, and goat knees.

bucked shins. Inflammation of the bone lining at the front of the cannon bone, occurring most often in young horses during hard training; this is often a temporary unsoundness, creating lameness.

bulb of heel. Rounded protrusion at the back of the foot on the heel; also called heel bulb.

bulldog mouth. Bottom teeth protrude more than the top teeth; also called sow mouth, monkey mouth, and undershot jaw.

bursa. Small fluid-filled sac that lubricates a moving part of the body to minimize friction.

bursitis. Inflammation of the bursa.

buttress foot. Misshapen hoof with bulge at the front of the foot and coronary band caused by low ringbone; also called pyramidal disease.

cadence. Rhythm and tempo of a horse's hoofbeats.

calcification. Hardening of a tissue due to deposits of calcium; replacement of soft tissue with bone.

calf knees. Conformational fault in which the knees bend backward, putting strain on the knee joint; also called back at the knees and sheep knees.

camped. Extended too far in a certain direction. A horse said to be "camped in front" if he stands with his front legs too far forward. A horse is said to be "camped out behind" if he stands with the hind feet too far behind himself; also called "out in the country." A horse is said to be "camped

under" if his legs are too far underneath his body.

canine teeth. Four small-diameter, long, sharp teeth in the interdental space of male horses; occasionally, smaller versions are found in female horses.

cannon. Area between the hock/knee and fetlock joint.

cannon bone. The long bone between hock/knee and fetlock joint; also called metacarpal (front leg) and metatarsal (hind).

capped elbow. Swelling at the point of the elbow due to trauma.

capped hock. Swelling at the point of the hock, usually caused by injury or trauma.

capped knee. Swelling over the knee due to inflammation of the joint capsules, caused by bruising or trauma.

caps. Temporary (baby) teeth that lodge on the incoming permanent tooth rather than falling out.

carpal. Pertaining to the knee.

carpal valgus. In at the knee; knock-kneed.

carpal varus. Out at the knee; bowlegged.

carpitis. Inflammation of the knee joint accompanied by swelling and pain.

carpus. Knee joint.

carriage. How the horse carries himself, especially his head, neck, and tail.

cartilage. A specialized fibrous connective tissue; flexible material at the end of a bone.

cast. A horse that is down and can't get up; he may be caught on his back against a stall wall or fence.

cat hammed. Inadequate muscling on the inner thighs between the hind legs.

caudal. Near the tail.

center of gravity. The balance point of a horse's weight. When a horse stands still, the center of gravity is about 6 inches behind the elbow.

centrals. The two frontmost incisors in the upper and lower jaw; first teeth to appear in foals.

cervical. Pertaining to the neck.

check ligament. A ligament that connects a bone to a tendon and limits the action of the tendon to hold the bone and tendon in proper position.

cheek teeth. Grinders; premolars and molars located in the cheek area of the mouth.

chest. The breast; the front part of a horse's body from which the front legs extend; also a term for the thorax or whole rib cage.

chestnut. Horny growth on the inner leg of the horse; large above the knees, small below the hocks.

chicken knuckle. Protrusion at the front of the hock joint; often found in post-legged horses with too-straight hocks.

chin. Lower part of the head between the lower lip and the front of the lower jaw.

chin groove. Area between the chin and the branches of the jaw where the curb strap of the bridle rests.

clean legs. No blemishes or unsoundnesses on the legs, especially from the knee or hock down.

cleft of the frog. The indentation dividing the frog into halves.

clicking. Forging; striking the front foot with the toe of the hind foot when walking or trotting.

close coupled. Short and strong; a horse with a short back and strong loins.

clubfoot. An abnormally upright hoof with a high heel and short toe; a short, stumpy, box-shaped foot in which the toe is nearly vertical.

coarse. Lacking in quality and refinement.

coarse bone. Large, clumsy cannon.

cob. A stout, short-legged horse with heavy bone and muscle, short neck, round barrel, and close coupling, usually less than 15.3 hands tall.

cobby. Stoutly built and close coupled.

cocked ankles. Fetlock joints cocked forward due to shortening of or pain in the tendons at the back of the lower leg; most common in hind legs.

coffin bone. The bone inside the hoof and connected to the short pastern above it; also called the pedal bone or third phalanx.

cold-blooded. Type of horse that originated in cold climates; this body type is better suited for retaining heat than dissipating heat. Usually heavy bodied; built for slow, steady work rather than for speed.

collateral. On both sides, such as collateral ligaments.

collected. Traveling in a well-balanced manner, with hocks underneath himself and carrying less weight on his front end; able to respond instantly and with agility to a rider's commands.

concave. Hollowed, rounded inward, such as a concave sole or back.

concussion. Shock from impact, as when a horse's foot hits the ground while traveling.

conformation. Shape or contour of body structures; overall structure of the horse and alignment of the body parts.

contracted. Narrowed, such as a contracted heel or foot.

contracted tendons. Shortening of the flexor tendon at the back of the leg, which hinders the normal extension of the fetlock joint or coffin joint inside the foot.

coon footed. Too much angulation in the pastern; the pastern slopes more than the hoof. This type of pastern is often long and weak.

corium. Specialized tissue that produces hoof horn.

corn. A bruise in the soft tissues underlying the sole of the foot, which often results in reddish discoloration of the sole and lameness.

cornea. Tough, transparent membrane that covers the lens of the eye.

corner teeth. Third (outermost) set of incisors; located next to the interdental space.

coronary band. The fleshy part of the top of the hoof, where the hairline meets the hoof.

coronet. Coronary band; also a white mark around the top of the hoof.

coupling. Area of the spine under the loin; the lumbar vertebrae; the space between the last rib and the hip. Also may refer to the lumbosacral joint between the last lumbar vertebrae and sacrum.

cow hocked. Poor hind leg conformation in which the hocks are too close together and the feet are typically too wide apart.

cranial. Near the head.

crest. Top line of the neck behind the head.

cribbing. Compulsive habit in which a horse grabs a surface (such as fence or manger) with his teeth, arches his neck, and sucks in air; causes abnormal wear of the incisors.

cross-firing. Interference that occurs when the inner edges of the diagonal feet strike one another — usually the inner toe or wall of the hind foot strikes the inner quarter or sole of the opposite front foot. This type of interference occurs mainly in pacers and long-backed horses.

croup. Highest point of the rump; some horsemen use the terms *croup* and *rump* interchangeably.

crown. Major portion of the horse's tooth; some of it protrudes from the gum.

cup. Indentation in the center of the biting surface of an incisor.

curb. Thickening of the plantar ligament at the back of the hock; enlargement below the point of the hock.

curby conformation. Sickle hocks.

cut out under the knee. Poor conformation characterized by an indentation below the knee at the front of the cannon.

deciduous teeth. Baby teeth, also called milk teeth, which are shed and replaced by permanent teeth as a horse matures.

deep flexor tendon. The tendon that runs down the back of the cannon bone to connect the muscles of the leg to the coffin bone in the foot.

degenerative joint disease. Progressive deterioration of structures within a joint.

dental star. A star or circular shape formed by secondary dentin on the wearing surface of the permanent incisors.

dentin. Hard inner tooth layer that is covered by enamel.

diagonal. Front foot and opposite hind foot. At the trot, diagonal legs move in unison.

diaphragm. Thin, strong sheet of muscle that separates the thorax from the abdomen; it contracts to pull air into the lungs.

digital cushion. Dense, spongy, shock-absorbing tissue inside the foot, at the heel area between the frog and the deeper tissues; also called plantar cushion.

digital extensor tendons. Tendons that connect the ends of the muscles of the upper leg to the bones of the foot and help move the foot forward and lift the toe.

dish-faced. A face profile featuring concavity below the eyes; it is seen most often in Arabians.

dished foot. A hoof that is concave in front rather than straight from the coronary band to the toe.

dishing. Paddling; swinging the feet outward while traveling.

dock. The upper part of the tail at the tail head.

dorsal. Pertaining to the upper or top surface.

dorsal spinous process. Projection at the top of a vertebra.

downhill balance. The backbone slants down from the hip joint to the base of the neck, making the horse heavy on his front end.

draft horse. A large heavy horse used for pulling.

drawn up in the flanks. Shallow rather than deep flanks; also called wasp waisted.

dropped sole. A sole that bulges down toward the ground rather than being concave or level.

dubbed off. Worn off.

easy keeper. A horse that stays fatter on less feed.

elbow. Bony protrusion at the back of the upper part of the foreleg; the joint between humerus and forearm that moves the leg forward.

elk nose. Sagging muzzle; top lip overhangs the lower one; also called elk nose.

enamel. The hard outer covering of a tooth; outside layer of the crown.

ergot. Small horny growth behind and beneath the fetlock joint.

ewe necked. The profile of the neck is concave rather than convex; upside down–looking neck.

exfoliation. The process of flaking off the dead layers of the sole of the foot.

extensor. Muscle that straightens, or extends, a joint.

fault. A conformation flaw, such as crooked legs, upright shoulder, or some other imperfection that might hinder athletic ability or predispose a horse to injury and unsoundness.

feathering. Long hair around the fetlocks; common in draft horses.

femur. Thigh bone between stifle and hip.

feral. Domestic animal gone wild.

fetlock. Hair at the back of the fetlock joint

fetlock joint. Joint between the cannon bone and pastern.

fibula. Small bone attached to the top of the outer aspect of the tibia in the hind leg.

fine. Light, refined; opposite of *coarse*.

fine boned. Bones too small in diameter for the size and weight of the horse.

first phalanx. Long pastern bone just below the fetlock joint.

fistula. An abnormal opening. Fistula of the withers is a continually draining abscess due to injury and bruising of a bursa and subsequent infection; a constantly draining bursa due to infection.

flank. Area in front of the stifle; back portion of the abdomen just ahead of the hind leg.

flare. Abnormal spread of the hoof wall at the ground due to uneven weight distribution on the foot; the sides of the hoof lack symmetry and the foot is unbalanced.

flat bone. Combination of cannon bone and tendons. When the tendons are set well back from the bone, the cannon is deep with a greater circumference than a cannon with "round" bone.

flat footed. The soles of the feet are flat or dropped instead of concave.

flexor. Muscle or tendon that flexes or bends a joint.

floating. Removing sharp points and edges of a tooth with a rasp; typically done by an equine dentist or veterinarian.

floating ribs. The last one or two ribs that are not connected to the sternum.

foot flight. The path of the foot as it makes a step.

forearm. The upper part of the front leg, from the elbow to the knee.

forehand. The front part of the horse: head, neck, shoulders, and front legs; the portion of the horse in front of the rider.

foreleg. Front leg.

forelock. Hair that grows down from the poll; the portion of the mane that hangs down over the forehead.

forging. Striking the toe of the hind foot or shoe against the bottom of the front foot on the same side.

founder. Laminitis. Inflammation of the laminae of the hoof, causing lameness and hoof changes: rings and ridges in the wall and sometimes a dropped or rotated coffin bone inside the hoof.

fox-trot. A fast walk/slow trot in which the horse brings each hind foot to the ground an instant before the diagonal front foot; a broken trot in which the horse appears to be walking in front and trotting behind.

frog. The triangular or wedge-shaped rubbery structure in the center of the sole (widest toward the heel of the foot) that serves as a cushion.

full mouth. Complete set of permanent teeth, which most horses have by age 5 or 6.

gait. Sequence of foot movements.

gaited horse. A horse or breed that performs gaits other than walk, trot, and gallop.

gallop. A four-beat gait; typically a horse's fastest gait.

Galvayne's groove. A line on the upper corner incisor that appears at the gum surface at age 10 and extends down the tooth as the horse ages. The groove extends halfway down the tooth by age 15 and to the grinding surface by age 20; it usually disappears, starting at the top, by age 30.

garde. A hard lump at the back of the hock and slightly to one side on the upper end of the splint bone.

gaskin. Muscled area of the hind leg above the hock.

gastrocnemius muscle. Large muscle at the back of the gaskin; similar to the calf muscle in a human leg.

girth. The area of the body behind the elbow; the circumference of the body measured around the barrel at this area.

glass eye. Eye without pigment; a bluish or white eye.

goat knees. Over at the knee; buck kneed.

good bone. Adequate amount of support under the horse; proper density and circumference of cannon bone — neither too fine nor too heavy.

goose rump. A sloping rump that is much lower at the buttocks than at the croup.

gotch eye. One eye is set at a different angle than the other eye.

ham. Rear part of the thigh muscle; muscle area below the buttock at the rear of the horse.

hammer-headed. Horse with a large, coarse head set on the neck at an abrupt angle.

hand. Unit of measure for describing the height of a horse. A hand is 4 inches, and a horse is measured from the ground to the withers. A horse 15½ hands is 15.2 hands, 15 hands, 2 inches.

hard keeper. A horse that stays relatively thin despite good feed, or one that requires a lot of feed to maintain his body weight.

haunch bone. Ilium; the part of the pelvis that sticks out to create the hip.

haunches. Hindquarters.

hay belly. Droopy, distended belly.

"heart." Willingness and desire to perform.

heart girth. Girth area; the circumference of the horse's body just behind the elbow.

heave line. A horizontal indentation on both sides of the lower abdomen caused by overdevelopment of the muscle from forcing air out of the lungs; a sign of a horse with heaves.

heaves. Chronic respiratory impairment in which a horse's lung capacity is diminished due to allergy/irritation from dust and mold spores; the horse wheezes and coughs with exertion and lacks stamina.

heel. The back of the hoof; the rearmost part of the hoof wall on each side of the foot.

heel bulb. The rounded portion of each heel at the back of the hoof below the coronary band.

hernia. Unusual protrusion of tissue. Some horses have umbilical hernias at the navel; some males have scrotal hernias.

herring gutted. Shallow in the flanks; wasp waisted.

high action. The horse lifts his legs high at each step, which reduces the length of stride.

high hocks. Hocks higher than halfway between the stifle and the ground; hocks higher than on the average horse.

high ringbone. Degenerative joint disease and subsequent new bone growth at the pastern joint between the first and second phalanx.

hindquarters. Rear end of the horse, including croup, rump, and hind legs.

hip. The large bone protruding just below and forward of the croup; the outer wing of the pelvis.

hip joint. The joint between the femur and the hip bone.

hock. The large joint in the hind leg (below the stifle and above the fetlock) that enables the lower leg to bend forward.

hoof. Horny wall and sole of the foot.

hoof bound. Condition created by a severely contracted foot in which the hoof wall presses in on the coffin bone and inner structures, causing pain and lameness.

hoof crack. A split in the hoof wall.

hoof rings. Irregularities (rings and ridges) that encircle the entire hoof.

hoof tester. Pincer-like instrument used to test for soreness and tenderness on the sole of the foot.

hook bone. Hip bone.

horn. Hard cutaneous material that makes up the outer hoof wall.

hot-blooded. Spirited, active type of horse whose ancestors originated in a hot climate. Body type is better suited for dissipating heat than for retaining it, and the bloodstream contains more red blood cells for greater oxygen-transportation capacity when exerting than does that of a cold-blooded horse.

hound gutted. Shallow in the flanks; wasp waisted.

humerus. Upper arm bone that joins the shoulder to the elbow.

iliosacral joint. Juncture between the ilium and sacrum; same as sacroiliac joint.

ilium. Pelvic bone that protrudes to form the hip; hook bone.

in at the knees. Carpal valgus; knock-kneed; knees are too close together.

incisors. Front teeth; the six top and six bottom teeth at the front of the mouth used for biting off grasses.

insensitive laminae. The tiny "leaves," or corrugations, on the inner hoof wall that interlock with the corresponding leaves on the inner, living portions of the foot.

interdental space. The space between the incisors and cheek teeth.

interference. Striking one foot or leg with the opposite foot.

interosseous ligament. The ligament that connects the splint bone to the cannon bone.

ischium. Lower part of the pelvis; the rearmost part of it forms the point of the buttocks.

jack spavin. An exceptionally large bone spavin on the hock.

jaw. Bone that supports the teeth.

jibbah. Bulge on the forehead of an Arabian horse.

joint. Union or junction between two bones.

joint capsule. Sac of lubricating synovial fluid surrounding a joint.

joint mouse. Small bone chip within a joint capsule.

jowl. Cheek bone; part of the jaw.

jug head. Horse with a large, coarse head.

jugular groove. The furrow on each side of the neck.

knee. Joint between forearm and cannon bone; the carpal joint.

knife neck. Unusually thin neck with little crest; sometimes due to poor conformation or emaciation and lack of muscle.

knock-kneed. Carpal valgus; in at the knees. Knees too close together, with cannon bones slanting out from the knees.

lameness. Abnormality of gait caused by the horse favoring a sore foot or leg.

laminae. Interlocking area of sensitive and insensitive tissues of the foot that connect the hoof wall to the inner tissues and coffin bone.

laminitis. Inflammation of the laminae beneath the hoof wall. In chronic cases the coffin bone drops and the horse is said to be foundered.

lateral. Pertaining to the sides or outside.

lateral gait. Gait in which both feet on one side move, then both feet on the other side move.

laterals. Second set of incisors to appear in the young horse; located between the central and corner incisors and sometimes called intermediates or middle incisors.

lead. Footfall pattern at the canter or gallop in which the legs on one side of the horse reach farther forward than the legs on the other side. When making a circle or turn, the horse should always lead with the inner legs.

ligament. Strong connective tissue that attaches bones together and supports joints.

light boned. Insufficient bone for the weight of the horse.

light horse. Horse built for speed and agility and used for riding or racing.

loaded shoulders. Shoulders too thick with muscle.

locked patella. Condition that occurs when the kneecap of the stifle slips out of place and locks the hind leg in an extended position.

loin. Muscular area of the back, between the last rib and the hip.

long pastern bone. The larger bone below the fetlock joint, between the fetlock joint and short pastern bone; first phalanx.

lordosis. Swayback.

low hocks. Hocks lower than halfway from stifle to ground; short cannons.

low ringbone. Degenerative joint disease and new bone growth at the coffin joint inside the hoof.

lumbar vertebrae. Vertebrae in the loin area behind the saddle; the portion of the backbone between the ribs and the pelvis.

lumbosacral joint. Area of the lower back, at the pelvis, where the last lumbar vertebra meets the sacrum.

malocclusion. Mismatch of upper and lower jaw, resulting in uneven wear of the teeth.

mandible. Lower jaw.

mastication. Chewing food.

maxilla. Upper jaw.

medial. Middle or inner; located toward the center of the body.

metacarpal. Pertaining to the cannon bone and splint bones in the front leg.

metacarpal periostitis. Bucked shins; inflammation of the lining on the front part of the cannon bone in the front leg.

metatarsal. Pertaining to the cannon bone and splint bones of the hind leg.

middle incisors. Laterals; incisors between the central and corner incisors.

milk teeth. Baby teeth that are smaller than permanent teeth; they are shed and replaced by age 5 in the horse.

mitbah. The juncture between the horse's head (jaw area) and the neck; the area of the neck just behind the head; also called throatlatch.

molars. Teeth behind the premolars that grind feed. A mature horse has twelve molars: three on each side, top and bottom.

monocular vision. Ability to see independently with each eye, viewing two different images at the same time.

muscle. Fibrous tissue that contracts to move a body part.

mutton withers. Low withers; usually a flat, broad area with very little bony definition at the withers.

muzzle. Lower end of the face comprising the nostrils, lips, and chin.

navicular bone. Small boat-shaped bone inside the foot, between the coffin bone and the short pastern bone.

navicular syndrome. Chronic inflammation involving the navicular bone and its surrounding structures, producing soreness in the heel area; previously called navicular disease.

near side. The left side of the horse.

neck. Portion of the horse measured from behind the head at the poll to the start of the withers, or from throatlatch to the union of the neck and breast.

nuchal ligament. Broad, thick ligament running from poll to withers at the top of the neck.

occlusion. Bite; the manner in which the top and lower jaw come into contact.

occult spavin. Blind spavin; typical spavin lameness without any obvious changes in the hock joint.

off. Slightly lame, such as being "off" on his right front foot.

off side. Right side (far side) of the horse.

offset cannons. Cannon bones set too far to the outside of the knee joints rather than located centrally; also called bench knees.

olecranon process. Point of the elbow.

osselet. Thickening and sometimes bony growth on the front surface at the top of the fetlock joint.

ossify. To change into bone

out at the knees. Carpal varus; bow-legged.

out in the country. Hind cannons are vertical as they should be but are set too far behind the horse.

over at the knees. The horse's knees are bent forward when he stands squarely; also called bucked knees, sprung knees, and goat knees.

overbite. Parrot mouth.

overreaching. Striking the front foot or lower leg with the hind feet; most often the toe of the hind foot strikes the rear of the front foot, hitting the heel bulb or shoe.

overshot jaw. Parrot mouth.

overstepping. The hind foot lands a good distance in front of the track left by the front foot.

pace. Two-beat lateral gait in which the front and hind foot on the same side move forward together.

paddling. Throwing the front feet outward rather than straight forward; gait defect commonly seen in horses that are pigeon-toed.

parrot mouth. Mismatch of upper and lower jaw in which the upper teeth protrude; the lower jaw is abnormally short.

paso. Smooth, lateral four-beat gait resembling a broken pace; the hind foot lands just before the front foot on the same side.

pastern. Area of the lower leg between the fetlock joint and the coronary band at the top of the hoof.

pastern joint. Joint between the long and short pastern bones.

patella. Small triangular-shaped bone at the front of the stifle joint, similar to the human kneecap.

pectoral. Pertaining to the front of the chest, or breast.

pedal bone. Coffin bone or third phalanx; the largest bone inside the hoof.

pelvis. Circle of bones connecting the hind legs to the spine.

periarticular. Around a joint.

periople. Narrow strip below the coronary band, similar to the cuticle on a human fingernail, which produces the waxy substance that covers the outer surface of the hoof wall.

periosteum. Bone lining.

periostitis. Inflammation of the bone lining, which often causes new bone growth.

permanent teeth. The large teeth that replace the shed baby teeth. They begin to erupt at 9 to 12 months and completely replace baby teeth by the time the horse is 5 years old.

phalanx. One of the three bones below the fetlock joint. Long pastern bone, short pastern bone, and coffin bone are lay terms for the first, second, and third phalanx.

pharynx. Portion of the throat between the mouth and esophagus that connects the nasal passages with the windpipe.

physitis. Inflammation of the specialized cartilage at the ends of the leg bones in young, fast-growing horses that causes pain and enlargement of the bone ends.

pigeon breasted. Front legs are set too far back under the horse, and the breast sticks out farther than normal.

pigeon-toed. Toes point inward toward one another rather than straight ahead.

pig eyed. Small, narrow, squinty eyes; the eyeball is set back farther in the head than normal.

pin bone. The bone at the rear of the pelvis that forms the point of the buttocks. Term occasionally used to refer to the hip bone; also called seat bone.

pisiform bone. Accessory carpal bone (trapezium) behind the knee.

plaiting. Placing one front foot directly in front of the other one when traveling, increasing the risk of stumbling and interference.

plantar. Pertaining to the sole of the foot or the back of the hind leg (below the hock).

plantar cushion. See *digital cushion*.

pointing. Standing with one front leg farther forward than the other, usually because putting weight on it is painful.

point of buttock. Most rearward part of the buttock formed by the pin bone (seat bone).

point of elbow. Bony point formed by the olecranon process of the ulna.

point of hip. Bony point formed by the wing of the pelvis. These protrusions at the front of the pelvis form the widest part of the rump.

point of hock. The slightly bulbous and rounded top part of the hock joint.

point of shoulder. Bony point formed by the end of the humerus where it joins the shoulder blade; the most forward part of the shoulder bones.

poll. Bony protrusion at the top of the skull between the ears; topmost part of the head.

pony. Technically, a small horse that is less than 14.2 hands in height at the withers. In actuality, body build differentiates a pony from a horse.

pop-eyed. Eyes that bulge more than normal.

popped knee. Swelling and inflammation that enlarges the knee joint; bony thickening may develop.

posterior. Toward the rear.

post-legged. Hind leg lacks sufficient angulation in the stifle and hock joints and looks too straight when viewed from the side.

premolars. The first three cheek teeth on each side, top and bottom, located in front of the three molars. The mature horse has twelve premolars.

pubis. The bone at the lowest part of the pelvis.

pyramidal disease. The front part of the foot protrudes forward, due to enlargement of the joint inside the hoof, just beneath the coronary band. Also called buttress foot, low ringbone.

quarter. One side of the rump. Also, portion of the hoof wall just forward of the heel.

quarter crack. Crack in the hoof wall in the back half of the hoof, toward the heel.

quarters. The rump. The area between the point of the croup to below the tail head, encompassing both sides of the backbone.

quick. Sensitive inner tissue underlying the sole.

quidding. Dropping wads of food out of the mouth, usually because of bad teeth.

quittor. A condition in which there is continual draining of an area (pus discharge) above the coronary band, usually due to a wound at the heel or rear quarter of the hoof.

rack. A fast four-beat gait in which each foot comes to the ground separately; one of the gaits of a five-gaited horse. Also called single-foot.

radius. The main bone of the forearm between the elbow joint and the knee.

ramp. High portion of a tooth that is larger than a hook and due to uneven length of the jaws and improper wear.

refinement. Horseman's term for slimmer lines, smaller leg bones, etc., — the qualities of a light horse exhibiting hot blood. Attributes needed for speed and agility rather than for ponderous, slow power.

ribbed up. The rear ribs are well arched and slant backward, making the horse close coupled. In a horse that is "well ribbed up," the ribs extend well back and the horse is deep through the flank.

ribs. Paired, curved bones extending out from the backbone to the bottom of the thorax; most horses have eighteen pairs.

ringbone. Bony enlargement in the pastern area or on the coffin bone.

roach back. Arched spine in the loin area behind the saddle.

road founder. Laminitis caused by concussion to the feet from fast gaits on hard surfaces.

roaring. Loud, raspy sound on exertion due to restriction of the horse's air passages.

Roman nose. A convex face profile.

rostral. Toward the nasal cavities; forward. A term pertaining to the teeth.

round bone. Tendons are too close to the cannon bone, making it round instead of flat and smaller in diameter than it should be.

rounding the back. Elevating the back by engaging the back muscles. The back arches up instead of dipping down, enabling the horse to drop his hindquarters and get his hind legs well under himself for better collection and weight carrying.

rump. The area from the croup to the tail head.

running walk. A four-beat gait that is faster than a walk but slower than a rack; the hind foot oversteps the track of the front foot by 4 to 18 inches, giving a gliding motion.

sacroiliac joints. Pair of joints on each side of the backbone, between the sacrum and the ilium of the hind leg, several inches below the croup.

sacrum. The five fused vertebrae that make up the final portion of the spine, excluding the tail.

sand cracks. Cracks in the hoof wall due to weak or brittle hoof horn or a long toe.

saphenous vein. Large vein that angles across the front of the hock joint.

scalping. Hitting the hairline at the top of the approaching hind foot (or even higher on the pastern or cannon) with the toe of the front foot as it is being picked up.

scapula. Shoulder blade.

sclera. The white of the eye.

scope. The degree of extension and flexion of the legs and body while the horse is in motion; length of stride.

seat bone. The rearmost part of the pelvis that defines the point of the buttocks.

second phalanx. Short pastern bone.

second thigh. Gaskin muscles.

seedy toe. Separation of the outer wall of the hoof from the inner, sensitive portion; also called white line disease.

sensitive laminae. Tiny corrugations in the inner, living surface of the foot that interlock with similar corrugations in the outer, insensitive hoof wall.

sesamoid bones. The two small bones at the rear of the fetlock joint.

shear mouth. Teeth worn at a steep angle, causing them to slide past one another rather than meeting properly for grinding.

sheared heel. Breakdown between the two heel bulbs (one is higher than the other and the tissue between them is torn) due to excessive pressure on one heel or chronic hoof imbalance.

sheep knees. Calf knees; back at the knees.

shelly feet. Feet with thin, brittle walls that break easily.

shin. Front part of the cannon bone.

shin buck. Inflammation of the bone lining at the front of the cannon bone; also called bucked shins.

shoe boil. Soft swelling over the point of the elbow due to injury and inflammation.

short pastern bone. The second phalanx; the smaller of the two pastern bones between the long pastern bone and the coffin bone.

shoulder. The front part of the body formed by the shoulder blade.

shoulder girdle. A group of large muscles that supports the shoulder joint.

shoulder joint. A shallow ball-and-socket joint between the lower end of the shoulder blade and the top of the humerus.

sickle hocks. Excessive angulation in the hock joint; the lower leg is angled in such a way that the feet are too far underneath the body.

sidebone. One or both of the cartilages on either side of the foot just above the coronary band turn to bone due to injury and inflammation.

single-foot. The rack.

slab sided. Narrow horse with little spring of ribs; the ribs are too short, too flat, or too upright. Also called bacon sided.

slack coupled. Too long in the loin.

slow pace. Slow, four-beat gait similar to the pace and the rack but with some hesitation between the left- and right-side strides.

smooth mouth. The cups in the upper and lower incisors have worn away and disappeared; the horse is older than 12 years.

sole. The horny covering of the bottom of the hoof, between the hoof wall and the frog.

sound. Healthy and free of any abnormal structure or injury that would interfere with the usefulness of the animal.

sow mouth. The lower jaw is longer than the upper jaw; also called monkey mouth and undershot jaw.

spavin. Disease of the hock joint characterized by swelling, bone inflammation, and bone spurs.

spavin test. A test in which the affected hind leg is held tightly flexed under the horse's belly for 2 minutes, after which the horse is trotted to see whether his first few steps show increased lameness.

speedy cutting. Limb interference at fast gaits.

spinal column. Backbone: neck, back, lumbar vertebra, sacrum, and tail bones.

splay footed. Feet turned out at the toes.

splint. Bony enlargement anywhere along the cannon bone or splint bones, usually due to excessive concussion or an injury.

splint bones. The two small bones below the knee (and hock), on either side of the cannon, extending partway down the cannon.

split up. Term referring to lack of muscling at the rear of the hindquarters, with daylight showing between the thighs when the horse is viewed from behind.

spring of rib. The degree to which the ribs are rounded; a horse with good spring of rib has well-rounded ribs.

sprinter. A horse built for a quick burst of speed; he can run fast for a short distance.

sprung knees. Over at the knees; bucked knees.

standing under. Leg placed too far under the horse when viewed from the side; also called camped under.

stargazer. Horse that holds his head too high and thrusts his nose upward, a problem that often occurs with a ewe-necked horse.

stay apparatus. The system of muscles, tendons, and ligaments that helps support the horse while standing, and acts to prevent overextension of the joints, and reduce concussion during movement.

stayer. A horse with exceptional endurance that can run for long distances without tiring.

staying power. Stamina.

step mouth. Abrupt change in the height of the cheek teeth that often occurs between the premolars and molars.

sternum. Breastbone; bone that starts between the front legs, defines the lower surface of the rib cage, and anchors the first ribs at their base.

stifle. The large joint between the thigh and the gaskin, just behind the flank, with a kneecap similar to that of a human.

straight and clean. Traveling straight: the feet move straight forward, do not paddle outward or wing inward, and there is no interference.

straight behind. Not enough angle in the stifles and hocks; the hind legs are too straight when viewed from the side. Also called post-legged.

straight gaited. A horse that does a walk, trot, and canter and no other gaits.

straight shoulder. Upright shoulder, lacking in slope.

stride. Length of step measured from the point at which a hoof leaves the ground to the spot where it returns to the ground.

stringhalt. Irregular jerking action of the hock up toward the belly when the horse is moving.

substance. Strength and density of bone, muscle, and tendons; conformation that gives the impression of stamina and hardiness.

suffraginis bone. Term once used for the long pastern bone or first phalanx.

sulci. The grooves along the edges of the frog.

superficial flexor tendon. Outer tendon at the back of the cannon that connects the muscles of the upper leg to the back of the pastern.

suspensory apparatus. The tendons and ligaments that support the fetlocks and keep them from hyperextending to the ground.

suspensory ligament. The ligament that holds up the fetlock joint.

swan neck. An overly long neck with a nice curve at the top but too much concavity toward the withers.

swaybacked. Having a downward dip in the back.

sweeny. Atrophy of the shoulder muscles due to a nerve injury, such as a blow to the shoulder or a tear when the leg slips suddenly.

synovial fluid. The lubricating fluid secreted by the membranes lining a joint cavity, bursa, or tendon sheath.

table. The grinding surface of a tooth.

tail. The dock and tail hair.

tail bones. The caudal vertebrae; an individual horse and breed may have from fifteen to twenty-one tail bones.

tail head. The top of the tail where it meets the hindquarters; also called dock.

tarsal. Pertaining to the hock.

temporary teeth. Teeth shed at various ages as the horse grows and replaced by permanent teeth; also called baby teeth or milk teeth.

tendon. Nonelastic fibrous tissue that connects a muscle to bone or cartilage.

tendon sheath. Protective membrane that envelops a tendon.

thigh. Muscled area covering the femur; the side of the hindquarter bordered by the rump at top, the hip at front, the buttocks at the rear, and the stifle at the bottom.

third phalanx. Coffin bone inside the hoof; also called pedal bone.

thoracic vertebrae. Vertebrae to which rib pairs attach.

thorax. Chest cavity enclosed by the rib cage and diaphragm.

thoroughpin. Soft, puffy swelling on the upper part of the hock.

throatlatch. Juncture between the jaw area of the head and the neck; the area of the neck just behind the head. Also called *mitbah*.

thrush. Infection along the edge of the frog, accompanied by black secretions and foul odor.

tibia. The main bone between the stifle and the hock.

tied in at the knee. Flexor tendons at the back of the knee are too close to the cannon bone.

tight elbows. Elbows turned in and too close to the body.

toe. Front part of the hoof.

toed in. Pigeon-toed with possible base-narrow conformation.

toed out. Splay footed with possible base-wide conformation.

topline. The top of the horse, from withers to tail.

transverse process. The wing of a vertebra; sideways projection.

trapezium. Small bone behind the knee joint; also called accessory carpal bone, pisiform bone.

trot. Two-beat diagonal gait in which the front foot and hind foot of opposite sides move forward in unison.

tushes. Canine teeth located behind the incisors in the interdental space; found in male horses and a few females. Also called tusks.

type. Classification of different kinds of horses. Horses having characteristics that contribute to usefulness for a specific purpose, such as stock-horse type, racing type, harness type.

ulna. The smaller bone of the forearm that is fused to the radius; it forms the elbow.

underline. The lower shape and length of the horse; the line from elbow to sheath or udder.

underrun heels. Abnormal foot with a low heel and more angle at the heel than at the front of the foot. Heel bulbs are too far back and the heel is too far forward.

undershot jaw. The lower jaw is longer than the upper jaw; also called monkey mouth and sow mouth.

unsound. A general term to indicate some form of damage (to bone, muscle, tendon, or ligaments), injury, or abnormality that reduces the horse's ability to perform.

unsoundness. An abnormality or injury that hinders serviceability.

upward fixation of the patella. The patella of the stifle joint catches over the femur, locking the patella in place with the leg in an extended position; the hind leg cannot flex. Usually associated with post-legged conformation.

uphill balance. The backbone slants up from the hip joint to the base of the neck. More weight is carried on the horse's hindquarters than is normal.

ventral. Located on or toward the lower or bottom surface.

vertebrae. The bones of the spine.

vestigial. Remaining from a previous stage of development; having no present-day function.

vulva. External opening of the mare's genital tract.

walk. A slow four-beat gait in which each foot strikes the ground at separate intervals in specific sequence: right hind, right front, left hind, left front.

wall. The outer horny covering of the foot that extends from the coronary band to the ground.

walleyed. Lack of pigment in the iris; the eye is blue or gray in color. Also called a china eye or glass eye.

warmblood. A cross between a hot-blooded breed and a cold-blooded breed.

wasp waisted. Tucked up and shallow in the flanks; herring gutted.

wave mouth. Uneven line of teeth due to uneven wear.

way of going. How a horse travels and moves his feet.

well-sprung ribs. Ribs that curve out from the backbone, projecting back and down, forming a wide rib cage.

white line. Junction at the bottom of the foot where the wall and sole meet.

white line disease. A condition in which the hoof wall separates from the underlying tissues, beginning at the ground surface at the white line; also called seedy toe.

whorlbone lameness. Lameness of a hind leg, due to inflammation of a bursa deep in the hip area; also called trochanteric bursitis.

wild horse. An undomesticated horse.

wind. Horseman's term for breathing capacity and endurance/stamina when running.

windpuffs. Enlargements of joint capsules and tendon sheaths in the fetlock joint area; caused by distention from too much fluid due to stress and strain. Also called wind gall.

winging. Swinging the hoof in at the walk or trot.

withers. Highest point over the shoulders; the bony projection of the backbone between the neck and the back.

wobbler syndrome. Incoordination of the hindquarters usually due to injury to the spinal cord, or malformed, narrow vertebrae that put pressure on the spinal cord.

wolf teeth. Small rudimentary teeth located just ahead of the premolars.

RECOMMENDED READING

BOOKS

There are a number of good books on horse conformation. Some of the most helpful ones include:

Adams, O. R. *Lameness in Horses*. Philadelphia: Lea & Febiger, 1962.

Bennett, Deb. *Principles of Conformation Analysis*, vol. 1. Gaithersburg, MD: Fleet Street Publishing, 1988.

———. *Principles of Conformation Analysis*, vol. 2. Gaithersburg, MD: Fleet Street Publishing , 1989.

———. *Principles of Conformation Analysis*, vol. 3. Gaithersburg, MD: Fleet Street Publishing, 1991.

Edwards, Gladys Brown. *Anatomy and Conformation of the Horse*. Croton-on-Hudson, NY: Dreenan, 1980.

Green, Ben K. *Horse Conformation*. Greenville, TX: self-published, 1969.

Hedges, Juliet, ed. *Equine Photos & Drawings for Conformation & Anatomy*. Tyler, TX: Equine Research, 1999.

Loving, Nancy S. *Conformation and Performance*. Millwood, NY: Breakthrough, 1997.

McBane, Susan. *Conformation for the Purpose*. Shrewsbury, Engl.: Swan Hill, 2000.

Sellnow, Les. *Understanding Equine Lameness*. Lexington, KY: The Bloodhorse, 1998.

Rooney, James R. *The Lame Horse: Causes, Symptoms and Treatment*. New York: A. S. Barnes, 1974.

Smythe, R. H. *What Makes a Good Horse: Its Structure and Performance*. London: Country Life Limited, 1957.

Way, Robert F., and Donald B. Lee. *The Anatomy of the Horse*. Millwood, NY: Breakthrough, 1983.

MAGAZINES

Occasionally, various equine magazines feature a series of articles or columns on conformation, and these can also be very helpful. Some of these articles focus on different aspects of conformation or describe how certain judges look at horses to evaluate them. Some discuss specific points of conformation, using photos of reader's horses that are sent in for evaluation. One authority on equine anatomy and conformation who has done a lot of writing on this subject for several magazines is Deb Bennett, PhD. She wrote a long series of articles in *EQUUS* during the late 1980s discussing conformation and evaluating readers' horses, some of which were later collected in the three-volume *Principles of Conformation Analysis* (Gaithersburg, MD: Fleet Street Publishing, 1988–1991).

OTHER STOREY TITLES YOU MIGHT ENJOY

Easy-Gaited Horses by Lee Ziegler. An in-depth guide to working with gaited horses by one of the world's leading experts on the subject. Includes line drawings and diagrams. 256 pages. ISBN 1-58017-562-7 (paperback); ISBN 1-58017-563-5 (hardcover).

The Horse Behavior Problem Solver by Jessica Jahiel. Using a friendly question-and-answer format and drawing on real-life case studies, Jahiel explains how a horse thinks and learns, why he acts the way he does, and how you should respond. 352 pages. ISBN 1-58017-524-4 (paperback); 1-58017-525-2 (hardcover).

The Horse Doctor Is In by Brent Kelley. Combining solid veterinary advice with enlightening stories from his Kentucky equine practice, Dr. Kelley educates readers about all aspects of horse health care, from fertility to fractures to foot care. 416 pages. Paperback. ISBN 1-58017-460-4.

Horse Handling & Grooming by Cherry Hill. This user-friendly guide offers a wealth of practical advice to help you master dozens of essential handling and grooming skills to keep your horse healthy. 160 pages. Paperback. ISBN 0-88266-956-7.

Horsekeeping on a Small Acreage: Designing and Maintaining Your Equine Facilities, 2nd ed. by Cherry Hill. Explains how to be a responsible steward of the land while providing horses with the best care possible. 320 pages, full color. ISBN 1-58017-535-X (paperback); 1-58017-603-8 (hardcover).

Storey's Guide to Feeding Horses by Melyni Worth. Healthy horses need proper diet and nutrition. Design balanced feeding programs according to the individual needs of your horses. Explains required nutrients, proper rations, herbal supplements, and more. 256 pages. Paperback. ISBN 1-58017-492-2.

Storey's Guide to Raising Horses by Heather Smith Thomas. Whether you are an experienced horse handler or are planning to own your first horse, this complete guide to intelligent horsekeeping covers all aspects of keeping a horse fit and healthy in body and spirit. 512 pages. Paperback. ISBN 1-58017-127-3.

Storey's Guide to Training Horses by Heather Smith Thomas. Covering everything from basic safety to retraining a horse that has acquired bad habits, this is an essential handbook for all horse owners. 512 pages. Paperback. ISBN 1-58017-467-1.

Storey's Horse Lover's Encyclopedia Deborah Burns, editor. This hefty, fully illustrated, comprehensive A-to-Z compendium is an indispensable answer book addressing every question you may have about horses and horse care. 480 pages. Paperback. ISBN 1-58017-317-9.

These and other Storey books are available wherever books are sold and directly from Storey Publishing, 210 MASS MoCA Way, North Adams, MA 01247, or by calling 1-800-441-5700. Or visit our Web site at www.storey.com.